MILITARY AIRCRAFT MARKINGS 1989

Peter R. March

LONDON

IAN ALLAN LTD

Contents

Photographs by Peter R. March (PRM) unless otherwise credited

This tenth edition published 1989

ISBN 0 7110 1834 0

Published by Ian Allan Ltd
and phototypeset and printed by Ian Allan Printing Ltd at their works
at Coombelands in Runnymede, England

Cover: ZH200; BAe Hawk 200. British Aerospace

Introduction

This tenth edition of *abc Military Aircraft Markings*, a companion to *abc Civil Aircraft Markings*, again sets out to list in alphabetical and numerical order all the aircraft which carry a United Kingdom military serial, and which are based, or might be seen, in the UK. The term 'aircraft' used here covers powered, manned aeroplanes, helicopters and gliders. Included are all the current Royal Air Force, Royal Navy, Army Air Corps, Ministry of Defence (Procurement Executive), manufacturers' test aircraft and civilian-owned aircraft with military markings, together with gliders of the services' gliding associations.

Aircraft withdrawn from operational use but which are retained in the UK for ground training purposes or otherwise preserved by the Services and in museums and collections are listed. The serials of some incomplete aircraft have been included, such as the cockpit sections of machines displayed by the RAF Exhibition Flight, aircraft used by airfield fire sections and for service battle damage repair training (BDRT), together with significant parts of aircraft held by preservation groups and societies. Many of these aircraft are allocated, and sometimes wear, a secondary identity, such as an RAF Support Command 'M' or a Royal Navy 'A' maintenance number. These numbers are listed against those aircraft to which they have been allocated, and cross-references are included.

A serial 'missing' is either because it was never issued as it formed part of a 'black-out block', or because the aircraft is written off, scrapped, sold, abroad or allocated an alternative marking. Aircraft used as targets on MoD ranges to which access is restricted, and un-manned target drones, are omitted.

In the main, the serials listed are those markings presently displayed on the aircraft. Aircraft which bear a **false** serial are quoted in *italic* type. The manufacturer and aircraft type are given, together with recent alternative, previous, secondary or civil identity shown in *round* brackets. Complete records of multiple previous identities are only included where space permits. The operating unit and its based location, along with any known unit and base code markings in *square* brackets, are given as accurately as possible. The unit markings are normally carried boldly on the sides of the fuselage or on the aircraft's fin. In the case of RAF and AAC machines currently in service, they are usually one or two letters or numbers, while the RN continues to use a well-established system of three-figure codes between 000 and 999 together with a fin letter code denoting the aircraft's operational base. RN squadrons, units and bases are allocated blocks of numbers from which individual aircraft codes are issued. To help identification of RN bases and landing platforms on ships, a list of tail-letter codes with their appropriate name, helicopter code number, ship pennant number and type of vessel is included; as is a helicopter code number/ships' tail-letter code grid cross-reference.

Codes change, for example when aircraft move between units, and therefore the markings currently painted on a particular aircraft might not be those shown in this edition because of subsequent events. Those airframes which may not appear in the next edition because of sale, accident, etc, have their fates, where known, given in italic type in the 'Locations' column.

A new feature in this tenth edition is a Guide to the location of operational bases of military aircraft in the UK, compiled by Wal Gandy. This includes all RAF, RN, AAC, MoD(PE) and civil airfields where the military aircraft listed are based or regularly operate from.

The Irish Army Air Corps fleet is listed, together with the serials of other overseas air arms whose aircraft might be seen visiting the UK from time to time. The serial numbers are as usually presented on the individual machine or as they are normally identified. Where possible, the aircraft's base and operating unit have been shown.

USAF, US Army and US Navy aircraft based in the UK and in Western Europe, and of types which regularly visit the UK from the USA, are each listed in separate sections by aircraft type. The serial number actually displayed on the aircraft is shown in full, with additional Fiscal Year (FY) or full serial information also provided. Where appropriate, details of the operating wing, squadron allocation and base are added.

Veteran and Vintage aircraft which carry overseas military markings but which are based in the UK have been separately listed showing the identity carried as a principal means of identification.

Information shown is believed to be correct at 31 January 1989, and significant changes can be monitored through the monthly 'Military Markings' column in *Aircraft Illustrated*.

Acknowledgements

The compiler wishes to thank the many people who have taken trouble to send comments, criticism and other useful information following the publication of the previous edition of *abc Military Aircraft Markings*. In particular the following correspondents: D. Braithwaite, S. Bushell, P. H. Butler, CU Friends, J. R. Cross, D. P. Curtis, G. Hall, J. Henderson, C. D. Madd, P.-J. Martin, T. Poole, M. C. Powney, L. P. Robinson.

This compilation has relied heavily on the publications of the following aviation groups and societies: *Air* (West London Aviation Group), *Air North*, *British Aviation Review* (British Aviation Research Group), *Clwyd Air Letter* (Clwyd Aviation Group), *Humberside Air Review* (Humberside Aviation Society), *Irish Air Letter*, *Norfolk Air Review* (Norfolk Aviation Group), *North-West Air News* (Air Britain, Merseyside), *Osprey* (Solent Aviation Society), *Prestwick Airport Letter* (Prestwick Airport Aviation Group), *Scotland Scanned* & *Scottish Air News* (Central Scotland Aviation Group), *Skyward* (Westcountry Aviation Society), *South West Aviation News* (South West Aviation Society), *Stansted Aviation Newsletter* (The Stansted Aviation Society), *Strobe* (East Anglia Aviation Group), *Ulster Airmail* (Ulster Aviation Society), together with these publications: *Military Aircraft Serials of Europe* (The Aviation Hobby Shop) and *Wrecks and Relics XI* (Midland Counties Publications).

The new edition of *abc Military Aircraft Markings* would not have been possible without considerable research and checking by Howard Curtis, Wal Gandy and Alison March to whom I am indebted.

PRM

Abbreviations

AAC	Army Air Corps	AvCo	Aviation Company
A&AEE	Aeroplane & Armament Experimental Establishment	AW	Armstrong Whitworth Aircraft/Aircraft Workshops
AAS	Aeromedical Airlift Squadron	AW&CS	Airborne Warning & Control Squadron/
ABS	Air Base Squadron	AW&CW	Wing
ABW	Air Base Wing	BAC	British Aircraft Corporation
ACCGS	Air Cadets Central Gliding School	BAe	British Aerospace Company
ACCS	Airborne Command and Control	BAOR	British Army of the Rhine
ACCW	Squadron/Wing	BAPC	British Aircraft Preservation Council
ACR	Armoured Cavalry Regiment		
AEF	Air Experience Flight	BATUS	British Army Training Unit Support
AES	Air Engineering School	BBMF	Battle of Britain Memorial Flight
AETW	Air Engineering Training Wing	BDRF	Battle Damage Repair Flight
AEW	Airborne Early Warning	BDRT	Battle Damage Repair Training
AFRES	Air Force Reserve	Bf	Bayerische Flugzeugwerke
AFSC	Air Force System Command	BFWF	Basic Fixed Wing Flight
AHB	Attack Helicopter Battalion	BGA	British Gliding & Soaring Association
AIU	Accident Investigation Unit		
AKG	Aufklärüngs Geschwader (Reconnaissance Wing)	BHC	British Hovercraft Corporation
		BP	Boulton & Paul
AMD-BA	Avions Marcel Dassault-Breguet Aviation	B-V	Boeing-Vertol
AMS	Air Movements School	BW	Bomber Wing
ANG	Air National Guard	CARG	Cotswold Aircraft Restoration Group
APS	Aircraft Preservation Society		
ARF	Aircraft Restoration Flight	CASA	Construcciones Aeronautics SA
ARG	Air Refuelling Group	CATCS	Central Air Traffic Control School
ARRS	Aerospace Rescue and Recovery	CBAS	Commando Brigade Air Squadron
ARRW	Squadron/Wing	CCF	Combined Cadet Force
ARS	Air Refuelling Squadron	CDE	Chemical Defence Establishment
ARW	Air Refuelling Wing	CFS	Central Flying School
ARWS	Advanced Rotary Wing Squadron	CinC	Commander in Chief
AS	Aggressor Squadron	Co	Company
ASF	Aircraft Servicing Flight	CSDE	Central Servicing Development Establishment
AS&RU	Aircraft Salvage and Repair Unit		
ATC	Air Training Corps	CTE	Central Training Establishment
ATCC	Air Traffic Control Centre	CTTS	Civilian Technical Training School
ATS	Aircrewman Training Squadron	CV	Chance-Vought

British Military Aircraft Serials

The Committee of Imperial Defence through its Air Committee introduced a standardised system of numbering aircraft in November 1912. The Air Department of the Admiralty was allocated the first batch 1-200 and used these to cover aircraft already in use and those on order. The Army was issued with the next block from 201-800, which included the number 304 which was given to the Cody Biplane now preserved in the Science Museum. By the outbreak of World War 1 the Royal Navy was on its second batch of serials 801-1600 and this system continued with alternating allocations between the Army and Navy until 1916 when number 10000, a Royal Flying Corps BE2C, was reached.

It was decided not to continue with five digit numbers but instead to start again from 1, prefixing RFC aircraft with the letter A and RNAS aircraft with the prefix N. The RFC allocations commenced with A1 an FE2D and before the end of the year had reached A9999 an Armstrong Whitworth FK8. The next group commenced with B1 and continued in logical sequence through the C, D, E and F prefixes. G was used on a limited basis to identity captured German aircraft, while H was the last block of wartime ordered aircraft. To avoid confusion I was not used, so the new postwar machines were allocated serials in the J range. A further minor change was made in the serial numbering system in August 1929 when it was decided to maintain four numerals after the prefix letter, thus omitting numbers 1 to 999. The new K series therefore commenced at K1000, which was allocated to an AW Atlas.

The Naval N prefix was not used in such a logical way. Blocks of numbers were allocated for specific types of aircraft such as seaplanes or flying boats. By the late 1920s the sequence had largely been used up and a new series using the prefix S was commenced. In 1930 separate naval allocations were stopped and subsequent serials were issued in the 'military' range which had by this time reached the K series. A further change in the pattern of allocations came in the L range. Commencing with L7272 numbers were issued in blocks with smaller blocks of serials between not used. These were known as blackout blocks. As M had already been used as a suffix for Maintenance Command instructional airframes it was not used as a prefix. Although N had previously been used for naval aircraft it was used again for serials allocated from 1937.

With the build-up to World War 2 the rate of allocations quickly accelerated and the prefix R was being used when war was declared. The letters O and Q were not allotted, and nor was S which had been used up to S1865 for naval aircraft before integration into the RAF series. By 1940 the serial Z9999 had been reached, as part of a blackout block, with the letters U and Y not used to avoid confusion. The option to recommence serial allocation at A1000 was not taken up; instead it was decided to use an alphabetical two-letter prefix with three numerals running from 100 to 999. Thus AA100 was allocated to a Blenheim IV.

This two-letter, three-numeral serial system which started in 1940 continues today with the current issue being in the ZH range. The letters C, I, O, Q, U and Y were, with the exception of NC, not used. For various reasons the following letter combinations were not issued: DA, DB, DH, EA, GA to GZ, HA, HT, JE, JH, JJ, KR to KT, MR, NW, NZ, SA to SK, SV, TN, TR and VE. The first postwar serials issued were in the VP range while the end of the WZs had been reached by the Korean War. At the current rate of issue the Z range should last out the remainder of this century.

Note: Whilst every effort has been made to ensure the accuracy of this publication, no part of the contents has been obtained from official sources. The compiler will be pleased to continue to receive comments, corrections and further information for inclusion in subsequent editions of *Military Aircraft Markings*. A monthly up-date of additions and amendments is published in *Aircraft Illustrated*.

British Military Aircraft Markings

A serial in *italics* denotes that it is not the genuine marking for that airframe.

Serial	Type (alternative identity)	Owner, Operator or Location	Notes
164	Bleriot Type XI (BAPC 106)	RAF Museum, Hendon	
168	Sopwith Tabloid Scout Replica (G-BFDE)	RAF Museum, Hendon	
304	Cody Biplane (BAPC 62)	Science Museum, South Kensington	
433	Bleriot Type XXVII (BAPC 107)	RAF Museum, Hendon	
687	RAF BE2b (BAPC 181)	RAF Museum Store, Cardington	
2345	Vickers FB5 Gunbus Replica (G-ATVP)	RAF Museum, Hendon	
2699	RAF BE2C	Imperial War Museum, Lambeth	
3066	Caudron GIII (G-AETA)	RAF Museum, Hendon	
5964	DH2 Replica (BAPC 112)	Museum of Army Flying, Middle Wallop	
5964	DH2 Replica (G-BFVH)	Privately owned, Duxford	
6232	RAF BE2C Replica (BAPC 41)	RAF St Athan Historic Aircraft Collection	
8151	Sopwith Baby Replica (BAPC 137)		
8359	Short 184	FAA Museum, RNAS Yeovilton	
A1325	RAF BE2e	Mosquito Aircraft Museum, London Colney	
A1742	Scout D Replica (BAPC 38)	RAF, St Mawgan	
A4850	RAF SE5A Replica (BAPC176)	South Yorkshire APS, Firbeck	
A8226	Sopwith 1½ Strutter Replica (G-BIDW)	RAF Museum, Hendon	
B1807	Sopwith Pup (G-EAVX) [A7]	Privately owned, Keynsham, Avon	
B4863	Eberhardt SE5E (G-BLXT) [G]	Privately owned, Booker	
B4863	RAF SE5A Replica (BAPC 113) [G]		
B6401	Sopwith Camel F1 Replica (G-AWYY/C1701)	FAA Museum, RNAS Yeovilton	
B7270	Sopwith Camel F1 Replica (G-BFCZ)	Privately owned, Booker	
C1904	RAF SE5A Replica (G-PFAP) [Z]	Privately owned, Bicester	
C4912	Bristol M1C Replica (G-BLWM)	RAF Museum Store, Cardington	
C4912	Bristol M1C Replica (BAPC 135)	Northern Aeroplane Workshops	
D3419	Sopwith Camel F1 Replica (BAPC 59)	RAF, St Mawgan	
D5329	Sopwith Dolphin	RAF Museum Store, Cardington	
D7560	Avro 504K	Science Museum, South Kensington	
D7889	Bristol F2b Fighter (G-AANM/BAPC 166)	Privately owned, St Leonards	
D8096	Bristol F2B Fighter (G-AEPH) [D]	Shuttleworth Collection, Old Warden	
E373	Avro 504K Replica (BAPC178)	Privately owned, Eccleston, Lancs	
E449	Avro 504K (G-EBJE)	RAF Museum, Hendon	
E2466	Bristol F2b (BAPC165)	RAF Museum, Hendon	
E2581	Bristol F2b Fighter	Imperial War Museum, Lambeth	
E6452	SNCAN Stampe SV4C (G-AXNW)	Privately owned, St Merryn	
F141	RAF SE5A Replica (G-SEVA) [C]	Privately owned, Boscombe Down	
F235	RAF SE5A Replica (G-BMDB) [B]	Privately owned, Boscombe Down	
F344	Avro 504K Replica	RAF Museum Store, Henlow	
F760	SE5A Microlight Replica [A]	Privately owned, Redhill	
F904	RAF SE5A (G-EBIA)	Shuttleworth Collection, Old Warden	
F938	RAF SE5A (G-EBIC)	RAF Museum, Hendon	
F939	RAF SE5A (G-EBIB/F937) [6]	Science Museum, South Kensington	
F943	RAF SE5A Replica (G-BIHF) [S]	Privately owned, Booker	
F943	RAF SE5A Replica (G-BKDT)	Privately owned, Elvington	
F1010	DH9A [19]	RAF Museum, Hendon	
F3556	RAF RE8	Imperial War Museum, Lambeth	
F4013	Sopwith Camel Replica	Privately owned, Coventry	
F5447	RAF SE5A Replica (G-BKER) [N]	Privately owned, Strathallan	
F5459	RAF SE5A Replica (BAPC 142) [11-Y]	Cornwall Aero Park, Helston	

7

Notes	Serial	Type (alternative identity)	Owner, Operator or Location
	F-5459	RAF SE5A Replica (G-INNY) [Y]	Privately owned, Old Sarum
	F6314	Sopwith Camel F1 [B]	RAF Museum, Hendon
	F8010	RAF SE5A Replica (G-BDWJ) [Z]	Privately owned, Booker
	F8614	Vickers Vimy Replica (G-AWAU)	RAF Museum, Hendon
	G1381	Avro 504K Replica [G] (BAPC 177)	Brooklands Museum, Weybridge
	H1968	Avro 504K Replica (BAPC 42)	RAF St Athan Historic Aircraft Collection
	H2311	Avro 504K (G-ABAA)	RAF Museum Store, Henlow
	H3426	Hawker Hurricane Replica (BAPC 68)	Midland Air Museum, Coventry
	H5199	Avro 504N (BK892, 3118M, G-ACNB, G-ADEV)	Shuttleworth Collection, Old Warden
	J7326	DH Humming Bird (G-EBQP)	Privately owned, Hemel Hempstead
	J8067	Pterodactyl 1a	Science Museum, South Kensington
	J9941	Hawker Hart 2 (G-ABMR)	RAF Museum, Hendon
	K1786	Hawker Tomtit (G-AFTA)	Shuttleworth Collection, Old Warden
	K1930	Hawker Fury Replica (G-BKBB)	Privately owned, Booker
	K2050	Hawker Fury Replica (G-ASCM)	Privately owned, Andrewsfield
	K2059	Isaacs Fury (G-PFAR)	Privately owned, Dunkeswell
	K2060	Isaacs Fury II (G-BKZM)	Privately owned, Huddersfield
	K2567	DH Tiger Moth (G-MOTH) (really DE306/7035M)	Russavia Collection, Duxford
	K2568	DH Tiger Moth (G-APMM) (really DE419)	Privately owned, Bedford
	K2571	DH Tiger Moth	Privately owned, Lutterworth
	K2572	DH Tiger Moth (G-AOZH) (really NM129)	Privately owned, Shoreham
	K3215	Avro Tutor (G-AHSA)	Shuttleworth Collection, Old Warden
	K3584	DH 82B Queen Bee (BAPC 186)	Mosquito Aircraft Museum, London Colney
	K3731	Isaacs Fury Replica (G-RODI)	Privately owned, Exeter
	K4232	Avro Rota I (SE-AZB)	RAF Museum, Hendon
	K4235	Avro Rota I (G-AHMJ)	Shuttleworth Collection, Old Warden
	K4972	Hawker Hart Trainer IIA (1764M)	RAF Museum Restoration Centre, Cardington
	K5054	Supermarine Spitfire Replica	Privately owned, Swindon
	K5414	Hawker Hind (G-AENP/ BAPC 78) [XV]	Shuttleworth Collection, Old Warden
	K6038	Westland Wallace II (2365M)	RAF Museum Store, Cardington
	K7271	Hawker Fury II Replica (BAPC 148)	RAF Cosford Aerospace Museum
	K8042	Gloster Gladiator II (8372M)	RAF Museum, Hendon
	K9942	VS Spitfire IA (8383M) [SD-V]	RAF Museum, Hendon
	L1592	Hawker Hurricane I [KW-Z]	Science Museum, South Kensington
	L1592	Hawker Hurricane I Replica (BAPC 63) [KW-Z]	Torbay Aircraft Museum, Paignton
	L2301	VS Walrus I (G-AIZG)	FAA Museum, RNAS Yeovilton
	L2940	Blackburn Skua I	FAA Museum, RNAS Yeovilton
	L5343	Fairey Battle I	RAF St Athan Historic Aircraft Collection
	L6906	Miles Magister I (G-AKKY/T9841) (BAPC 44)	Brooklands Museum, Weybridge
	L7775	Vickers Wellington IA (fuselage)	South Yorkshire Aircraft Museum, Firbeck, Notts
	L8032	Gloster Gladiator (G-AMRK)	Shuttleworth Collection, Old Warden
	L8756	Bristol Bolingbroke IVT (RCAF 10001) [XD-E]	RAF Hendon
	N248	Supermarine S6A	Southampton Hall of Aviation
	N1671	Boulton Paul Defiant I (8370M) [EW-D]	Battle of Britain Museum, Hendon
	N1854	Fairey Fulmar II (G-AIBE)	FAA Museum, RNAS Yeovilton
	N2078	Sopwith Baby	FAA Museum, RNAS Yeovilton
	N2276	Gloster Gladiator II (really N5903) [H]	FAA Museum, RNAS Yeovilton
	N3289	VS Spitfire Replica [OW-K] (BAPC65)	Kent Battle of Britain Museum, Hawkinge
	N2980	Vickers Wellington IA [R]	Brooklands Museum, Weybridge
	N3788	Miles Magister I (G-AKPF) (really G-ANLT)	Privately owned, Cambridge
	N4389	Fairey Albacore I [4M] (really N4172)	FAA Museum, RNAS Yeovilton

Serial	Type (alternative identity)	Owner, Operator or Location	Notes
N4877	Avro Anson I (G-AMDA) [VX-F]	Skyfame Collection, Duxford	
N5180	Sopwith Pup (G-EBKY)	Shuttleworth Collection, Old Warden	
N5182	Sopwith Pup Replica (G-APUP)	RAF Museum, Hendon	
N5195	Sopwith Pup (G-ABOX)	Museum of Army Flying, Middle Wallop	
N5492	Sopwith Triplane Replica (BAPC 111)	FAA Museum, RNAS Yeovilton	
N5628	Gloster Gladiator II	RAF Museum, Hendon	
N5912	Sopwith Triplane (8385M)	RAF Museum, Hendon	
N6004	Short Stirling 1	RAeS Medway Branch, Rochester	
N6160	Sopwith Pup	Privately owned, Tattershall Thorpe	
N6452	Sopwith Pup Replica (G-BIAU)	FAA Museum, RNAS Yeovilton	
N6466	DH Tiger Moth (G-ANKZ)	Privately owned, Barton	
N6720	DH Tiger Moth (7014M) [RUO-B]	No 1940 Sqn ATC, Levenshulme	
N6812	Sopwith Camel	Imperial War Museum, Lambeth	
N6847	DH Tiger Moth (G-APAL)	Privately owned, Little Gransden	
N6848	DH Tiger Moth (G-BALX)	Privately owned, Sedlescombe	
N6985	DH Tiger Moth (G-AHMN)	Museum of Army Flying, Middle Wallop	
N9191	DH Tiger Moth (G-ALND)	Privately owned, Shipdham	
N9238	DH Tiger Moth (G-ANEL)	Privately owned, Oxford	
N9389	DH Tiger Moth (G-ANJA)	Privately owned, Shipmeadow, Suffolk	
N9510	DH Tiger Moth (G-AOEL)	Royal Scottish Museum of Flight, East Fortune	
N9899	Supermarine Southampton I	RAF Museum Restoration Centre, Cardington	
P2183	Fairey Battle I	RAF St Athan Historic Aircraft Collection	
P2617	Hawker Hurricane I (8373M) [AF-F]	RAF Museum, Hendon	
P3059	Hawker Hurricane Replica [SD-N] (BAPC64)	Kent Battle of Britain Museum, Hawkinge	
P3175	Hawker Hurricane I (Wreckage)	RAF Museum, Hendon	
P4139	Fairey Swordfish II [5H] (really HS618/A2001)	FAA Museum, RNAS Yeovilton	
P5865	CCF Harvard 4 (N13631)	Privately owned, North Weald	
P6382	Miles M.14A Hawk Trainer (G-AJRS)	Shuttleworth Collection, Old Warden	
P7350	VS Spitfire IIA (G-AWIJ) [UO-T]	RAF Battle of Britain Memorial Flight, Coningsby	
P7540	VS Spitfire IIA [DU-W]	Dumfries & Galloway Aviation Museum Tinwald Downs	
P9390	VS Spitfire I Replica (BAPC 71) [KL-B]	Norfolk & Suffolk Aviation Museum, Flixton	
P9444	VS Spitfire IA [RN-D]	Science Museum, South Kensington	
R1914	Miles Magister (G-AHUJ)	Strathallan Aircraft Collection	
R3950	Fairey Battle I (RCAF 1899) [RA-L]	Privately owned, Duxford	
R4907	DH Tiger Moth (G-ANCS)	Privately owned, Moulton St Mary	
R4959	DH Tiger Moth (G-ARAZ) [59]	Privately owned, Goodwood	
R5086	DH Tiger Moth (G-APIH)	Privately owned, Little Gransden	
R5250	DH Tiger Moth (G-AODT)	Privately owned, Swanton Morley	
R5868	Avro Lancaster I (7325M) [RO-S]	Bomber Command Museum, Hendon	
R6915	VS Spitfire I	Imperial War Museum, Lambeth	
R9125	Westland Lysander III (8377M) [LX-L]	Battle of Britain Museum, Hendon	
S1287	Fairey Flycatcher Replica (G-BEYB) [5]	Privately owned, Stockbridge	
S1595	Supermarine S6B	Science Museum, South Kensington	
S1595	Supermarine S6B Replica (BAPC 156)	Privately owned, North Weald	
S3398	Spad XIII Replica (G-BFYO) [2]	FAA Museum, RNAS Yeovilton	
S4523	Spad XIII [I] (N4727V)	Imperial War Museum, Lambeth	
T5424	DH Tiger Moth (G-AJOA)	Privately owned, Chiseldon	
T5493	DH Tiger Moth (G-ANEF)	Privately owned, Cranwell North	
T5672	DH Tiger Moth (G-ALRI)	Privately owned, Chalmington	
T5854	DH Tiger Moth (G-ANKK)	Privately owned, Halfpenny Green	
T5879	DH Tiger Moth (G-AXBW)	Privately owned, Tongham	
T5968	DH Tiger Moth (G-ANNN)	Privately owned, Kilkerran	
T6099	DH Tiger Moth (G-AOGR/XL714)	Privately owned, Clacton	
T6296	DH Tiger Moth (8387M)	RAF Museum, Hendon	

Notes	Serial	Type (alternative identity)	Owner, Operator or Location
	T6313	DH Tiger Moth (G-AHVU)	Privately owned, Denham
	T6553	DH Tiger Moth (G-APIG) [N]	Privately owned, Avignon
	T6818	DH Tiger Moth (G-ANKT)	Shuttleworth Collection, Old Warden
	T7281	DH Tiger Moth (G-ARTL)	Privately owned, Egton, nr Whitby
	T7404	DH Tiger Moth (G-ANMV)	Privately owned, Booker
	T7909	DH Tiger Moth (G-ANON)	Privately owned, Sherburn-in-Elmet
	T7997	DH Tiger Moth (G-AOBH)	Privately owned, Benington
	T8191	DH Tiger Moth	RN Historic Flight, RNAS Yeovilton
	T9707	Miles Magister (G-AKKR/8378M/T9708)	Greater Manchester Museum of Science and Industry
	T9738	Miles Hawk Trainer III (G-AKAT)	Privately owned, Hillam
	V3388	Airspeed Oxford (G-AHTW)	Skyfame Collection, Duxford
	V7350	Hawker Hurricane I	Robertsbridge Aviation Society
	V7767	Hawker Hurricane Replica (BAPC 72)	Air Museum, North Weald
	V9281	WS Lysander III (G-BCWL) [RU-M]	Privately owned, Henstridge
	V9300	WS Lysander III (RCAF 1558/ G-LIZY)	British Aerial Museum, Duxford
	V9441	WS Lysander IIIA (RCAF2355/G-AZWT) [AR-A]	Strathallan Aircraft Collection
	W1048	HP Halifax II (8465M) [TL-S]	RAF Museum, Hendon
	W4041	Gloster E28/39 [G]	Science Museum, South Kensington
	W4050	DH Mosquito 1	Mosquito Aircraft Museum, London Colney
	W5856	Fairey Swordfish II (G-BMGC)	Strathallan Aircraft Collection
	W5984	Fairey Swordfish II	See P4139
	X4590	VS Spitfire I (8384M) [PR-F]	RAF Museum, Hendon
	Z2033	Fairey Firefly I (G-ASTL)	Skyfame Collection, Duxford
	Z7015	Hawker Sea Hurricane IB (G-BKTH)	Shuttleworth Collection, Duxford
	Z7197	Percival Proctor III (G-AKZN/ 8380M)	RAF St Athan Historic Aircraft Collection
	Z7258	DH Dragon Rapide (G-AHGD) (really NR786)	Privately owned, Old Warden
	AB910	VS Spitfire VB [BP-O]	RAF Battle of Britain Memorial Flight, Coningsby
	AE436	HP Hampden (parts)	RAFM c/o Lincolnshire Aviation Heritage Centre, East Kirkby
	AL246	Grumman Martlet I	FAA Museum, RNAS Yeovilton
	AM561	Lockheed Hudson V (remains)	Cornwall Aero Park, Helston
	AP507	Cierva C30A (G-ACWP) [KX-P]	Science Museum, South Kensington
	AR213	VS Spitfire IA (G-AIST) [PR-D]	Privately owned, Booker
	AR501	VS Spitfire VC (G-AWII) [NN-D]	Shuttleworth Collection, Duxford
	BB807	DH Tiger Moth (G-ADWO)	Southampton Hall of Aviation
	BB814	DH Tiger Moth (G-AFWI)	RN Gliding Club, Lee-on-Solent
	BL614	VS Spitfire VB (4354M) [ZD-F]	Greater Manchester Museum of Science and Industry
	BM597	VS Spitfire VB (5718M) [PR-O]	RAF Church Fenton, on gate
	BN230	Hawker Hurricane IIC (5466M) (really LF751) [FT-A]	RAF Manston, Memorial Pavilion
	DE208	DH Tiger Moth (G-AGYU)	Privately owned, Nayland
	DE363	DH Tiger Moth (G-ANFC)	Military Aircraft Preservation Group, Hadfield, Derbyshire
	DE373	DH Tiger Moth T2 (A680/ A2127)	Privately owned
	DE623	DH Tiger Moth (G-ANFI)	Privately owned, St Athan
	DE638	DH Tiger Moth (G-ANEJ)	Privately owned, Bilton, Humbs
	DE673	DH Tiger Moth (G-ADNZ/ 6948M)	Privately owned, Hampton
	DE992	DH Tiger Moth (G-AXXV)	Privately owned, Wellesbourne Mountford
	DF128	DH Tiger Moth (G-AOJJ) [RCO-U]	Privately owned, Abingdon
	DF130	DH Tiger Moth (G-BACK)	Sold to Chile
	DF155	DH Tiger Moth (G-ANFV)	Privately owned, Lossiemouth
	DF198	DH Tiger Moth (G-BBRB)	Privately owned, Biggin Hill
	DG202	Gloster F9/40 Meteor (5758M) [G]	RAF Cosford Aerospace Museum
	DG590	Miles Hawk Major (G-ADMW/8379M)	RAF Museum Store, Henlow
	DP872	Fairey Barracuda II	FAA Museum, Yeovilton

Serial	Type (alternative identity)	Owner, Operator or Location	Notes
DR613	FW Wicko GM1 (G-AFJB)	Privately owned, Berkswell	
DR628	Beech D.17s (N18V) [PB-1]	Privately owned, Duxford	
DV372	Avro Lancaster I (nose only)	Imperial War Museum, Lambeth	
EE416	Gloster Meteor III (nose only)	Science Museum, South Kensington	
EE531	Gloster Meteor F4 (7090M)	Midland Air Museum, Coventry	
EE549	Gloster Meteor F4 (7008M)	RAF St Athan Historic Aircraft Collection	
EE606	VS Spitfire VC (G-MKVC) [D-B]	Privately owned, Micheldever	
EJ693	Hawker Tempest V [SA-J]	Privately owned	
EM720	DH Tiger Moth (G-AXAN)	Privately owned, Staverton	
EM727	DH Tiger Moth (G-AOXN)	Privately owned, Yeovil	
EM903	DH Tiger Moth (G-APBI)	Privately owned, Audley End	
EN398	VS Spitfire IX Replica (BAPC184) [JE-J]	Aces High Ltd, North Weald	
EP120	VS Spitfire VB (5377M/8070M) [QV-H]	RAF Wattisham, on display	
EX280	NA Harvard IIA (G-TEAC) [G]	Privately owned, North Weald	
EX976	NA Harvard III	FAA Museum, RNAS Yeovilton	
EZ259	NA Harvard III (G-BMJW)	Privately owned, Bracknell	
EZ407	NA Harvard III	RN Historic Flight, Lee-on-Solent	
FE905	NA Harvard IIB (LN-BNM/12392)	RAF Museum Restoration Centre, Cardington	
FE992	NA Harvard IIB (G-BDAM)	Privately owned, Henstridge	
FH153	NA Harvard IIB (G-BBHK) [GW-A]	Privately owned, Cardiff	
FR870	Curtiss Kittyhawk III (NL1009N) [GA-S]	Privately owned, Duxford	
FS728	NA Harvard IIB (G-BAFM)	Privately owned, Booker	
FS890	NA Harvard IIB (7554M)	A&AEE, stored Boscombe Down	
FT239	NA Harvard IV (G-BIWX)	Privately owned, White Waltham	
FT323	NA Harvard III (really P.AF.1513)	Vintage Aircraft Team, Cranfield	
FT375	NA Harvard IIB	MoD(PE) A&AEE Boscombe Down	
FT391	NA Harvard IIB (G-AZBN)	Privately owned, Duxford	
FX301	NA Harvard III (G-JUDI) (really EX915)	Privately owned, Parham, Essex	
FX442	NA Harvard IIB	Privately owned, Bournemouth	
HA457	Hawker Tempest (fuselage)	RAF Museum Restoration Centre, Cardington	
HB275	Be.C-45 Expeditor II (N5063N)	Privately owned, White Waltham	
HB751	Fairchild Argus III (G-BCBL)	Privately owned, Little Gransden	
HD368	NA TB-25J Mitchell [VO-A] (really 44-30861) N90892/G-BKXW)	Aces High Ltd, North Weald	
HH379	GAL48 Hotspur II (rear fuselage only)	Museum of Army Flying, Middle Wallop	
HJ711	DH Mosquito NFII [VI-C]	Yorkshire Air Museum, Elvington	
HM354	Percival Proctor III (G-ANPP)	Privately owned, Stansted	
HR792	HP Halifax GR II	Yorkshire Air Museum, Elvington	
HS503	Fairey Swordfish IV (BAPC 108)	RAF Museum Store, Henlow	
HX922	DH Mosquito TT35 (G-AWJV) [EG-F] (really TA634)	Mosquito Aircraft Museum, London Colney	
JV482	Grumman Wildcat V	Ulster Aviation Society, Newtownards	
JV928	PBY-5A Catalina (G-BLSC) [Y]	Plane Sailing, Duxford	
KB889	Avro Lancaster B10 (G-LANC)	Imperial War Museum, Duxford	
KB976	Avro Lancaster B10 (G-BCOH) [LQ-K]	Privately owned, Cranfield	
KB994	Avro Lancaster B10 (fuselage)	Privately owned, Bedford	
KD431	CV Corsair IV [E2-M]	FAA Museum, RNAS Yeovilton	
KE209	Grumman Hellcat II	FAA Museum, RNAS Yeovilton	
KE418	Hawker Tempest (rear fuselage)	RAF Museum Store, Cardington	
KF183	NA Harvard IIB	MoD(PE) A&AEE Boscombe Down	
KF388	NA Harvard IIB (nose only)	Wessex Aviation Society, Wimborne	
KF423	NA Harvard II	Booker Aviation Museum	
KF435	NA Harvard IIB	Booker Air Museum	
KF594	NA Harvard IIB (cockpit section)	Newark Air Museum, Winthorpe	
KG374	Douglas Dakota C-4 [YS] (really KN645/8355M)	RAF Cosford Aerospace Museum	
KK995	Sikorsky Hoverfly I [E]	RAF Museum, Hendon	
KL161	NA B-25D Mitchell II (N88972)	The Fighter Collection, Duxford	
KN448	Douglas Dakota C4 (nose only)	Science Museum, South Kensington	
KN751	Consolidated Liberator VI [F]	RAF Cosford Aerospace Museum	
KP208	Douglas Dakota C-4 [YS]	Airborne Forces Museum, Aldershot	

Notes	Serial	Type (alternative identity)	Owner, Operator or Location
	KX829	Hawker Hurricane IV [JV-I]	Birmingham Museum of Science & Industry
	LA198	VS Spitfire F21 (7118M) [RAI-G]	RAF Leuchars, on display
	LA226	VS Spitfire F21 (7119M)	RAF, stored Shawbury
	LA255	VS Spitfire F21 (6490M) [JX-U]	RAF No 1 Sqn, Wittering
	LA564	VS Seafire F46	Privately owned, Newport Pagnell
	LB294	Taylorcraft Plus D (G-AHWJ)	Museum of Army Flying, Middle Wallop
	LB312	Taylorcraft Plus D (G-AHXE)	Privately owned, Shoreham
	LB375	Taylorcraft Plus D (G-AHGW)	Privately owned, Coventry
	LF363	Hawker Hurricane IIC [NV-L]	RAF Battle of Britain Memorial Flight, Coningsby
	LF738	Hawker Hurricane IIC (5405M)	RAF, RAeS Medway Branch, Rochester
	LF751	Hawker Hurricane IIC (5466M)	See BN230
	LF858	DH Queen Bee (G-BLUZ)	Privately owned, Meppershall
	LH208	Airspeed Horsa I (parts only)	Museum of Army Flying, Middle Wallop
	LS326	Fairey Swordfish II (G-AJVH) [L2]	RN Historic Flight, RNAS Yeovilton
	LZ551	DH Sea Vampire I [G]	FAA Museum, RNAS Yeovilton
	LZ766	Percival Proctor III (G-ALCK)	Skyfame Collection, Duxford
	MD497	WS 51 Widgeon (G-ANLW) [NE-X]	Privately owned, Wellingborough
	MF628	Vickers Wellington T10	Bomber Command Museum, Hendon
	MH434	VS Spitfire IX (G-ASJV)	Privately owned, Duxford
	MJ627	VS Spitfire TIX (G-ASOZ/ G-BMSB)	Privately owned, Kenilworth
	MJ730	VS Spitfire LFIX (G-BLAS)	Privately owned, East Midlands Airport
	MK356	VS Spitfire IX (5690M) [21-V]	RAF St Athan Historic Aircraft Collection
	ML407	VS Spitfire T9 (G-LFIX) [OU-V]	Privately owned, Goodwood
	ML417	VS Spitfire LFIXe (G-BJSG)	Privately owned, Duxford
	ML427	VS Spitfire IX (6457M) [I-ST]	Birmingham Museum of Science & Industry
	ML796	Short Sunderland V	Imperial War Museum, Duxford
	ML824	Short Sunderland V [NS-Z]	RAF Museum, Hendon
	MN235	Hawker Typhoon IB	RAF Museum, Hendon
	MP425	Airspeed Oxford I (G-AITB)	RAF Museum Store, Cardington
	MT438	Auster III (G-AREI)	Privately owned, Chessington
	MT719	VS Spitfire VIII (I-SPIT)	Privately owned, Coningsby
	MT847	VS Spitfire FRXIVe (6960M)	RAF Cosford Aerospace Museum
	MV154	VS Spitfire HF VIII (G-BKMI/ A58-671)	Privately owned, Charfield, Glos
	MV262	VS Spitfire XIV [42-G] (G-CCVV)	Privately owned, Micheldever
	MV363	VS Spitfire XIV (G-SPIT/G-BGHB) (really MV293)	Privately owned, Duxford
	MV370	VS Spitfire XIV (G-FXIV) [AV-L]	Privately owned, North Weald
	MW100	Avro York C1 (G-AGNV/TS798)	RAF Cosford Aerospace Museum
	NF370	Fairey Swordfish II	Imperial War Museum, Lambeth
	NF389	Fairey Swordfish III [5B]	FAA Museum, Fleetlands
	NF875	DH Dragon Rapide 6 (G-AGTM) [603/CH]	Russavia Collection, Duxford
	NH238	VS Spitfire IX (N238V/ G-MKIX)	Warbirds of GB, Biggin Hill
	NH799	VS Spitfire XIV	Privately owned, Duxford
	NJ673	Auster 5D (G-AOCR)	Privately owned, Wyberton
	NJ695	Auster 4 (G-AJXV)	Privately owned, Leicester East
	NJ703	Auster 5 (G-AKPI)	Privately owned, Doncaster
	NJ719	Auster 5 (G-ANFU) (really TW385)	North East Aircraft Museum, Usworth
	NL879	DH Tiger Moth (G-AVPJ)	Privately owned, Wellesbourne Mountford
	NL985	DH Tiger Moth (7015M)	Vintage Aircraft Team, Cranfield
	NP181	Percival Proctor IV (G-AOAR)	Privately owned, Biggin Hill
	NP184	Percival Proctor IV (G-ANYP) [K]	Torbay Aircraft Museum, Paignton
	NP294	Percival Proctor IV [TB-M]	Lincolnshire Aviation Museum, East Kirkby
	NP303	Percival Proctor IV (G-ANZJ)	Privately owned, Byfleet, Surrey
	NR747	DH Dragon Rapide (G-AJHO)	Privately owned, near Bassingbourn
	NV778	Hawker Tempest V (8386M)	RAF Museum, Hendon
	NX611	Avro Lancaster VII (G-ASXX/ 8375M) [YF-C]	Lincolnshire Aviation Heritage Center, East Kirkby
	PA474	Avro Lancaster I [PM-M^2]	RAF Battle of Britain Memorial Flight, Coningsby
	PF179	HS Gnat T1 (XR541/8602M)	RAF St Athan, CTTS

Serial	Type (alternative identity)	Owner, Operator or Location	Notes
PG617	DH Tiger Moth (G-AYVY)	*Sold in Sweden*	
PG651	DH Tiger Moth (G-AYUX)	*To I-EDAI*	
PG671	DH Tiger Moth (N82AM) [26]	*To Holland*	
PK624	VS Spitfire F22 (8072M) [RAU-T]	RAF Abingdon, at main gate	
PK664	VS Spitfire F22 (7759M) (V6-B)	RAF Binbrook, at main gate	
PK683	VS Spitfire F24 (7150M)	Southampton Hall of Aviation	
PK724	VS Spitfire F24 (7288M)	RAF Museum, Hendon	
PL344	VS Spitfire IX (G-IXCC)	Privately owned, Micheldever	
PL965	VS Spitfire XI [3-W]	RAeS, Rochester	
PL983	VS Spitfire XI (G-PRXI)	Warbirds of GB, Biggin Hill	
PM631	VS Spitfire XIX [DL-E]	RAF Battle of Britain Memorial Flight, Coningsby	
PM651	VS Spitfire XIX (7758M)	RAF Benson, at main gate	
PN323	HP Halifax VII (nose only)	Imperial War Museum, Duxford	
PP972	VS Seafire LIII	Warbirds of GB, Biggin Hill	
PS853	VS Spitfire XIX	RAF Battle of Britain Memorial Flight, Coningsby	
PS915	VS Spitfire XIX (7548M/7711M)	RAF Battle of Britain Memorial Flight, Coningsby	
PT462	VS Spitfire TIX (G-CTIX)	Privately owned, Micheldever, Hants	
PV202	VS Spitfire TIX (G-TRIX)	Privately owned, Micheldever, Hants	
PV260	VS Spitfire IX (really BR601) [DB-P]	Warbirds of GB, Biggin Hill	
PZ865	Hawker Hurricane IIc (G-AMAU) [RF-U]	RAF Battle of Britain Memorial Flight, Coningsby	
RA848	Slingsby Cadet TX1	Privately owned, Leeds	
RA854	Slingsby Cadet TX1	The Aeroplane Collection store, Wigan	
RA897	Slingsby Cadet TX1	Newark Air Museum store, Hucknall	
RD253	Bristol Beaufighter TF10 (7931M)	RAF Museum, Hendon	
RF342	Avro Lincoln B2 (G-29-1/ G-APRJ)	Aces High Ltd, Bedford	
RF398	Avro Lincoln B2 (8376M)	RAF Cosford Aerospace Museum	
RG333	Miles Messenger IIA (G-AIEK)	Privately owned, Felton, Bristol	
RG333	Miles Messenger IIA (G-AKEZ)	Torbay Aircraft Museum, Paignton	
RH377	Miles Messenger 4A (G-ALAH)	The Aeroplane Collection, RAF Henlow	
RH746	Bristol Brigand TF1	North East Aircraft Museum, Usworth	
RL962	DH Dragon Rapide (G-AHED)	RAF Museum Store, Cardington	
RM221	Percival Proctor IV (G-ANXR)	Privately owned, Biggin Hill	
RM689	VS Spitfire XIV (G-ALGT) [MN-E]	Rolls-Royce, Filton	
RR232	VS Spitfire IXC	Privately owned, Micheldever, Hants	
RR299	DH Mosquito T3 (G-ASKH) [HT-E]	British Aerospace, Hawarden	
RT188	Isaacs Spitfire Replica (G-BBJI) [R]	Privately owned, Langham	
RT520	Auster 5 (G-ALYB)	South Yorkshire Air Museum, Firbeck	
RT610	Auster 5A (G-AKWS)	Privately owned, Exeter	
RW382	VS Spitfire XVIe (7245M/ 8075M) [NG-C]	Privately owned, Earls Colne, Essex	
RW386	VS Spitfire XVIe (6944M/ G-BXVI) [RAK-A]	Warbirds of GB, Bitteswell	
RW388	VS Spitfire XVIe (6946M) [U4-U]	Stoke-on-Trent City Museum, Hanley	
RW393	VS Spitfire XVIe (7293M) [XT-A]	RAF Turnhouse, at main gate	
SL542	VS Spitfire XVIe (8390M) [4M-N]	RAF Coltishall, at main gate	
SL674	VS Spitfire XVIe [RAS-H] (8392M)	RAF Memorial Chapel, Biggin Hill	
SM832	VS Spitfire XIV (G-WWII)	Privately owned, Duxford	
SM969	VS Spitfire XVIII (G-BRAF)	Warbirds of GB, Bitteswell	
SX137	VS Seafire XVII	FAA Museum, RNAS Yeovilton	
SX300	VS Seafire XVII (A646/A696/ A2054)	Privately owned, Warwick	
SX336	VS Seafire XVII (A2055)	Privately owned, Twyford, Bucks	
TA122	DH Mosquito FBVI [UP-G]	Mosquito Aircraft Museum, London Colney	
TA634	DH Mosquito B35 (G-AWJV)	Mosquito Aircraft Museum, London Colney	
TA639	DH Mosquito TT35 [AZ-E] (7806M)	RAF Cosford Aerospace Museum	
TA719	DH Mosquito TT35 (G-ASKC) [6T]	Skyfame Collection, Duxford	

Notes	Serial	Type (alternative identity)	Owner, Operator or Location
	TB252	VS Spitfire XVIe (7257M/7281M/ 8073M) [GW-H]	Privately owned, Earls Colne, Essex
	TB382	VS Spitfire XVIe (7244M)	RAF Exhibition Flight, Abingdon
	TB752	VS Spitfire XVIe (7256M/ 7279M/8086M) [KH-Z]	RAF Manston, Memorial Hall
	TB863	VS Spitfire XVIe (G-CDAN)	*Sold to New Zealand, Oct 1988*
	TB885	VS Spitfire LFXVIe	Shoreham Aircraft Preservation Society
	TD248	VS Spitfire XVIe (7246M) [DW-A]	Privately owned, Earls Colne, Essex
	TE184	VS Spitfire LF XVI (6850M)	Privately owned, Micheldever, Hants
	TE311	VS Spitfire XVIe (7241M)	RAF Exhibition Flight, Abingdon
	TE356	VS Spitfire XVIe (7001M) (G-SXVI)	Warbirds of GB, Biggin Hill
	TE392	VS Spitfire XVIe (7000M/8074M)	Warbirds of GB, Biggin Hill
	TE462	VS Spitfire XVIe (7243M)	Royal Scottish Museum of Flight, East Fortune
	TE476	VS Spitfire XVIe (7451M/ 8071M)	RAF Northolt at main gate
	TE517	VS Spitfire LFIX (2046/G-BIXP/ G-CCIX)	Privately owned, Micheldever, Hants
	TE566	VS Spitfire LFIX (G-BLCK)	Privately owned, Ludham
	TF956	Hawker Sea Fury FB11 [123/T]	RN Historic Flight, RNAS Yeovilton
	TG263	Saro SRA1 (G-12-1) [P]	Science Museum, Wroughton
	TG511	HP Hastings T5 (8554M)	RAF Cosford Aerospace Museum
	TG517	HP Hastings T5 (517)	Newark Air Museum, Winthorpe
	TG528	HP Hastings C1A	Skyfame Collection, Duxford
	TG568	HP Hastings C1A	RAE Bedford Fire Section
	TJ118	DH Mosquito TT35 (nose only)	Mosquito Aircraft Museum store
	TJ138	DH Mosquito B35 (7607M) [VO-L]	RAF St Athan Historic Aircraft Collection
	TJ343	Auster 5 (G-AJXC)	Privately owned, Popham
	TJ398	Auster AOP5 (BAPC 70)	Aircraft Preservation Society of Scotland, East Fortune
	TJ457	Auster 5C (G-AKSZ)	Privately owned, RAF Halton
	TJ569	Auster 5 (G-AKOW)	Museum of Army Flying, Middle Wallop
	TJ672	Auster 5 (G-ANIJ)	Privately owned, Thruxton
	TJ704	Auster 5 [JA]	Yorkshire Air Museum, Elvington
	TK777	GAL Hamilcar I	Museum of Army Flying, Middle Wallop
	TL615	Airspeed Horsa II	Robertsbridge Aviation Society
	TL659	Airspeed Horsa (BAPC 80) [74]	Museum of Army Flying, Middle Wallop
	TP298	VS Spitfire XIV (fuselage)	Privately owned, Ludham
	TS291	Slingsby Cadet TX1 (BGA852)	Museum of Flight, East Fortune
	TV959	DH Mosquito T3 [AF-V]	Imperial War Museum, Lambeth
	TW117	DH Mosquito T3 (7805M)	Bomber Command Museum, Hendon
	TW385	Auster 5 (G-ANFU)	*See NJ719*
	TW439	Auster 5 (G-ANRP)	Privately owned, Dorchester
	TW467	Auster 5 (G-ANIE)	Privately owned, Cranfield
	TW511	Auster 5 (G-CMAL/G-APAF)	Privately owned, Skegness
	TW536	Auster AOP6 (7704M/G-BNGE) [TS-V]	AAC Historic Aircraft Flight, Middle Wallop
	TW591	Auster 6A (G-ARIH) [N]	Privately owned, Burnaston
	TW641	Auster AOP6 (G-ATDN)	Privately owned, Biggin Hill
	TX183	Avro Anson C19	Privately owned, Arbroath
	TX192	Avro Anson C19	Guernsey Airport Fire Section
	TX213	Avro Anson C19 (G-AWRS)	North East Aircraft Museum, Usworth
	TX214	Avro Anson C19 (7817M)	RAF Cosford Aerospace Museum
	TX226	Avro Anson C19 (7865M)	Imperial War Museum, Duxford
	TX228	Avro Anson C19	City of Norwich Aviation Museum
	TX235	Avro Anson C19	Snowdon Mountain Aviation, Llandwrog
	VD165	Slingsby T7 Kite	Russavia Collection, Dunstable
	VF301	DH Vampire F1 (7060M) [RAL-B]	Midland Air Museum, Coventry
	VF516	Auster AOP6 (G-ASMZ) [T]	Museum of Army Flying, Middle Wallop
	VF548	Beagle Terrier 1 (G-ASEG)	Privately owned, Liverpool
	VF611	Beagle A61 Terrier 2 (G-ATBU)	Privately owned, Hucknall
	VH127	Fairey Firefly TT4	FAA Museum, stored Wroughton
	VL348	Avro Anson C19 (G-AVVO)	Newark Air Museum, Winthorpe
	VL349	Avro Anson C19 (G-AWSA)	Norfolk & Suffolk Aviation Museum, Flixton
	VM325	Avro Anson C19	Midland Air Museum, Coventry
	VM360	Avro Anson C19 (G-APHV)	Royal Scottish Museum of Flight, East Fortune
	VM791	Slingsby Cadet TX3 (really XA312) (8876M)	No 135 Redhill & Reigate Sqn ATC, RAF Kenley

Serial	Type (alternative identity)	Owner, Operator or Location	Notes
VN148	Grunau Baby IIb (BAPC 33) (BGA 2400)	Russavia Collection, Duxford	
VP293	Avro Shackleton T4	Strathallan Aircraft Collection	
VP519	Avro Anson C19 (nose only) (G-AVVR)	Military Aircraft Preservation Group, Hadfield, Derbyshire	
VP952	DH Devon C2 (8820M)	RAF Cosford Aerospace Museum	
VP953	DH Devon C2	FSCTE, RAF Manston	
VP955	DH Devon C2 (G-DVON)	Privately owned, Bournemouth	
VP956	DH Devon C2	FSCTE, RAF Manston	
VP957	DH Devon C2 (8822M)	RAF Bishop's Court NI, BDRT	
VP958	DH Devon C2 [DC] (8795M)	Sold to New Zealand	
VP959	DH Devon C2 [L]	MoD(PE) RAE West Freugh	
VP960	DH Devon C2	FSCTE, RAF Manston	
VP961	DH Devon C2 (G-ALFM)	Privately owned, Leavesden	
VP962	DH Devon C2 (G-BLRB)	Privately owned, RAF Kemble	
VP963	DH Devon C2	FSCTE, RAF Manston	
VP965	DH Devon C2 [DE] (8823M)	FSCTE, RAF Manston	
VP967	DH Devon C2 (G-KOOL)	East Surrey Technical College, Redhill	
VP968	DH Devon C2	A&AEE Boscombe Down Fire Section	
VP971	DH Devon C2 (8824M)	RAF FF&SS, Catterick	
VP975	DH Devon C2 [M]	Science Museum, Wroughton	
VP976	DH Devon C2 (8784M)	RAF Northolt Fire Section	
VP977	DH Devon C2 (G-ALTS)	RAE West Freugh Fire Section	
VP981	DH Devon C2	RAF Battle of Britain Flight, Coningsby	
VR137	Westland Wyvern TF1	FAA Museum, RNAS Yeovilton	
VR192	Pervical Prentice T1 (G-APIT)	Second World War Aircraft Preservation Society, Lasham	
VR249	Percival Prentice T1 (G-APIY) [FA-EL]	Newark Air Museum, Winthorpe	
VR259	Percival Prentice T1 (G-APJB)	Aircraft Radio Museum, Coventry	
VR930	Hawker Sea Fury FB11 (8382M)	FAA Museum, stored Lee-on-Solent	
VS356	Percival Prentice T1 (G-AOLU)	Scottish Aircraft Collection Trust, Perth	
VS562	Avro Anson T21 (8012M)	Privately owned, Portsmouth	
VS610	Percival Prentice T1 (G-AOKL) [K-L]	Privately owned, Southend	
VS623	Percival Prentice T1 (G-AOKZ) [KQ-F]	Midland Air Museum, Coventry	
VT229	Gloster Meteor F4 (7151M) [60]	Privately owned, Winthorpe	
VT260	Gloster Meteor F4 (8813M) [67]	Imperial War Museum, Duxford	
VT409	Fairey Firefly AS5 (really WD889)	North East Aircraft Museum, Usworth	
VT812	DH Vampire F3 (7200M) [N]	RAF Museum, Hendon	
VT921	Grunau Baby	Privately owned, Honington	
VT935	Boulton Paul P111A (VT769)	Midland Air Museum, Coventry	
VV106	VS517 (7175M)	RAF Cosford Aerospace Museum	
VV119	Supermarine 535 (nose only) (7285M)	Lincolnshire Aviation Museum, East Kirkby	
VV217	DH Vampire FB5 (7323M)	No 301 Sqn ATC, Bury St Edmunds	
VV901	Avro Anson T21	Pennine Aviation Museum, Bacup	
VV950	Avro Anson T21	RAF Kinloss Fire Section	
VW453	Gloster Meteor T7 (8703M)	Cotswold Aircraft Restoration Group, RAF Innsworth	
VW985	Auster AOP6 (G-ASEF)	Privately owned, Upper Arncott, Oxon	
VX118	Auster 6A (G-ASNB)	Privately owned, Keevil	
VX185	EE Canberra B(I)8 (nose only) (7631M)	Science Museum, South Kensington	
VX250	DH Sea Hornet 21 [48] (rear fuselage)	Mosquito Aircraft Museum, London Colney	
VX272	Hawker P1052 (7174M)	RAF Cosford Aerospace Museum	
VX275	Slingsby Sedbergh TX1 (8884M) (BGA 572)	RAF Museum Store, Cardington	
VX461	DH Vampire FB5 (7646M)	RAF Museum Store, Henlow	
VX573	Vickers Valetta C2 (8389M)	RAF Cosford Aerospace Museum	
VX577	Vickers Valetta C2	North East Aircraft Museum, Usworth	
VX580	Vickers Valetta C2	Norfolk & Suffolk Aviation Museum Flixton	
VX595	WS51 Dragonfly HR1 [29]	RAF Museum Store, Henlow	
VX653	Hawker Sea Fury FB11	RAF Museum, Hendon	
VZ304	DH Vampire FB5 (7630M)	Vintage Aircraft Team, Cranfield	
VZ345	Hawker Sea Fury T20S	A&AEE Boscombe Down (on rebuild)	
VZ462	Gloster Meteor F8	Second World War Aircraft Preservation Society, stored	
VZ467	Gloster Meteor F8 [01]	RAF, stored Scampton	

Notes	Serial	Type (alternative identity)	Owner, Operator or Location
	VZ477	Gloster Meteor F8 (nose only) (7741M)	Kimbolton School CCF, Cambs
	VZ608	Gloster Meteor FR9	Newark Air Museum, Winthorpe
	VZ634	Gloster Meteor T7 (8657M)	Newark Air Museum, Winthorpe
	VZ638	Gloster Meteor T7 (G-JETM) [HF]	Privately owned, Charlwood, Surrey
	VZ728	RS4 Desford Trainer (G-AGOS)	Scottish Aircraft Collection Trust, Perth
	VZ962	WS51 Dragonfly HR1 [904]	International Helicopter Museum, Weston-super-Mare
	VZ965	WS51 Dragonfly HR5	FAA Museum, at RNAS Culdrose
	WA473	VS Attacker F1 [102/J]	FAA Museum, RNAS Yeovilton
	WA576	Bristol Sycamore 3 (G-ALSS/ 7900M)	Dumfries & Galloway Aviation Museum, Tinwald Downs
	WA577	Bristol Sycamore 3 (G-ALST/ 7718M)	North East Aircraft Museum, Usworth
	WA591	Gloster Meteor T7 (7917M) [W]	RAF Woodvale, on display
	WA634	Gloster Meteor T7/8	RAF Cosford Aerospace Museum
	WA638	Gloster Meteor T7	Martin Baker Aircraft, Chalgrove
	WA662	Gloster Meteor T7	MoD(PE) RAE Farnborough
	WA984	Gloster Meteor F8 [A]	Southampton Hall of Aviation
	WB188	Hawker Hunter F3 (7154M)	RAF Cosford Aerospace Museum
	WB271	Fairey Firefly AS5 [204/R]	RN Historic Flight, RNAS Yeovilton
	WB440	Fairey Firefly AS6	Greater Manchester Museum of Science and Industry
	WB491	Avro Ashton 2 (nose only) (TS897/G-AJJW)	Wales Aircraft Museum, Cardiff
	WB530	DH Devon C2 (8825M)	*Burned at RAF Swinderby*
	WB531	DH Devon C2 (G-BLRN)	*To USA as N531WB*
	WB533	DH Devon C2 (G-DEVN) [DA]	Privately owned, Shoreham
	WB550	DH Chipmunk T10 [F]	RAF EFTS, Swinderby
	WB556	DH Chipmunk T10	RAFGSA, Bicester
	WB560	DH Chipmunk T10	RAF No 4 AEF, Exeter
	WB565	DH Chipmunk T10 [X]	AAC BFWF, Middle Wallop
	WB567	DH Chipmunk T10	RAF No 12 AEF, Turnhouse
	WB569	DH Chipmunk T10	RAF No 1 AEF, Manston
	WB575	DH Chipmunk T10 [907]	RN Flying Grading Flt, Plymouth
	WB584	DH Chipmunk T10 PAX (7706M)	No 327 Sqn ATC, Kilmarnock
	WB585	DH Chipmunk T10 (G-AOSY) [RCU-X]	Privately owned, Blackbushe
	WB586	DH Chipmunk T10 [A]	RAF No 6 AEF, Abingdon
	WB588	DH Chipmunk T10 (G-AOTD) [D]	Shuttleworth Collection, Old Warden
	WB615	DH Chipmunk T10 [E]	AAC BFWF, Middle Wallop
	WB624	DH Chipmunk T10 PAX	The Aeroplane Collection, Warmingham
	WB626	DH Chipmunk T10 PAX	Privately owned, Swanton Morley
	WB627	DH Chipmunk T10 [N]	RAF No 5 AEF, Cambridge
	WB647	DH Chipmunk T10 [R]	AAC BFWF, Middle Wallop
	WB652	DH Chipmunk T10 [V]	RAF No 5 AEF, Cambridge
	WB654	DH Chipmunk T10 [14]	RAF No 10 AEF, Woodvale
	WB657	DH Chipmunk T10 [908]	RN Flying Grading Flt, Plymouth
	WB660	DH Chipmunk T10 (G-ARMB)	Privately owned, Henstridge
	WB670	DH Chipmunk T10 (8361M)	Newark Air Museum, Winthorpe
	WB671	DH Chipmunk T10 [910]	RN Flying Grading Flt, Plymouth
	WB685	DH Chipmunk T10 PAX	North East Aircraft Museum, Usworth
	WB693	DH Chipmunk T10 [S]	AAC BFWF, Middle Wallop
	WB697	DH Chipmunk T10 [O]	RAF No 3 AEF, Filton
	WB732	DH Chipmunk T10 (G-AOJZ/ G-ASTD)	Air Service Training, Perth
	WB739	DH Chipmunk T10 [8]	RAF No 8 AEF, Shawbury
	WB754	DH Chipmunk T10 [H]	AAC BFWF, Middle Wallop
	WB758	DH Chipmunk T10 (7729M) [P]	Torbay Aircraft Museum, Paignton
	WB763	DH Chipmunk T10 (G-BBMR) [14]	Southall Technical College
	WD289	DH Chipmunk T10 [N]	RAF EFTS, Swinderby
	WD293	DH Chipmunk T10 PAX (7645M)	No 2308 Sqn ATC, Cwmbran
	WD305	DH Chipmunk T10 (G-ARGG)	Privately owned, Meppershall
	WD310	DH Chipmunk T10 [H]	RAF EFTS, Swinderby
	WD318	DH Chipmunk T10 PAX (8207M)	No 145 Sqn ATC, Timperley
	WD325	DH Chipmunk T10 [N]	AAC BFWF, Middle Wallop

Serial	Type (alternative identity)	Owner, Operator or Location	Notes
WD331	DH Chipmunk T10 [A] [6]	RAF EFTS, Swinderby	
WD335	DH Chipmunk T10 PAX	No 1955 Sqn ATC, Wells, Somerset	
WD356	DH Chipmunk T10 (7625M)	Privately owned, Huntingdon	
WD363	DH Chipmunk T10 (G-BCIH) [5]	Privately owned, Stansted	
WD373	DH Chipmunk T10 [12]	RAF No 2 AEF, Hurn	
WD374	DH Chipmunk T10 [903]	RN Flying Grading Flt, Plymouth	
WD379	DH Chipmunk T10 (really WB696/G-APLO) [K]	Privately owned, Jersey	
WD390	DH Chipmunk T10 [68]	RAF No 9 AEF, Finningley	
WD413	Avro Anson C 21 (G-BFIR/ 7881M)	Privately owned, Strathallan	
WD496	HP Hastings C2	A&AEE Boscombe Down Fire Section	
WD646	Gloster Meteor TT20 (8189M) [R]	No 2030 Sqn ATC, Sheldon	
WD686	Gloster Meteor NF11	Imperial War Museum, Duxford	
WD790	Gloster Meteor NF11 (8743M) (nose only)	North East Aircraft Museum, Usworth	
WD889	Fairey Firefly AS6	North East Aircraft Museum, Usworth	
WD931	EE Canberra B2 (nose only)	No 425 Sqn ATC, Aldridge, W Midlands	
WD935	EE Canberra B2 (8440M)	RAF St Athan Historic Aircraft Collection	
WD954	EE Canberra B2 (nose only)	Lincolnshire Aviation Museum, East Kirkby	
WD955	EE Canberra T17A	RAF No 360 Sqn, Wyton	
WE113	EE Canberra B2 [BJ]	RAF No 231 OCU, Wyton	
WE122	EE Canberra TT18	MoD(PE) RAE Llanbedr	
WE139	EE Canberra PR3 (8369M)	RAF Museum, Hendon	
WE146	EE Canberra PR3 (cockpit only)	MoD(PE) RAE Farnborough	
WE168	EE Canberra PR3 (8049M)	RAF Manston, on display	
WE173	EE Canberra PR3 (8740M)	RAF Coltishall, BDRT	
WE188	EE Canberra T4	Solway Aviation Society, Carlisle	
WE192	EE Canberra T4 [92]	Solway Aviation Society, Carlisle	
WE539	Beagle A.61 Terrier I (G-ATHU)	Privately owned, Luton	
WE402	DH Venom FB50 (G-VIDI)	Vintage Aircraft Team, Cranfield	
WE569	Auster T7 (G-ASAJ)	Privately owned, Middle Wallop	
WE600	Auster T7 (mod) (7602M)	RAF St Athan Historic Aircraft Collection	
WE925	Gloster Meteor F8	Wales Aircraft Museum, Cardiff	
WE982	Slingsby Prefect TX1 (8781M)	RAF Museum, Hendon	
WF122	Sea Prince T1 (A2673) [575/CU]	Cornwall Aero Park, Helston	
WF125	Sea Prince T1 (A2674) [CU]	RN Predannack Fire School	
WF128	Sea Prince T1 (8611M) [CU]	Norfolk & Suffolk Aviation Museum, Flixton	
WF137	Sea Prince C1	Second World War Aircraft Preservation Society, Lasham	
WF219	Hawker Sea Hawk F1 (A2439)	FAA Museum, RNAS Yeovilton	
WF225	Hawker Sea Hawk F1 (A2645) [CU]	RNAS Culdrose, at main gate	
WF259	Hawker Sea Hawk F2 (A2483) [171/A]	Royal Scottish Museum of Flight, East Fortune	
WF369	Vickers Varsity T1 [F]	Newark Air Museum, Winthorpe	
WF372	Vickers Varsity T1 [T]	Brooklands Aviation Museum	
WF376	Vickers Varsity T1	Bristol Airport Fire Section	
WF408	Vickers Varsity T1 (8395M)	RAF Cosford Aerospace Museum	
WF410	Vickers Varsity T1 [F]	Brunel Technical College, Bristol	
WF413	Vickers Varsity T1 [V]	CTE, RAF Manston	
WF425	Vickers Varsity T1	Imperial War Museum, Duxford	
WF643	Gloster Meteor F8 [X]	Norfolk & Suffolk Aviation Museum, Flixton	
WF714	Gloster Meteor F8 (Really WK914)	Privately owned, Duxford	
WF784	Gloster Meteor T7 (7895M)	RAF Quedgeley, at main gate	
WF791	Gloster Meteor T7 (8354M)	Crashed Coventry 30 May 1988	
WF825	Gloster Meteor T7 (8359M) [Z]	Avon Aviation Museum, Monkton Farleigh	
WF877	Gloster Meteor T7	Aces High, North Weald	
WF890	EE Canberra T17A [EJ]	RAF No 360 Sqn, Wyton	
WF911	EE Canberra B2 (nose only)	Privately owned, Preston	
WF916	EE Canberra T17 [EL]	RAF No 360 Sqn, Wyton	
WF922	EE Canberra PR3	Midland Air Museum, Coventry	
WG300	DH Chipmunk T10 PAX	RAFGSA, Bicester	

Notes	Serial	Type (alternative identity)	Owner, Operator or Location
	WG303	DH Chipmunk T10 PAX (8208M)	RAFGSA, Bicester
	WG307	DH Chipmunk T10 (G-BCYJ)	Privately owned, Lossiemouth
	WG308	DH Chipmunk T10 [W]	RAF No 7 AEF, Newton
	WG316	DH Chipmunk T10 (G-BCAH)	Privately owned, Shoreham
	WG321	DH Chipmunk T10 [G]	AAC BFWF, Middle Wallop
	WG323	DH Chipmunk T10 [F]	AAC BFWF, Middle Wallop
	WG348	DH Chipmunk T10 (G-BBMV)	Privately owned, Moulton St Mary
	WG350	DH Chipmunk T10 (G-BPAL)	Privately owned, Old Sarum
	WG362	DH Chipmunk T10 PAX (8437M/ 8630M)	RAF EFTS, Swinderby
	WG403	DH Chipmunk T10 [O]	AAC BFWF, Middle Wallop
	WG407	DH Chipmunk T10 [67]	RAF No 9 AEF, Finningley
	WG418	DH Chipmunk T10 PAX (8209M/G-ATDY)	RAF No 10 AEF, Woodvale
	WG419	DH Chipmunk T10 PAX (8206M)	No 1053 Sqn ATC, Armthorpe
	WG422	DH Chipmunk T10 (G-BFAX/ 8394M) [16]	Privately owned, Biggin Hill
	WG430	DH Chipmunk T10	RAF No 1 AEF, Manston
	WG432	DH Chipmunk T10 [L]	AAC BFWF, Middle Wallop
	WG458	DH Chipmunk T10 [Z]	RAF, No 34 AEF, Exeter
	WG463	DH Chipmunk T10 PAX (8363M/G-ATDX)	No 188 Sqn ATC, Ipswich
	WG464	DH Chipmunk T10 PAX (8364M/G-ATEA)	No 131 Sqn ATC Jesmond Barracks, Newcastle
	WG465	DH Chipmunk T10 (G-BCEY)	Privately owned, Southend
	WG466	DH Chipmunk T10	RAF Gatow Station Flight, Berlin
	WG469	DH Chipmunk T10 [X]	RAF No 7 AEF, Newton
	WG471	DH Chipmunk T10 PAX (8210M)	No 301 Sqn ATC, Bury St Edmunds
	WG477	DH Chipmunk T10 PAX (8362M/G-ATDI/G-ATDP)	No 281 Sqn ATC, Birkdale
	WG478	DH Chipmunk T10 [L]	RAF EFTS, Swinderby
	WG479	DH Chipmunk T10 [K]	RAF EFTS, Swinderby
	WG480	DH Chipmunk T10 [D]	RAF EFTS, Swinderby
	WG486	DH Chipmunk T10	RAF Gatow Station Flight, Berlin
	WG511	Avro Shackleton T4 (fuselage only)	Cornwall Aero Park, Helston
	WG655	Hawker Sea Fury T20 [910/GN]	RN Historic Flight, RNAS Yeovilton
	WG718	WS51 Dragonfly HR3 (A2531) [934/-]	Wales Aircraft Museum, Cardiff
	WG719	WS51 Dragonfly HR5 (G-BRMA) [902]	International Helicopter Museum, Weston-super-Mare
	WG724	WS51 Dragonfly HR5 [932]	North East Aircraft Museum, Usworth
	WG725	WS51 Dragonfly HR3 (7703M)	Cornwall Aero Park, Helston
	WG751	WS51 Dragonfly HR5	Privately owned, Ramsgreave, Lancs
	WG752	WS51 Dragonfly HR3	Imperial War Museum, Duxford
	WG760	EE P1A (7755M)	RAF Cosford Aerospace Museum
	WG763	EE P1A (7816M)	Greater Manchester Museum of Science and Industry
	WG768	Short SB5 (8005M)	RAF Cosford Aerospace Museum
	WG774	BAC 221	Science Museum, RNAS Yeovilton
	WG777	Fairey FD2 (7986M)	RAF Cosford Aerospace Museum
	WG789	EE Canberra B2/6	Privately owned, Burgess Hill
	WH132	Gloster Meteor T7 (7906M) [J]	No 276 Sqn ATC, Chelmsford
	WH166	Gloster Meteor T7 (8052M)	RAF Digby, at main gate
	WH291	Gloster Meteor F8	Second World War Aircraft Preservation Society, Lasham
	WH301	Gloster Meteor F8 (7930M) [T]	RAF Museum, Hendon
	WH364	Gloster Meteor F8 (8169M)	RAF Kemble, at main gate
	WH453	Gloster Meteor D16 [L]	MoD(PE) RAE Llanbedr
	WH646	EE Canberra T17A [EG]	RAF No 360 Sqn, Wyton
	WH657	EE Canberra B2	Brenzett Aeronautical Collection
	WH664	EE Canberra T17 [EH]	RAF No 360 Sqn, Wyton
	WH665	EE Canberra T17 (8763M) [J]	Rolls-Royce Technical College, Filton
	WH670	EE Canberra B2 [CB]	RAF No 100 Sqn, Wyton
	WH699	EE Canberra B2T (8755M) (really WJ637)	RAFC Cranwell, Trenchard Hall on display
	WH703	EE Canberra B2 (8490M) [S]	RAF Abingdon, BDRF
	WH718	EE Canberra TT18 [CW]	RAF No 100 Sqn, Wyton
	WH724	EE Canberra T19 (nose only)	RAF Shawbury Fire Section
	WH725	EE Canberra B2	Imperial War Museum, Duxford
	WH734	EE Canberra B(TT)2	Flight Refuelling Ltd, Llanbedr

Serial	Type (alternative identity)	Owner, Operator or Location	Notes
WH740	EE Canberra T17 (8762M) [X-K]	RAF No 2 SoTT, Cosford	
WH773	EE Canberra PR7 (8696M)	No 2331 Sqn ATC, RAF Wyton	
WH774	EE Canberra PR7	MoD(PE) RAE Farnborough Fire Section	
WH775	EE Canberra PR7 [O] (8128M/8868M)	RAF No 2 SoTT, Cosford	
WH779	EE Canberra PR7 [CK]	RAF No 100 Sqn, Wyton	
WH780	EE Canberra T22 [853]	RN, stored St Athan	
WH791	EE Canberra PR7 (8165M/8176M/ 8187M)	RAF Cottesmore, at main gate	
WH794	EE Canberra PR7 (8652M)	RAF FF&SS, Catterick	
WH796	EE Canberra PR7 (nose only)	Bomber County Aviation Museum, Hemswell	
WH797	EE Canberra T22 [851]	RN, stored St Athan	
WH798	EE Canberra PR7 (8130M)	Wales Aircraft Museum, Cardiff	
WH801	EE Canberra T22 [850]	RN, stored St Athan	
WH803	EE Canberra T22 [856]	RN, stored St Athan	
WH840	EE Canberra T4 (8350M)	RAF Locking, at main gate	
WH844	EE Canberra T4 (8914M)	*To Pendine Ranges*	
WH846	EE Canberra T4	Yorkshire Air Museum, Elvington	
WH848	EE Canberra T4 [BD]	RAF No 231 OCU, Wyton	
WH849	EE Canberra T4 [BE]	RAF No 231 OCU, Wyton	
WH850	EE Canberra T4	Macclesfield Historical Aviation Society, Chelford, Cheshire	
WH854	EE Canberra T4 (nose only)	Martin Baker Aircraft, Chalgrove	
WH863	EE Canberra T17 (8693M)	RAF Marham, BDRT	
WH869	EE Canberra B2 (8515M)	RAF Abingdon, BDRF	
WH876	EE Canberra D14	MoD(PE) Boscombe Down, stored	
WH887	EE Canberra TT18 [847]	BAe Warton	
WH902	EE Canberra T17A [EK]	RAF No 360 Sqn, Wyton	
WH903	EE Canberra B2 (8584M) (nose only)	RAF Exhibition Flight, Abingdon	
WH904	EE Canberra T19 [04]	Newark Air Museum, Winthorpe	
WH914	EE Canberra B2 (G-27-373) [U]		
WH919	EE Canberra B2	RAF, stored St Athan	
WH946	EE Canberra B6 (Mod) (8185M) (nose only)	Privately owned, Tetney, Grimsby	
WH952	EE Canberra B6	Royal Artillery Museum, Woolwich	
WH953	EE Canberra B6	MoD(PE) RAE Bedford	
WH957	EE Canberra E15 (8869M) [V]	RAF No 2 SoTT, Cosford	
WH960	EE Canberra B15 (8344M) [A]	RAF No 2 SoTT, Cosford	
WH964	EE Canberra E15 (8870M) [CX]	RAF No 2 SoTT, Cosford	
WH972	EE Canberra E15 [CM]	RAF No 100 Sqn, Wyton	
WH981	EE Canberra E15 [CN]	RAF No 100 Sqn, Wyton	
WH983	EE Canberra E15 [CP]	RAF No 100 Sqn, Wyton	
WH984	EE Canberra B15 (8101M) nose only	RAF CTTS, St Athan	
WH984	EE Canberra B15 (8101M) [E] (fuselage etc)	RAF No 2 SoTT, Cosford	
WH991	WS51 Dragonfly HR3	Privately owned, Storwood, East Yorks	
WJ231	Hawker Sea Fury FB11 [115/O]	FAA Museum, RNAS Yeovilton	
WJ237	WAR Sea Fury Replica (G-BLTG) [113/O]	Privately owned, Little Gransden	
WJ288	Hawker Sea Fury FB11 (G-SALY) [029]	Privately owned, Duxford	
WJ329	HP Hastings C2	*Burnt at RAF Leeming*	
WJ350	Percival Sea Prince C2	Guernsey Airport Fire Section	
WJ358	Auster AOP6 (G-ARYD)	Museum of Army Flying, Middle Wallop	
WJ565	EE Canberra T17 (8871M) [C]	RAF No 2 SoTT, Cosford	
WJ567	EE Canberra B2 [CC]	RAF No 100 Sqn, Wyton	
WJ573	EE Canberra B2 (7656M)	RAF Museum Store, Henlow	
WJ574	EE Canberra TT18 [844]	RN, stored St Athan	
WJ576	EE Canberra T17	Wales Aircraft Museum, Cardiff	
WJ581	EE Canberra T17	Wales Aircraft Museum, Cardiff	
WJ603	EE Canberra B2 (8664M) [G]	RAF Wattisham Fire Section	
WJ607	EE Canberra T17A [EB]	RAF No 360 Sqn, Wyton	
WJ614	EE Canberra TT18 [846]	RN FRADU, Yeovilton	
WJ629	EE Canberra TT18 (8747M) [845]	RAF Chivenor, BDRT	

Notes	Serial	Type (alternative identity)	Owner, Operator or Location
	WJ630	EE Canberra T17 [ED]	RAF No 360 Sqn, Wyton
	WJ633	EE Canberra T17A [EF]	RAF No 360 Sqn, Wyton
	WJ635	EE Canberra B2 (nose)	RAF Chivenor, Fire Section
	WJ636	EE Canberra TT18 [CX]	RAF No 100 Sqn, Wyton
	WJ639	EE Canberra TT18 [39]	North East Aircraft Museum, Usworth
	WJ640	EE Canberra B2 (8722M) [L]	RAF No 2 SoTT, Cosford
	WJ657	EE Canberra B2	Brezzett Aeronautical Collection
	WJ676	EE Canberra B2 (7796M)	Princess Alexandra RAF Hospital, Wroughton
	WJ677	EE Canberra B2 (nose only)	RNAS Yeovilton Fire Section
	WJ678	EE Canberra B2 (8864M) [CF]	RAF Abingdon, BDRF
	WJ680	EE Canberra TT18 [CT]	RAF No 100 Sqn, Wyton
	WJ681	EE Canberra B2T (8735M)	Scrapped at RAF Brawdy
	WJ682	EE Canberra TT18 [CU]	RAF No 100 Sqn, Wyton
	WJ715	EE Canberra TT18 [CV]	RAF No 100 Sqn, Wyton
	WJ717	EE Canberra TT18 [841]	RN, stored St Athan
	WJ721	EE Canberra TT18 [21]	Pennine Aviation Museum, Bacup
	WJ722	EE Canberra B2	Lovaux, Macclesfield
	WJ728	EE Canberra B2	RAE Farnborough, derelict
	WJ731	EE Canberra B2T [BK]	RAF No 231 OCU, Wyton
	WJ756	EE Canberra E15 [CL]	RAF No 2 SoTT, Cosford
	WJ775	EE Canberra B6 (8581M) [Z]	CSDE, RAF Swanton Morley
	WJ815	EE Canberra PR7 (8729M)	RAF Coningsby Fire Section
	WJ817	EE Canberra PR7 (8695M) [FO]	RAF Wyton, BDRT
	WJ821	EE Canberra PR7 (8668M)	Bassingbourn, on display
	WJ857	EE Canberra T4 (nose only)	BAe Warton Fire Section
	WJ861	EE Canberra T4 [BF]	RAF, stored St Athan
	WJ863	EE Canberra T4 (nose only)	Cambridge Airport Fire Section
	WJ865	EE Canberra T4	RAE Apprentice School, Farnborough
	WJ866	EE Canberra T4 [BL]	RAF No 231 OCU, Wyton
	WJ867	EE Canberra T4 (8643M)	RAF FF&SS, Catterick
	WJ870	EE Canberra T4 (8683M)	RAF St Mawgan, BDRT
	WJ872	EE Canberra T4 (8492M) (nose only)	No 327 Sqn ATC, Kilmarnock
	WJ874	EE Canberra T4 [BM]	RAF No 231 OCU, Wyton
	WJ876	EE Canberra T4 (nose only)	RAF Exhibition Flight, Abingdon
	WJ877	EE Canberra T4 [BG]	RAF No 231 OCU, Wyton
	WJ879	EE Canberra T4 [BH]	RAF No 231 OCU, Wyton
	WJ880	EE Canberra T4 (8491M) [39] (nose only)	No 2263 Sqn ATC, North Weald
	WJ893	Vickers Varsity T1	RAE Aberporth Fire Section
	WJ902	Vickers Varsity T1 [C]	RAF Wittering Fire Section
	WJ903	Vickers Varsity T1 [C] (nose only)	Dumfries & Galloway Aviation Museum, Tinwald Downs
	WJ907	Vickers Varsity T1 [G]	Norwich Airport Fire Section
	WJ944	Vickers Varsity T1	Wales Aircraft Museum, Cardiff
	WJ945	Vickers Varsity T1 (G-BEDV) [21]	Duxford Aviation Society
	WJ975	EE Canberra T19 [S]	Bomber County Aviation Museum, Hemswell
	WJ977	EE Canberra T17 (8761M) [R]	Scrapped at Wyton
	WJ981	EE Canberra T17A [EN]	RAF No 360 Sqn, Wyton
	WJ986	EE Canberra T17 [EP]	RAF No 360 Sqn, Wyton
	WJ992	EE Canberra T4	MoD(PE) RAE Bedford
	WK102	EE Canberra T17 [EQ] (8780M)	RAF No 2 SoTT, Cosford
	WK111	EE Canberra T17 [EA]	RAF No 360 Sqn, Wyton
	WK118	EE Canberra TT18 [CQ]	RAF No 100 Sqn, Wyton
	WK122	EE Canberra TT18 [22]	Cornwall Aero Park, Helston
	WK123	EE Canberra TT18 [CY]	RAF No 100 Sqn, Wyton
	WK124	EE Canberra TT18 [CR]	RAF No 100 Sqn, Wyton
	WK126	EE Canberra TT18 [843]	RN FRADU, Yeovilton
	WK127	EE Canberra TT18 [CS]	RAF No 100 Sqn, Wyton
	WK128	EE Canberra B2	Flight Refuelling Ltd, RAE Llanbedr
	WK142	EE Canberra TT18 [848]	RN FRADU, Yeovilton
	WK143	EE Canberra B2	RAE Llanbedr Fire Section
	WK144	EE Canberra B2 (8689M)	RAF St Athan Fire Section
	WK145	EE Canberra B2	RAE Llanbedr Fire Section
	WK146	EE Canberra B2 (nose only)	RAF Exhibition Flight, Abingdon
	WK162	EE Canberra B2 [CA] (8887M)	RAF Wyton Fire Section
	WK163	EE Canberra B6	MoD(PE) RAE Bedford
	WK198	VS Swift F4 (7428M)	North East Aircraft Museum, Usworth
	WK275	VS Swift F4	Privately owned, Upper Hill, nr Leominster

Serial	Type (alternative identity)	Owner, Operator or Location	Notes
WK277	VS Swift FR5 (7719M) [N]	Newark Air Museum, Winthorpe	
WK281	VS Swift FR5 (7712M) [S]	RAF St Athan Historic Aircraft Collection	
WK511	DH Chipmunk T10	RN, stored Shawbury	
WK512	DH Chipmunk T10 [A]	AAC BFWF, Middle Wallop	
WK517	DH Chipmunk T10 [84]	RAF No 11 AEF, stored Shawbury	
WK518	DH Chipmunk T10	RAF Battle of Britain Flight, Coningsby	
WK522	DH Chipmunk T10 (G-BCOU)	Privately owned, High Easter	
WK549	DH Chipmunk T10 [Y]	Privately owned, Currock Hill	
WK550	DH Chipmunk T10 [J]	RAF EFTS, Swinderby	
WK554	DH Chipmunk T10	RAF No 5 AEF, Cambridge	
WK559	DH Chipmunk T10 [M]	AAC BFWF, Middle Wallop	
WK562	DH Chipmunk T10 [T]	RAF No 3 AEF, Filton	
WK570	DH Chipmunk T10 PAX (8211M)	RAF No 2 AEF, Lee-on-Solent	
WK572	DH Chipmunk T10 [X]	RAF No 3 AEF, Filton	
WK574	DH Chipmunk T10	RNAS Yeovilton Station Flight	
WK575	DH Chipmunk T10 PAX [F]	No 301 Sqn ATC, Bury St Edmunds	
WK576	DH Chipmunk T10 PAX (8357M)	No 1206 Sqn ATC, Lichfield	
WK585	DH Chipmunk T10	RAF No 12 AEF, Turnhouse	
WK586	DH Chipmunk T10 [X]	RAF EFTS, Swinderby	
WK587	DH Chipmunk T10 PAX (8212M)	St Ignatius Coll, Enfield	
WK589	DH Chipmunk T10 [C]	RAF No 6 AEF, Abingdon	
WK590	DH Chipmunk T10 [69]	RAF No 9 AEF, Finningley	
WK608	DH Chipmunk T10 [906]	RN Flying Grading Flt, Plymouth	
WK609	DH Chipmunk T10 [L]	RAF No 3 AEF, Filton	
WK611	DH Chipmunk T10 (G-ARWB)	Privately owned, Shoreham	
WK613	DH Chipmunk T10 [P]	Pennine Aviation Museum, Bacup	
WK620	DH Chipmunk T10 [T]	AAC BFWF, Middle Wallop	
WK622	DH Chipmunk T10 (G-BCZH)	Privately owned, Norwich	
WK624	DH Chipmunk T10 [12]	RAF No 10 AEF, Woodvale	
WK626	DH Chipmunk T10 PAX (8213M)	No 3585 Sqn ATC, Welling, London	
WK628	DH Chipmunk T10 (G-BBMW)	Privately owned, Shoreham	
WK630	DH Chipmunk T10 [11]	RAF No 2 AEF, Hurn	
WK633	DH Chipmunk T10 [B]	RAF EFTS, Swinderby	
WK634	DH Chipmunk T10 [902]	RN Flying Grading Flt, Plymouth	
WK635	DH Chipmunk T10	RNAS Yeovilton Station Flight	
WK638	DH Chipmunk T10 [83]	RAF No 11 AEF, Leeming	
WK639	DH Chipmunk T10 [10]	RAF No 10 AEF, Woodvale	
WK640	DH Chipmunk T10 [C]	RAF EFTS, Swinderby	
WK642	DH Chipmunk T10 [M]	RAF No 3 AEF, Filton	
WK643	DH Chipmunk T10 [G]	RAF EFTS, Swinderby	
WK654	Gloster Meteor F8 (8092M) [X]	RAF Neatishead, at main gate	
WK800	Gloster Meteor D16 [Z]	MoD(PE) RAE Llanbedr	
WK864	Gloster Meteor F8 (really WL168) [C]	RAF Finningley on display	
WK935	Gloster Meteor Prone Pilot (7869M)	RAF Cosford Aerospace Museum	
WK991	Gloster Meteor F8 (7825M)	Imperial War Museum, Duxford	
WL131	Gloster Meteor F8 (nose only) (7751M)	4th Guernsey (Forest) Air Scouts, Guernsey Airport	
WL181	Gloster Meteor F8 [X]	North East Aircraft Museum, Usworth	
WL332	Gloster Meteor T7	Wales Aircraft Museum, Cardiff	
WL345	Gloster Meteor T7	Privately owned, Hollington, East Sussex	
WL349	Gloster Meteor T7 [Z]	Staverton Airport, on display	
WL360	Gloster Meteor T7 (7920M) [G]	RAF Locking, at main gate	
WL375	Gloster Meteor T7	Dumfries & Galloway Aviation Museum, Tinwald Downs	
WL405	Gloster Meteor T7	North East Aircraft Museum, Usworth	
WL419	Gloster Meteor T7	Martin Baker Aircraft, Chalgrove	
WL505	DH Vampire FB9 (7705M)	RAF St Athan Historic Aircraft Collection	
WL626	Vickers Varsity T1 (G-BHDD) [P]	East Midlands Aeropark	
WL627	Vickers Varsity T1 (8488M) [D]	RAF Newton, Fire Section	
WL635	Vickers Varsity T1	RAF Machrihanish Police School	
WL679	Vickers Varsity T1	MoD(PE) RAE Farnborough	

21

Notes	Serial	Type (alternative identity)	Owner, Operator or Location
	WL732	BP Sea Balliol T21	RAF Cosford Aerospace Museum, store
	WL738	Avro Shackleton MR2C (8567M)	RAF Lossiemouth, at main gate
	WL747	Avro Shackleton AEW2	RAF No 8 Sqn, Lossiemouth
	WL756	Avro Shackleton AEW2	RAF No 8 Sqn, Lossiemouth
	WL757	Avro Shackleton AEW2	RAF No 8 Sqn, Lossiemouth
	WL790	Avro Shackleton AEW2	RAF No 8 Sqn, Lossiemouth
	WL795	Avro Shackleton AEW2 (8753M)	RAF St Mawgan, on display
	WL798	Avro Shackleton MR2C (8114M) [Z]	RAF Lossiemouth (wfu)
	WL925	Slingsby Cadet TX3 (really WV925)	Air Cadet Recruiting Team, Cosford
	WM145	AW Meteor NF11 (nose only)	N. Yorks Recovery Group, Chop Gate
	WM167	AW Meteor NF11 (G-LOSM) [M]	Privately owned, Bournemouth
	WM223	AW Meteor TT20	Second World War Aircraft Preservation Society, Lasham
	WM224	AW Meteor TT20 (8177M)	Privately owned, North Weald
	WM292	AW Meteor TT20 [841]	Wales Aircraft Museum, Cardiff
	WM366	AW Meteor NF13 (4X-FNA)	Second World War Aircraft Preservation Society, Lasham
	WM367	AW Meteor NF13	Privately owned, Powick, Hereford & Worcs
	WM571	DH Sea Venom FAW 21 [742/VL]	Southampton Hall of Aviation
	WM705	DH Vampire NF10 (pod)	Privately owned, Bingley
	WM711	DH Vampire NF10 (pod)	Privately owned, Bingley
	WM712	DH Vampire NF10 (pod)	Privately owned, Bingley
	WM713	DH Vampire NF10 (pod)	Privately owned, Bingley
	WM714	DH Vampire NF10 (pod)	Privately owned, Bingley
	WM727	DH Vampire NF10 (pod)	Privately owned, Bingley
	WM729	DH Vampire NF10 (pod only) [A]	Privately owned Ruislip
	WM730	DH Vampire NF10 (pod)	Privately owned, Bingley
	WM913	Hawker Sea Hawk FB5 [456-J] (A2510/8162M)	Newark Air Museum, Winthorpe
	WM961	Hawker Sea Hawk FB5 [J] (A2517)	Torbay Aircraft Museum, Paignton
	WM969	Hawker Sea Hawk FB5 (A2530)	Imperial War Museum, Duxford
	WM983	Hawker Sea Hawk FGA6 (really XE489)	Chilton Cantelo House School, Somerset
	WM993	Hawker Sea Hawk FB5 (A2522) [034]	Privately owned, Peasedown St John, Avon
	WM994	Hawker Sea Hawk FB5 (A2503/G-SEAH)	Privately owned, Charlwood, Surrey
	WN105	Hawker Sea Hawk FB3 (A2662/A2509/8164M) (really WF299)	Cornwall Aero Park, Helston
	WN108	Hawker Sea Hawk FB5 [033]	Shorts Apprentice School, Belfast
	WN149	BP Balliol T2 (nose only)	Privately owned, Preston
	WN464	Fairey Gannet AS4 (A2540)	Cornwall Aero Park, Helston
	WN493	WS51 Dragonfly HR5	FAA Museum, RNAS Yeovilton
	WN499	WS51 Dragonfly HR5 [Y]	Torbay Aircraft Museum, Paignton
	WN516	BP Balliol T2	North East Aircraft Museum, Usworth
	WN534	BP Balliol T2 (nose only)	Privately owned, Preston
	WN901	Hawker Hunter F2 (7543M)	*Burned at RAF Newton*
	WN904	Hawker Hunter F2 (7544M) [3]	Imperial War Museum, Duxford
	WN907	Hawker Hunter F2 (7416M)	Staravia, Ascot
	WP180	Hawker Hunter F5 (7582M/8473M) [K] (really WP190)	RAF Stanbridge, at main gate
	WP185	Hawker Hunter F5 (7583M)	RAF Museum, Hendon
	WP232	DH Vampire NF10 (pod) [T]	Privately owned, Bingley
	WP239	DH Vampire NF10 (pod)	Privately owned, Bingley
	WP250	DH Vampire NF10 (nose only)	Friends of Biggin Hill, Sevenoaks
	WP242	DH Vampire NF10 (pod)	Privately owned, Bingley
	WP255	DH Vampire NF10 (pod)	Privately owned, Ecclesfield
	WP270	EoN Eton TX1 (8598M)	Greater Manchester Museum of Science and Industry
	WP271	EoN Eton TX1	Stored Keevil

Serial	Type (alternative identity)	Owner, Operator or Location	Notes
WP309	Percival Sea Prince T1 [570/CU]	RNAS Yeovilton Fire Section	
WP313	Percival Sea Prince T1 [568/CU]	FAA Museum, stored Wroughton	
WP314	Percival Sea Prince T1 (8634M) [573/CU]	RAF Police Dog School, Syerston	
WP320	Percival Sea Prince T1 [573/CU]	RAF Leuchars Fire Section	
WP321	Percival Sea Prince T1 (G-BRFC) [750/CU]	Privately owned, Bourn	
WP503	WS51 Dragonfly HR3 [901]	Privately owned, Storwood, East Yorks	
WP515	EE Canberra B2 [CD]	RAF No 100 Sqn, Wyton	
WP772	DH Chipmunk T10 [Q]	AAC BFWF, Middle Wallop	
WP776	DH Chipmunk T10 [817]	RN No 771 Sqn, Culdrose	
WP784	DH Chipmunk T10 PAX	Privately owned, Wellingborough	
WP786	DH Chipmunk T10 [D]	RAF No 6 AEF, Abingdon	
WP788	DH Chipmunk T10 (G-BCHL)	Privately owned, Sleap	
WP790	DH Chipmunk T10 (G-BBNC) [T]	Mosquito Aircraft Museum, London Colney	
WP795	DH Chipmunk T10 [901]	RN Flying Grading Flt, Plymouth	
WP801	DH Chipmunk T10 [911]	RN Flying Grading Flt, Plymouth	
WP803	DH Chipmunk T10	RAF No 8 Sqn, Lossiemouth	
WP805	DH Chipmunk T10 [D]	RAF No 6 AEF, Abingdon	
WP808	DH Chipmunk T10 (G-BDEU)	Privately owned, Binham	
WP809	DH Chipmunk T10 [78]	RN Yeovilton Station Flight	
WP833	DH Chipmunk T10	RAF No 4 AEF, Exeter	
WP835	DH Chipmunk T10 (G-BDCB)	Privately owned, Booker	
WP837	DH Chipmunk T10 [L]	RAF No 5 AEF, Cambridge	
WP839	DH Chipmunk T10 [A]	RAF, stored Shawbury	
WP840	DH Chipmunk T10 [9]	RAF No 2 AEF, Hurn	
WP843	DH Chipmunk T10 (G-BDBP)	Privately owned, Tollerton	
WP844	DH Chipmunk T10	RAF No 11 AEF, Teesside	
WP845	DH Chipmunk T10 PAX	No 1329 Sqn ATC, Stroud	
WP855	DH Chipmunk T10 [11]	RAF stored, Shawbury	
WP856	DH Chipmunk T10 [904]	RN Flying Grading Flt, Plymouth	
WP857	DH Chipmunk T10 (G-BDRJ) [24]	Privately owned, Elstree	
WP859	DH Chipmunk T10 [E]	RAF No 8 AEF, Shawbury	
WP860	DH Chipmunk T10	RAF No 12 AEF, Turnhouse	
WP863	DH Chipmunk T10 PAX (8360M/G-ATJI)	No 1304 Sqn ATC, Chippenham	
WP864	DH Chipmunk T10 PAX (8214M)	RAF No 7AEF, Newton	
WP869	DH Chipmunk T10 PAX (8215M)	RAF	
WP871	DH Chipmunk T10 [W]	AAC BFWF, Middle Wallop	
WP872	DH Chipmunk T10	RAF No 12 AEF, Turnhouse	
WP896	DH Chipmunk T10 [11]	RAF No 10 AEF, Woodvale	
WP900	DH Chipmunk T10 [15]	RAF No 10 AEF, Woodvale	
WP901	DH Chipmunk T10 [B]	RAF No 6 AEF, Abingdon	
WP903	DH Chipmunk T10 (G-BCGC)	RN Gliding Club, Culdrose	
WP904	DH Chipmunk T10 [909]	RN Flying Grading Flt, Plymouth	
WP906	DH Chipmunk T10	RN No 771 Sqn, Culdrose	
WP907	DH Chipmunk T10 PAX (7970M)	Privately owned, Reading	
WP912	DH Chipmunk T10 (8467M)	RAF Cosford Aerospace Museum	
WP914	DH Chipmunk T10 [E]	RAF No 6 AEF, Abingdon	
WP920	DH Chipmunk T10 [10]	RAF No 2 AEF, Hurn	
WP925	DH Chipmunk T10 [C]	AAC BFWF, Middle Wallop	
WP927	DH Chipmunk T10 PAX (8216M/G-ATJK)	No 247 Sqn ATC, Woodvale	
WP928	DH Chipmunk T10 [D]	AAC BFWF, Middle Wallop	
WP929	DH Chipmunk T10 [F]	RAF No 8 AEF, Shawbury	
WP930	DH Chipmunk T10 [J]	AAC BFWF, Middle Wallop	
WP962	DH Chipmunk T10 [V]	RAF No 3 AEF, Filton	
WP964	DH Chipmunk T10	AAC BFWF, Middle Wallop	
WP967	DH Chipmunk T10	RAF No 12 AEF, Turnhouse	
WP970	DH Chipmunk T10 [T]	RAF No 5 AEF, Cambridge	
WP971	DH Chipmunk T10 (G-ATHD)	Privately owned, Cranfield	
WP972	DH Chipmunk T10 PAX (8667M)	CSDE, RAF Swanton Morley	
WP974	DH Chipmunk T10 [N]	RAF No 3 AEF, Filton	
WP977	DH Chipmunk T10 (G-BHRD)	Privately owned, Kidlington	
WP978	DH Chipmunk T10 PAX (7467M)	RAF No 2 AEF, Bournemouth	
WP979	DH Chipmunk T10 [J]	CSDE, RAF Swanton Morley	
WP980	DH Chipmunk T10 [E]	RAF EFTS, Swinderby	
WP981	DH Chipmunk T10 [D]	RAF No 5AEF, Cambridge	

Notes	Serial	Type (alternative identity)	Owner, Operator or Location
	WP983	DH Chipmunk T10 [B]	AAC BFWF, Middle Wallop
	WP984	DH Chipmunk T10 [Y]	RAF No 7 AEF, Newton
	WR410	DH Venom FB54 (really J1790/ G-BLKA)	Vintage Aircraft Team, Cranfield
	WR539	DH Venom FB4 (8399M) [F]	Wales Aircraft Museum, Cardiff
	WR960	Avro Shackleton AEW2 (8772M)	Greater Manchester Museum of Science and Industry
	WR963	Avro Shackleton AEW2	RAF No 8 Sqn, Lossiemouth
	WR965	Avro Shackleton AEW2	RAF No 8 Sqn, Lossiemouth
	WR967	Avro Shackleton MR2C (8398M)	RAF Lossiemouth, simulator
	WR971	Avro Shackleton MR3 (8119M) [Q]	RAF No 2 SoTT, Cosford
	WR974	Avro Shackleton MR3 (8117M) [K]	RAF Cosford Aerospace Museum
	WR977	Avro Shackleton MR3 (8186M) [B]	Newark Air Museum, Winthorpe
	WR982	Avro Shackleton MR3 (8106M) [J]	RAF No 2 SoTT, Cosford
	WR985	Avro Shackleton MR3 (8103M) [H]	RAF No 2 SoTT, Cosford
	WS103	Gloster Meteor T7 [709/VL]	FAA Museum, stored Wroughton
	WS692	Gloster Meteor NF12 (7605M) [C]	Newark Air Museum, Winthorpe
	WS726	Gloster Meteor NF14 (7960M) [G]	No 1855 Sqn ATC, Royton
	WS739	Gloster Meteor NF14 (7961M)	Newark Air Museum, Winthorpe
	WS760	Gloster Meteor NF14 (7964M)	Vintage Aircraft Team, Cranfield
	WS774	Gloster Meteor NF14 (7959M)	RAF Hospital, Ely, at main gate
	WS776	Gloster Meteor NF14 (7716M) [K]	RAF North Luffenham, at main gate
	WS792	Gloster Meteor NF14 (7965M) [K]	RAF Carlisle, at main gate
	WS807	Gloster Meteor NF14 (7973M) [N]	RAF Watton, at main gate
	WS832	Gloster Meteor NF14 [W]	Solway Aviation Society, Carlisle Airport
	WS838	Gloster Meteor NF14	Midland Air Museum, Coventry
	WS840	Gloster Meteor NF14 (7969M)	RAF Aldergrove for display
	WS843	Gloster Meteor NF14 (7937M) [Y]	RAF St Athan Historic Aircraft Collection
	WS844	Gloster Meteor NF14 (7967M) [JCF] (really WS788)	RAF Leeming, at main gate
	WT121	Douglas Skyraider AEW1 [415/CU] (really WT983)	FAA Museum, RNAS Yeovilton
	WT212	EE Canberra B2	Lovaux Ltd, Macclesfield
	WT301	EE Canberra B6 (Mod)	Defence School, Chattenden
	WT305	EE Canberra B6 (8511M)	RAF Wyton, at main gate
	WT308	EE Canberra B(I)6	MoD(PE), Apprentice School RAE Farnborough
	WT309	EE Canberra B(I)6	MoD(PE) A&AEE, stored Boscombe Down
	WT327	EE Canberra B(I)8	MoD(PE) RAE Bedford
	WT333	EE Canberra B(I)8	RAE Bedford
	WT339	EE Canberra B(I)8 (8198M)	RAF Barkston Heath Fire Section
	WT346	EE Canberra B(I)8 (8197M)	RAF Cosford Aerospace Museum
	WT478	EE Canberra T4 [BA]	RAF No 231 OCU, Wyton
	WT480	EE Canberra T4 [BC]	RAF No 231 OCU, Wyton
	WT483	EE Canberra T4 [83]	Stratford Aircraft Collection, Long Marston
	WT486	EE Canberra T4 (8102M) [C]	Aldergrove Fire Section
	WT488	EE Canberra T4	BAe Dunsfold
	WT507	EE Canberra PR7 (8131M/8548M) [44] (nose only)	No 384 Sqn ATC, Mansfield
	WT509	EE Canberra PR7 [CG]	RAF No 100 Sqn, Wyton
	WT510	EE Canberra T22 [854]	RN, stored St Athan
	WT518	EE Canberra PR7 (8133M/8691M) (rear fuselage only)	Wales Aircraft Museum, Cardiff
	WT519	EE Canberra PR7 [CH]	RAF No 100 Sqn, Wyton
	WT520	EE Canberra PR7 (8094M/8184M) [20]	RAF Swinderby

Serial	Type (alternative identity)	Owner, Operator or Location	Notes
WT525	EE Canberra T22 [855]	RN, stored St Athan	
WT532	EE Canberra PR7 (8728M/ 8890M)	RAF No 2 SoTT, Cosford	
WT534	EE Canberra PR7 (8549M) [43] (nose only)	No 492 Sqn ATC, Shirley, W. Mids	
WT535	EE Canberra T22 [852]	RN, stored St Athan	
WT536	EE Canberra PR7 (8063M) [F]	RAF No 2 SoTT, Cosford	
WT537	EE Canberra PR7	BAe Samlesbury, on display	
WT538	EE Canberra PR7 [CJ]	RAF No 100 Sqn, Wyton	
WT555	Hawker Hunter F1 (7499M)	RAF Cosford Aerospace Museum	
WT569	Hawker Hunter F1 (7491M)	No 2117 Sqn ATC, Kenfig Hill, Mid-Glamorgan	
WT612	Hawker Hunter F1 (7496M)	RAF Henlow on display	
WT619	Hawker Hunter F1 (7525M)	Greater Manchester Museum of Science and Industry	
WT648	Hawker Hunter F1 (7530M) (nose section)	RAF St Athan Fire Section	
WT651	Hawker Hunter F1 (7532M) [C]	ROC Lawford Heath, Warwicks, on display	
WT660	Hawker Hunter F1 (7421M) [C]	RAF Carlisle, at main gate	
WT680	Hawker Hunter F1 (7533M) [Z]	No 1429 Sqn ATC at RAE Aberporth	
WT684	Hawker Hunter F1 (7422M)	RAF Brize Norton Fire Section	
WT694	Hawker Hunter F1 (7510M)	RAF Newton, at main gate	
WT711	Hawker Hunter GA11 (833/DD]	RNAS Culdrose, SAH	
WT722	Hawker Hunter T8C [878/VL]	RN FRADU, Yeovilton	
WT723	Hawker Hunter PR11 [866/VL]	RN FRADU, Yeovilton	
WT744	Hawker Hunter GA11 [868/VL]	RN FRADU, Yeovilton	
WT745	Hawker Hunter T8C (8893M) [745] (rear fuselage)	Scrapped at RAF Coltishall	
WT746	Hawker Hunter F4 (7770M) [A]	RAF No 1 SoTT, Halton	
WT799	Hawker Hunter T8C [879/-]	RN, stored Shawbury	
WT804	Hawker Hunter GA11 [831/DD]	RNAS Culdrose, SAH	
WT806	Hawker Hunter GA11	RAF No 2 TWU, Chivenor, preserved	
WT809	Hawker Hunter GA11 [867/VL]	Crashed nr Ilchester (14 June 1988)	
WT933	Bristol Sycamore 3 (G-ALSW/7709M)	Newark Air Museum, Winthorpe	
WV106	Douglas Skyraider AEW1	Cornwall Aero Park, Helston	
WV198	S55 Sikorsky HAR21 (G-BJWY/A2576) [K]	Helicopter Museum of GB, Squires Gate	
WV256	Hawker Hunter GA11 [862/VL]	RN FRADU, Yeovilton	
WV267	Hawker Hunter GA11 [836/DD]	RNAS Culdrose, SAH	
WV276	Hawker Hunter F4 (7847M) [D]	RAF No 1 SoTT, Halton	
WV318	Hawker Hunter T7B	RAF No 208 Sqn, Lossiemouth	
WV322	Hawker Hunter T8C	RAF No 237 OCU, Lossiemouth	
WV332	Hawker Hunter F4 (7673M) (nose only)	No 1254 Sqn ATC, Godalming	
WV363	Hawker Hunter T8C [872/VL]	RN FRADU, Yeovilton	
WV372	Hawker Hunter T7 [877/VL]	RN, stored Shawbury	
WV381	Hawker Hunter GA11 [732/VL]	UKAEA, Culham, Oxon	
WV382	Hawker Hunter GA11 [830/VL]	RN Lee-on-Solent, BDRT	
WV383	Hawker Hunter T7	MoD(PE) RAE Farnborough	
WV396	Hawker Hunter T8C [879/VL]	RN FRADU, Yeovilton	
WV483	Percival Provost T1 (7693M) [N-E]	Privately owned,	
WV486	Percival Provost T1 (7694M) [N-D]	Privately owned, Grazeley, Berks	
WV493	Percival Provost T1 (G-BDYG/7696M) [29]	Royal Scottish Museum of Flight, East Fortune	
WV495	Percival Provost T1 (7697M) [P-C]	Vintage Aircraft Team, Cranfield	
WV499	Percival Provost T1 (7698M) [P-G]	RAF St Athan Historic Aircraft Collection	
WV544	Percival Provost T1 (7700M)	AAC Netheravon Fire Section	
WV562	Percival Provost T1 (7606M) [P-C]	RAF Cosford Aerospace Museum	
WV605	Percival Provost T1 [T-B]	Norfolk & Suffolk Aviation Museum, Flixton	
WV606	Percival Provost T1 (7622M) [P-B]	Newark Air Museum, Winthorpe	
WV679	Percival Provost T1 (7615M) [O-J]	Torbay Aircraft Museum, Paignton	
WV686	Percival Provost T1 (7621M) (G-BLFT) [O-P]	Privately owned, Slough	

Notes	Serial	Type (alternative identity)	Owner, Operator or Location
	WV703	Percival Pembroke C1 (8108M) (G-IIIM)	Privately owned, Tattershall Thorpe
	WV705	Percival Pembroke C1 (nose only)	Southampton Hall of Aviation
	WV746	Percival Pembroke C1 (8938M)	RAF Cosford Aerospace Museum
	WV753	Percival Pembroke C1 (8113M)	Wales Aircraft Museum, Cardiff
	WV781	Bristol Sycamore HR12 (G-ALTD/7839M)	Snowdon Mountain Aviation Collection, Caernarfon
	WV783	Bristol Sycamore HR12 (G-ALSP/7841M)	RAF Museum Store, Henlow
	WV787	EE Canberra B2/8 (8799M)	Newark Air Museum, Winthorpe
	WV795	Hawker Sea Hawk FGA6 (A2661/8151M)	Privately owned, Peasedown St John, Avon
	WV797	Hawker Sea Hawk FGA6 (A2637/8155M)	Midland Air Museum, Coventry
	WV798	Hawker Sea Hawk FGA6 (A2557) [028/CU]	Second World War Aircraft Preservation Society, Lasham
	WV826	Hawker Sea Hawk FGA6 (A2532) [147/Z]	Wales Aircraft Museum, Cardiff
	WV843	Hawker Sea Hawk FGA4 (nose only)	Torbay Aircraft Museum, Paignton
	WV856	Hawker Sea Hawk FGA6 [163]	FAA Museum, RNAS Yeovilton
	WV903	Hawker Sea Hawk FGA6 (A2632/8153M) [128/C] [SAH-8]	RN, Fleetlands
	WV908	Hawker Sea Hawk FGA6 (A2660/8154M) [188/A]	RN Historic Flight, RNAS Yeovilton
	WV911	Hawker Sea Hawk FGA4 (A2526) [115/C]	RN AES, Lee-on-Solent
	WW138	DH Sea Venom FAW22 [227/O]	FAA Museum, RNAS Yeovilton
	WW145	DH Sea Venom FAW22 [680/LM]	Royal Scottish Museum of Flight, East Fortune
	WW217	DH Sea Venom FAW22 [736]	Newark Air Museum, Winthorpe
	WW388	Percival Provost T1 (7616M) [O-F]	Wales Aircraft Museum, Cardiff
	WW397	Percival Provost T1 (8060M/ G-BKHP) [N-E]	Privately owned, RAF Lyneham
	WW421	Percival Provost T1 (7688M) [O]	Lincolnshire Aviation Museum, East Kirkby
	WW442	Percival Provost T1 (7618M) [N]	Privately owned, Leverstock Green, Herts
	WW444	Percival Provost T1 [D]	Privately owned, Sibson
	WW447	Percival Provost T1	Privately owned, Grazeley, Berks
	WW453	Percival Provost T1 [W-S]	Air Service Training, Perth
	WW654	Hawker Hunter GA11 [834/DD]	RNAS Culdrose, SAH
	WX660	Hover-Air HA-5 Hoverhawk III (really XW660)	Privately owned, Cheltenham
	WX788	DH Venom NF3	Wales Aircraft Museum, Cardiff
	WX853	DH Venom NF3 (7443M)	De Havilland Heritage Collection, Hatfield
	WX905	DH Venom NF3 (7458M)	RAF Museum Store, Henlow
	WZ415	DH Vampire T11 [72]	No 2 Sqn ATC, Leavesden
	WZ425	DH Vampire T11	Wales Aircraft Museum, Cardiff
	WZ450	DH Vampire T11 (pod only) [23]	No 2371 Sqn ATC, Tile Cross, W. Mids
	WZ464	DH Vampire T11 (N62430) [40]	Vintage Aircraft Team, Cranfield
	WZ476	DH Vampire T11 (really XE985)	Mosquito Aircraft Museum, stored Hatfield
	WZ507	DH Vampire T11 (G-VTII)	Vintage Aircraft Team, Cranfield
	WZ514	DH Vampire T11	Privately owned, Meols, Merseyside
	WZ515	DH Vampire T11 [60]	Skyfame Collection, stored
	WZ518	DH Vampire T11	North East Aircraft Museum, Usworth
	WZ549	DH Vampire T11 [F] (8118M)	Lincolnshire Aviation Museum, RAF Coningsby
	WZ550	DH Vampire T11 (7902M) [R]	Booker Aircraft Museum
	WZ553	DH Vampire T11 [40]	No 1461 Sqn ATC, Wigston, Leics
	WZ557	DH Vampire T11	N Yorks Recovery Group, Chop Gate
	WZ559	DH Vampire T11 (7736M)	RAF Halton Fire Section
	WZ576	DH Vampire T11 (8174M)	To Canada
	WZ581	DH Vampire T11 [77]	Privately owned, Ruislip

Serial	Type (alternative identity)	Owner, Operator or Location	Notes
WZ584	DH Vampire T11 [K]	St Albans College of FE	
WZ589	DH Vampire T11 [19]	Lashenden Air Warfare Museum, Headcorn	
WZ590	DH Vampire T11 [19]	Imperial War Museum, Duxford	
WZ608	DH Vampire T11 [56] (nose only)	Kibworth Aviation Group, Market Harborough	
WZ616	DH Vampire T11 [60]	Vintage Aircraft Team, Cranfield	
WZ662	Auster AOP9 (G-BKVK)	Privately owned, Swanton Morley	
WZ706	Auster AOP9 (7851M)	Royal Military College of Science, Shrivenham	
WZ711	Auster 9/Beagle E3 (G-AVHT)	Privately owned, Middle Wallop	
WZ721	Auster AOP9	Museum of Army Flying, Middle Wallop	
WZ724	Auster AOP9 (7432M)	AAC Middle Wallop, at main gate	
WZ736	Avro 707A (7868M)	Greater Manchester Museum of Science and Industry	
WZ744	Avro 707C (7932M)	RAF Cosford Aerospace Museum	
WZ753	Slingsby Grasshopper TX1	Southampton Hall of Aviation	
WZ767	Slingsby Grasshopper TX1	North East Aircraft Museum, Usworth	
WZ791	Slingsby Grasshopper TX1 (8944M)	RAF ACCGS Syerston, preserved	
WZ798	Slingsby Grasshopper TX1	Stratford Aircraft Collection, Long Marston	
WZ822	Slingsby Grasshopper TX1	Robertsbridge Aviation Society, E. Sussex	
WZ826	Vickers Valiant B(K)1 (7872M) (nose only) (really XD826)	Wales Aircraft Museum, Cardiff	
WZ845	DH Chipmunk T10	RAF No 1 AEF, Manston	
WZ846	DH Chipmunk T10 PAX (G-BCSC/8439M)	No 1404 Sqn ATC, Chatham	
WZ847	DH Chipmunk T10 [F]	RAF No 6 AEF, Abingdon	
WZ856	DH Chipmunk T10 [Z]	RAF No 7 AEF, Newton	
WZ862	DH Chipmunk T10 [M]	RAF EFTS, Swinderby	
WZ866	DH Chipmunk T10 PAX (8217M) (G-ATEB)	No 2296 Sqn ATC, Dunoon, Strathclyde	
WZ868	DH Chipmunk T10 (G-BCIW) [H]	Privately owned, Duxford	
WZ869	DH Chipmunk T10 PAX (8019M) [R]	No 391 Sqn ATC, Handforth	
WZ872	DH Chipmunk T10 [E]	RAF No 5 AEF, Cambridge	
WZ876	DH Chipmunk T10 (G-BBWN)	Privately owned, Netherthorpe	
WZ877	DH Chipmunk T10	RAF No 7AEF, Newton	
WZ878	DH Chipmunk T10 [86]	RAF No 11 AEF, Leaming	
WZ879	DH Chipmunk T10 [L]	RAF Scampton	
WZ882	DH Chipmunk T10 [K]	AAC BFWF, Middle Wallop	
WZ884	DH Chipmunk T10 [P]	AAC BFWF, Middle Wallop	
XA109	DH Sea Vampire T22	Royal Scottish Museum of Flight, East Fortune	
XA127	DH Sea Vampire T22 (nose only)	FAA Museum, RNAS Yeovilton	
XA129	DH Sea Vampire T22	FAA Museum, stored Wroughton	
XA231	Slingsby Grasshopper TX1 (8888M)	E. Cheshire & S. Manchester Wing 4TC HQ, RAF Sealand	
XA243	Slingsby Grasshopper TX1 (8886M)	RAF St Athan, ground instruction	
XA282	Slingsby Cadet TX3	Snowdon Mountain Aviation Collection, Caernarfon	
XA293	Slingsby Cadet TX3	Stratford Aircraft Collection, Long Marston	
XA454	Fairey Gannet COD4	RNAS Yeovilton Fire Section	
XA459	Fairey Gannet ECM6 (A2608) [E/-]	Wales Aircraft Museum, Cardiff	
XA460	Fairey Gannet ECM6 [768/BY]	North East Wales Institute of HE	
XA466	Fairey Gannet COD4 [777/LM]	FAA Museum, stored Wroughton	
XA508	Fairey Gannet T2 (A2472) [627/GN]	Midland Air Museum, Coventry	
XA549	Gloster Javelin FAW1 (7717M) [E]	RAF Museum Store, Swinderby	
XA553	Gloster Javelin FAW1 (7470M)	RAF Stanmore Park, on display	
XA564	Gloster Javelin FAW1 (7464M)	RAF Cosford Aerospace Museum	
XA571	Gloster Javelin FAW1 (nose only) (7663M/7722M)	Booker Air Museum	
XA634	Gloster Javelin FAW4 (7641M) [L]	RAF Leeming on display	
XA699	Gloster Javelin FAW5 (7809M)	Midland Air Museum, Coventry	
XA801	Gloster Javelin FAW2 (7739M)	RAF Stafford, at main gate	
XA847	EE P1B (8371M)	Privately owned,	

Notes	Serial	Type (alternative identity)	Owner, Operator or Location
	XA862	WS55 Whirlwind HAR1 (A2542/G-AMJT) [9]	Midland Air Museum, Coventry
	XA864	WS55 Whirlwind HAR1	FAA Museum, stored Wroughton
	XA870	WS55 Whirlwind HAR1 (A2543)	Cornwall Aero Park, Helston
	XA879	DH Devon C2	RAE, stored Llanbedr
	XA880	DH Devon C2	MoD(PE) RAE Llanbedr
	XA893	Avro Vulcan B1 (8591M) (nose only)	RAF Cosford Aerospace Museum
	XA900	Avro Vulcan B1 (7896M) (cockpit section)	*Scrapped at Cosford*
	XA903	Avro Vulcan B1 (nose only)	Wales Aircraft Museum, Cardiff
	XA917	HP Victor B1 (7827M) (nose only)	RAF Marham, ground instruction
	XB259	Blackburn Beverley C1 (G-AOAI)	Museum of Army Transport, Beverley
	XB261	Blackburn Beverley C1	Southend Airport Hotel
	XB285	Blackburn Beverley C1	Privately owned, Worminghall, Bucks
	XB288	Blackburn Beverley C1	Privately owned, Worminghall, Bucks
	XB446	Grumman Avenger ECM6B [992/C]	FAA Museum, RNAS Yeovilton
	XB480	Hiller HT1 (A2577) [537]	FAA Museum, RNAS Yeovilton
	XB733	Canadair Sabre 4 (G-ATBF)	Privately owned, Much Hoole, Lancs
	XD145	Saro SR53	RAF Cosford Aerospace Museum
	XD163	WS55 Whirlwind HAR10 (8645M) [X]	International Helicopter Museum, Wroughton
	XD165	WS55 Whirlwind HAR10 (8673M) [B]	RAF No 1 SoTT, Halton
	XD182	WS55 Whirlwind HAR10 (8612M)	RAF *scrapped 1988*
	XD186	WS55 Whirlwind HAR10 (8730M)	RAF Chivenor, on display
	XD234	VS Scimitar F1 [834]	RAE, derelict Farnborough
	XD235	VS Scimitar F1	*To Foulness Ranges*
	XD317	VS Scimitar F1 [112/R]	FAA Museum, RNAS Yeovilton
	XD332	VS Scimitar F1 (A2574) [612]	Cornwall Aero Park, Helston
	XD375	DH Vampire T11 (7887M)	City of Norwich Aviation Museum
	XD377	DH Vampire T11 (8203M) [A]	RAF Cosford
	XD382	DH Vampire T11 (8033M)	RAF Shawbury, at main gate
	XD425	DH Vampire T11 [16]	Dumfries & Galloway Aviation Museum, Tinwald Downs
	XD429	DH Vampire T11 (7604M) [28] (really XD542)	RAF Cranwell, at main gate
	XD434	DH Vampire T11 [25]	Manchester University, Barton
	XD435	DH Vampire T11 [26]	No 480 Sqn ATC, Kenilworth, Warwicks
	XD445	DH Vampire T11 [51]	Bomber County Aviation Museum, Hemswell
	XD447	DH Vampire T11 [50]	Stratford Aircraft Collection, Long Marston
	XD452	DH Vampire T11 (7990M) [66]	Privately owned, Whitchurch, Salop
	XD453	DH Vampire T11 (7890M) [64]	No 58 Sqn ATC, Yorkshire Air Museum, Elvington
	XD459	DH Vampire T11 [63]	Privately owned, Benington
	XD463	DH Vampire T11 (8023M)	No 1360 Sqn ATC, Stapleford, Notts
	XD506	DH Vampire T11 (7983M)	RAF Swinderby, on display
	XD515	DH Vampire T11 (7998M)	*See XM515*
	XD525	DH Vampire T11 (7882M) (pod only)	Campbell College CCF, Belfast
	XD527	DH Vampire T11 [46]	CTE, RAF Manston
	XD528	DH Vampire T11 (8159M)	No 2415 Sqn ATC, Penkridge, Staffs
	XD534	DH Vampire T11 [41]	Military Aircraft Preservation Group, Hadfield, Derbys
	XD535	DH Vampire T11	Friends of Biggin Hill, Sevenoaks store
	XD536	DH Vampire T11 (7734M)	Southall Technical College
	XD547	DH Vampire T11 [Z] (pod only)	Scotland West Aircraft Investigation Group, Strathallan
	XD593	DH Vampire T11 [50]	Newark Air Museum, Winthorpe
	XD595	DH Vampire T11 (pod only)	Privately owned, Altrincham
	XD596	DH Vampire T11 (7939M)	Southampton Hall of Aviation
	XD599	DH Vampire T11 [A]	Snowdon Mountain Aviation Collection, Caernarfon

Serial	Type (alternative identity)	Owner, Operator or Location	Notes
XD602	DH Vampire T11 (7737M)	Privately owned, Southall	
XD613	DH Vampire T11 (8122M) [M]	RAF Cosford	
XD616	DH Vampire T11 [56]	No 1239 Sqn ATC, Hoddesdon, Herts	
XD622	DH Vampire T11 (8160M)	No 2214 Sqn ATC, Usworth	
XD624	DH Vampire T11 [O]	Macclesfield Technical College	
XD626	DH Vampire T11 [Q]	Midland Air Museum, Coventry	
XD674	Hunting Jet Provost T1 (7570M) [T]	RAF Cosford Aerospace Museum	
XD816	Vickers Valiant B(K)1 (nose only)	Brooklands Museum	
XD818	Vickers Valiant B(K)1 (7894M)	RAF Museum, Hendon	
XD826	Vickers Valiant B(K)1 (7872M) (nose only)	See WZ826	
XD875	Vickers Valiant B(K)1 (nose only)	No 163 Sqn ATC, Coventry	
XE317	Bristol Sycamore HR14 (G-AMWO) [S-N]	Newark Air Museum, Winthorpe	
XE327	Hawker Sea Hawk FGA6 (A2556) [644/LH]	Privately owned, Kings Langley, Herts	
XE339	Hawker Sea Hawk FGA6 (8156M/A2635) [149/E] [SAH-7]	RNAS, stored Lee-on-Solent	
XE340	Hawker Sea Hawk FGA6 [131/Z]	Strathallan Aircraft Collection	
XE368	Hawker Sea Hawk FGA6 (A2534) [200/J]	Cornwall Aero Park, Helston	
XE369	Hawker Sea Hawk FGA6 [5] (A2580/8158M/A2633)	RNAS Yeovilton Fire Section	
XE489	Hawker Sea Hawk FGA6 (composite with WM983/A2511) (G-JETH)	Privately owned, Charlwood, Surrey	
XE521	Fairey Rotodyne Y	International Helicopter Museum, Weston-super-Mare	
XE531	Hawker Hunter T12	RAE Farnborough Fire Section	
XE584	Hawker Hunter FGA9 (front fuselage)	Macclesfield Historical Av Soc, Chelford, Cheshire	
XE587	Hawker Hunter F6 [7]	MoD(PE), stored RAE Farnborough	
XE597	Hawker Hunter FGA9 (8874M)	RAF No 1 SoTT, Halton	
XE601	Hawker Hunter FGA9	MoD(PE) A&AEE Boscombe Down	
XE624	Hawker Hunter FGA9 (8875M) [G]	RAF Brawdy, on display	
XE627	Hawker Hunter F6A	Imperial War Museum, Duxford	
XE643	Hawker Hunter FGA9 (8586M) (nose only)	RAF Exhibition Flight, Abingdon	
XE650	Hawker Hunter FGA9 (G-9-449)	Lovaux Ltd, Macclesfield	
XE653	Hawker Hunter F6A (8829M) [D]	RAF TMTS, Scampton	
XE656	Hawker Hunter F6 (8678M)	RAF No 1 SoTT, Halton	
XE665	Hawker Hunter T8C [876/VL]	RN FRADU, Yeovilton	
XE668	Hawker Hunter GA11 [832/DD]	RNAS Culdrose, SAH	
XE670	Hawker Hunter F4 (7762M/ 8585M) (nose only)	RAF Exhibition Flight, Abingdon	
XE673	Hawker Hunter GA11 (8846M) (tail from XE689) [680/VL]	RAF Bawdsey, BDRT	
XE677	Hawker Hunter F4	Lincolnshire Aviation Museum, East Kirkby	
XE682	Hawker Hunter GA11	RNAS Culdrose Fire Section	
XE685	Hawker Hunter GA11 [861/VL]	RN FRADU, Yeovilton	
XE689	Hawker Hunter GA11 [864/VL]	RN FRADU, Yeovilton	
XE707	Hawker Hunter GA11 [865/VL]	RN FRADU, Yeovilton	
XE712	Hawker Hunter GA11 [708]	RN Predannack Fire School	
XE793	Slingsby Cadet TX3 (8666M)	RAF St Athan, instructional use	
XE799	Slingsby Cadet TX3 [R] (8943M)	ACCGS Syerston, preserved	
XE849	DH Vampire T11 (7928M) [V3]	Avon Aviation Museum, Monkton Farleigh	
XE852	DH Vampire T11 [30]	No 2247 Sqn ATC, Hawarden	
XE855	DH Vampire T11	Midland Air Museum, Coventry	
XE856	DH Vampire T11	Second World War Aircraft Preservation Society, Lasham	
XE864	DH Vampire T11	No 480 Sqn ATC, Studley, Warwicks	
XE872	DH Vampire T11 [62]	Midland Air Museum, Coventry	
XE874	DH Vampire T11 (8582M) [61]	RAF Valley on display	
XE897	DH Vampire T11 (really XD403)	Strathallan Aircraft Collection	
XE920	DH Vampire T11 (8196M) [D]	RAF, stored Scampton	

Notes	Serial	Type (alternative identity)	Owner, Operator or Location
	XE921	DH Vampire T11 [64]	Privately owned, Keevil
	XE928	DH Vampire T11 [76]	Privately owned, Keevil
	XE935	DH Vampire T11 [30]	S Yorks Air Museum, Firbeck
	XE946	DH Vampire T11 (7473M) (nose only)	RAF Museum Store, Cardington
	XE956	DH Vampire T11	St Albans College of FE
	XE979	DH Vampire T11 [54]	Privately owned, Standish
	XE982	DH Vampire T11 (7564M)	No 124 Sqn ATC, RAF Credenhill, Hereford
	XE993	DH Vampire T11 (8161M)	RAF Cosford Fire Section
	XE995	DH Vampire T11 [53]	Torbay Aircraft Museum, Paignton
	XE998	DH Vampire T11 [36]	Privately owned, Charlwood, Surrey
	XF113	VS Swift F7 (nose only) [19]	Privately owned, Peasedown St John, Avon
	XF114	VS Swift F7	Jet Heritage, Bournemouth
	XF274	Gloster Meteor T7	RAE/AIU on display, Farnborough
	XF289	Hawker Hunter T8C [875/VL]	RN FRADU, Yeovilton
	XF300	Hawker Hunter GA11 [860/VL]	RN FRADU, Yeovilton
	XF301	Hawker Hunter GA11 [834/VL]	RN store, Yeovilton
	XF310	Hawker Hunter T7 [869/VL]	RN FRADU, Yeovilton
	XF314	Hawker Hunter F51 [N] (really E-412)	Tangmere Military Aviation Museum
	XF319	Hawker Hunter F4 (7849M) [B]	RAF No 1 SoTT, Halton
	XF321	Hawker Hunter T7	RNEC Manadon
	XF357	Hawker Hunter T8C [871/VL]	RN FRADU, Yeovilton
	XF358	Hawker Hunter T8C [870]	RN FRADU, Yeovilton
	XF368	Hawker Hunter GA11 [863/VL]	RN FRADU, Yeovilton
	XF375	Hawker Hunter F6 (8736M) [05]	SIF, RAFC Cranwell
	XF382	Hawker Hunter F6A [15]	Midland Air Museum, Coventry
	XF383	Hawker Hunter F6 (8706M) [V]	RAF Wittering, BDRT
	XF383	Hawker Hunter F51 [71] (really E-409)	Wales Aircraft Museum, Cardiff
	XF435	Hawker Hunter FGA9 (8880M) [52]	RAF Brawdy, BDRT
	XF445	Hawker Hunter FGA9 (8715M) [T] (really XG264)	RAF Brawdy Fire Section
	XF509	Hawker Hunter F6 (8708M) [73]	RAF Chivenor, at main gate
	XF515	Hawker Hunter F6A (8830M) [C]	RAF TMTS, Scampton
	XF516	Hawker Hunter F6A (8685M) [66]	SIF, RAFC Cranwell
	XF519	Hawker Hunter FGA9 [J] (8677M/ 8738M) (composite with XJ695)	FSCTE, RAF Manston
	XF522	Hawker Hunter F6 (nose only)	No 1365 Sqn ATC, Aylesbury
	XF526	Hawker Hunter F6 (8679M) [78/E]	RAF St Athan Fire Section
	XF527	Hawker Hunter F6 (8680M)	RAF Halton, on display
	XF545	Percival Provost T1 (7957M) [O-K]	RAF Linton-on-Ouse, at main gate
	XF597	Percival Provost T1 (G-BKFW) [A-H]	Privately owned, Aldermaston
	XF603	Percival Provost T1 [H]	Rolls-Royce Tech Coll, Filton
	XF690	Percival Provost T1 (G-BGKA/ (8041M)	Privately owned, Newton
	XF708	Avro Shackleton MR3 [203/C]	Imperial War Museum, Duxford
	XF785	Bristol 173 (G-ALBN/7648M)	RAF Museum Store, Henlow
	XF799	Percival Pembroke C1PR	RAF No 60 Sqn, Wildenrath
	XF836	Percival Provost T1 (8043M/ G-AWRY) [JG]	Privately owned, Popham
	XF844	Percival Provost T1 [30]	RAE Farnborough Apprentice School
	XF877	Percival Provost T1 (G-AWVF) [JX]	Privately owned, Compton Abbas
	XF898	Percival Provost T1 [Z]	Booker Fire Section
	XF914	Percival Provost T1 [P-V]	Vintage Aircraft Team, Cranfield
	XF926	Bristol 188 (8368M)	RAF Cosford Aerospace Museum
	XF967	Hawker Hunter T8C	RAF No 237 OCU, Lossiemouth
	XF974	Hawker Hunter F4 (7949M) [C]	RAF No 1 SoTT, Halton
	XF979	Hawker Hunter F51 (really E-408)	RAF Sealand, on display
	XF985	Hawker Hunter T8C [873/VL]	RN, stored Shawbury
	XF990	Hawker Hunter F6 (8007M) (nose only)	RAF FF&SS, Catterick
	XF994	Hawker Hunter T8C [873/VL]	RN FRADU, Yeovilton
	XF995	Hawker Hunter T8B [W]	RAF No 12 Sqn, Lossiemouth

Serial	Type (alternative identity)	Owner, Operator or Location	Notes
XG151	Hawker Hunter FGA9 (8798M) (nose only) [H]	*Scrapped at Lossiemouth*	
XG154	Hawker Hunter FGA9 (8863M) [54]	RAF, stored St Athan	
XG158	Hawker Hunter F6A (8686M) [21]	RAE Farnborough Apprentice School	
XG160	Hawker Hunter F6A [B] (8831M)	RAF TMTS, Scampton	
XG164	Hawker Hunter F6 (8681M)	RAF No 1 SoTT, Halton	
XG172	Hawker Hunter F6A [A] (8832M)	RAF TMTS, Scampton	
XG194	Hawker Hunter FGA9 [55] (8839M)	RAF North Luffenham Training Area	
XG195	Hawker Hunter FGA9 (composite with XG297)	Bomber County Aviation Museum, Hemswell	
XG196	Hawker Hunter F6A (8702M)	RAF Bracknell, on gate	
XG209	Hawker Hunter F6 [69] (8709M)	RAFC Engineering Wing, Cranwell	
XG210	Hawker Hunter F6	RAE Apprentice School, Bedford	
XG225	Hawker Hunter F6A (8713M) [S]	RAF Cosford on display	
XG226	Hawker Hunter F6A (8800M) (fuselage, etc)	Privately owned, Faygate	
XG226	Hawker Hunter F6A (8800M) [28] (nose only)	Privately owned, Faygate	
XG252	Hawker Hunter FGA9 (8840M) [U]	RAF Credenhill, on display	
XG254	Hawker Hunter FGA9 (8881M)	RAF Coltishall, BDRT	
XG274	Hawker Hunter F6 [71] (8710M)	RAF No 1 SoTT, Halton	
XG290	Hawker Hunter F6 [74] (8711M)	RAF Bentley Priory, on display	
XG297	Hawker Hunter FGA9 (nose only)	Privately owned, Preston	
XG325	EE Lightning F1 (nose only)	No 1476 Sqn ATC, Rayleigh, Essex	
XG327	EE Lightning F1 (8188M)	FSCTE, RAF Manston	
XG329	EE Lightning F1 (8050M)	RAF Swinderby	
XG331	EE Lightning F1 (nose only)	No 2342 Sqn ATC, CARG store, RAF Innsworth	
XG337	EE Lightning F1 (8056M) [M]	RAF Cosford Aerospace Museum	
XG452	Bristol Belvedere HC1 (G-BRMB/7997M)	International Helicopter Museum, Weston-super-Mare	
XG454	Bristol Belvedere HC1 (8366M)	Greater Manchester Museum of Science and Industry	
XG474	Bristol Belvedere HC1 (8367M) [O]	RAF Museum, Hendon	
XG502	Bristol Sycamore HR14	Museum of Army Flying, Middle Wallop	
XG506	Bristol Sycamore HR14 (7852M)	Bomber County Aviation Museum, Hemswell	
XG518	Bristol Sycamore HR14 (8009M) [S-E]	North East Aircraft Museum, Usworth	
XG540	Bristol Sycamore HR14 (7899M/8345M) [Y-S]	Privately owned, Drighlington, Yorks	
XG544	Bristol Sycamore HR14	Torbay Aircraft Museum, Paignton	
XG547	Bristol Sycamore HR14 (G-HAPR/8010M) [S-T]	International Helicopter Museum, Weston-super-Mare	
XG573	WS55 Whirlwind HAR3	CDE, Porton Down, Wilts	
XG574	WS55 Whirlwind HAR3 (A2575) [752/PO]	FAA Museum, RNAS Yeovilton	
XG577	WS55 Whirlwind HAR3 (A2571)	RE 39 Regt, Waterbeach, on display	
XG592	WS55 Whirlwind HAS7 [54]	Wales Aircraft Museum, Cardiff	
XG594	WS55 Whirlwind HAS7 [517/PO]	Strathallan Aircraft Collection	
XG596	WS55 Whirlwind HAS7 (A2651) [66]	International Helicopter Museum, Weston-super-Mare	
XG613	DH Sea Venom FAW21	Imperial War Museum, Duxford	
XG629	DH Sea Venom FAW22	Torbay Aircraft Museum, Paignton	
XG680	DH Sea Venom FAW22 [735/VL]	North East Aircraft Museum, Usworth	
XG691	DH Sea Venom FAW22 [493/J]	Cornwall Aero Park, Helston	
XG692	DH Sea Venom FAW22 [668/LM]	Midland Warplane Museum, Long Marston	
XG730	DH Sea Venom FAW22 [499/A]	Mosquito Aircraft Museum, London Colney	
XG734	DH Sea Venom FAW22	*Dismantled*	
XG736	DH Sea Venom FAW22	Ulster Aviation Society, Newtownards	
XG737	DH Sea Venom FAW22 [220/Z]	Wales Aircraft Museum, Cardiff	
XG743	DH Sea Vampire T22 [597/LM]	Imperial War Museum, Duxford	

Notes	Serial	Type (alternative identity)	Owner, Operator or Location
	XG797	Fairey Gannet ECM6 [766/BY]	Imperial War Museum, Duxford
	XG831	Fairey Gannet ECM6 (A2539)	Cornwall Aero Park, Helston
	XG882	Fairey Gannet T5 (8754M) [771/LM]	RAF Lossiemouth on display
	XG883	Fairey Gannet T5 [773/BY]	Wales Aircraft Museum, Cardiff
	XG888	Fairey Gannet T5 [-/LM]	RNAS, stored Lee-on-Solent
	XG900	Short SC1	Science Museum, Wroughton
	XG905	Short SC1	Ulster Folk & Transport Museum, County Down
	XH124	Blackburn Beverley C1 (8025M)	RAF Museum, Hendon
	XH131	EE Canberra PR9 [AF]	RAF No 1 PRU, Wyton
	XH132	Short SC9 Canberra (8915M)	RAF St Mawgan, BDRT
	XH133	EE Canberra PR9	RAF, stored St Athan
	XH134	EE Canberra PR9 [AA]	RAF No 1 PRU, Wyton
	XH135	EE Canberra PR9 [AG]	RAF No 1 PRU, Wyton
	XH136	EE Canberra PR9 (8782M) [W]	RAF No 2 SoTT, Cosford
	XH165	EE Canberra PR9	RAF, stored St Athan
	XH168	EE Canberra PR9 [AB]	RAF No 1 PRU, Wyton
	XH169	EE Canberra PR9 [AC]	RAF No 1 PRU, Wyton
	XH170	EE Canberra PR9 (8739M)	RAF Wyton, on gate
	XH171	EE Canberra PR9 (8746M) [U]	RAF No 2 SoTT, Cosford
	XH174	EE Canberra PR9 [AD]	RAF No 1 PRU, Wyton
	XH175	EE Canberra PR9 [AE]	RAF No 1 PRU, Wyton
	XH177	EE Canberra PR9 (nose only)	Wales Aircraft Museum, Cardiff
	XH274	DH Vampire T11	RAF Ternhill Fire Section
	XH278	DH Vampire T11 (8595M/ 7866M)	No 2482 Sqn ATC, RAF Henlow
	XH312	DH Vampire T11 [18]	Privately owned, Chester
	XH313	DH Vampire T11 [E]	St Albans College of FE
	XH318	DH Vampire T11 [64] (7761M)	No 424 Sqn ATC, Hants
	XH328	DH Vampire T11 [66]	Privately owned, Cranfield
	XH329	DH Vampire T11 [70]	Privately owned, Keevil
	XH330	DH Vampire T11 [73]	Privately owned, Bridgnorth
	XH537	Avro Vulcan B2 MRR (8749M)	RAF Abingdon, on display
	XH539	Avro Vulcan B2	*Scrapped RAF Waddington 1988*
	XH558	Avro Vulcan B2	RAF Vulcan Display Flight, Scampton
	XH560	Avro Vulcan K2	RAF Marham Fire Section
	XH567	EE Canberra B6(mod)	MoD(PE) RAE Bedford
	XH568	EE Canberra B6(mod)	MoD(PE) RAE Bedford
	XH583	EE Canberra T4 (G-27-374) (nose only)	NEAM, Usworth
	XH590	HP Victor K1A	CTE, RAF Manston
	XH592	HP Victor K1A (8429M) [L]	RAF Cosford Aerospace Museum
	XH593	HP Victor K1A (8428M) [T]	RAF No 2 SoTT, Cosford
	XH616	HP Victor K1A	CTE, RAF Manston
	XH648	HP Victor K1A	Imperial War Museum, Duxford
	XH669	HP Victor K2	RAF No 55 Sqn, Marham
	XH670	HP Victor SR2 (nose only)	Lincolnshire Aviation Museum, East Kirkby
	XH671	HP Victor K2	RAF No 55 Sqn, Marham
	XH672	HP Victor K2	RAF No 55 Sqn, Marham
	XH673	HP Victor K2 (8911M)	RAF Marham, on display
	XH675	HP Victor K2	RAF No 55 Sqn, Marham
	XH764	Gloster Javelin FAW9 (7972M)	RAF Manston, on display
	XH767	Gloster Javelin FAW9 (7955M) [K]	Avon Aviation Museum, Monkton Farleigh Mines, Bath
	XH837	Gloster Javelin FAW7 (8032M) (nose only)	Snowdon Mountain Aviation Collection, Caernarfon
	XH892	Gloster Javelin FAW9 (7982M) [J]	Norfolk & Suffolk Aviation Museum, Flixton
	XH897	Gloster Javelin FAW9	Imperial War Museum, Duxford
	XH903	Gloster Javelin FAW9 (7938M)	RAF Innsworth, at main gate
	XH980	Gloster Javelin FAW8 (7867M) [A]	RAF West Raynham, at main gate
	XH992	Gloster Javelin FAW8 (7829M) [P]	Newark Air Museum, Winthorpe
	XJ314	RR Thrust Measuring Rig	Royal Scottish Museum of Flight, East Fortune

Serial	Type (alternative identity)	Owner, Operator or Location	Notes
XJ319	DH Sea Devon C20 (G-AMXP) [CU18]	RN, No 771 Sqn Culdrose	
XJ324	DH Sea Devon C20 (G-AMXZ)	RN, stored Kemble	
XJ348	DH Sea Devon C20 (G-AMXX/ G-NAVY)	Privately owned, Staverton	
XJ380	Bristol Sycamore HR14 (8628M)	Privately owned, Drighlington, Yorks	
XJ389	Fairey Jet Gyrodyne (XD759/ G-AJJP)	RAF Cosford Aerospace Museum	
XJ393	WS55 Whirlwind HAR3 (A2538)	Torbay Aircraft Museum, Paignton	
XJ396	WS55 Whirlwind HAR10	RAE Farnborough Fire Section	
XJ402	WS55 Whirlwind HAR3 (A2572) [61]	RNAS Yeovilton, Fire Section	
XJ407	WS55 Whirlwind HAR10	*Privately owned, RAF Lakenheath as N7013H*	
XJ409	WS55 Whirlwind HAR10	Wales Aircraft Museum, Cardiff	
XJ411	WS55 Whirlwind HAR10 [Z]	*To Pendine Ranges*	
XJ430	WS55 Whirlwind HAR10	CTE, RAF Manston	
XJ435	WS55 Whirlwind HAR10 (8671M) [V]	RAF No 1 SoTT, Halton	
XJ445	WS55 Whirlwind HAR5	CDE, Porton Down, Wilts	
XJ476	DH Sea Vixen FAW1 (nose section)	No 424 Sqn ATC, Southampton Hall of Aviation	
XJ481	DH Sea Vixen FAW1 [VL]	On display Ocean Village, Southampton	
XJ482	DH Sea Vixen FAW1 (A2598) [713/VL]	Norfolk & Suffolk Aviation Museum, Flixton	
XJ494	DH Sea Vixen FAW2	Privately owned, Kings Langley, Herts	
XJ560	DH Sea Vixen FAW2 (8142M) [242]	Newark Air Museum, Winthorpe	
XJ565	DH Sea Vixen FAW2 [127/E]	Mosquito Aircraft Museum, London Colney	
XJ571	DH Sea Vixen FAW2 (8140M) [242/R]	Privately owned, Southampton Airport	
XJ575	DH Sea Vixen FAW2 (A2611) [-/VL] [SAH-13]	Cornwall Aero Park, Helston	
XJ580	DH Sea Vixen FAW2 [131/E]	Christchurch Memorial Group	
XJ582	DH Sea Vixen FAW2 (8139M) [702]	RAF Cottesmore Fire Section	
XJ584	DH Sea Vixen FAW2 (A2621) [SAH-16]	Cornwall Aero Park, Helston	
XJ604	DH Sea Vixen FAW2 (8222M)	*To Otterburn Ranges*	
XJ607	DH Sea Vixen FAW2 (8171M) [701-VL]	Privately owned, Southampton	
XJ608	DH Sea Vixen FAW2 (8802M)	RAF North Luffenham Training Area	
XJ609	DH Sea Vixen FAW2 (8172M) painted 8171M [702/VL]	RAF Abingdon Fire Section	
XJ634	Hawker Hunter F6A (8684M) [29]	SIF, RAFC Cranwell	
XJ639	Hawker Hunter F6A (8687M) [31]	SIF, RAFC Cranwell	
XJ676	Hawker Hunter F6A [32] (8844M)	*Scrapped at RAF Lyneham*	
XJ690	Hawker Hunter FGA9 (composite with XG195)	Lovaux Ltd, Macclesfield	
XJ723	WS55 Whirlwind HAR10	OPITB, Montrose	
XJ726	WS55 Whirlwind HAR10 [F]	Snowdon Mountain Aviation Collection, Caernarfon	
XJ727	WS55 Whirlwind HAR10 (8661M) [L]	RAF No 1 SoTT, Halton	
XJ729	WS55 Whirlwind HAR10 (8732M)	RAF Finningley, for display	
XJ763	WS55 Whirlwind HAR10 (G-BKHA)	Privately owned, Thronicombe, Dorset	
XJ772	DH Vampire T11 [H]	Brooklands Technical College	
XJ782	Avro Vulcan B2 MRR (8766M)	*Scrapped at Finningley, May 1988*	
XJ823	Avro Vulcan B2A	Privately owned, Carlisle Airport	
XJ824	Avro Vulcan B2A	Imperial War Museum, Duxford	
XJ825	Avro Vulcan K2 (8810M)	RAF Waddington, BDRT	
XJ917	Bristol Sycamore HR14 [H-S]	Cornwall Aero Park, Helston	
XJ918	Bristol Sycamore HR14 (8190M)	RAF Cosford Aerospace Museum	
XK149	Hawker Hunter F6A [34] (8714M)	SIF, RAFC Cranwell	

Notes	Serial	Type (alternative identity)	Owner, Operator or Location
	XK412	Auster AOP9	Privately owned, Wootton Bassett
	XK416	Auster AOP9 (G-AYUA/ 7855M)	Vintage Aircraft Team, Cranfield
	XK417	Auster AOP9 (G-AVXY)	Privately owned, Leicester
	XK418	Auster AOP9 (7976M)	Second World War Aircraft Preservation Society, Lasham
	XK421	Auster AOP9 (8365M)	Cotswold Aircraft Restoration Group, RAF Innsworth
	XK482	Saro Skeeter AOP12 (7840M/ G-BJWC) [C]	Helicopter Museum of GB, Squires Gate
	XK488	Blackburn Buccaneer S1	FAA Museum, RNAS Yeovilton
	XK526	Blackburn Buccaneer S2 (8648M)	RAF Honington, at main gate
	XK530	Blackburn Buccaneer S1	RAE Bedford Fire Section
	XK531	Blackburn Buccaneer S1 (8403M) [LM]	Defence School, Winterbourne Gunner
	XK532	Blackburn Buccaneer S1 (8867M/A2581) [632/LM]	RAF Lossiemouth, on display
	XK533	Blackburn Buccaneer S1 (nose only)	Museum of Flight, East Fortune
	XK590	DH Vampire T11 [V]	Wellesbourne Aviation Group
	XK623	DH Vampire T11 [56] (G-VAMP)	Snowdon Mountain Aviation Collection, Caernarfon
	XK624	DH Vampire T11 [32]	Norfolk & Suffolk Aviation Museum, Flixton
	XK625	DH Vampire T11 [12]	Privately owned, North Weald
	XK627	DH Vampire T11	Pennine Aviation Museum, Bacup
	XK632	DH Vampire T11 [67]	No 1187 Sqn ATC, Hemel Hempstead
	XK637	DH Vampire T11 [56]	No 1855 Sqn ATC, Royton, Greater Manchester
	XK655	DH Comet 2R (G-AMXA)	Strathallan Aircraft Collection
	XK659	DH Comet 2 (nose only)	Privately owned, Elland, W. Yorks
	XK695	DH Comet 2R (G-AMXH)	Imperial War Museum, Duxford
	XK699	DH Comet C2 (7971M)	RAF Lyneham on display
	XK724	Folland Gnat F1 (7715M)	RAF Cosford Aerospace Museum
	XK740	Folland Gnat F1 (8396M)	Southampton Hall of Aviation
	XK741	Folland Gnat F1	Midland Air Museum, Coventry
	XK776	ML Utility 1	Museum of Army Flying, Middle Wallop
	XK824	Slingsby Grasshopper TX1	Privately owned, King's Lynn
	XK884	Percival Pembroke C1 (G-BNPG)	To Sweden as SE-BKH
	XK895	DH Sea Devon C20	RN, No 771 Sqn, Culdrose
	XK906	WS55 Whirlwind HAS7	AAC Netheravon Fire Section
	XK907	WS55 Whirlwind HAS7 [U]	Midland Air Museum, Coventry
	XK911	WS55 Whirlwind HAS7 (A2603) [519/PO]	RN, stored Wroughton
	XK912	WS55 Whirlwind HAS7 [60/CU]	Privately owned, Crudwell, Wilts
	XK936	WS55 Whirlwind HAS7 [62]	Imperial War Museum, Duxford
	XK940	WS55 Whirlwind HAS7 (G-AYXT)	Helicopter Museum of GB, Squires Gate
	XK943	WS55 Whirlwind HAS7 (A2653/8796M) [57]	RAF Abingdon, Fire Section
	XK944	WS55 Whirlwind HAS7 (A2607)	No 617 Sqn ATC, Malpas School, Cheshire
	XK968	WS55 Whirlwind HAR10 (8445M) [E]	CTE, RAF Manston
	XK969	WS55 Whirlwind HAR10 (8646M)	CTE, RAF Manston
	XK970	WS55 Whirlwind HAR10 (8789M)	RAF Odiham, BDRT
	XK986	WS55 Whirlwind HAR10 (8790M)	RAF Odiham, BDRT
	XK987	WS55 Whirlwind HAR10 (8393M)	MoD Swynnerton, Staffs
	XK988	WS55 Whirlwind HAR10 (A2646) [N]	Museum of Army Flying, Middle Wallop
	XL149	Blackburn Beverley C1 (fuselage etc) (7988M)	RAF Museum, Hendon
	XL149	Blackburn Beverley C1 (nose only) (7988M)	Newark Air Museum, Winthorpe
	XL158	HP Victor K2	RAF No 55 Sqn, Marham
	XL160	HP Victor K2 (8910M)	RAF Marham Fire Section
	XL161	HP Victor K2	RAF No 55 Sqn, Marham
	XL162	HP Victor K2	RAF No 55 Sqn, Marham
	XL163	HP Victor K2 (8916M)	RAF St Athan Fire Section
	XL164	HP Victor K2	RAF No 55 Sqn, Marham

Serial	Type (alternative identity)	Owner, Operator or Location	Notes
XL188	HP Victor K2	RAF No 55 Sqn, Marham	
XL189	HP Victor K2 (8912M)	RAF Waddington on display	
XL190	HP Victor K2	RAF No 55 Sqn, Marham	
XL192	HP Victor K2	RAF No 55 Sqn, Marham	
XL231	HP Victor K2	RAF No 55 Sqn, Marham	
XL233	HP Victor K2 (89..M)	*Scrapped at RAF St Athan*	
XL318	Avro Vulcan B2 (8733M)	Bomber Command Museum, Hendon	
XL319	Avro Vulcan B2	North East Aircraft Museum, Usworth	
XL360	Avro Vulcan B2A	Midland Air Museum, Coventry	
XL384	Avro Vulcan B2 (8505M/ 8670M)	RAF Scampton Fire Section	
XL386	Avro Vulcan B2A (8760M)	CTE, RAF Manston	
XL388	Avro Vulcan B2 (nose only)	Privately owned, Walpole, Suffolk	
XL391	Avro Vulcan B2	Privately owned, Blackpool	
XL392	Avro Vulcan B2 (8745M)	RAF Valley Fire Section	
XL426	Avro Vulcan B2 (G-VJET)	Privately owned, Southend	
XL427	Avro Vulcan B2 (8756M)	RAF Machrihanish Fire Section	
XL445	Avro Vulcan K2 (8811M)	RAF Lyneham Fire Section	
XL449	Fairey Gannet AEW3	Wales Aircraft Museum, Cardiff	
XL471	Fairey Gannet AEW3 [043/R]	*Scrapyard at Lichfield*	
XL472	Fairey Gannet AEW3 [044/R]	A&AEE Boscombe Down, derelict	
XL497	Fairey Gannet AEW3 [041/R]	HMS *Gannet*, Prestwick, at gate	
XL500	Fairey Gannet AEW3 (A2701) [LM]	RNAS, stored Lee-on-Solent	
XL502	Fairey Gannet AEW3 (8610M) (G-BMYP)	Privately owned, Carlisle	
XL503	Fairey Gannet AEW3 [070/E]	FAA Museum, RNAS Yeovilton	
XL511	HP Victor K2	CTE, RAF Manston	
XL512	HP Victor K2	RAF No 55 Sqn, Marham	
XL563	Hawker Hunter T7	MoD(PE) RAE/IAM Farnborough	
XL564	Hawker Hunter T7 [4]	MoD(PE) ETPS Boscombe Down	
XL565	Hawker Hunter T7	RAF, stored Lossiemouth	
XL567	Hawker Hunter T7 (8723M) [84] (fuselage only)	RAF Chivenor, BDRT	
XL568	Hawker Hunter T7A [N]	RAF No 237 OCU, Lossiemouth	
XL569	Hawker Hunter T7 (8833M) [80]	RAF Abingdon, BDRF	
XL572	Hawker Hunter T7	Jet Heritage, Bournemouth	
XL573	Hawker Hunter T7	RAF No 12 Sqn, Lossiemouth	
XL576	Hawker Hunter T7	*Sold to USA*	
XL577	Hawker Hunter T7 (8676M) [01]	SIF, RAFC Cranwell	
XL578	Hawker Hunter T7 [77]	RAF, stored St Athan	
XL580	Hawker Hunter T8M [723]	RN No 899 Sqn, Yeovilton	
XL586	Hawker Hunter T7 [85]	MoD(PE) BAe Warton	
XL587	Hawker Hunter T7 (8807M) [Z]	RAF TMTS, Scampton	
XL591	Hawker Hunter T7	RAF No 237 OCU, Lossiemouth	
XL592	Hawker Hunter T7 (8836M) [Y]	RAF TMTS, Scampton	
XL595	Hawker Hunter T7 [78]	RAF, stored St Athan	
XL598	Hawker Hunter T8C [880]	RN FRADU, Yeovilton	
XL600	Hawker Hunter T7 [57/FL]	RNAY Fleetlands Apprentice School	
XL601	Hawker Hunter T7 [874/VL]	RN store, Yeovilton	
XL602	Hawker Hunter T8M	MoD(PE) BAe Dunsfold	
XL603	Hawker Hunter T8M [724]	RN No 899 Sqn, Yeovilton	
XL609	Hawker Hunter T7 (8866M) [YF]	RAF Lossiemouth, BDRT	
XL612	Hawker Hunter T7 [2]	MoD(PE) ETPS Boscombe Down	
XL613	Hawker Hunter T7A [613]	RAF No 237 OCU, Lossiemouth	
XL614	Hawker Hunter T7 [O]	RAF No 237 OCU, Lossiemouth	
XL616	Hawker Hunter T7	RAF No 208 Sqn, Lossiemouth	
XL617	Hawker Hunter T7	Jet Heritage, Bournemouth	
XL618	Hawker Hunter T7 (8892M) [05]	RAF Cottesmore, BDRT	
XL621	Hawker Hunter T7 (G-BNCX)	Lovaux Ltd, Hurn	
XL623	Hawker Hunter T7 [90] (8770M)	RAF Newton, BDRF	
XL629	EE Lightning T4	A&AEE Boscombe Down, at main gate	
XL703	SAL Pioneer CC1 (8034M)	Greater Manchester Museum of Science and Industry	
XL717	DH Tiger Moth (G-AOXG/T7291) [LM]	FAA Museum, RNAS Yeovilton	
XL728	WS58 Wessex HAS1	RAF Brawdy Fire Section	
XL735	Saro Skeeter AOP12	Privately owned, Little Staughton	
XL738	Saro Skeeter AOP12 (7860M)	AAC Centre, Middle Wallop, on display	
XL762	Saro Skeeter AOP12 (8017M)	Royal Scottish Museum of Flight, East Fortune	
XL763	Saro Skeeter AOP12	Southall Technical College	
XL764	Saro Skeeter AOP12 (7940M)	Newark Air Museum, Winthorpe	
XL765	Saro Skeeter AOP12	Privately owned, Pimlico	

Notes	Serial	Type (alternative identity)	Owner, Operator or Location
	XL770	Saro Skeeter AOP12 (8046M)	Southampton Hall of Aviation
	XL809	Saro Skeeter AOP12 (G-BLIX/ PH-HOF)	Privately owned, Sywell
	XL811	Saro Skeeter AOP12 [157]	The Aircraft Collection, Warmingham
	XL812	Saro Skeeter AOP12 (G-SARO)	Privately owned, Old Buckenham
	XL813	Saro Skeeter AOP12	Museum of Army Flying, Middle Wallop
	XL814	Saro Skeeter AOP12	AAC Historic Aircraft Flight, Middle Wallop
	XL824	Bristol Sycamore HR14 (8021M)	Greater Manchester Museum of Science and Industry
	XL829	Bristol Sycamore HR14	Bristol Industrial Museum
	XL836	WS55 Whirlwind HAS7 (A2642) [65]	RN Yeovilton, Fire Section
	XL840	WS55 Whirlwind HAS7 [56]	City of Norwich Aviation Museum
	XL846	WS55 Whirlwind HAS7 (A2625) [85]	RN Predannack Fire School
	XL847	WS55 Whirlwind HAS7 (A2626) [83]	AAC Middle Wallop, Fire Section
	XL853	WS55 Whirlwind HAS7 (A2630)	Southampton Hall of Aviation
	XL875	WS55 Whirlwind HAR9	Air Service Training, Perth
	XL880	WS55 Whirlwind HAR9 (A2714) [433/ED]	RN Lee-on-Solent, BDRT
	XL898	WS55 Whirlwind HAR9 (8654M) [30/ED]	Boscombe Down, A&AEE derelict
	XL899	WS55 Whirlwind HAR9 [587/CU]	RN Predannack Fire School
	XL929	Percival Pembroke C1 (G-BNPU)	Chelsea College, Shoreham
	XL954	Percival Pembroke C1	RAF No 60 Sqn, Wildenrath
	XL993	SAL Twin Pioneer CC1 (8388M)	RAF Cosford Aerospace Museum
	XM135	BAC Lightning F1 [135]	Imperial War Museum, Duxford
	XM144	BAC Lightning F1 (8417M) [J]	RAF Leuchars, at main gate
	XM169	BAC Lightning F1A (8422M) [W]	RAF Leuchars decoy
	XM172	BAC Lightning F1A (8427M) [B]	RAF Coltishall, at main gate
	XM173	BAC Lightning F1A (8414M) [A]	RAF Bentley Priory, at main gate
	XM178	BAC Lightning F1A (8418M) [Y]	RAF Leuchars decoy
	XM191	BAC Lightning F1A (7854M/ 8590M) (nose only)	RAF Exhibition Flight, Abingdon
	XM192	BAC Lightning F1A (8413M) [K]	RAF Wattisham, at main gate
	XM223	DH Devon C2	MoD(PE) RAE West Freugh
	XM279	EE Canberra B(I)8 (nose only)	S Yorks Air Museum, Firbeck
	XM296	DH Heron C4	RN FONAC, RNAS Yeovilton
	XM300	WS58 Wessex HAS1	Wales Aircraft Museum, Cardiff
	XM326	WS58 Wessex HAS1 [515]	RNAS Portland Fire Section
	XM327	WS58 Wessex HAS3 [401/KE]	College of Nautical Studies, Warsash
	XM328	WS58 Wessex HAS3	RNAS Culdrose, SAH
	XM329	WS58 Wessex HAS1 (A2609)	RN Predannack Fire School
	XM330	WS58 Wessex HAS1	MoD(PE) RAE Farnborough, stored
	XM331	WS58 Wessex HAS3	RN Predannack Fire School
	XM349	Hunting Jet Provost T3A [H] (89--M)	RAF No 2 SoTT, Cosford
	XM350	Hunting Jet Provost T3A [89]	RAF No 7 FTS, Church Fenton
	XM351	Hunting Jet Provost T3 [Y] (8078M)	RAF No 2 SoTT, Cosford
	XM352	Hunting Jet Provost T3A [21]	RAF No 1 FTS, Linton-on-Ouse
	XM355	Hunting Jet Provost T3 (8229M) [D]	RAF No 1 SoTT, Halton
	XM357	Hunting Jet Provost T3A [45]	RAF No 1 FTS, Linton-on-Ouse
	XM358	Hunting Jet Provost T3A [53]	RAF No 1 FTS, Linton-on-Ouse
	XM362	Hunting Jet Provost T3 (8230M)	RAF No 1 SoTT, Halton
	XM365	Hunting Jet Provost T3A [37]	RAF No 1 FTS, Linton-on-Ouse
	XM367	Hunting Jet Provost T3 [Z] (8083M)	RAF No 2 SoTT, Cosford
	XM369	Hunting Jet Provost T3 (8084M) [07]	RAF No 1 SoTT, Halton
	XM370	Hunting Jet Provost T3A [10]	RAF No 1 FTS, Linton-on-Ouse
	XM371	Hunting Jet Provost T3A [K] (89--M)	RAF No 1 SoTT, Halton
	XM372	Hunting Jet Provost T3A [55] (8917M)	RAF Linton-on-Ouse Fire Section
	XM374	Hunting Jet Provost T3A [18]	RAF No 1 FTS, Linton-on-Ouse

Serial	Type (alternative identity)	Owner, Operator or Location	Notes
XM375	Hunting Jet Provost T3 (8231M) [B]	RAF No 1 SoTT, Halton	
XM376	Hunting Jet Provost T3A [27]	RAF No 1 FTS, Linton-on-Ouse	
XM378	Hunting Jet Provost T3A [3/8]	RAF No 1 FTS, Linton-on-Ouse	
XM379	Hunting Jet Provost T3	Army Apprentice College, Arborfield	
XM381	Hunting Jet Provost T3 (8232M) [O]	RAF No 1 SoTT, Halton	
XM383	Hunting Jet Provost T3A [90]	RAF No 7 FTS, Church Fenton	
XM386	Hunting Jet Provost T3 (8076M) [08]	RAF No 1 SoTT, Halton	
XM387	Hunting Jet Provost T3 [I]	RAF CFS, Scampton	
XM401	Hunting Jet Provost T3A [17]	RAF No 1 FTS, Linton-on-Ouse	
XM402	Hunting Jet Provost T3 (8055AM) [J]	RAF No 1 SoTT, Halton	
XM403	Hunting Jet Provost T3A [A]	RAF CFS, Scampton	
XM404	Hunting Jet Provost T3 (8055BM)	RAF No 1 SoTT, Halton	
XM405	Hunting Jet Provost T3A [42]	RAF No 1 FTS, Linton-on-Ouse	
XM408	Hunting Jet Provost T3 (8233M) [P]	RAF No 1 SoTT, Halton	
XM409	Hunting Jet Provost T3 (8082M) [A]	RAF No 1 SoTT, Halton	
XM410	Hunting Jet Provost T3 (8054AM) [C]	RAF No 1 SoTT, Halton	
XM411	Hunting Jet Provost T3 (8434M)	RAF No 1 SoTT, Halton	
XM412	Hunting Jet Provost T3A [41]	RAF No 1 FTS, Linton-on-Ouse	
XM413	Hunting Jet Provost T3	Army Apprentice College, Arborfield	
XM414	Hunting Jet Provost T3A [101]	RAF No 7 FTS, Church Fenton	
XM417	Hunting Jet Provost T3 (8054BM) [D]	RAF No 1 SoTT, Halton	
XM419	Hunting Jet Provost T3A [102]	RAF No 7 FTS, Church Fenton	
XM424	Hunting Jet Provost T3A [30]	RAF No 1 FTS, Linton-on-Ouse	
XM425	Hunting Jet Provost T3A [88]	RAF No 7 FTS, Church Fenton	
XM426	Hunting Jet Provost T3 (nose only)	Privately owned, Lutterworth	
XM455	Hunting Jet Provost T3A [K]	RAF No 2 SoTT, Cosford	
XM458	Hunting Jet Provost T3A [B]	RAF CFS, Scampton	
XM459	Hunting Jet Provost T3A [104]	RAF No 7 FTS, Church Fenton	
XM461	Hunting Jet Provost T3A [11]	RAF No 1 FTS, Linton-on-Ouse	
XM463	Hunting Jet Provost T3A	RAF No 1 FTS, Linton-on-Ouse	
XM464	Hunting Jet Provost T3A [23]	RAF No 1 FTS, Linton-on-Ouse	
XM465	Hunting Jet Provost T3A [85]	RAF No 7 FTS, Church Fenton	
XM466	Hunting Jet Provost T3A [31]	RAF No 1 FTS, Linton-on-Ouse	
XM467	Hunting Jet Provost T3 (8085M) [06] [69]	RAF No 1 SoTT, Halton	
XM468	Hunting Jet Provost T3 (8081M) [B]	RAF No 1 SoTT, Halton	
XM470	Hunting Jet Provost T3A [M]	RAF CFS, Scampton	
XM471	Hunting Jet Provost T3A [L] (89--M)	RAF No 2 SoTT, Cosford	
XM472	Hunting Jet Provost T3A [22]	RAF No 1 FTS, Linton-on-Ouse	
XM473	Hunting Jet Provost T3A [81]	RAF No 7 FTS, Church Fenton	
XM474	Hunting Jet Provost T3 (8121M)	No 1330 Sqn ATC, Warrington	
XM475	Hunting Jet Provost T3A [96]	RAF No 7 FTS, Church Fenton	
XM478	Hunting Jet Provost T3A [33]	RAF No 1 FTS, Linton-on-Ouse	
XM479	Hunting Jet Provost T3A [54]	RAF No 1 FTS, Linton-on-Ouse	
XM480	Hunting Jet Provost T3 [02] (8080M)	RAF No 1 SoTT, Halton	
XM515	DH Vampire T11 (7998M) (really XD515)	Newark Air Museum, Winthorpe	
XM529	Saro Skeeter AOP12 (7979M/ G-BDNS)	Privately owned, Handforth	
XM553	Saro Skeeter AOP12 (G-AWSV)	Privately owned, Middle Wallop	
XM555	Saro Skeeter AOP12 (8027M)	RAF Cosford Aerospace Museum	
XM556	Saro Skeeter AOP12 (G-HELI/7870M) [V]	International Helicopter Museum, Weston-super-Mare	
XM561	Saro Skeeter AOP12 (7980M)	Lincolnshire Aviation Museum, East Kirkby	
XM564	Saro Skeeter AOP12	Royal Armoured Corps, Bovington	
XM569	Avro Vulcan B2	Wales Aircraft Museum, Cardiff	
XM575	Avro Vulcan B2A (G-BLMC)	East Midlands Aeropark	

Notes	Serial	Type (alternative identity)	Owner, Operator or Location
	XM594	Avro Vulcan B2	Newark Air Museum, Winthorpe
	XM597	Avro Vulcan B2	Royal Scottish Museum of Flight, East Fortune
	XM598	Avro Vulcan B2 (8778M)	RAF Cosford Aerospace Museum
	XM602	Avro Vulcan B2 (8771M)	RAF St Athan Historic Aircraft Collection
	XM603	Avro Vulcan B2	Avro Aircraft Restoration Society, Woodford
	XM607	Avro Vulcan B2 (8779M)	RAF Waddington, on display
	XM612	Avro Vulcan B2	City of Norwich Aviation Museum
	XM652	Avro Vulcan B2 (nose only)	Privately owned, Burntwood, Staffs
	XM655	Avro Vulcan B2 (G-VULC/ N655AV)	Privately owned, Wellesbourne Mountford
	XM656	Avro Vulcan B2 (8757M) (nose only)	RAF Cottesmore Fire Section
	XM657	Avro Vulcan B2A (8734M)	CTE, RAF Manston
	XM660	WS55 Whirlwind HAS7 [78]	North East Aircraft Museum, Usworth
	XM665	WS55 Whirlwind HAS7	Booker Aircraft Museum
	XM667	WS55 Whirlwind HAS7 (A2629) [56/CU]	RN Predannack Fire School
	XM685	WS55 Whirlwind HAS7 (G-AYZJ) [513/PO]	Newark Air Museum, Winthorpe
	XM693	HS Gnat T1 (7891M)	BAe Hamble on display
	XM694	HS Gnat T1	RAE Bedford Apprentice School
	XM697	HS Gnat T1	No 1349 Sqn ATC, Woking
	XM706	HS Gnat T1 (8572M) [12]	RAF No 1 SoTT, Halton
	XM708	HS Gnat T1 (8573M)	RAF Locking, on display
	XM709	HS Gnat T1 (8617M) [67]	RAF No 1 SoTT, Halton
	XM715	HP Victor K2	RAF No 55 Sqn, Marham
	XM717	HP Victor K2	RAF No 55 Sqn, Marham
	XM832	WS58 Wessex HAS1	*Scrapped at Yeovilton*
	XM833	WS58 Wessex HAS3	Second World War Aircraft Preservation Society, Lasham
	XM836	WS58 Wessex HAS3 [651/PO]	RNAY Fleetlands, instructional use
	XM838	WS58 Wessex HAS3	RN Predannack Fire School
	XM841	WS58 Wessex HAS1 [510]	RN Predannack Fire School
	XM843	WS58 Wessex HAS1 (A2693) [527/LS]	RNAS Lee-on-Solent on display
	XM845	WS58 Wessex HAS1 (A2682) [530/PO]	RNAS Yeovilton Fire Section
	XM868	WS58 Wessex HAS1 (A2706) [517/PO]	RN AES, Lee-on-Solent
	XM870	WS58 Wessex HAS3 [PO]	RN NACDS, Culdrose
	XM874	WS58 Wessex HAS1 (A2689) [521/CU]	RNAS Culdrose, SAH
	XM916	WS58 Wessex HAS3 [666/PO]	RAF Wroughton Fire Section
	XM917	WS58 Wessex HAS1 (A2692) [528/PO]	RNAS Lee-on-Solent Fire Section
	XM919	WS58 Wessex HAS3 [55]	RNAY Fleetlands Apprentice School
	XM923	WS58 Wessex HAS3	*Scrapped at RNAY Fleetlands*
	XM926	WS58 Wessex HAS1	*To Pendine Ranges*
	XM927	WS58 Wessex HAS3 (8814M) [660/PO]	RAF Shawbury, BDRT
	XM969	BAC Lightning T4 (8592M)	*Scrapped at Binbrook*
	XM987	BAC Lightning T4	RAF Coningsby, BDRT
	XM997	BAC Lightning T4	RAF FF&SS, Catterick
	XN126	WS55 Whirlwind HAR10 (8655M) [S]	RAF No 1 SoTT, Halton
	XN132	Sud Alouette AH2	AAC UNFICYP, Nicosia
	XN137	Hunting Jet Provost T3 [95] (nose only)	RAF Exhibition Flight, Abingdon
	XN185	Slingsby Sedbergh TX1 (8942M)	RAF ACCGS Syerston, preserved
	XN239	Slingsby Cadet TX3 [G] (8889M)	ATC Regional HQ, Henlow
	XN246	Slingsby Cadet TX3	Southampton Hall of Aviation
	XN258	WS55 Whirlwind HAR9 [589/CU]	Cornwall Aero Park, Helston
	XN263	WS55 Whirlwind HAS7	Royal Military College of Science, stored, Shrivenham
	XN297	WS55 Whirlwind HAR9 [12] (really XN311/A2643)	Privately owned, Hull
	XN298	WS55 Whirlwind HAR9 [810/LS]	Privately owned, Stoke-on-Trent
	XN299	WS55 Whirlwind HAS7 [758]	Torbay Aircraft Museum, Paignton

Serial	Type (alternative identity)	Owner, Operator or Location	Notes
XN302	WS55 Whirlwind HAS7 (A2654) [LS]	RNAS Lee-on-Solent Fire Section	
XN304	WS55 Whirlwind HAS7 [64]	Norfolk & Suffolk Aviation Museum, Flixton	
XN306	WS55 Whirlwind HAR9 [434/ED]	RNAS Portland Fire Section	
XN308	WS55 Whirlwind HAS7 (A2605) [510/PO]	RNAS Yeovilton Fire Section	
XN309	WS55 Whirlwind HAR9 (A2663) [590/CU]	Second World War Aircraft Preservation Society, Lasham	
XN314	WS55 Whirlwind HAS7 (A2614)	RN Predannack Fire School	
XN332	Saro P531 (G-APNV/A2579) [759]	International Helicopter Museum, Weston-super-Mare	
XN334	Saro P531 (A2525)	International Helicopter Museum, under restoration, Crawley C.o.T.	
XN341	Saro Skeeter AOP12 (8022M)	RAF St Athan Historic Aircraft Collection	
XN344	Saro Skeeter AOP12 (8018M)	Science Museum, South Kensington	
XN351	Saro Skeeter AOP12 (G-BKSC)	Privately owned, Shempston, Lossiemouth	
XN359	WS55 Whirlwind HAR9 (A2712) [434/ED]	RNAS Lee-on-Solent, BDRT	
XN380	WS55 Whirlwind HAS7 [67]	Lashenden Air Warfare Museum, Headcorn	
XN382	WS55 Whirlwind HAS7	*To Bofors, Sweden, 88*	
XN385	WS55 Whirlwind HAS7	RN Historic Flight, stored Wroughton	
XN386	WS55 Whirlwind HAR9 [435/ED] (A2713)	Privately owned, Blackpool	
XN387	WS55 Whirlwind HAR9 (8564M)	RAF Odiham, BDRT	
XN412	Auster AOP9	Cotswold Aircraft Restoration Group, RAF Innsworth	
XN435	Auster AOP9 (G-BGBU)	Privately owned, Egham	
XN437	Auster AOP9 (G-AXWA)	Privately owned, Welling, Kent	
XN441	Auster AOP9 (G-BGKT)	Privately owned, Reymerston Hall	
XN453	DH Comet 2e	RAE Farnborough Fire Section	
XN458	Hunting Jet Provost T3 [19] (8234M)	RAF CTTS, St Athan	
XN459	Hunting Jet Provost T3A [N]	RAF CFS, Scampton	
XN461	Hunting Jet Provost T3A [28]	RAF No 1 FTS, Linton-on-Ouse	
XN462	Hunting Jet Provost T3A [87]	RAF No 7 FTS, Church Fenton	
XN466	Hunting Jet Provost T3A [29]	RAF No 1 FTS, Linton-on-Ouse	
XN467	Hunting Jet Provost T4 (8559M) [F]	RAF No 1 SoTT, Halton	
XN470	Hunting Jet Provost T3A [84]	RAF No 7 FTS, Church Fenton	
XN471	Hunting Jet Provost T3A [24]	RAF No 1 FTS, Linton-on-Ouse	
XN472	Hunting Jet Provost T3A [J] (89--M)	RAF No 2 SoTT, Cosford	
XN473	Hunting Jet Provost T3A (8862M) [98] (cockpit only)	RAF Church Fenton Fire Section	
XN492	Hunting Jet Provost T3 [X] (8079M)	RAF No 2 SoTT, Cosford	
XN493	Hunting Jet Provost T3 (nose only)	No 1075 Sqn ATC, Camberley	
XN494	Hunting Jet Provost T3A [43]	RAF No 1 FTS, Linton-on-Ouse	
XN495	Hunting Jet Provost T3A [102] (8786M)	RAF Abingdon, BDRF	
XN497	Hunting Jet Provost T3A [52]	RAF No 1 FTS, Linton-on-Ouse	
XN498	Hunting Jet Provost T3A [16]	RAF No 1 FTS, Linton-on-Ouse	
XN499	Hunting Jet Provost T3A [L]	RAF CFS, Scampton	
XN500	Hunting Jet Provost T3A [80]	RAF No 7 FTS, Church Fenton	
XN501	Hunting Jet Provost T3A [S]	RAF No 2 SoTT, Cosford	
XN502	Hunting Jet Provost T3A [D]	RAF CFS, Scampton	
XN503	Hunting Jet Provost T3 (nose only)	RAF Exhibition Flight, Abingdon	
XN505	Hunting Jet Provost T3A [25]	RAF No 1 FTS, Linton-on-Ouse	
XN506	Hunting Jet Provost T3A [19]	RAF No 1 FTS, Linton-on-Ouse	
XN508	Hunting Jet Provost T3A [98]	RAF No 7 FTS, Church Fenton	
XN509	Hunting Jet Provost T3A [50]	RAF No 1 FTS, Linton-on-Ouse	
XN510	Hunting Jet Provost T3A [40]	RAF No 1 FTS, Linton-on-Ouse	
XN511	Hunting Jet Provost T3 [21] (nose only)	No 177 Sqn ATC, Blackpool Airport	
XN512	Hunting Jet Provost T3 (8435M)	RAF No 1 SoTT, Halton	

Notes	Serial	Type (alternative identity)	Owner, Operator or Location
	XN547	Hunting Jet Provost T3A [48]	RAF No 1 FTS, Linton-on-Ouse
	XN548	Hunting Jet Provost T3A [103]	RAF No 7 FTS, Church Fenton
	XN549	Hunting Jet Provost T3 (8235M) [R]	RAF No 1 SoTT, Halton
	XN551	Hunting Jet Provost T3A [100]	RAF No 7 FTS, Church Fenton
	XN552	Hunting Jet Provost T3A [32]	RAF No 1 FTS, Linton-on-Ouse
	XN553	Hunting Jet Provost T3A	RAF St Athan Station Flight
	XN554	Hunting Jet Provost T3 (8436M) [K]	RAF No 1 SoTT, Halton
	XN574	Hunting Jet Provost T3A [21]	RAF No 1 FTS, Linton-on-Ouse
	XN577	Hunting Jet Provost T3A [89]	RAF No 7 FTS, Church Fenton
	XN579	Hunting Jet Provost T3A [14]	RAF No 1 FTS, Linton-on-Ouse
	XN581	Hunting Jet Provost T3A [C]	RAF CFS, Scampton
	XN582	Hunting Jet Provost T3A [H] (89--M)	RAF No 2 SoTT, Cosford
	XN584	Hunting Jet Provost T3A [E]	RAF CFS, Scampton
	XN585	Hunting Jet Provost T3A [12]	RAF Linton-on-Ouse Fire Section
	XN586	Hunting Jet Provost T3A [91]	RAF No 7 FTS, Church Fenton
	XN589	Hunting Jet Provost T3A [46]	RAF No 1 FTS, Linton-on-Ouse
	XN592	Hunting Jet Provost T3 (nose only)	No 1105 Sqn ATC, Winchester
	XN593	Hunting Jet Provost T3A [97]	RAF No 7 FTS, Church Fenton
	XN594	Hunting Jet Provost T3 [W] (8077M)	RAF No 2 SoTT, Cosford
	XN595	Hunting Jet Provost T3A [82]	RAF No 7 FTS, Church Fenton
	XN600	Hunting Jet Provost T3A (nose only)	N. Yorks Recovery Group, Chop Gate
	XN602	Hunting Jet Provost T3 (8088M)	CTE, RAF Manston
	XN605	Hunting Jet Provost T3A [J]	RAF CFS, Scampton
	XN606	Hunting Jet Provost T3A [36]	RAF No 1 FTS, Linton-on-Ouse
	XN629	Hunting Jet Provost T3A [39]	RAF No 1 FTS, Linton-on-Ouse
	XN632	Hunting Jet Provost T3 (8352M)	RAF St Athan, CTTS
	XN634	Hunting Jet Provost T3A [94]	RAF No 7 FTS, Church Fenton
	XN635	Hunting Jet Provost T3 [57] (nose only)	RN Predannack Fire School
	XN636	Hunting Jet Provost T3A [15]	RAF No 1 FTS, Linton-on-Ouse
	XN637	Hunting Jet Provost T3 (G-BKOU)	Vintage Aircraft Team, Cranfield
	XN640	Hunting Jet Provost T3A [99]	RAF No 7 FTS, Church Fenton
	XN641	Hunting Jet Provost T3A (8865M) [47]	RAF Newton Fire Section
	XN643	Hunting Jet Provost T3A (8704M) [26] (cockpit only)	RAFC Cranwell, instructional use
	XN643	Hunting Jet Provost T3A (8704M) (fuselage only)	BAe Warton Fire Section
	XN647	DH Sea Vixen FAW2 (A2610) [707-VL]	Cornwall Aero Park, Helston
	XN649	DH Sea Vixen FAW2 [126]	MoD(PE), stored RAE Farnborough
	XN650	DH Sea Vixen FAW2 (A2612/ A2620/A2639) [VL]	Wales Aircraft Museum, Cardiff
	XN651	DH Sea Vixen FAW2 (A2616) (nose only)	Privately owned, Pucklechurch, Avon
	XN652	DH Sea Vixen FAW2 (8817M)	RAF FF&SS, Catterick
	XN657	DH Sea Vixen D3 [TR-1]	MoD(PE) RAE Llanbedr Fire Section
	XN685	DH Sea Vixen FAW2 (8173M) [P] [-/VL]	BAe Hawarden Apprentice School
	XN688	DH Sea Vixen FAW2 (8141M)	RAE Farnborough Fire Section
	XN691	DH Sea Vixen FAW2 [N] [247-H] (8143M)	Midland Air Museum, Coventry
	XN692	DH Sea Vixen FAW2 (A2624) [125/E]	RNAS Yeovilton on display, FONAC
	XN694	DH Sea Vixen FAW2	MoD(PE) RAF Llanbedr
	XN696	DH Sea Vixen FAW2 [751] cockpit	Privately owned, Suffolk
	XN699	DH Sea Vixen FAW2 [752] (8224M)	RAF North Luffenham
	XN714	Hunting H126	RAF Cosford Aerospace Museum
	XN724	EE Lightning F2A [F] (8513M)	Privately owned, Newcastle-on-Tyne
	XN728	EE Lightning F2A (8546M) [V]	Privately owned, Balderton, Notts
	XN734	EE Lightning F3A (8346M/ G-27-239/G-BNCA)	Vintage Aircraft Team, Cranfield
	XN769	EE Lightning F2 (8402M) [Z]	London ATCC, West Drayton

Serial	Type (alternative identity)	Owner, Operator or Location	Notes
XN774	EE Lightning F2A (8551M) [F]	RAF Coningsby, decoy	
XN776	EE Lightning F2A [B] (8535M)	Royal Scottish Museum of Flight, East Fortune	
XN781	EE Lightning F2A (8538M) [B]	RAF Leuchars Fire Section	
XN816	AW Argosy E1 (8489M)	*Sold to New Zealand for spares*	
XN817	AW Argosy C1	MoD(PE) RAE West Freugh Fire Section	
XN819	AW Argosy C1 (8205M) (nose only)	Newark Air Museum, Winthorpe	
XN855	AW Argosy E1 (8556M)	FSCTE, RAF Manston	
XN923	HS Buccaneer S1	Boscombe Down, A&AEE derelict	
XN925	HS Buccaneer S1 (8087M/ A2602)	RAF FF&SS, Catterick	
XN928	HS Buccaneer S1 (8179M)	Wales Aircraft Museum, Cardiff	
XN929	HS Buccaneer S1 (8051M) (nose only)	RAF Lossiemouth procedures trainer	
XN930	HS Buccaneer S1 (8180M) [632/LM]	RAF Honington, Fire Section	
XN934	HS Buccaneer S1 (A2600) [631]	RN Predannack Fire School	
XN953	HS Buccaneer S1 (A2655/ 8182M)	RN Predannack Fire School	
XN957	HS Buccaneer S1 [630/LM]	FAA Museum, RNAS Yeovilton	
XN964	HS Buccaneer S1 [613/LM]	Newark Air Museum, Winthorpe	
XN967	HS Buccaneer S1 (A2627) [103/E]	Cornwall Aero Park, Helston	
XN972	HS Buccaneer S1 (8183M) (nose only) (really XN962)	RAF Exhibition Flight, Abingdon	
XN973	HS Buccaneer S1 (nose only) [633]	BAe Warton Fire Section	
XN974	HS Buccaneer S2A	MoD(PE) BAe Warton	
XN976	HS Buccaneer S2B	RAF No 12 Sqn, Lossiemouth	
XN977	HS Buccaneer S2B [G]	RAF, stored Shawbury	
XN979	HS Buccaneer S2 (nose only)	Cranfield Institute of Technology	
XN981	HS Buccaneer S2B [981]	RAF No 12 Sqn, Lossiemouth	
XN982	HS Buccaneer S2C	MoD(PE) BAe Brough	
XN983	HS Buccaneer S2B	RAF No 208 Sqn, Lossiemouth	
XP107	WS58 Wessex HAS1 (A2527)	RN Predannack Fire School	
XP110	WS58 Wessex HAS3 [55/FL]	RNAY Fleetlands Apprentice School	
XP116	WS58 Wessex HAS3 (A2618) [520]	RN AES, Lee-on-Solent	
XP137	WS58 Wessex HAS3 [CU]	RN NACDS, Culdrose	
XP140	WS58 Wessex HAS3 (8806M) [653/PO]	RAF Chilmark, BDRT	
XP142	WS58 Wessex HAS3	FAA Museum, RNAS Yeovilton	
XP149	WS58 Wessex HAS1 (A2669)	RN Predannack Fire School	
XP150	WS58 Wessex HAS3 [406/AN]	RN AES, Lee-on-Solent	
XP151	WS58 Wessex HAS1 (A2684) [047/R]	RN Lee-on-Solent Fire Section	
XP155	WS58 Wessex HAS1 (A2640)	RNAS Culdrose Fire Section	
XP157	WS58 Wessex HAS1 (A2680)	RN AES, Lee-on-Solent	
XP158	WS58 Wessex HAS1 (A2688) [522/CU]	RN AES, Lee-on-Solent	
XP159	WS58 Wessex HAS1 (8877M) [047/R]	RAF Odiham, BDRT	
XP160	WS58 Wessex HAS1 (A2650) [521/CU]	RN AES, Lee-on-Solent	
XP165	WS Scout AH1	International Helicopter Museum, Weston-super-Mare	
XP166	WS Scout AH1 (G-APVL)	MoD(PE) RAE Farnborough, in store	
XP167	WS Scout AH1	RAE Farnborough Fire Section	
XP190	WS Scout AH1	AAC, stored Wroughton	
XP191	WS Scout AH1	AAC Middle Wallop, BDRT	
XP226	Fairey Gannet AEW3 (A2667) [073/E]	Newark Air Museum, Winthorpe	
XP241	Auster AOP9	Tagmore Nurseries, Rabley Heath, Herts	
XP242	Auster AOP9	Museum of Army Flying, stored Middle Wallop	

Notes	Serial	Type (alternative identity)	Owner, Operator or Location
	XP244	Auster AOP9 (7864M) [M7922]	Army Apprentice College, Arborfield
	XP248	Auster AOP9 (7822M)	Vintage Aircraft Team, Cranfield
	XP279	Auster AOP9 (G-BWKK)	Privately owned, Goodwood
	XP280	Auster AOP9	Leicester Museum of Technology store
	XP281	Auster AOP9	Imperial War Museum, Duxford
	XP282	Auster AOP9 (G-BGTC)	Privately owned, Swanton Morley
	XP283	Auster AOP9 (7859M)	Vintage Aircraft Team, Cranfield
	XP299	WS55 Whirlwind HAR10 (8726M)	RAF Cosford Aerospace Museum
	XP328	WS55 Whirlwind HAR10 (G-BKHC)	Privately owned, RAF Lakenheath
	XP329	WS55 Whirlwind HAR10 [V] (8791M) [UN]	Privately owned, Tattershall Thorpe
	XP330	WS55 Whirlwind HAR10	CAA Fire School, Teesside Airport
	XP333	WS55 Whirlwind HAR10 (8650M) [G]	RAF FSCTE, Manston
	XP338	WS55 Whirlwind HAR10 (8647M) [N]	RAF No 2 SoTT, Cosford
	XP344	WS55 Whirlwind HAR10 (8764M) [X]	RAF North Luffenham
	XP345	WS55 Whirlwind HAR10 [UN] (8792M)	Privately owned, Storwood, East Yorks
	XP346	WS55 Whirlwind HAR10 (8793M)	Stratford Aircraft Collection, Long Marston
	XP350	WS55 Whirlwind HAR10	Cornwall Aero Park, Helston
	XP351	WS55 Whirlwind HAR10 (8672M) [Z]	RAF Shawbury, gate guardian
	XP352	WS55 Whirlwind HAR10 (8701M)	*To Hermeskeil Museum, West Germany*
	XP354	WS55 Whirlwind HAR10 (8721M)	RAF No 1 SoTT, Halton
	XP355	WS55 Whirlwind HAR10 (8463M/G-BEBC) [A]	City of Norwich Aviation Museum
	XP356	WS55 Whirlwind HAR10	*Burnt at Farnborough*
	XP357	WS55 Whirlwind HAR10 (8499M)	CTE, RAF Manston
	XP359	WS55 Whirlwind HAR10 (8447M)	RAF Stafford, fire section
	XP360	WS55 Whirlwind HAR10 [V]	Second World War Aircraft Preservation Society, Lasham
	XP361	WS55 Whirlwind HAR10 (8731M)	RAF Valley, preserved at gate
	XP393	WS55 Whirlwind HAR10 [U]	RAE Farnborough Fire Section
	XP394	WS55 Whirlwind HAR10 [C]	CTE, RAF Manston
	XP395	WS55 Whirlwind HAR10 (8674M) [A]	Privately owned, Tattershall Thorpe
	XP398	WS55 Whirlwind HAR10 (8794M)	Privately owned, Charlwood, Surrey
	XP399	WS55 Whirlwind HAR10	Privately owned, Tor View Garage, Glastonbury, Som
	XP400	WS55 Whirlwind HAR10 (8444M) [N]	CTE, RAF Manston
	XP404	WS55 Whirlwind HAR10 (8682M)	RAF SAREW, Finningley
	XP405	WS55 Whirlwind HAR10 (8656M) [Y]	RAF No 1 SoTT, Halton
	XP411	AW Argosy C1 (8442M) [C]	RAF Cosford Aerospace Museum
	XP439	AW Argosy E1 (8558M)	*Scrapped at Lossiemouth*
	XP442	AW Argosy T2 (8454M) [55]	RAF No 1 SoTT, Halton
	XP444	AW Argosy C1 (8455M)	*Sold to New Zealand for spares*
	XP458	Slingsby Grasshopper TX1	City of Norwich Aviation Museum
	XP502	HS Gnat T1 (8576M) [02]	RAF St Athan, CTTS
	XP503	HS Gnat T1 (8568M) [73]	RAF No 1 SoTT, Halton
	XP504	HS Gnat T1 (8618M) [68] [04]	RAF No 1 SoTT, Halton
	XP505	HS Gnat T1 [05]	Science Museum, South Kensington
	XP511	HS Gnat T1 (8619M) [65]	RAF No 1 SoTT, Halton
	XP514	HS Gnat T1 (8635M)	Privately owned, Leavesden
	XP516	HS Gnat T1 (8580M) [16]	MoD(PE) RAE Farnborough
	XP530	HS Gnat T1 (8606M) [60]	RAF No 1 SoTT, Halton
	XP532	HS Gnat T1 (8577M/8615M) [32]	MoD(PE) RAE Farnborough
	XP533	HS Gnat T1 (8632M) [Q]	RAF No 2 SoTT, Cosford
	XP534	HS Gnat T1 (8620M) [64]	RAF No 1 SoTT, Halton
	XP535	HS Gnat T1 (A2679) [SAH-1]	*To G-BOXP, Cranfield*
	XP538	HS Gnat T1 (8607M) [P]	RAF No 2 SoTT, Cosford

Serial	Type (alternative identity)	Owner, Operator or Location	Notes
XP540	HS Gnat T1 (8608M) [62]	RAF No 1 SoTT, Halton	
XP541	HS Gnat T1 (8616M) [41]	Privately owned	
XP542	HS Gnat T1 (8575M) [42]	RAF St Athan, CTTS	
XP547	Hunting Jet Provost T4 [04]	RAF No 1 TWU/79 Sqn, Brawdy	
XP556	Hunting Jet Provost T4 [B]	RAF CATCS, Shawbury	
XP557	Hunting Jet Provost T4 (8494M)	RAF No 1 SoTT, Halton	
XP558	Hunting Jet Provost T4 (8627M/A2628) [20]	RAF St Athan, CTTS	
XP563	Hunting Jet Provost T4 [C]	RAF CATCS, Shawbury	
XP567	Hunting Jet Provost T4 (8510M) [23]	RAF No 1 SoTT, Halton	
XP573	Hunting Jet Provost T4 (8236M) [19]	RAF No 1 SoTT, Halton	
XP585	Hunting Jet Provost T4 (8407M) [24]	RAF No 1 SoTT, Halton	
XP627	Hunting Jet Provost T4	North East Aircraft Museum, Usworth	
XP629	Hunting Jet Provost T4 [P]	RAF CATCS, Shawbury	
XP638	Hunting Jet Provost T4 [A]	RAF CATCS, Shawbury	
XP640	Hunting Jet Provost T4 (8501M) [E]	RAF No 1 SoTT, Halton	
XP672	Hunting Jet Provost T4 (8458M) [27]	RAF No 1 SoTT, Halton	
XP677	Hunting Jet Provost T4 (8587M) (nose only)	No 2530 Sqn ATC, Headley Court, Uckfield, East Sussex	
XP680	Hunting Jet Provost T4 (8460M)	RAF St Athan, BDRT	
XP686	Hunting Jet Provost T4 (8401M/8502M) [G]	RAF No 1 SoTT, Halton	
XP688	Hunting Jet Provost T4 [E]	RAF CATCS, Shawbury	
XP693	BAC Lightning F6	MoD(PE) BAe Warton	
XP694	BAC Lightning F3	*To Otterburn Ranges*	
XP701	BAC Lightning F3 (8924M) [DD]	Kent Battle of Britain Museum, Hawkinge	
XP702	BAC Lightning F3	*To Otterburn Ranges*	
XP703	BAC Lightning F3 (nose only)	BAe Warton Fire Section	
XP706	BAC Lightning F3 (8925M)	Lincolnshire Lightning Preservation Society, Strubby	
XP707	BAC Lightning F3 [DB]	*Written off 19 March 1987*	
XP741	BAC Lightning F3 [AR] (8939M)	CTE, RAF Manston	
XP745	BAC Lightning F3 (8453M) [H]	RAF Boulmer, at main gate	
XP748	BAC Lightning F3 (8446M)	*To Wembury Ranges*	
XP749	BAC Lightning F3 (8926M)	Privately owned, Sutton-on-the-Forest	
XP750	BAC Lightning F3 (8927M)	Privately owned, Sutton-on-the-Forest	
XP751	BAC Lightning F3 (8928M)		
XP761	BAC Lightning F3 (8438M) [N]	*Scrapped at Binbrook*	
XP764	BAC Lightning F3 [DC] (8929M)	Privately owned, Sutton-on-the-Forest	
XP769	DHC Beaver AL1	AAC, Aldergrove	
XP771	DHC Beaver AL1	AAC store, Shawbury	
XP772	DHC Beaver AL1	Museum of Army Transport, Beverley	
XP775	DHC Beaver AL1	AAC, stored Shawbury	
XP778	DHC Beaver AL1	AAC Beaver Training Flt, Middle Wallop	
XP779	DHC Beaver AL1	AAC, stored Shawbury	
XP804	DHC Beaver AL1	*Sold to Canada*	
XP806	DHC Beaver AL1	Army Apprentice College, Arborfield	
XP810	DHC Beaver AL1	AAC, stored Shawbury	
XP814	DHC Beaver AL1	AAC, stored Shawbury	
XP820	DHC Beaver AL1	AAC Beaver Training Flt, Middle Wallop	
XP821	DHC Beaver AL1 [MCO]	Museum of Army Flying, Middle Wallop	
XP822	DHC Beaver AL1	Museum of Army Flying, Middle Wallop	
XP823	DHC Beaver AL1	*Sold to Canada*	
XP825	DHC Beaver AL1	AAC, Aldergrove	
XP827	DHC Beaver AL1	AAC Netheravon Fire Section	
XP831	Hawker P1127 (8406M)	RAF Museum, Hendon	
XP841	Handley-Page HP115	Concorde Museum, RNAS Yeovilton	
XP846	WS Scout AH1 [B]	AAC, stored Wroughton	
XP847	WS Scout AH1	Museum of Army Flying, Middle Wallop	
XP848	WS Scout AH1	AAC AETW, Middle Wallop	
XP849	WS Scout AH1	MoD(PE) ETPS Boscombe Down	
XP850	WS Scout AH1	AAC, stored Wroughton	
XP852	WS Scout AH1 (89--M)	*AAC, 1 Regt Hildesheim, BDRT*	
XP853	WS Scout AH1	AAC AETW, Middle Wallop	
XP854	WS Scout AH1 (7898M/TAD043)	AAC AETW, Middle Wallop	

Notes	Serial	Type (alternative identity)	Owner, Operator or Location
	XP855	WS Scout AH1	AAC, stored Wroughton
	XP856	WS Scout AH1	AAC, Middle Wallop BDRT
	XP857	WS Scout AH1	AAC Middle Wallop Fire Section
	XP883	WS Scout AH1	AAC No 658 Sqn, Netheravon
	XP884	WS Scout AH1	AAC AETW, Middle Wallop
	XP885	WS Scout AH1 [Y]	AAC No 666 (TA) Sqn, Netheravon
	XP886	WS Scout AH1	Army Apprentice College, Arborfield
	XP887	WS Scout AH1 [C]	AAC, Sek Kong
	XP888	WS Scout AH1	AAC AETW, Middle Wallop
	XP890	WS Scout AH1 [G]	AAC, stored Wroughton
	XP891	WS Scout AH1 [S]	AAC No 666 (TA) Sqn, Netheravon
	XP893	WS Scout AH1	AAC, stored Wroughton
	XP894	WS Scout AH1 [D]	AAC, Sek Kong
	XP897	WS Scout AH1	*AAC No 3 Regt, Soest, BDRT*
	XP898	WS Scout AH1	*AAC No 664 Sqn Minden, BDRT*
	XP899	WS Scout AH1 [D]	Army Apprentice College, Arborfield
	XP900	WS Scout AH1 [Z]	AAC, stored Wroughton
	XP901	WS Scout AH1 [E]	AAC, Sek Kong
	XP902	WS Scout AH1	AAC, stored Wroughton
	XP903	WS Scout AH1	AAC, stored Wroughton
	XP905	WS Scout AH1	AAC AETW, Middle Wallop
	XP908	WS Scout AH1	AAC No 660 Sqn, Brunei
	XP909	WS Scout AH1	AAC, stored Wroughton
	XP910	WS Scout AH1	AAC No 658 Sqn, Netheravon
	XP915	DH Comet 3B (G-ANLO)	Scrapped at Woodford
	XP919	DH Sea Vixen FAW2 (8163M) [706/VL]	City of Norwich Aviation Museum
	XP921	DH Sea Vixen FAW2 (8226M) [753]	RAF North Luffenham Training Area
	XP924	DH Sea Vixen D3	MoD(PE) RAE Llanbedr
	XP925	DH Sea Vixen FAW2 (nose only) [752]	RAE Farnborough
	XP967	Sud Alouette AH2	AAC
	XP980	Hawker P.1127 (A2700)	RNAS Culdrose, SAH
	XP984	Hawker P.1127 (A2658)	RNEC Manadon, for instruction
	XR107	AW Argosy T2 (8441M)	*Sold to New Zealand for spares*
	XR137	AW Argosy E1	Snowdon Mountain Aviation Collection, Caernarfon
	XR140	AW Argosy E1 (8579M) (fuselage only)	RAF Halton, Fire Section
	XR220	BAC TSR2 (7933M)	RAF Cosford Aerospace Museum
	XR222	BAC TSR2	Imperial War Museum, Duxford
	XR232	Sud Alouette AH2 (F-WEIP)	AAC Historic Aircraft Flight, Middle Wallop
	XR240	Auster AOP9 (G-BDFH)	Privately owned, Booker
	XR241	Auster AOP9 (G-AXRR)	Privately owned, Duxford
	XR243	Auster AOP9 (8057M)	RAF St Athan Historic Aircraft Collection
	XR244	Auster AOP9	AAC Historic Aircraft Flight, Middle Wallop
	XR246	Auster AOP9 (7862M/ G-AZBU)	Privately owned, Reymerston Hall
	XR267	Auster AOP9 (G-BJXR)	Cotswold Aircraft Restoration Group, RAF Innsworth
	XR269	Auster AOP9 (G-BDXY)	Privately owned, Old Buckenham
	XR271	Auster AOP9	Museum of Artillery, Woolwich
	XR363	SC5 Belfast C1 (G-OHCA)	Privately owned, Southend
	XR371	SC5 Belfast C1	RAF Cosford Aerospace Museum
	XR376	Sud Alouette AH2	AAC
	XR378	Sud Alouette AH2	AAC
	XR379	Sud Alouette AH2	AAC
	XR382	Sud Alouette AH2	AAC
	XR385	Sud Alouette AH2	AAC
	XR386	Sud Alouette AH2	AAC
	XR396	DH Comet 4C (8882M) (G-BDIU)	RAF Kinloss BDRT
	XR436	Saro Scout AH1	AAC Middle Wallop, BDRT
	XR441	DH Sea Heron C1 (G-AORG)	RNAS Yeovilton, Station Flight
	XR442	DH Sea Heron C1 (G-AORH)	RNAS Yeovilton, Station Flight
	XR443	DH Sea Heron C1 (G-ARKU)	RNAS Yeovilton, Station Flight
	XR445	DH Sea Heron C1 (G-ARKW)	RNAS Yeovilton, Station Flight
	XR453	WS55 Whirlwind HAR10 (8873M) [A]	RAF Odiham, on gate
	XR458	WS55 Whirlwind HAR10 (8662M) [H]	RAF No 1 SoTT, Halton

Serial	Type (alternative identity)	Owner, Operator or Location	Notes
XR478	WS55 Whirlwind HAR10	Defence School, Winterbourne Gunner	
XR479	WS55 Whirlwind HAR10 [A]	*To Pendine Ranges*	
XR481	WS55 Whirlwind HAR10	RAF, stored Wroughton	
XR482	WS55 Whirlwind HAR10 [G]	Defence School, Winterbourne Gunner	
XR483	WS55 Whirlwind HAR10	RAF, stored Wroughton	
XR485	WS55 Whirlwind HAR10 [Q]	Norfolk & Suffolk Aviation Museum, Flixton	
XR486	WS55 Whirlwind HCC12 (8727M)	RAF St Athan Historic Aircraft Collection	
XR493	Saro Scout AH1 (G-APVM/8040M)	*Scraped at Farnborough*	
XR497	WS58 Wessex HC2	RAF No 22 Sqn SAR*	
XR498	WS58 Wessex HC2 [X]	RAF No 72 Sqn, Aldergrove	
XR499	WS58 Wessex HC2 [W]	RAF No 72 Sqn, Aldergrove	
XR501	WS58 Wessex HC2	RAF No 22 Sqn SAR*	
XR502	WS58 Wessex HC2 [Z]	RAF No 72 Sqn, Aldergrove	
XR503	WS58 Wessex HC2	MoD(PE) RAE Bedford	
XR504	WS58 Wessex HC2	RAF No 22 Sqn SAR*	
XR505	WS58 Wessex HC2 [WA]	RAF No 2 FTS, Shawbury	
XR506	WS58 Wessex HC2 [V]	RAF No 72 Sqn, Aldergrove	
XR507	WS58 Wessex HC2	RAF No 22 Sqn SAR*	
XR508	WS58 Wessex HC2 [D]	RAF No 28 Sqn, Sek Kong	
XR509	WS58 Wessex HC2 (8752M)	RAF Benson, BDRT	
XR511	WS58 Wessex HC2 [L]	RAF No 72 Sqn, Aldergrove	
XR515	WS58 Wessex HC2 [B]	RAF No 28 Sqn, Sek Kong	
XR516	WS58 Wessex HC2 [WB]	RAF No 2 FTS, Shawbury	
XR517	WS58 Wessex HC2 [N]	RAF No 72 Sqn, Aldergrove	
XR518	WS58 Wessex HC2	RAF No 22 Sqn SAR*	
XR519	WS58 Wessex HC2 [WC]	RAF No 2 FTS, Shawbury	
XR520	WS58 Wessex HC2	RAF No 22 Sqn SAR*	
XR521	WS58 Wessex HC2 [WD]	RAF No 2 FTS, Shawbury	
XR522	WS58 Wessex HC2 [A]	RAF No 28 Sqn, Sek Kong	
XR523	WS58 Wessex HC2 [M]	RAF No 72 Sqn, Aldergrove	
XR524	WS58 Wessex HC2	RAF No 22 Sqn SAR*	
XR525	WS58 Wessex HC2 [G]	RAF No 72 Sqn, Aldergrove	
XR526	WS58 Wessex HC2 (8147M)	Westlands, Sherborne	
XR527	WS58 Wessex HC2 [K]	RAF No 72 Sqn, Aldergrove	
XR528	WS58 Wessex HC2 [T]	RAF No 72 Sqn, Aldergrove	
XR529	WS58 Wessex HC2 [E]	RAF No 72 Sqn, Aldergrove	
XR534	HS Gnat T1 (8578M) [65]	RAF Valley on display	
XR535	HS Gnat T1 (8569M) [05]	RAF No 1 SoTT, Halton	
XR537	HS Gnat T1 (8642M) [T]	RAF No 2 SoTT, Cosford	
XR538	HS Gnat T1 (8621M) [69]	RAF No 1 SoTT, Halton	
XR541	HS Gnat T1 (8602M)	To 'PF179'	
XR544	HS Gnat T1	RAE Farnborough Fire Section	
XR569	HS Gnat T1 (8560M) [08]	RAF No 1 SoTT, Halton	
XR571	HS Gnat T1 (8493M)	RAF *Red Arrows* Scampton on display	
XR572	HS Gnat T1 (A2676) [SAH-3]	*To Colorado, USA*	
XR574	HS Gnat T1 (8631M) [72]	RAF No 1 SoTT, Halton	
XR588	WS58 Wessex HC2	RAF No 22 Sqn SAR*	
XR595	WS Scout AH1 [M]	AAC No 666 (TA) Sqn, Netheravon	
XR597	WS Scout AH1	AAC AETW, Middle Wallop	
XR600	WS Scout AH1 (89--M)	AAC Aldergrove, BDRT	
XR601	WS Scout AH1	Army Apprentice College, Arborfield	
XR602	WS Scout AH1	AAC, stored Wroughton	
XR603	WS Scout AH1 [A]	*Royal Australian Navy Museum, Nowra*	
XR604	WS Scout AH1	AAC Middle Wallop, BDRT	
XR627	WS Scout AH1	AAC, stored Wroughton	
XR629	WS Scout AH1	AAC, stored Wroughton	
XR630	WS Scout AH1 [U] (really XP907)	AAC Middle Wallop Fire Section	
XR632	WS Scout AH1 [Q]	AAC No 666 (TA) Sqn, Netheravon	
XR635	WS Scout AH1	AAC AETW, Middle Wallop	
XR637	WS Scout AH1	AAC, stored Wroughton	
XR639	WS Scout AH1 [X]	AAC, stored Wroughton	
XR643	Hunting Jet Provost T4 (8516M) [26]	RAF No 1 SoTT, Halton	
XR650	Hunting Jet Provost T4 (8459M) [28]	RAF No 1 SoTT, Halton	

Note: *The SAR Wing and SAREW are based at RAF Finningley. No 22 Sqn SAR has detached flights: A Flt—RAF Chivenor; B Flt—RAF Leuchars; C Flt and SARTU—RAF Valley; E Flt—RAF Coltishall.

Notes	Serial	Type (alternative identity)	Owner, Operator or Location
	XR651	Hunting Jet Provost T4 (8431M) [A]	RAF No 1 SoTT, Halton
	XR653	Hunting Jet Provost T4 [H]	RAF CATCS, Shawbury
	XR654	Hunting Jet Provost T4 (fuselage)	Macclesfield Historical Av Soc, Chelford, Cheshire
	XR658	Hunting Jet Provost T4	Jet Heritage, Bournemouth
	XR662	Hunting Jet Provost T4 (8410M) [25]	RAF No 1 SoTT, Halton
	XR669	Hunting Jet Provost T4 (8062M) [02] (nose only)	RAF No 1 SoTT, Halton
	XR670	Hunting Jet Provost T4 (8498M)	RAF No 1 SoTT, Halton
	XR672	Hunting Jet Provost T4 (8495M) [C]	RAF No 1 SoTT, Halton
	XR673	Hunting Jet Provost T4 [L]	RAF CATCS, Shawbury
	XR674	Hunting Jet Provost T4 [D]	RAF CATCS, Shawbury
	XR679	Hunting Jet Provost T4 [04]	RAF No 1 TWU/79 Sqn Brawdy
	XR681	Hunting Jet Provost T4 (8588M) (nose only)	No 1349 Sqn ATC, Odiham
	XR700	Hunting Jet Provost T4 (8589M) (nose only)	RAF Exhibition Flight, Aldergrove
	XR701	Hunting Jet Provost T4 [K]	RAF CATCS, Shawbury
	XR704	Hunting Jet Provost T4 (8506M) [30]	RAF No 1 SoTT, Halton
	XR713	EE Lightning F3 (8935M)	RAF No 111 Sqn on display, Leuchars
	XR716	EE Lightning F3 [AQ] (8940M)	RAF Cottesmore, BDRT
	XR717	EE Lightning F3	*Scrapped at Boscombe Down*
	XR718	EE Lightning F3 [DA] (8932M)	RAF Wattisham
	XR720	EE Lightning F3 (8930M)	Privately owned, Sutton-on-the-Forest
	XR724	EE Lightning F6 [BC]	MoD(PE)/BAe Warton
	XR725	EE Lightning F6	Privately owned, Rossington
	XR726	EE Lightning F6	Privately owned, Rossington
	XR727	EE Lightning F6 (8962M)	*To RAF Wildenrath for BDRT*
	XR728	EE Lightning F6 [JS]	Lightning Preservation Group, Bruntingthorpe
	XR747	EE Lightning F6	Privately owned, Rossington
	XR749	EE Lightning F3 [Q] (8934M)	RAF Leuchars, BDRT
	XR751	EE Lightning F3	Privately owned, Lower Tremar, Cornwall
	XR753	EE Lightning F6 [BP] (89--M)	RAF Leeming, gate guardian
	XR754	EE Lightning F6 [BC] (89--M)	RAF Honington BDRT
	XR755	EE Lightning F6	Privately owned, Callington, Cornwall
	XR756	EE Lightning F6	*To Shoeburyness Ranges*
	XR757	EE Lightning F6	Privately owned, Rossington
	XR758	EE Lightning F6 [BF] (89--M)	*RAF Laarbruch, BDRT*
	XR759	EE Lightning F6	Privately owned, Rossington
	XR769	EE Lightning F6 [AM]	*Ditched 11 April 1988 North Sea*
	XR770	EE Lightning F6 [JS]	Privately owned, Laceby
	XR771	EE Lightning F6	Midland Air Museum, Coventry
	XR773	EE Lightning F6 [BR]	A&AEE, stored Boscombe Down
	XR777	WS Scout AH1 (really XT625)	St George's Barracks, Sutton Coldfield
	XR806	BAC VC10 C1	RAF No 10 Sqn, Brize Norton
	XR807	BAC VC10 C1	RAF No 10 Sqn, Brize Norton
	XR808	BAC VC10 C1	RAF No 10 Sqn, Brize Norton
	XR810	BAC VC10 C1	RAF No 10 Sqn, Brize Norton
	XR944	Wallis WA116 (G-ATTB)	Privately owned, Reymerston Hall
	XR951	HS Gnat T1 (8603M) [26]	RAF
	XR953	HS Gnat T1 (8609M) [63]	RAF No 1 SoTT, Halton
	XR954	HS Gnat T1 (8570M) [30]	RAF No 1 SoTT, Halton
	XR955	HS Gnat T1 (A2678) [SAH-2]	Privately owned, Leavesden
	XR977	HS Gnat T1 (8640M)	RAF Cosford Aerospace Museum
	XR980	HS Gnat T1 (8622M) [70]	RAF No 1 SoTT, Halton
	XR984	HS Gnat T1 (8571M)	RAF No 1 SoTT, Halton
	XR987	HS Gnat T1 (8641M) [S]	Privately owned, Leavesden
	XR991	HS Gnat T1 (8637M/A2709) [SAH-6] (G-BOXO)	*To G-BOXO, Cranfield*
	XR998	HS Gnat T1 (8623M) [71]	RAF No 1 SoTT, Halton
	XS100	HS Gnat T1 (8561M) [57]	RAF No 1 SoTT, Halton
	XS101	HS Gnat T1 (8638M) (G-GNAT)	Privately owned, Cranfield
	XS102	HS Gnat T1 (8624M) [66]	RAF No 2 SoTT, Cosford
	XS104	HS Gnat T1 (8604M) [44]	Privately owned, Leavesden
	XS105	HS Gnat T1 (8625M) [V]	RAF No 2 SoTT, Cosford

Serial	Type (alternative identity)	Owner, Operator or Location	Notes
XS107	HS Gnat T1 (8639M) [U]	RAF No 2 SoTT, Cosford	
XS109	HS Gnat T1 (8626M) [75]	RAF No 1 SoTT, Halton	
XS110	HS Gnat T1 (8562M) [20]	RAF No 1 SoTT, Halton	
XS119	WS58 Wessex HAS3 [55]	RN Predannack Fire School	
XS120	WS58 Wessex HAS1 (8653M) [520/CU]	RAF Wroughton Fire Section	
XS122	WS58 Wessex HAS3 (A2707) [655/PO]	RNEC Manadon, for instruction	
XS125	WS58 Wessex HAS1 (A2648)	RN Predannack Fire School	
XS128	WS58 Wessex HAS1 (A2670)	RNAS Yeovilton, BDRT	
XS149	WS58 Wessex HAS3 [661/GL]	International Helicopter Museum, Weston-super-Mare, Avon	
XS153	WS58 Wessex HAS3 [662/PO]	RNEC Manadon, for instruction	
XS176	Hunting Jet Provost T4 (8514M) [N]	RAF No 1 SoTT, Halton	
XS177	Hunting Jet Provost T4 [N]	RAF IWTU, Brawdy	
XS178	Hunting Jet Provost T4 [05]	RAF No 1 TWU/79 Sqn, Brawdy	
XS179	Hunting Jet Provost T4 (8237M) [20]	RAF No 1 SoTT, Halton	
XS180	Hunting Jet Provost T4 (8238M) [21]	RAF No 1 SoTT, Halton	
XS181	Hunting Jet Provost T4 [F]	RAF No 1 TWU, Brawdy	
XS186	Hunting Jet Provost T4 (8408M) [M]	RAF No 1 SoTT, Halton	
XS209	Hunting Jet Provost T4 (8409M) [29]	RAF No 1 SoTT, Halton	
XS210	Hunting Jet Provost T4 (8239M) [22]	RAF No 1 SoTT, Halton	
XS215	Hunting Jet Provost T4 (8507M) [17]	RAF No 1 SoTT, Halton	
XS216	Hunting Jet Provost T4 (nose only)	RAF SAREW Finningley, for rescue training	
XS217	Hunting Jet Provost T4 [O]	RAF CATCS, Shawbury	
XS218	Hunting Jet Provost T4 (8508M) [18]	RAF No 1 SoTT, Halton	
XS219	Hunting Jet Provost T4 [06]	RAF No 1 TWU/79 Sqn, Brawdy	
XS230	BAC Jet Provost T5P	MoD(PE) ETPS Boscombe Down	
XS231	BAC Jet Provost T5 (G-ATAJ)	RAF, Scampton, instructional use	
XS235	HS Comet 4C	MoD(PE) A&AEE Boscombe Down	
XS241	WS58 Wessex HU5	MoD(PE) stored, Wroughton	
XS416	EE Lightning T5	Privately owned, Rossington	
XS417	EE Lightning T5	Newark Air Museum, Winthorpe	
XS419	EE Lightning T5	Privately owned, Rossington	
XS420	EE Lightning T5	Privately owned, Lincoln	
XS422	EE Lightning T5	MoD(PE), stored Boscombe Down	
XS451	EE Lightning T5 (8503M)	To Flight Systems Inc, USA	
XS452	EE Lightning T5 [BT] (G-BPFE)	Privately owned, Cranfield	
XS456	EE Lightning T5	Privately owned, King's Lynn	
XS457	EE Lightning T5 (nose only)	Museum of Weapon Technology, Grimsby	
XS458	EE Lightning T5 [DY]	Privately owned, Cranfield	
XS459	EE Lightning T5	Privately owned, King's Lynn	
XS463	WS Wasp HAS1 (A2647)	RN Predannack Fire School	
XS463	WS Wasp HAS1 (really XT431)	International Helicopter Museum, Weston-super-Mare	
XS479	WS58 Wessex HU5 [XF] (8819M)	RAF Brize Norton JATE	
XS481	WS58 Wessex HU5	RN, stored Wroughton	
XS482	WS58 Wessex HU5 [A-D]	RAE Farnborough Apprentice School	
XS483	WS58 Wessex HU5 [T]	RN AES, Lee-on-Solent	
XS484	WS58 Wessex HU5 [821/CU]	RN, stored Wroughton	
XS485	WS58 Wessex HC5C (Hearts)	RAF No 84 Sqn, Akrotiri	
XS486	WS58 Wessex HU5 [825/CU]	RN stored, Wroughton	
XS488	WS58 Wessex HU5 [XK]	RN, stored Wroughton	
XS489	WS58 Wessex HU5 [R]	RN, stored Wroughton	
XS491	WS58 Wessex HU5 [XM]	RN, stored Wroughton	
XS492	WS58 Wessex HU5 [623]	RN, stored Wroughton	
XS493	WS58 Wessex HU5	Department of Naval Recruitment, (846 Sqn), Fleetlands	
XS496	WS58 Wessex HU5 [625/PO]	RN AES, Lee-on-Solent	
XS498	WS58 Wessex HC5C (Joker)	RAF No 84 Sqn, Akrotiri	
XS506	WS58 Wessex HU5 [XE]	RN, stored Wroughton	
XS507	WS58 Wessex HU5 [627/PO]	RN AES, Lee-on-Solent	
XS508	WS58 Wessex HU5	RNAS Yeovilton	

Notes	Serial	Type (alternative identity)	Owner, Operator or Location
	XS509	WS58 Wessex HU5 (A2597)	MoD(PE) ETPS Boscombe Down
	XS510	WS58 Wessex HU5 [626/PO]	RN AES, Lee-on-Solent
	XS511	WS58 Wessex HU5 [M]	RN AES, Lee-on-Solent
	XS513	WS58 Wessex HU5 [419/PO]	RN AES, Lee-on-Solent
	XS514	WS58 Wessex HU5 [L]	RN AES, Lee-on-Solent
	XS515	WS58 Wessex HU5 [N]	RN AES, Lee-on-Solent
	XS516	WS58 Wessex HU5 [Q]	RN AES, Lee-on-Solent
	XS517	WS58 Wessex HC5C (Diamonds)	RAF No 84 Sqn, Akrotiri
	XS520	WS58 Wessex HU5 [F]	RN AES, Lee-on-Solent
	XS521	WS58 Wessex HU5 [YB]	Army, Saighton, Cheshire
	XS522	WS58 Wessex HU5 [ZL/VL]	RN AES, Lee-on-Solent
	XS523	WS58 Wessex HU5 [824/CU]	RN, stored Wroughton
	XS527	WS Wasp HAS1	FAA Museum, RNAS Yeovilton
	XS529	WS Wasp HAS1 [461]	RN AES, Lee-on-Solent
	XS535	WS Wasp HAS1 [432]	RAOC, West Moors, Dorset
	XS537	WS Wasp HAS1 (A2672) [582]	RNAS Portland BDRT
	XS538	WS Wasp HAS1 [451]	RN Lee-on-Solent, BDRT
	XS539	WS Wasp HAS1 [435/E]	RN AES, Lee-on-Solent
	XS541	WS Wasp HAS1 [602]	RN, stored Wroughton
	XS545	WS Wasp HAS1 (A2702) [635]	RN AES, Lee-on-Solent
	XS562	WS Wasp HAS1 [605]	RN, stored Wroughton
	XS565	WS Wasp HAS1 [445]	To Foulness Ranges
	XS566	WS Wasp HAS1 [607]	RN
	XS567	WS Wasp HAS1 [434/E]	RN AES, Lee-on-Solent
	XS568	WS Wasp HAS1 [441]	RNAY Fleetlands Apprentice School
	XS569	WS Wasp HAS1	RNAY Fleetlands Apprentice School
	XS570	WS Wasp HAS1 (A2699) [P]	RN AES, Lee-on-Solent
	XS572	WS Wasp HAS1 (8845M) [414]	RAF Stafford Fire Section (No 16 MU)
	XS576	DH Sea Vixen FAW2 [125/E]	Imperial War Museum, Duxford
	XS577	DH Sea Vixen D3	MoD(PE) RAE Llanbedr
	XS587	DH Sea Vixen FAW(TT)2 (G-VIXN/8828M)	Privately owned, Hurn
	XS590	DH Sea Vixen FAW2 [131/E]	FAA Museum, RNAS Yeovilton
	XS596	HS Andover C1	RAF No 115 Sqn, Benson
	XS597	HS Andover C1	RAF No 60 Sqn, Wildenrath
	XS598	HS Andover C1 [E] (fuselage)	RAF AMS, Brize Norton
	XS603	HS Andover E3	RAF No 115 Sqn, Benson
	XS605	HS Andover E3	RAF No 115 Sqn, Benson
	XS606	HS Andover C1	MoD(PE) ETPS Boscombe Down
	XS607	HS Andover C1	MoD(PE) RAE West Freugh
	XS610	HS Andover E3	RAF No 115 Sqn, Benson
	XS637	HS Andover C1	RAF No 60 Sqn, Wildenrath
	XS639	HS Andover E3A	RAF No 115 Sqn, Benson
	XS640	HS Andover E3	RAF No 115 Sqn, Benson
	XS641	HS Andover E3A	RAF No 115 Sqn, Benson
	XS642	HS Andover C1 [C] (8785M)	RAF Benson Fire Section
	XS643	HS Andover E3A	RAF No 115 Sqn, Benson
	XS644	HS Andover E3A	RAF No 115 Sqn, Benson
	XS646	HS Andover C1 (med)	MoD(PE) RAE Farnborough
	XS650	Slingsby Swallow TX1 (8801M)	RAF St Athan Historic Aircraft Collection
	XS674	WS58 Wessex HC2 [R]	RAF No 72 Sqn, Aldergrove
	XS675	WS58 Wessex HC2	RAF No 22 Sqn SAR*
	XS676	WS58 Wessex HC2 [WJ]	RAF No 2 FTS, Shawbury
	XS677	WS58 Wessex HC2 [WK]	RAF No 2 FTS, Shawbury
	XS679	WS58 Wessex HC2 [WG]	RAF No 2 FTS, Shawbury
	XS695	HS Kestrel FGA1 (A2619) [SAH-6]	RNAS Culdrose, SAH
	XS709	HS Dominie T1 [M]	RAF No 6 FTS, Finningley
	XS710	HS Dominie T1 [O]	RAF No 6 FTS, Finningley
	XS711	HS Dominie T1 [L]	RAF No 6 FTS, Finningley
	XS712	HS Dominie T1 [A]	RAF No 6 FTS, Finningley
	XS713	HS Dominie T1 [C]	RAF No 6 FTS, Finningley
	XS714	HS Dominie T1 [P]	RAF No 6 FTS, Finningley
	XS726	HS Dominie T1 [T]	RAF No 6 FTS, Finningley
	XS727	HS Dominie T1 [D]	RAF No 6 FTS, Finningley
	XS728	HS Dominie T1 [E]	RAF No 6 FTS, Finningley
	XS729	HS Dominie T1 [G]	RAF No 6 FTS, Finningley
	XS730	HS Dominie T1 [H]	RAF No 6 FTS, Finningley
	XS731	HS Dominie T1 [J]	RAF No 6 FTS, Finningley
	XS732	HS Dominie T1 [B]	RAF No 6 FTS, Finningley

Serial	Type (alternative identity)	Owner, Operator or Location	Notes
XS733	HS Dominie T1 [Q]	RAF No 6 FTS, Finningley	
XS734	HS Dominie T1 [N]	RAF No 6 FTS, Finningley	
XS735	HS Dominie T1 [R]	RAF No 6 FTS, Finningley	
XS736	HS Dominie T1 [S]	RAF No 6 FTS, Finningley	
XS737	HS Dominie T1 [K]	RAF No 6 FTS, Finningley	
XS738	HS Dominie T1 [U]	RAF No 6 FTS, Finningley	
XS739	HS Dominie T1 [F]	RAF No 6 FTS, Finningley	
XS743	Beagle Basset CC1	MoD(PE) ETPS Boscombe Down	
XS765	Beagle Basset CC1	To G-BSET	
XS770	Beagle Basset CC1	RAF Cosford Aerospace Museum	
XS789	HS Andover CC2	RAF No 32 Sqn, Northolt	
XS790	HS Andover CC2	RAF Queen's Flight, Benson	
XS791	HS Andover CC2	RAF No 32 Sqn, Northolt	
XS792	HS Andover CC2	RAF No 32 Sqn, Northolt	
XS793	HS Andover CC2	RAF No 60 Sqn, Wildenrath	
XS794	HS Andover CC2	RAF No 32 Sqn, Northolt	
XS862	WS58 Wessex HAS3 [650]	RNAS Lee-on-Solent, at gate	
XS863	WS58 Wessex HAS1	Imperial War Museum, Duxford	
XS865	WS58 Wessex HAS1 (A2694) [529/CU]	RNAS Lee-on-Solent Fire Section	
XS866	WS58 Wessex HAS1 (A2705) [520/CU]	RN SAH, Culdrose	
XS867	WS58 Wessex HAS1 (A2671)	RNAS Lee-on-Solent Fire Section	
XS868	WS58 Wessex HAS1 (A2691)	RNAY Fleetlands, on gate	
XS869	WS58 Wessex HAS1 (A2649) [508/PO]	FAA Air Medical School, Seafield Park, rescue training	
XS870	WS58 Wessex HAS1 (A2697) [-/PO]	RN BDRT, Lee-on-Solent	
XS871	WS58 Wessex HAS1 (8457M) [AI]	RAF Odiham Fire Section	
XS872	WS58 Wessex HAS1 (A2666) [572/CU]	RNAY Fleetlands Apprentice School	
XS873	WS58 Wessex HAS1 (A2686) [525/CU]	RN Predannack Fire School	
XS876	WS58 Wessex HAS1 (A2695) [523]	RN SAH, Culdrose	
XS877	WS58 Wessex HAS1 (A2687) [16/PO]	RNE Culdrose, Engineering Training School	
XS878	WS58 Wessex HAS1 (A2683)	RN AES, Lee-on-Solent	
XS881	WS58 Wessex HAS1 (A2675) [046/CU]	FAA Museum, stored Wroughton	
XS882	WS58 Wessex HAS1 (A2696) [524]	RN HMS Naviad, Portsmouth	
XS885	WS58 Wessex HAS1 (A2668) [12/CU]	RN Exhibition Flight, Lee-on-Solent	
XS886	WS58 Wessex HAS1 (A2685) [527/CU]	No 492 Sqn ATC, Shirley, W. Mids	
XS887	WS58 Wessex HAS1 (A2690) [514/PO]	Cornwall Aero Park, Helston	
XS888	WS58 Wessex HAS1 [521]	RN Exhibition Unit, Fleetlands	
XS895	EE Lightning F6	To Shoeburyness Ranges	
XS897	EE Lightning F6	Privately owned, Rossington	
XS898	EE Lightning F6 [BD]	Privately owned, Cranfield	
XS899	EE Lightning F6 [BL]	Privately owned, Cranfield	
XS901	EE Lightning F6 [BK] (89--M)	RAF Bruggen for BDRT	
XS903	EE Lightning F6 [BA]	Yorkshire Air Museum, Elvington	
XS904	EE Lightning F6	MoD(PE)/BAe, Warton	
XS919	EE Lightning F6	Privately owned, Liskeard	
XS922	EE Lightning F6 [BJ] (89--M)	RAF Wattisham, BDRT	
XS923	EE Lightning F6 [BE]	Privately owned, Cranfield	
XS925	EE Lightning F6 [BA]	RAF Museum, Hendon	
XS927	EE Lightning F6	To Shoeburyness Ranges	
XS928	EE Lightning F6 [AD]	MoD(PE)/BAe, Warton	
XS929	EE Lightning F6 [BG] (89--M)	To RAF Akrotiri as gate guardian	
XS932	EE Lightning F6	Privately owned, Rossington	
XS933	EE Lightning F6 (cockpit only)	Privately owned, Lincoln	
XS935	EE Lightning F6	Privately owned, Rossington	
XS936	EE Lightning F6	Privately owned, Liskeard, Cornwall	
XT108	Agusta-Bell Sioux AH1 [U]	Museum of Army Flying, Middle Wallop	
XT131	Agusta-Bell Sioux AH1 [B]	AAC Historic Aircraft Flight, Middle Wallop	
XT133	Agusta-Bell Sioux AH1 (7923M)	Royal Engineers' Museum, Chatham	

Notes	Serial	Type (alternative identity)	Owner, Operator or Location
	XT140	Agusta-Bell Sioux AH1	Air Service Training, Perth
	XT141	Agusta-Bell Sioux AH1 (8509M)	RAF AMS, Brize Norton
	XT148	Agusta-Bell Sioux AH1	Privately owned, Panshanger
	XT150	Agusta-Bell Sioux AH1 (7883M) [R]	Museum of Army Flying, Middle Wallop
	XT151	WS Sioux AH1 [W]	Museum of Army Flying store, Middle Wallop
	XT175	WS Sioux AH1 (TAD175)	CSE Oxford for ground instruction
	XT176	WS Sioux AH1 [U]	FAA Museum, RNAS Yeovilton
	XT190	WS Sioux AH1	Museum of Army Flying, Middle Wallop
	XT200	WS Sioux AH1 [F]	Newark Air Museum, Winthorpe
	XT236	WS Sioux AH1 (frame only)	Museum of Army Flying, Middle Wallop
	XT255	WS58 Wessex HAS3 (8751M)	RAF No 14 MU, Carlisle, BDRT
	XT256	WS58 Wessex HAS3 (A2615)	*Sold to Sweden*
	XT257	WS58 Wessex HAS3 (8719M)	RAF No 1 SoTT, Halton
	XT270	HS Buccaneer S2B	RAF, stored Shawbury
	XT271	HS Buccaneer S2A	RAF No 237 OCU, Lossiemouth
	XT272	HS Buccaneer S2	MoD(PE) RAE Farnborough
	XT273	HS Buccaneer S2B	RAF No 12 Sqn, Lossiemouth
	XT274	HS Buccaneer S2A (8856M) [E]	RAF Abingdon, BDRF
	XT275	HS Buccaneer S2B [A]	RAF, stored Shawbury
	XT276	HS Buccaneer S2B [S]	RAF, stored Shawbury
	XT277	HS Buccaneer S2A (8853M) [F/M]	RAF No 2 SoTT, Cosford
	XT279	HS Buccaneer S2B	RAF No 208 Sqn, Lossiemouth
	XT280	HS Buccaneer S2B	BAe Woodford
	XT281	HS Buccaneer S2B (8705M) [ET]	RAF Lossiemouth, ground instruction
	XT283	HS Buccaneer S2B	MoD(PE) ETPS, Boscombe Down
	XT284	HS Buccaneer S2A (8855M) [H]	RAF Abingdon, BDRF
	XT286	HS Buccaneer S2B	RAF No 208 Sqn, Lossiemouth
	XT287	HS Buccaneer S2B	RAF No 208 Sqn, Lossiemouth
	XT288	HS Buccaneer S2B	RAF No 12 Sqn, Lossiemouth
	XT415	WS Wasp HAS1	Airwork Ltd, Bournemouth
	XT416	WS Wasp HAS1	*Written off 20th July 1977*
	XT420	WS Wasp HAS1 [606]	RN, stored Wroughton
	XT421	WS Wasp HAS1 [FIR4]	RN, stored Wroughton
	XT422	WS Wasp HAS1 [324]	Privately owned, Burgess Hill
	XT423	WS Wasp HAS1 [434/E]	*AAC Falklands, ground instruction*
	XT426	WS Wasp HAS1 [FIR2]	RN, stored Wroughton
	XT427	WS Wasp HAS1	Cornwall Aero Park, Helston
	XT429	WS Wasp HAS1 [445/PLY]	RN, Portland
	XT430	WS Wasp HAS1 [444]	Defence School, Winterbourne Gunner
	XT432	WS Wasp HAS1 [609]	RN, Portland
	XT434	WS Wasp HAS1 [455]	RN AES, Lee-on-Solent
	XT437	WS Wasp HAS1 [423]	RN AES, Lee-on-Solent
	XT439	WS Wasp HAS1 [605]	Cranfield Institute of Technology
	XT441	WS Wasp HAS1 (A2703)	RN Predannack Fire School
	XT443	WS Wasp HAS1 [422]	RN, stored Wroughton
	XT449	WS58 Wessex HU5 [C]	RN AES, Lee-on-Solent
	XT450	WS58 Wessex HU5 [V]	RN Predannack Fire School
	XT451	WS58 Wessex HU5 [XN]	RN, stored Wroughton
	XT453	WS58 Wessex HU5 [A]	RN AES, Lee-on-Solent
	XT455	WS58 Wessex HU5 [U]	RN AES, Lee-on-Solent
	XT456	WS58 Wessex HU5 [XZ] (89--M)	RAF No 72 Sqn Aldergrove, BDRT
	XT458	WS58 Wessex HU5 [622]	RN AES, Lee-on-Solent
	XT459	WS58 Wessex HU5 [D]	RNAS Lee-on-Solent Fire Section
	XT460	WS58 Wessex HU5 [K]	RN, stored Wroughton
	XT463	WS58 Wessex HC5C (*Clubs*)	RAF No 84 Sqn, Akrotiri
	XT466	WS58 Wessex HU5 [XV] (8921M)	RAF No 2 SoTT, Cosford
	XT468	WS58 Wessex HU5 [628/PO]	RN store, Wroughton
	XT469	WS58 Wessex HU5 (8920M)	RAF Stafford ground instruction
	XT470	WS58 Wessex HU5 [A]	AAC Netheravon Fire Section
	XT471	WS58 Wessex HU5	RN, stored Wroughton
	XT472	WS58 Wessex HU5 [XC]	International Helicopter Museum, Weston-super-Mare
	XT474	WS58 Wessex HU5 [820/CU]	RN, stored Wroughton
	XT475	WS58 Wessex HU5 [624/PO]	RN AES, Lee-on-Solent
	XT479	WS58 Wessex HC5C (*Spades*)	RAF No 84 Sqn, Akrotiri
	XT480	WS58 Wessex HU5 [XQ]	RN, stored Wroughton
	XT481	WS58 Wessex HU5 [XF]	RN, stored Wroughton
	XT482	WS58 Wessex HU5 [ZM]	RN AES, Lee-on-Solent

Serial	Type (alternative identity)	Owner, Operator or Location	Notes
XT484	WS58 Wessex HU5 [H]	RN AES, Lee-on-Solent	
XT485	WS58 Wessex HU5 [621]	RN AES, Lee-on-Solent	
XT486	WS58 Wessex HU5 [XR] (8919M)	RAF JATE, Brize Norton	
XT487	WS58 Wessex HU5 (A2723) [815/LS]	RNAS Lee-on-Solent Fire Section	
XT548	WS Sioux AH1 [D]	Army Apprentice College, Arborfield	
XT550	WS Sioux AH1 [D]	Museum of Army Flying, Middle Wallop	
XT575	Vickers Viscount (OE-LAG)	MoD(PE) RS&RE Bedford	
XT595	McD Phantom FG1 (nose only) (8550M/8851M)	RAF Exhibition Flight, Abingdon	
XT595	McD Phantom FGI (fuselage) (8550M/8551M)	RAF Wattisham, BDRT	
XT596	McD Phantom FG1	FAA Museum, RNAS Yeovilton	
XT597	McD Phantom FG1	MoD(PE) A&AEE Boscombe Down	
XT601	WS58 Wessex HC2	RAF No 22 Sqn SAR*	
XT602	WS58 Wessex HC2	RAF No 22 Sqn SAR*	
XT603	WS58 Wessex HC2 [WF]	RAF No 2 FTS, Shawbury	
XT604	WS58 Wessex HC2	RAF No 22 Sqn SAR*	
XT605	WS58 Wessex HC2 [E]	RAF No 28 Sqn, Sek Kong	
XT606	WS58 Wessex HC2	RAF No 22 Sqn SAR*	
XT607	WS58 Wessex HC2 [P]	RAF No 72 Sqn, Aldergrove	
XT614	WS Scout AH1 [C]	AAC No 660 Sqn, Sek Kong	
XT616	WS Scout AH1	AAC, stored Wroughton	
XT617	WS Scout AH1	AAC, stored Wroughton	
XT618	WS Scout AH1 [K]	AAC, Sek Kong	
XT620	WS Scout AH1 (89--M)	AAC Aldergrove, BDRT	
XT621	WS Scout AH1	Royal Military College of Science, Shrivenham	
XT623	WS Scout AH1	AAC, stored Wroughton	
XT624	WS Scout AH1 [D]	AAC No 660 Sqn, Sek Kong	
XT626	WS Scout AH1	AAC, stored Wroughton	
XT627	WS Scout AH1 [H]	AAC, Sek Kong	
XT628	WS Scout AH1 [E]	AAC No 660 Sqn, Sek Kong	
XT630	WS Scout AH1	AAC No 660 Sqn, Brunei	
XT631	WS Scout AH1	MoD(PE) A&AEE Boscombe Down	
XT632	WS Scout AH1 [U]	AAC No 666 (TA) Sqn, Netheravon	
XT633	WS Scout AH1	AAC, stored Wroughton	
XT634	WS Scout AH1 [T]	AAC No 666 (TA) Sqn, Netheravon	
XT636	WS Scout AH1 [F]	AAC No 660 Sqn, Sek Kong	
XT637	WS Scout AH1	AAC, stored Wroughton	
XT638	WS Scout AH1 [N]	AAC, stored Wroughton	
XT639	WS Scout AH1 [Y]	AAC, stored Wroughton	
XT640	WS Scout AH1	AAC AETW, Middle Wallop	
XT642	WS Scout AH1	AAC, stored Wroughton	
XT643	WS Scout AH1 [B]	AAC No 660 Sqn, Sek Kong	
XT644	WS Scout AH1 [Y]	AAC Historic Aircraft Flight, Middle Wallop	
XT645	WS Scout AH1	AAC, stored Wroughton	
XT646	WS Scout AH1 [Z]	AAC No 666 (TA) Sqn, Netheravon	
XT648	WS Scout AH1	AAC, stored Wroughton	
XT649	WS Scout AH1 [Y]	AAC No 658 Sqn, Netheravon	
XT657	BHC SR.N6 Winchester 5	British Hovercraft Corpn	
XT661	Vickers Viscount (9G-AAV)	MoD(PE) RS&RE Bedford	
XT667	WS58 Wessex HC2 [F]	RAF No 28 Sqn, Sek Kong	
XT668	WS58 Wessex HC2 [S]	RAF No 72 Sqn, Aldergrove	
XT669	WS58 Wessex HC2 (8894M) [T]	RAF Aldergrove instructional use	
XT670	WS58 Wessex HC2	RAF No 22 Sqn SAR*	
XT671	WS58 Wessex HC2 [D]	RAF No 72 Sqn, Aldergrove	
XT672	WS58 Wessex HC2 [WE]	RAF No 2 FTS, Shawbury	
XT673	WS58 Wessex HC2 [G]	RAF No 28 Sqn, Sek Kong	
XT674	WS58 Wessex HC2	Remains stored at Leuchars	
XT675	WS58 Wessex HC2 [C]	RAF No 28 Sqn, Sek Kong	
XT676	WS58 Wessex HC2 [I]	RAF No 72 Sqn, Aldergrove	
XT677	WS58 Wessex HC2 (8016M)	RAF Brize Norton fire section	
XT678	WS58 Wessex HC2 [H]	RAF No 28 Sqn, Sek Kong	
XT680	WS58 Wessex HC2	RAF No 22 Sqn SAR*	
XT681	WS58 Wessex HC2 [U]	RAF No 72 Sqn, Aldergrove	
XT752	Fairey Gannet T5 [-/LM] (G-APYO/WN365)	RNAS, stored Lee-on-Solent	
XT755	WS58 Wessex HU5 [V]	RN, stored Wroughton	
XT756	WS58 Wessex HU5 [ZJ]	RN, stored Wroughton	
XT757	WS58 Wessex HU5 (A2722)	RN Predannack Fire School	
XT759	WS58 Wessex HU5 [XY]	RN, stored Wroughton	

Notes	Serial	Type (alternative identity)	Owner, Operator or Location
	XT760	WS58 Wessex HU5 [618/PO]	RN, Portland
	XT761	WS58 Wessex HU5 (A27--)	RN AES, Lee-on-Solent
	XT762	WS58 Wessex HU5	RNAS Culdrose, SAH
	XT764	WS58 Wessex HU5 [G]	RN, stored Wroughton
	XT765	WS58 Wessex HU5 [J]	RN AES, Lee-on-Solent
	XT766	WS58 Wessex HU5 [822/CU]	RN, stored Wroughton
	XT768	WS58 Wessex HU5	RN, stored Wroughton
	XT769	WS58 Wessex HU5 [823/CU]	RN, stored Wroughton
	XT770	WS58 Wessex HU5 [VL]	RN, stored Wroughton
	XT771	WS58 Wessex HU5 (A27--)	RN AES, Lee-on-Solent
	XT772	WS58 Wessex HU5 (8805M)	RAF Valley, BDRT
	XT773	WS58 Wessex HU5	RN, stored Wroughton
	XT778	WS Wasp HAS1 [430] (A27--)	RN AES, Lee-on-Solent
	XT779	WS Wasp HAS1 [582]	RN Portland Fire Section
	XT780	WS Wasp HAS1 [636]	RNAY Fleetlands Apprentice School
	XT782	WS Wasp HAS1 [324]	RN, stored Wroughton
	XT783	WS Wasp HAS1 [470]	RN, stored Wroughton
	XT784	WS Wasp HAS1 [FIR3]	RN, stored Wroughton
	XT785	WS Wasp HAS1 [FIR1]	RN Portland
	XT786	WS Wasp HAS1 [441]	RN Portland Fire Section
	XT788	WS Wasp HAS1 [442] (G-BMIR) (XT793)	Privately owned, Tattershall Thorpe
	XT790	WS Wasp HAS1 [608]	RN Portland
	XT791	WS Wasp HAS1 [433]	RN Portland
	XT793	WS Wasp HAS1 [456]	RN, stored Wroughton
	XT795	WS Wasp HAS1 [476/LE]	RN Lee-on-Solent, on gate
	XT803	WS Sioux AH1 [Y]	Privately owned, Panshanger
	XT827	WS Sioux AH1 [D]	Army Apprentice College, Arborfield
	XT852	McD Phantom FGR2	MoD(PE) BAe Scampton
	XT853	McD Phantom FGR2	MoD(PE) BAe Scampton
	XT857	McD Phantom FG1 [MP] (8913M)	RAF Leuchars ground instruction
	XT858	McD Phantom FG1	MoD(PE) BAe Brough (structures test)
	XT859	McD Phantom FG1 [BK]	RAF No 111 Sqn, Leuchars
	XT860	McD Phantom FG1 [AL]	Crashed 20 April 1988 into North Sea
	XT863	McD Phantom FG1 [AS]	RAF No 43 Sqn, Leuchars
	XT864	McD Phantom FG1 [BJ]	RAF No 111 Sqn, Leuchars
	XT865	McD Phantom FG1	RAF No 111 Sqn, Leuchars
	XT867	McD Phantom FG1 [BH]	RAF No 111 Sqn, Leuchars
	XT870	McD Phantom FG1 [BS]	RAF No 111 Sqn, Leuchars
	XT872	McD Phantom FG1 [BT]	RAF No 111 Sqn, Leuchars
	XT873	McD Phantom FG1 [BA]	RAF No 111 Sqn, Leuchars
	XT874	McD Phantom FG1 [BE]	RAF No 111 Sqn, Leuchars
	XT875	McD Phantom FG1 [AK]	RAF No 43 Sqn, Leuchars
	XT891	McD Phantom FGR2 [CZ]	RAF No 64 Sqn/228 OCU, Leuchars
	XT892	McD Phantom FGR2 [CQ]	RAF No 64 Sqn/228 OCU, Leuchars
	XT893	McD Phantom FGR2 [W]	RAF No 56 Sqn, Wattisham
	XT894	McD Phantom FGR2 [CP]	RAF No 64 Sqn/228 OCU, Leuchars
	XT895	McD Phantom FGR2 [CH]	RAF, stored St Athan
	XT896	McD Phantom FGR2 [CY]	RAF No 64 Sqn/228 OCU, Leuchars
	XT897	McD Phantom FGR2 [Y]	RAF No 56 Sqn, Wattisham
	XT898	McD Phantom FGR2	RAF No 64 Sqn/228 OCU, Leuchars
	XT899	McD Phantom FGR2 [K]	RAF No 19 Sqn, Wildenrath
	XT900	McD Phantom FGR2 [CO]	RAF No 64 Sqn/228 OCU, Leuchars
	XT901	McD Phantom FGR2 [Y]	RAF store, St Athan
	XT902	McD Phantom FGR2 [K]	RAF No 19 Sqn, Wildenrath
	XT903	McD Phantom FGR2 [CM]	RAF No 64 Sqn/228 OCU, Leuchars
	XT905	McD Phantom FGR2 [CU]	RAF No 64 Sqn/228 OCU, Leuchars
	XT906	McD Phantom FGR2 [CH]	RAF No 64 Sqn/228 OCU, Leuchars
	XT907	McD Phantom FGR2 [CT]	RAF No 64 Sqn/228 OCU, Leuchars
	XT908	McD Phantom FGR2 [CW]	RAF No 64 Sqn/228 OCU, Leuchars
	XT909	McD Phantom FGR2	RAF No 19 Sqn, Wildenrath
	XT910	McD Phantom FGR2 [CJ]	RAF No 64 Sqn/228 OCU, Leuchars
	XT911	McD Phantom FGR2 [T]	RAF, stored St Athan
	XT914	McD Phantom FGR2 [CV]	RAF No 64 Sqn/228 OCU, Leuchars
	XV101	BAC VC10 C1	RAF No 10 Sqn, Brize Norton
	XV102	BAC VC10 C1	RAF No 10 Sqn, Brize Norton
	XV103	BAC VC10 C1	RAF No 10 Sqn, Brize Norton
	XV104	BAC VC10 C1	RAF No 10 Sqn, Brize Norton
	XV105	BAC VC10 C1	RAF No 10 Sqn, Brize Norton
	XV106	BAC VC10 C1	RAF No 10 Sqn, Brize Norton
	XV107	BAC VC10 C1	RAF No 10 Sqn, Brize Norton
	XV108	BAC VC10 C1	RAF No 10 Sqn, Brize Norton
	XV109	BAC VC10 C1	RAF No 10 Sqn, Brize Norton

Serial	Type (alternative identity)	Owner, Operator or Location	Notes
XV118	WS Scout AH1	AAC, stored Wroughton	
XV119	WS Scout AH1 [T]	AAC, stored Wroughton	
XV121	WS Scout AH1 [V]	AAC No 658 Sqn, Netheravon	
XV122	WS Scout AH1	AAC, stored Wroughton	
XV123	WS Scout AH1	AAC, stored Wroughton	
XV124	WS Scout AH1	AAC, stored Wroughton	
XV126	WS Scout AH1 [X]	AAC No 666 (TA) Sqn, Netheravon	
XV127	WS Scout AH1	AAC Recruiting Team, Middle Wallop	
XV128	WS Scout AH1	AAC D&TS, Middle Wallop	
XV129	WS Scout AH1 [V]	AAC No 666 (TA) Sqn, Netheravon	
XV130	WS Scout AH1 [R]	AAC No 666 (TA) Sqn, Netheravon	
XV131	WS Scout AH1 [X]	AAC No 660 Sqn, Brunei	
XV134	WS Scout AH1 [P]	AAC No 666 (TA) Sqn, Netheravon	
XV135	WS Scout AH1	AAC, stored Wroughton	
XV136	WS Scout AH1 [X]	AAC No 666 (TA) Sqn, Netheravon	
XV137	WS Scout AH1 [W]	AAC No 658 Sqn, Netheravon	
XV138	WS Scout AH1	AAC, stored Wroughton	
XV139	WS Scout AH1	Army Apprentice College, Arborfield	
XV140	WS Scout AH1 [K]	AAC No 666 (TA) Sqn, Netheravon	
XV141	WS Scout AH1	Army Apprentice College, Arborfield	
XV147	HS Nimrod MR1 (Mod)	MoD(PE) stored RAE Farnborough	
XV148	HS Nimrod MR1 (Mod)	MoD(PE) BAe Woodford	
XV152	HS Buccaneer S2A (8776M) [A]	*Scrapped at RAF Swanton Morley*	
XV154	HS Buccaneer S2A (8854M)	RAF Lossiemouth, ground instruction	
XV155	HS Buccaneer S2B (8716M)	BAe Brough Apprentice School	
XV156	HS Buccaneer S2A (8773M)	RAF St Athan Fire Section	
XV157	HS Buccaneer S2B	RAF, stored Shawbury	
XV161	HS Buccaneer S2B	RAF No 12 Sqn, Lossiemouth	
XV163	HS Buccaneer S2A	RAF No 237 OCU, Lossiemouth	
XV165	HS Buccaneer S2B	RAF No 12 Sqn, Lossiemouth	
XV168	HS Buccaneer S2B	RAF No 237 OCU, Lossiemouth	
XV176	Lockheed Hercules C3P	RAF Lyneham Transport Wing	
XV177	Lockheed Hercules C1P	RAF Lyneham Transport Wing	
XV178	Lockheed Hercules C3P	RAF Lyneham Transport Wing	
XV179	Lockheed Hercules C1P	RAF Lyneham Transport Wing	
XV181	Lockheed Hercules C1	RAF Lyneham Transport Wing	
XV182	Lockheed Hercules C1P	RAF Lyneham Transport Wing	
XV183	Lockheed Hercules C3P	RAF Lyneham Transport Wing	
XV184	Lockheed Hercules C3P	RAF Lyneham Transport Wing	
XV185	Lockheed Hercules C1P	RAF Lyneham Transport Wing	
XV186	Lockheed Hercules C1P	RAF Lyneham Transport Wing	
XV187	Lockheed Hercules C1P	RAF Lyneham Transport Wing	
XV188	Lockheed Hercules C3P	RAF Lyneham Transport Wing	
XV189	Lockheed Hercules C3P	RAF Lyneham Transport Wing	
XV190	Lockheed Hercules C3P	RAF Lyneham Transport Wing	
XV191	Lockheed Hercules C1P	RAF Lyneham Transport Wing	
XV192	Lockheed Hercules C1K	RAF Lyneham Transport Wing	
XV193	Lockheed Hercules C3P	RAF Lyneham Transport Wing	
XV195	Lockheed Hercules C1P	RAF Lyneham Transport Wing	
XV196	Lockheed Hercules C1P	RAF Lyneham Transport Wing	
XV197	Lockheed Hercules C3P	RAF Lyneham Transport Wing	
XV199	Lockheed Hercules C3P	RAF Lyneham Transport Wing	
XV200	Lockheed Hercules C1P	RAF Lyneham Transport Wing	
XV201	Lockheed Hercules C1K	RAF No 1312 Flt, Mount Pleasant, FI	
XV202	Lockheed Hercules C3P	RAF Lyneham Transport Wing	
XV203	Lockheed Hercules C1K	RAF No 1312 Flt, Mount Pleasant, FI	
XV204	Lockheed Hercules C1K	RAF No 1312 Flt, Mount Pleasant, FI	
XV205	Lockheed Hercules C1P	RAF No 1312 Flt, Mount Pleasant, FI	
XV206	Lockheed Hercules C1P	RAF Lyneham Transport Wing	
XV207	Lockheed Hercules C3P	RAF Lyneham Transport Wing	
XV208	Lockheed Hercules W2	MoD(PE) MRF Farnborough	
XV209	Lockheed Hercules C3	RAF Lyneham Transport Wing	
XV210	Lockheed Hercules C1P	MoD(PE) A&AEE Boscombe Down	
XV211	Lockheed Hercules C1P	RAF Lyneham Transport Wing	
XV212	Lockheed Hercules C3P	RAF Lyneham Transport Wing	
XV213	Lockheed Hercules C1K	RAF No 1312 Flt, Mount Pleasant, FI	
XV214	Lockheed Hercules C3P	RAF Lyneham Transport Wing	
XV215	Lockheed Hercules C1P	RAF Lyneham Transport Wing	
XV217	Lockheed Hercules C3P	RAF Lyneham Transport Wing	
XV218	Lockheed Hercules C1P	RAF Lyneham Transport Wing	
XV219	Lockheed Hercules C3P	RAF Lyneham Transport Wing	
XV220	Lockheed Hercules C3P	RAF Lyneham Transport Wing	
XV221	Lockheed Hercules C3	RAF Lyneham Transport Wing	
XV222	Lockheed Hercules C3P	RAF Lyneham Transport Wing	

Notes	Serial	Type (alternative identity)	Owner, Operator or Location
	XV223	Lockheed Hercules C3P	RAF Lyneham Transport Wing
	XV226	HS Nimrod MR2	RAF No 42 Sqn, St Mawgan
	XV227	HS Nimrod MR2P	RAF Kinloss MR Wing
	XV228	HS Nimrod MR2P	RAF No 42 Sqn, St Mawgan
	XV229	HS Nimrod MR2P	RAF No 42 Sqn, St Mawgan
	XV230	HS Nimrod MR2P	RAF Kinloss MR Wing
	XV231	HS Nimrod MR2	RAF No 42 Sqn, St Mawgan
	XV232	HS Nimrod MR2P	RAF Kinloss MR Wing
	XV233	HS Nimrod MR2	RAF No 42 Sqn, St Mawgan
	XV234	HS Nimrod MR2	RAF Kinloss MR Wing
	XV235	HS Nimrod MR2	RAF Kinloss MR Wing
	XV236	HS Nimrod MR2P	RAF No 42 Sqn, St Mawgan
	XV237	HS Nimrod MR2P	RAF No 42 Sqn, St Mawgan
	XV238	HS Nimrod MR2P	RAF Kinloss MR Wing
	XV239	HS Nimrod MR2P	RAF Kinloss MR Wing
	XV240	HS Nimrod MR2	RAF No 42 Sqn, St Mawgan
	XV241	HS Nimrod MR2	RAF Kinloss MR Wing
	XV242	HS Nimrod MR2	RAF Kinloss MR Wing
	XV243	HS Nimrod MR2P	RAF Kinloss MR Wing
	XV244	HS Nimrod MR2	RAF Kinloss MR Wing
	XV245	HS Nimrod MR2P	RAF No 42 Sqn, St Mawgan
	XV246	HS Nimrod MR2	RAF No 42 Sqn, St Mawgan
	XV247	HS Nimrod MR2P	RAF Kinloss MR Wing
	XV248	HS Nimrod MR2P	RAF Kinloss MR Wing
	XV249	HS Nimrod MR2	RAF No 42 Sqn, St Mawgan
	XV250	HS Nimrod MR2P	RAF No 42 Sqn, St Mawgan
	XV251	HS Nimrod MR2	RAF No 42 Sqn, St Mawgan
	XV252	HS Nimrod MR2	RAF Kinloss MR Wing
	XV253	HS Nimrod MR2P	RAF No 42 Sqn, St Mawgan
	XV254	HS Nimrod MR2P	RAF Kinloss MR Wing
	XV255	HS Nimrod MR2P	RAF Kinloss MR Wing
	XV257	HS Nimrod MR2	MoD(PE), stored BAe Woodford
	XV258	HS Nimrod MR2	RAF No 42 Sqn, St Mawgan
	XV259	BAe Nimrod AEW3	RAF, stored Waddington
	XV260	HS Nimrod MR2P	RAF Kinloss MR Wing
	XV261	BAe Nimrod AEW3	RAF, stored Abingdon
	XV262	BAe Nimrod AEW3	RAF, stored Abingdon
	XV263	BAe Nimrod AEW3P (8967M)	RAF Finningley, Air Engineer Sqn
	XV268	DHC Beaver AL1	AAC, stored Shawbury
	XV269	DHC Beaver AL1 (8011M)	AAC AETW, Middle Wallop NIEF
	XV270	DHC Beaver AL1	AAC, Beaver Training Flight, Middle Wallop
	XV271	DHC Beaver AL1	AAC, Aldergrove
	XV272	DHC Beaver AL1 (fuselage only)	AAC Middle Wallop, BDRT
	XV277	HS Harrier GR3	MoD(PE) Rolls-Royce, Filton
	XV279	HS Harrier GR1 [44] (8566M)	RAF Wittering BDRT
	XV281	HS Harrier GR3 (89...M)	RAF Wittering Fire Section
	XV290	Lockheed Hercules C3P	RAF Lyneham Transport Wing
	XV291	Lockheed Hercules C1P	RAF Lyneham Transport Wing
	XV292	Lockheed Hercules C1P	RAF Lyneham Transport Wing
	XV293	Lockheed Hercules C1P	RAF Lyneham Transport Wing
	XV294	Lockheed Hercules C3P	RAF Lyneham Transport Wing
	XV295	Lockheed Hercules C1P	RAF Lyneham Transport Wing
	XV296	Lockheed Hercules C1K	RAF Lyneham Transport Wing
	XV297	Lockheed Hercules C1P	RAF Lyneham Transport Wing
	XV298	Lockheed Hercules C1P	RAF Lyneham Transport Wing
	XV299	Lockheed Hercules C3P	RAF Lyneham Transport Wing
	XV300	Lockheed Hercules C1P	RAF Lyneham Transport Wing
	XV301	Lockheed Hercules C3P	RAF Lyneham Transport Wing
	XV302	Lockheed Hercules C3P	RAF Lyneham Transport Wing
	XV303	Lockheed Hercules C3P	RAF Lyneham Transport Wing
	XV304	Lockheed Hercules C3P	RAF Lyneham Transport Wing
	XV305	Lockheed Hercules C3P	RAF Lyneham Transport Wing
	XV306	Lockheed Hercules C1P	RAF Lyneham Transport Wing
	XV307	Lockheed Hercules C3	RAF Lyneham Transport Wing
	XV328	EE Lightning T5 [BZ]	Privately owned, Cranfield
	XV332	HS Buccaneer S2B	RAF No 237 OCU, Lossiemouth
	XV333	HS Buccaneer S2B	BAe Woodford
	XV334	HS Buccaneer S2B	RAF, stored Shawbury
	XV336	HS Buccaneer S2A	RAF, stored Shawbury
	XV337	HS Buccaneer S2C (8852M)	RAF Abingdon, BDRF
	XV338	HS Buccaneer S2A (fuselage etc) (8774M)	RAF Honington ground instruction
	XV338	HS Buccaneer S2A (nose only) (8774M)	RAF Exhibition Flight, Abingdon

Serial	Type (alternative identity)	Owner, Operator or Location	Notes
XV341	HS Buccaneer S2A	RAF Lossiemouth Fire Section	
XV342	HS Buccaneer S2B	RAF No 208 Sqn, Lossiemouth	
XV344	HS Buccaneer S2C	MoD(PE) RAE Farnborough	
XV349	HS Buccaneer S2B	RAF, stored Shawbury	
XV350	HS Buccaneer S2B	MoD(PE) BAe Scampton	
XV352	HS Buccaneer S2B [FC]	RAF No 237 OCU, Lossiemouth	
XV353	HS Buccaneer S2B	RAF No 208 Sqn, Lossiemouth	
XV355	HS Buccaneer S2A	RAF No 208 Sqn, Lossiemouth	
XV356	HS Buccaneer S2A [B]	RAF, stored Shawbury	
XV359	HS Buccaneer S2B [359]	RAF No 208 Sqn, Lossiemouth	
XV361	HS Buccaneer S2B	RAF No 208 Sqn, Lossiemouth	
XV370	Sikorsky SH-3D (G-ATYU)	MoD(PE) ETPS Boscombe Down	
XV371	WS61 Sea King HAS1	MoD(PE) RAE Farnborough	
XV372	WS61 Sea King HAS1	Westlands, Yeovil for ground instruction	
XV373	WS61 Sea King HAS1	*To Foulness Ranges*	
XV393	McD Phantom FGR2	RAF No 64 Sqn/228 OCU, Leuchars	
XV394	McD Phantom FGR2 [T]	RAF No 92 Sqn, Wildenrath	
XV396	McD Phantom FGR2 [D]	RAF, stored St Athan	
XV398	McD Phantom FGR2 [Cl]	RAF No 64 Sqn/228 OCU, Leuchars	
XV399	McD Phantom FGR2 [L]	RAF No 56 Sqn, Wattisham	
XV400	McD Phantom FGR2 [D]	RAF No 56 Sqn, Wattisham	
XV401	McD Phantom FGR2	RAF No 56 Sqn, Wattisham	
XV402	McD Phantom FGR2	RAF, BAe Brough	
XV404	McD Phantom FGR2 [I]	RAF No 19 Sqn, Wildenrath	
XV406	McD Phantom FGR2 [AV]	RAF No 43 Sqn, Leuchars	
XV407	McD Phantom FGR2 [CL]	RAF No 64 Sqn/228 OCU, Leuchars	
XV408	McD Phantom FGR2	RAF No 92 Sqn, Wildenrath	
XV409	McD Phantom FGR2	RAF, stored St Athan	
XV410	McD Phantom FGR2	RAF No 56 Sqn, Wattisham	
XV411	McD Phantom FGR2 [G]	RAF No 19 Sqn, Wildenrath	
XV412	McD Phantom FGR2 [P]	RAF, No 92 Sqn, Wildenrath	
XV414	McD Phantom FGR2 [R]	RAF Wattisham, BDRT	
XV415	McD Phantom FGR2 [CB]	RAF No 64 Sqn/228 OCU, Leuchars	
XV419	McD Phantom FGR2 [A]	RAF No 1435 Flt, Mount Pleasant, FI	
XV420	McD Phantom FGR2 [T]	RAF No 56 Sqn, Wattisham	
XV421	McD Phantom FGR2 [AN]	RAF No 9 Sqn, Wildenrath	
XV422	McD Phantom FGR2 [J]	RAF No 19 Sqn, Wildenrath	
XV423	McD Phantom FGR2	RAF BAe Brough	
XV424	McD Phantom FGR2 [Q]	RAF No 56 Sqn, Wattisham	
XV425	McD Phantom FGR2 [CD]	RAF No 64 Sqn/288 OCU, Leuchars	
XV426	McD Phantom FGR2 [P]	RAF No 56 Sqn, Wattisham	
XV428	McD Phantom FGR2 [CC]	*Crashed at Abingdon 23rd September 1988*	
XV429	McD Phantom FGR2 [K]	BAe Scampton	
XV430	McD Phantom FGR2 [A]	RAF No 19 Sqn, Wildenrath	
XV432	McD Phantom FGR2 [H]	RAF No 56 Sqn, Wattisham	
XV433	McD Phantom FGR2 [B]	RAF No 1435 Flt, Mount Pleasant, FI	
XV435	McD Phantom FGR2 [R]	RAF No 92 Sqn, Wildenrath	
XV436	McD Phantom FGR2 [E] (8850M)	RAF Abingdon, BDRF	
XV437	McD Phantom FGR2 [Y]	*Crashed West Germany 18 October 1988*	
XV438	McD Phantom FGR2 [C]	RAF No 1435 Flt, Mount Pleasant, FI	
XV439	McD Phantom FGR2 [D]	RAF No 19 Sqn, Wildenrath	
XV442	McD Phantom FGR2	RAF No 19 Sqn, Wildenrath	
XV460	McD Phantom FGR2 [N]	RAF No 92 Sqn, Wildenrath	
XV461	McD Phantom FGR2 [G]	RAF No 56 Sqn, Wattisham	
XV462	McD Phantom FGR2	RAF No 92 Sqn, Wildenrath	
XV464	McD Phantom FGR2 [N]	RAF No 56 Sqn, Wattisham	
XV465	McD Phantom FGR2 [F]	RAF No 19 Sqn, Wildenrath	
XV466	McD Phantom FGR2 [R]	RAF No 56 Sqn, Wattisham	
XV467	McD Phantom FGR2 [Q]	RAF No 92 Sqn, Wildenrath	
XV468	McD Phantom FGR2 [E]	RAF No 19 Sqn, Wildenrath	
XV469	McD Phantom FGR2 [AO]	RAF No 92 Sqn, Wildenrath	
XV470	McD Phantom FGR2 [AW]	RAF No 43 Sqn, Leuchars	
XV472	McD Phantom FGR2 [A]	RAF No 56 Sqn, Wattisham	
XV473	McD Phantom FGR2 [K]	RAF No 56 Sqn, Wattisham	
XV474	McD Phantom FGR2 [M]	RAF No 56 Sqn, Wattisham	
XV475	McD Phantom FGR2 [H]	RAF No 19 Sqn, Wildenrath	
XV476	McD Phantom FGR2 [S]	RAF No 56 Sqn, Wattisham	
XV478	McD Phantom FGR2 [C]	RAF No 19 Sqn, Wildenrath	
XV480	McD Phantom FGR2 [I]	RAF No 56 Sqn, Wattisham	
XV481	McD Phantom FGR2 [X]	RAF No 92 Sqn, Wildenrath	
XV482	McD Phantom FGR2	RAF No 92 Sqn, Wildenrath	
XV485	McD Phantom FGR2 [M]	RAF No 19 Sqn, Wildenrath	

Notes	Serial	Type (alternative identity)	Owner, Operator or Location
	XV486	McD Phantom FGR2 [N]	RAF, stored St Athan
	XV487	McD Phantom FGR2 [AA]	RAF No 19 Sqn, Wildenrath
	XV488	McD Phantom FGR2 [O]	RAF No 92 Sqn, Wildenrath
	XV489	McD Phantom FGR2 [S]	RAF No 92 Sqn, Wildenrath
	XV490	McD Phantom FGR2 [CG]	RAF No 64 Sqn/228 OCU, Leuchars
	XV492	McD Phantom FGR2 [W]	RAF No 92 Sqn, Wildenrath
	XV494	McD Phantom FGR2 [L]	RAF No 19 Sqn, Wildenrath
	XV495	McD Phantom FGR2	RAF, stored St Athan
	XV496	McD Phantom FGR2 [V]	RAF No 92 Sqn, Wildenrath
	XV497	McD Phantom FGR2 [D]	RAF No 1435 Flt, Mount Pleasant, Fl
	XV498	McD Phantom FGR2 [U]	RAF No 92 Sqn, Wildenrath
	XV499	McD Phantom FGR2 [CF]	RAF No 64 Sqn/228 OCU, Leuchars
	XV500	McD Phantom FGR2 [J]	RAF No 56 Sqn, Wattisham
	XV501	McD Phantom FGR2 [B]	*Crashed nr Le Mans 2nd August 1988*
	XV567	McD Phantom FG1 [AI]	RAF No 43 Sqn, Leuchars
	XV568	McD Phantom FG1 [AT]	RAF No 43 Sqn, Leuchars
	XV569	McD Phantom FG1 [BQ]	RAF No 111 Sqn, Leuchars
	XV570	McD Phantom FG1 [BN]	RAF No 111 Sqn, Leuchars
	XV571	McD Phantom FG1 [A]	RAF No 43 Sqn, Leuchars
	XV572	McD Phantom FG1 [AN]	RAF No 43 Sqn, Leuchars
	XV573	McD Phantom FG1 [BD]	RAF No 111 Sqn, Leuchars
	XV574	McD Phantom FG1 [Z]	RAF No 111 Sqn, Leuchars
	XV575	McD Phantom FG1 [BO]	RAF No 111 Sqn, Leuchars
	XV576	McD Phantom FG1 [AD]	RAF No 43 Sqn, Leuchars
	XV577	McD Phantom FG1 [AM]	RAF No 43 Sqn, Leuchars
	XV579	McD Phantom FG1 [AR]	RAF No 43 Sqn, Leuchars
	XV581	McD Phantom FG1 [AE]	RAF No 43 Sqn, Leuchars
	XV582	McD Phantom FG1 [AF]	RAF No 43 Sqn, Leuchars
	XV583	McD Phantom FG1 [BB]	RAF No 111 Sqn, Leuchars
	XV584	McD Phantom FG1 [BF]	RAF No 111 Sqn, Leuchars
	XV585	McD Phantom FG1 [AP]	RAF No 43 Sqn, Leuchars
	XV586	McD Phantom FG1 [AJ]	RAF No 43 Sqn, Leuchars
	XV587	McD Phantom FG1 [AG]	RAF No 43 Sqn, Leuchars
	XV588	McD Phantom FG1 [007] (nose only)	RNAS Culdrose Fire Section
	XV588	McD Phantom FG1 (forward fuselage only)	RAF Leuchars, BDRT
	XV590	McD Phantom FG1 [AX]	RAF No 43 Sqn, Leuchars
	XV591	McD Phantom FG1 [MP]	RAF St Athan Fire Section
	XV592	McD Phantom FG1 [BL]	RAF No 111 Sqn, Leuchars
	XV615	BHC SR.N6 Winchester 2	RN Hong Kong
	XV623	WS Wasp HAS1 [601]	RN Portland, BDRT
	XV624	WS Wasp HAS1 [YM]	RN Portland Fire Section
	XV625	WS Wasp HAS1 [471]	RNEC Manadon, for instruction
	XV626	WS Wasp HAS1 [325/HR]	RN, stored Wroughton
	XV629	WS Wasp HAS1	AAC Middle Wallop, BDRT
	XV631	WS Wasp HAS1	MoD(PE) RAE Farnborough
	XV632	WS Wasp HAS1 [610]	*To Malaysian Navy as M499-01*
	XV634	WS Wasp HAS1 [462]	RN No 829 Sqn, Portland
	XV636	WS Wasp HAS1 [600]	RN, stored Wroughton
	XV638	WS Wasp HAS1 (8826M) [A/430]	RAF AMS, Brize Norton
	XV639	WS Wasp HAS1 [612]	RN, stored Wroughton
	XV642	WS61 Sea King AEW2A	MoD(PE) Westlands, Yeovil
	XV643	WS61 Sea King HAS5 [015]	RN No 820 Sqn, Culdrose
	XV644	WS61 Sea King HAS1 (A2664) [644]	RN AES, Lee-on-Solent
	XV647	WS61 Sea King HAR5 [820/CU]	RN No 771 Sqn, Culdrose
	XV648	WS61 Sea King HAS5 [582]	RN No 706 Sqn, Culdrose
	XV649	WS61 Sea King AEW2A [183/R]	RN No 849 Sqn, Culdrose
	XV650	WS61 Sea King AEW2A [180]	RN No 849 Sqn, Culdrose
	XV651	WS61 Sea King HAS5 [131]	RN Fleetlands
	XV652	WS61 Sea King HAS5 [132]	*Ditched in Mediterranean, 3 Feb 1988*
	XV653	WS61 Sea King HAS5 [509]	RN No 810 Sqn, Culdrose
	XV654	WS61 Sea King HAS5 [018/R]	RN No 820 Sqn, Culdrose
	XV655	WS61 Sea King HAS5 [272]	RN No 814 Sqn, Culdrose
	XV656	WS61 Sea King AEW2A [186/L]	RN No 849 Sqn, Culdrose
	XV657	WS61 Sea King HAS6 [255]	RN No 824 Sqn, Prestwick
	XV659	WS61 Sea King HAS5 [266]	RN No 814 Sqn, Culdrose
	XV660	WS61 Sea King HAS5 [507]	RN No 810 Sqn, Culdrose
	XV661	WS61 Sea King HAS5 [135]	RN No 826 Sqn, Culdrose
	XV663	WS61 Sea King HAS5 [703]	RN No 819 Sqn, Prestwick
	XV664	WS61 Sea King AEW2A [181]	RN No 849 Sqn, Culdrose
	XV665	WS61 Sea King HAS5 [508]	RN No 810 Sqn, Culdrose

Serial	Type (alternative identity)	Owner, Operator or Location	Notes
XV666	WS61 Sea King HAR5 [823/CU]	RN No 771 Sqn, Culdrose	
XV669	WS61 Sea King HAS1 [10] (A2659)	RNAS Culdrose, Engineering Training School	
XV670	WS61 Sea King HAS5 [592]	RN Fleetlands	
XV671	WS61 Sea King AEW2A	RN NASU, Culdrose	
XV672	WS61 Sea King AEW2A [182/R]	RN No 849 Sqn, Culdrose	
XV673	WS61 Sea King HAS5 [588]	RN Fleetlands	
XV674	WS61 Sea King HAS5 [274]	RN No 814 Sqn, Culdrose	
XV675	WS61 Sea King HAS5	RN Fleetlands	
XV676	WS61 Sea King HAS6 [252-PW]	RN No 824 Sqn, Prestwick	
XV677	WS61 Sea King HAS5 [705]	RN No 819 Sqn, Prestwick	
XV696	WS61 Sea King HAS5 [503]	RN No 810 Sqn, Culdrose	
XV697	WS61 Sea King AEW2A [184/R]	RN No 849 Sqn, Culdrose	
XV699	WS61 Sea King HAS5 [134]	RN No 826 Sqn, Culdrose	
XV700	WS61 Sea King HAS5 [011/R]	RN No 820 Sqn, Culdrose	
XV701	WS61 Sea King HAS5 [706]	RN No 819 Sqn, Prestwick	
XV703	WS61 Sea King HAS5 [586]	Westlands, Yeovil, under repair	
XV704	WS61 Sea King AEW2A	RN No 849 Sqn, Culdrose	
XV705	WS61 Sea King HAR5 [821-CU]	RN No 771 Sqn, Culdrose	
XV706	WS61 Sea King HAS5 [597]	RN No 706 Sqn, Culdrose	
XV707	WS61 Sea King AEW2A [185/L]	RN No 849 Sqn, Culdrose	
XV708	WS61 Sea King HAS5 [596]	RN No 706 Sqn, Culdrose	
XV709	WS61 Sea King HAS5 [585]	RN No 706 Sqn, Culdrose	
XV710	WS61 Sea King HAS5 [267/L]	RN No 814 Sqn, Culdrose	
XV711	WS61 Sea King HAS5 [273/L]	RN No 814 Sqn, Culdrose	
XV712	WS61 Sea King HAS5 [270]	RN No 814 Sqn, Culdrose	
XV713	WS61 Sea King HAS5	RN No 706 Sqn, Culdrose	
XV714	WS61 Sea King AEW2A [187/L]	RN No 849 Sqn, Culdrose	
XV719	WS58 Wessex HC2 [B]	RAF No 72 Sqn, Aldergrove	
XV720	WS58 Wessex HC2	RAF No 22 Sqn SAR*	
XV721	WS58 Wessex HC2 [H]	RAF No 72 Sqn, Aldergrove	
XV722	WS58 Wessex HC2 [WH]	RAF No 2 FTS, Shawbury	
XV723	WS58 Wessex HC2 [Q]	RAF No 72 Sqn, Aldergrove	
XV724	WS58 Wessex HC2	RAF No 22 Sqn SAR*	
XV725	WS58 Wessex HC2 [C]	RAF No 72 Sqn, Aldergrove	
XV726	WS58 Wessex HC2 [J]	RAF No 72 Sqn, Aldergrove	
XV728	WS58 Wessex HC2 [A]	RAF No 72 Sqn, Aldergrove	
XV729	WS58 Wessex HC2	RAF No 22 Sqn SAR*	
XV730	WS58 Wessex HC2	RAF No 22 Sqn SAR*	
XV731	WS58 Wessex HC2 [Y]	RAF No 72 Sqn, Aldergrove	
XV732	WS58 Wessex HCC4	RAF Queen's Flight, Benson	
XV733	WS58 Wessex HCC4	RAF Queen's Flight, Benson	
XV738	HS Harrier GR3 [B]	RAF No 4 Sqn, Gutersloh	
XV740	HS Harrier GR3	RAF No 1 Sqn, Wittering	
XV741	HS Harrier GR3 [I]	RAF No 233 OCU, Wittering (wfu)	
XV744	HS Harrier GR3	RAF HSF, Wittering	
XV747	HS Harrier GR3	RAF Coltishall, BDRT	
XV748	HS Harrier GR3 [07]	RAF No 1 Sqn, Wittering	
XV751	HS Harrier GR3 [U]	RAF No 3 Sqn, Gutersloh	
XV752	HS Harrier GR3 [G]	RAF No 3 Sqn, Gutersloh	
XV753	HS Harrier GR3	RAF No 1 Sqn, Wittering	
XV755	HS Harrier GR3 [M]	RAF No 233 OCU, Wittering	
XV758	HS Harrier GR3 [V]	RAF No 3 Sqn, Gutersloh	
XV759	HS Harrier GR3 [O]	RAF No 233 OCU, Wittering	
XV760	HS Harrier GR3 [K]	RAF No 3 Sqn, Gutersloh	
XV762	HS Harrier GR3 [09]	RAF ASF, Wittering	
XV778	HS Harrier GR3 [08]	RAF No 1 Sqn, Wittering	
XV779	HS Harrier GR3 (8931M) [01/A]	RAF Wittering on display	
XV782	HS Harrier GR3	RAF CSDE, Swanton Morley	
XV783	HS Harrier GR3 [N]	RAF No 233 OCU, Wittering	
XV784	HS Harrier GR3 (8909M) [C]	RAF Abingdon, BDRT	
XV786	HS Harrier GR3 [S]	RAF No 3 Sqn, Gutersloh	
XV789	HS Harrier GR3 [07]	RAF No 1 Sqn, Wittering	
XV793	HS Harrier GR3	RAF CSDE, Swanton Morley	
XV804	HS Harrier GR3 [D]	RAF No 3 Sqn, Gutersloh	
XV806	HS Harrier GR3 [N]	RAF No 3 Sqn, Gutersloh	
XV808	HS Harrier GR3 [L]	RAF No 233 OCU, Wittering	
XV809	HS Harrier GR3 [F]	Written off 20 May 1988	
XV810	HS Harrier GR3 [K]	RAF No 233 OCU, Wittering	
XV814	DH Comet 4 (G-APDF)	MoD(PE) RAE Farnborough	
XV859	BHC SR.N6 Winchester 6	RN NHTU, Lee-on-Solent	
XV863	HS Buccaneer S2B	BAe Woodford	
XV864	HS Buccaneer S2B	RAF No 12 Sqn, Lossiemouth	
XV865	HS Buccaneer S2B	RAF No 208 Sqn, Lossiemouth	

Notes	Serial	Type (alternative identity)	Owner, Operator or Location
	XV866	HS Buccaneer S2B	RAF, stored Shawbury
	XV867	HS Buccaneer S2B	RAF No 12 Sqn, Lossiemouth
	XV868	HS Buccaneer S2B	RAF No 12 Sqn, Lossiemouth
	XV869	HS Buccaneer S2B	RAF No 12 Sqn, Lossiemouth
	XW175	HS Harrier T4A	MoD(PE) RAE Bedford
	XW179	WS Sioux AH1 (composite)	Privately owned, Stoke-on-Trent
	XW198	WS Puma HC1 [DL]	RAF No 230 Sqn, Gutersloh
	XW199	WS Puma HC1 [DU]	RAF No 230 Sqn, Gutersloh
	XW200	WS Puma HC1 [FA]	RAF No 240 OCU, Odiham
	XW201	WS Puma HC1 [FB]	RAF No 240 OCU, Odiham
	XW202	WS Puma HC1 [CE]	RAF No 33 Sqn, Odiham
	XW204	WS Puma HC1 [CA]	RAF No 33 Sqn, Odiham
	XW206	WS Puma HC1 [CC]	RAF No 33 Sqn, Odiham
	XW207	WS Puma HC1 [CD]	RAF No 33 Sqn, Odiham
	XW208	WS Puma HC1 [DP]	RAF No 230 Sqn, Gutersloh
	XW209	WS Puma HC1 [CF]	RAF No 33 Sqn, Odiham
	XW210	WS Puma HC1 [CG]	RAF No 33 Sqn, Odiham
	XW211	WS Puma HC1 [CH]	RAF No 33 Sqn, Odiham
	XW212	WS Puma HC1	RAF No 240 OCU, Odiham
	XW213	WS Puma HC1 [CJ]	RAF No 33 Sqn, Odiham
	XW214	WS Puma HC1 [CK]	RAF No 33 Sqn, Odiham
	XW215	WS Puma HC1 [DM]	RAF No 230 Sqn, Gutersloh
	XW216	WS Puma HC1 [CL]	RAF No 33 Sqn, Odiham
	XW217	WS Puma HC1 [DA]	RAF No 230 Sqn, Gutersloh
	XW218	WS Puma HC1 [DT]	RAF No 33 Sqn, Odiham
	XW219	WS Puma HC1 [DC]	RAF No 230 Sqn, Gutersloh
	XW220	WS Puma HC1 [DD]	RAF No 230 Sqn, Gutersloh
	XW221	WS Puma HC1 [DE]	RAF No 230 Sqn, Gutersloh
	XW222	WS Puma HC1 [DF]	RAF No 230 Sqn, Gutersloh
	XW223	WS Puma HC1 [CB]	RAF No 33 Sqn, Odiham
	XW224	WS Puma HC1 [DH]	RAF No 230 Sqn, Gutersloh
	XW225	WS Puma HC1 [FE]	RAF No 240 OCU, Odiham
	XW226	WS Puma HC1 [DK]	RAF No 230 Sqn, Gutersloh
	XW227	WS Puma HC1 [DN]	RAF No 230 Sqn, Gutersloh
	XW229	WS Puma HC1 [DB]	RAF No 230 Sqn, Gutersloh
	XW231	WS Puma HC1 [FD]	RAF No 240 OCU, Odiham
	XW232	WS Puma HC1 [DJ]	RAF No 230 Sqn, Gutersloh
	XW233	WS Puma HC1 [CN]	RAF No 33 Sqn, Odiham
	XW234	WS Puma HC1 [CO]	RAF No 33 Sqn, Odiham
	XW235	WS Puma HC1 [CP]	RAF No 33 Sqn, Odiham
	XW236	WS Puma HC1 [CQ]	RAF No 1563 Flt, Belize
	XW237	WS Puma HC1 [CR]	RAF No 33 Sqn, Odiham
	XW241	Sud SA330E Puma (F-ZJUX)	MoD(PE) RAE Bedford (wfu)
	XW249	Cushioncraft CC7	Cornwall Aero Park, Helston
	XW255	BHC BH-7 Wellington	RN NHTU, Lee-on-Solent
	XW264	HS Harrier T2 (forward fuselage)	CARG store, RAF Innsworth
	XW265	HS Harrier T4A [V]	RAF No 233 OCU, Wittering
	XW266	HS Harrier T4A [5]	RAF St Athan
	XW267	HS Harrier T4 [SA]	MoD(PE) SAOEU, Boscombe Down
	XW268	HS Harrier T4A [U]	RAF No 233 OCU, Wittering
	XW269	HS Harrier T4 [Y]	RAF No 4 Sqn, Gutersloh
	XW270	HS Harrier T4 [T]	RAF No 4 Sqn, Gutersloh
	XW271	HS Harrier T4 [Z]	RAF No 3 Sqn, Gutersloh
	XW272	HS Harrier T4 (8783M) (nose only)	Cranfield Institute of Technology
	XW276	Aerospatiale SA341 (F-ZWRI)	Science Museum, Wroughton
	XW280	WS Scout AH1	AAC No 660 Sqn, Brunei
	XW281	WS Scout AH1 [U]	AAC No 666 (TA) Sqn, Netheravon
	XW282	WS Scout AH1 [W]	AAC No 666 (TA) Sqn, Netheravon
	XW283	WS Scout AH1 [X]	AAC No 658 Sqn, Netheravon
	XW284	WS Scout AH1 [A] (fuselage only)	AAC, stored Wroughton
	XW287	BAC Jet Provost T5 [P]	RAF No 6 FTS, Finningley
	XW289	BAC Jet Provost T5A [61]	RAF No 1 FTS, Linton-on-Ouse
	XW290	BAC Jet Provost T5A [41]	RAF College, Cranwell
	XW291	BAC Jet Provost T5 [N]	RAF No 6 FTS, Finningley
	XW292	BAC Jet Provost T5A [32]	RAF College, Cranwell
	XW293	BAC Jet Provost T5 [Z]	RAF No 6 FTS, Finningley
	XW294	BAC Jet Provost T5A [45]	RAF College, Cranwell
	XW295	BAC Jet Provost T5A [29]	RAF College, Cranwell
	XW296	BAC Jet Provost T5 [Q]	RAF No 6 FTS, Finningley
	XW298	BAC Jet Provost T5 [O]	RAF No 6 FTS, Finningley

Serial	Type (alternative identity)	Owner, Operator or Location	Notes
XW299	BAC Jet Provost T5A [60]	RAF No 1 FTS, Linton-on-Ouse	
XW301	BAC Jet Provost T5A [63]	RAF No 1 FTS, Linton-on-Ouse	
XW302	BAC Jet Provost T5 [T]	RAF No 6 FTS, Finningley	
XW303	BAC Jet Provost T5A [127]	RAF No 7 FTS, Church Fenton	
XW304	BAC Jet Provost T5A [X]	RAF No 6 FTS, Finningley	
XW305	BAC Jet Provost T5A [42]	RAF College, Cranwell	
XW306	BAC Jet Provost T5 [Y]	RAF No 6 FTS, Finningley	
XW307	BAC Jet Provost T5 [S]	RAF No 6 FTS, Finningley	
XW309	BAC Jet Provost T5 [V]	RAF No 6 FTS, Finningley	
XW310	BAC Jet Provost T5A [37]	RAF College, Cranwell	
XW311	BAC Jet Provost T5 [W]	RAF No 6 FTS, Finningley	
XW312	BAC Jet Provost T5A [64]	RAF No 1 FTS, Linton-on-Ouse	
XW313	BAC Jet Provost T5A [30]	RAF College, Cranwell	
XW315	BAC Jet Provost T5A [63] (fuselage only)	RAF Abingdon, BDRF	
XW316	BAC Jet Provost T5A [135]	RAF No 7 FTS, Church Fenton	
XW317	BAC Jet Provost T5A [25]	RAF College, Cranwell	
XW318	BAC Jet Provost T5A [12]	RAF College, Cranwell	
XW319	BAC Jet Provost T5A [57]	RAF No 3 FTS, Scampton	
XW320	BAC Jet Provost T5A [71]	RAF No 1 FTS, Linton-on-Ouse	
XW321	BAC Jet Provost T5A [132]	RAF No 7 FTS, Church Fenton	
XW322	BAC Jet Provost T5A [43]	RAF College, Cranwell	
XW323	BAC Jet Provost T5A [44]	RAF College, Cranwell	
XW324	BAC Jet Provost T5 [U]	RAF No 6 FTS, Finningley	
XW325	BAC Jet Provost T5A [33]	RAF College, Cranwell	
XW326	BAC Jet Provost T5A [62]	RAF No 1 FTS, Linton-on-Ouse	
XW327	BAC Jet Provost T5A [134]	RAF No 7 FTS, Church Fenton	
XW328	BAC Jet Provost T5A [128]	RAF No 7 FTS, Church Fenton	
XW329	BAC Jet Provost T5A [48] (8741M) (cockpit only)	RAF Church Fenton Fire Section	
XW330	BAC Jet Provost T5A [10]	RAF College, Cranwell	
XW332	BAC Jet Provost T5A [34]	RAF College, Cranwell	
XW333	BAC Jet Provost T5A [61]	RAF No 3 FTS, Scampton	
XW334	BAC Jet Provost T5A [131]	RAF No 7 FTS, Church Fenton	
XW335	BAC Jet Provost T5A [27]	RAF College, Cranwell	
XW336	BAC Jet Provost T5A [6]	RAF College, Cranwell	
XW351	BAC Jet Provost T5A [31]	RAF College, Cranwell	
XW352	BAC Jet Provost T5 [R]	RAF No 6 FTS, Finningley	
XW353	BAC Jet Provost T5A [51]	RAF No 3 FTS, Scampton	
XW354	BAC Jet Provost T5A [7]	RAF College, Cranwell	
XW355	BAC Jet Provost T5A [20]	RAF College, Cranwell	
XW357	BAC Jet Provost T5A [5]	RAF College, Cranwell	
XW358	BAC Jet Provost T5A [130]	RAF No 7FTS, Church Fenton	
XW359	BAC Jet Provost T5A [65]	RAF No 1 FTS, Linton-on-Ouse	
XW360	BAC Jet Provost T5A [129]	RAF No 7 FTS, Church Fenton	
XW361	BAC Jet Provost T5A [21]	RAF College, Cranwell	
XW362	BAC Jet Provost T5A [17]	RAF College, Cranwell	
XW363	BAC Jet Provost T5A [36]	RAF College, Cranwell	
XW364	BAC Jet Provost T5A [35]	RAF College, Cranwell	
XW365	BAC Jet Provost T5A [73]	RAF No 1 FTS, Linton-on-Ouse	
XW366	BAC Jet Provost T5A [75]	RAF No 1 FTS, Linton-on-Ouse	
XW367	BAC Jet Provost T5A [26]	RAF College, Cranwell	
XW368	BAC Jet Provost T5A [L/55]	RAF No 6 FTS, Finningley	
XW369	BAC Jet Provost T5A [9]	RAF College, Cranwell	
XW370	BAC Jet Provost T5A [72]	RAF No 1 FTS, Linton-on-Ouse	
XW372	BAC Jet Provost T5A [M/121]	RAF No 6 FTS, Finningley	
XW373	BAC Jet Provost T5A [11]	RAF College, Cranwell	
XW374	BAC Jet Provost T5A [38]	RAF College, Cranwell	
XW375	BAC Jet Provost T5A [52]	RAF No 3 FTS, Scampton	
XW404	BAC Jet Provost T5A [77]	RAF No 1 FTS, Linton-on-Ouse	
XW405	BAC Jet Provost T5A [J]	RAF No 6 FTS, Finningley	
XW406	BAC Jet Provost T5A [23]	RAF College, Cranwell	
XW408	BAC Jet Provost T5A [24]	RAF College, Cranwell	
XW409	BAC Jet Provost T5A [123]	RAF No 7 FTS, Church Fenton	
XW410	BAC Jet Provost T5A [80]	RAF No 1 FTS, Linton-on-Ouse	
XW412	BAC Jet Provost T5A [15]	RAF College, Cranwell	
XW413	BAC Jet Provost T5A [69]	RAF No 1 FTS, Linton-on-Ouse	
XW415	BAC Jet Provost T5A [53]	RAF No 3 FTS, Scampton	
XW416	BAC Jet Provost T5A [19]	RAF College, Cranwell	
XW418	BAC Jet Provost T5A [126]	RAF No 7 FTS, Church Fenton	
XW419	BAC Jet Provost T5A [125]	RAF No 7 FTS, Church Fenton	
XW420	BAC Jet Provost T5A [8]	RAF College, Cranwell	
XW421	BAC Jet Provost T5A [60]	RAF No 3 FTS, Scampton	
XW422	BAC Jet Provost T5A [3]	RAF College, Cranwell	

Notes	Serial	Type (alternative identity)	Owner, Operator or Location
	XW423	BAC Jet Provost T5A [14]	RAF College, Cranwell
	XW424	BAC Jet Provost T5A [62]	Privately owned, Misson, Notts
	XW425	BAC Jet Provost T5A [H]	RAF No 6 FTS, Finningley
	XW427	BAC Jet Provost T5A [56]	RAF No 3 FTS, Scampton
	XW428	BAC Jet Provost T5A [39]	RAF College, Cranwell
	XW429	BAC Jet Provost T5A [66]	RAF No 1 FTS, Linton-on-Ouse
	XW430	BAC Jet Provost T5A [58]	RAF No 3 FTS, Scampton
	XW431	BAC Jet Provost T5A [A]	RAF No 6 FTS, Finningley
	XW432	BAC Jet Provost T5A [76]	RAF No 1 FTS, Linton-on-Ouse
	XW433	BAC Jet Provost T5A [124]	RAF No 7 FTS, Church Fenton
	XW434	BAC Jet Provost T5A [78]	RAF No 1 FTS, Linton-on-Ouse
	XW435	BAC Jet Provost T5A [4]	RAF College, Cranwell
	XW436	BAC Jet Provost T5A [62]	RAF No 3 FTS, Scampton
	XW437	BAC Jet Provost T5A [1]	RAF College, Cranwell
	XW438	BAC Jet Provost T5A [B]	RAF 6 FTS, Finningley
	XW527	HS Buccaneer S2B	RAF No 12 Sqn, Lossiemouth
	XW528	HS Buccaneer S2B (8861M) [C]	RAF Coningsby, BDRT
	XW529	HS Buccaneer S2B	MoD(PE) BAe Scampton
	XW530	HS Buccaneer S2B	RAF No 12 Sqn, Lossiemouth
	XW533	HS Buccaneer S2B	RAF No 237 OCU, Lossiemouth
	XW534	HS Buccaneer S2B	MoD(PE) BAe Scampton
	XW538	HS Buccaneer S2B (8660M) [T]	*Scrapped at Lossiemouth*
	XW541	HS Buccaneer S2B (8858M)	*To Shoebury Ranges, 11 Oct 88*
	XW542	HS Buccaneer S2B	RAF No 237 OCU, Lossiemouth
	XW543	HS Buccaneer S2B	RAF No 12 Sqn, Lossiemouth
	XW544	HS Buccaneer S2B (8857M) [Y]	RAF No 2 SoTT, Cosford
	XW545	HS Buccaneer S2B (8859M)	RAF St Athan, BDRT
	XW546	HS Buccaneer S2B	MoD(PE) BAe Woodford
	XW547	HS Buccaneer S2B	RAF No 12 Sqn, Lossiemouth
	XW549	HS Buccaneer S2B (8860M)	RAF Kinloss, BDRT
	XW550	HS Buccaneer S2B [X]	RAF, stored St Athan
	XW566	SEPECAT Jaguar T2	MoD(PE) RAE Farnborough store
	XW612	WS Scout AH1 [A]	AAC No 660 Sqn, Sek Kong
	XW613	WS Scout AH1 [B]	AAC No 660 Sqn, Sek Kong
	XW614	WS Scout AH1	AAC, stored Wroughton
	XW615	WS Scout AH1 (89--M)	*AAC No 4 Rgt Detmold, BDRT*
	XW616	WS Scout AH1	AAC, stored Wroughton
	XW626	HS Comet 4AEW (G-APDS)	MoD(PE), RAE Bedford apprentice school
	XW630	HS Harrier GR3 [M]	RAF No 4 Sqn, Gutersloh
	XW635	Beagle D5/180 (G-AWSW)	RAF No 5 AEF, Teversham
	XW660	Hover-Air HA5 Hoverhawk III	Privately owned, Cheltenham
	XW664	HS Nimrod R1P	RAF No 51 Sqn, Wyton
	XW665	HS Nimrod R1	RAF No 51 Sqn, Wyton
	XW666	HS Nimrod R1	RAF No 51 Sqn, Wyton
	XW750	HS748 Series 107 (G-ASJT)	MoD(PE) RAE Bedford
	XW763	HS Harrier GR3 [02]	RAF No 1 Sqn, Wittering
	XW764	HS Harrier GR3	RAF St Athan
	XW768	HS Harrier GR3 [N]	RAF No 4 Sqn, Gutersloh
	XW788	HS125 CC1	RAF No 32 Sqn, Northolt
	XW789	HS125 CC1	RAF No 32 Sqn, Northolt
	XW790	HS125 CC1	RAF No 32 Sqn, Northolt
	XW791	HS125 CC1	RAF No 32 Sqn, Northolt
	XW795	WS Scout AH1	AAC, stored Fleetlands
	XW796	WS Scout AH1 [V]	AAC No 660 Sqn, Sek Kong
	XW797	WS Scout AH1 [G]	AAC No 660 Sqn, Sek Kong
	XW798	WS Scout AH1 [H]	AAC No 660 Sqn, Sek Kong
	XW799	WS Scout AH1 [Z]	AAC No 658 Sqn, Netheravon
	XW836	WS Lynx	AAC Middle Wallop, BDRT
	XW838	WS Lynx [TAD 009]	AAC AETW, Middle Wallop
	XW839	WS Lynx	RNEC Manadon
	XW843	WS Gazelle AH1	AAC No 2 Flt, Netheravon
	XW844	WS Gazelle AH1	AAC No 661 Sqn, Hildesheim
	XW845	WS Gazelle HT2 [47/CU]	RN No 705 Sqn, Culdrose
	XW846	WS Gazelle AH1	AAC, stored Wroughton
	XW847	WS Gazelle AH1	AAC D&TS, Middle Wallop
	XW848	WS Gazelle AH1 [D]	AAC No 670 Sqn, Middle Wallop
	XW849	WS Gazelle AH1 [G]	RM 3 CBAS, Yeovilton
	XW851	WS Gazelle AH1 [H]	RM 3 CBAS, Yeovilton
	XW852	WS Gazelle HT3	RAF No 32 Sqn, Northolt
	XW853	WS Gazelle HT2 [53/CU]	RN No 705 Sqn, Culdrose
	XW854	WS Gazelle HT2 [46/CU]	RN No 705 Sqn, Culdrose
	XW855	WS Gazelle HT3	RAF No 32 Sqn, Northolt

Serial	Type (alternative identity)	Owner, Operator or Location	Notes
XW856	WS Gazelle HT2 [49/CU]	RN No 705 Sqn, Culdrose	
XW857	WS Gazelle HT2 [55/CU]	RN No 705 Sqn, Culdrose	
XW858	WS Gazelle HT3 [C]	RAF No 2 FTS, Shawbury	
XW860	WS Gazelle HT2 [44/CU]	RN, stored Wroughton	
XW861	WS Gazelle HT2 [59/CU]	RN No 705 Sqn, Culdrose	
XW862	WS Gazelle HT3 [D]	RAF No 2 FTS, Shawbury	
XW863	WS Gazelle HT2 [42/CU]	RN, stored Wroughton	
XW864	WS Gazelle HT2 [54/CU]	RN, No 705 Sqn, Culdrose	
XW865	WS Gazelle AH1 [C]	AAC No 670 Sqn, Middle Wallop	
XW866	WS Gazelle HT3 [E]	RAF No 2 FTS, Shawbury	
XW868	WS Gazelle HT2 [50/CU]	RN No 705 Sqn, Culdrose	
XW870	WS Gazelle HT3 [F]	RAF No 2 FTS, Shawbury	
XW871	WS Gazelle HT2 [44/CU]	RN No 705 Sqn, Culdrose	
XW884	WS Gazelle HT2 [41/CU]	RN No 705 Sqn, Culdrose	
XW885	WS Gazelle AH1 [B]	AAC No 670 Sqn, Middle Wallop	
XW886	WS Gazelle HT2 [48/CU]	RN No 705 Sqn, Culdrose	
XW887	WS Gazelle HT2 [57/CU]	RN, stored Wroughton	
XW888	WS Gazelle AH1	AAC AETW, Middle Wallop	
XW889	WS Gazelle AH1	AAC AETW, Middle Wallop	
XW890	WS Gazelle HT2 [53/CU]	RN, stored Wroughton	
XW891	WS Gazelle HT2 [49/CU]	Crashed Predannack 25 November 1987	
XW892	WS Gazelle AH1	AAC No 662 Sqn, Soest	
XW893	WS Gazelle AH1	AAC Garrison Air Sqn, FI	
XW894	WS Gazelle HT2 [52/CU]	RN No 705 Sqn, Culdrose	
XW895	WS Gazelle HT2 [51/CU]	RN No 705 Sqn, Culdrose	
XW897	WS Gazelle AH1	AAC No 669 Sqn, Minden	
XW898	WS Gazelle HT3 [G]	RAF No 2 FTS, Shawbury	
XW899	WS Gazelle AH1	AAC, stored Wroughton	
XW900	WS Gazelle AH1 (TAD-900)	AAC AETW, Middle Wallop	
XW902	WS Gazelle HT3 [H]	RAF No 2 FTS, Shawbury	
XW903	WS Gazelle AH1 [E]	AAC No 670 Sqn, Middle Wallop	
XW904	WS Gazelle AH1	AAC No 664 Sqn, Minden	
XW906	WS Gazelle HT3 [J]	RAF No 2 FTS, Shawbury	
XW907	WS Gazelle HT2 [40/CU]	RN No 705 Sqn, Culdrose	
XW908	WS Gazelle AH1	AAC No 653 Sqn, Soest	
XW909	WS Gazelle AH1	AAC No 659 Sqn, Detmold	
XW910	WS Gazelle HT3 [K]	RAF No 2 FTS, Shawbury	
XW911	WS Gazelle AH1 [I]	AAC No 670 Sqn, Middle Wallop	
XW912	WS Gazelle AH1	AAC AETW, Middle Wallop	
XW913	WS Gazelle AH1	AAC No 664 Sqn, Minden	
XW916	HS Harrier GR3 [W]	RAF Wittering Fire Section	
XW917	HS Harrier GR3 [L] [89--M]	RAF Gutersloh on display	
XW919	HS Harrier GR3 [04]	RAF No 1 Sqn, Wittering	
XW921	HS Harrier GR3 [E]	Crashed nr Gutersloh 18 August 1988	
XW922	HS Harrier GR3 (8885M) [B]	MoD ROF, Enfield	
XW923	HS Harrier GR3 (cockpit) (8724M)	RAF Wittering for rescue training	
XW924	HS Harrier GR3 [G]	RAF No 4 Sqn, Gutersloh	
XW925	HS Harrier T4 [R]	RAF St Athan	
XW927	HS Harrier T4	RAF No 3 Sqn, Gutersloh	
XW930	HS125 (G-ATPC)	MoD(PE) RAE Bedford	
XW934	HS Harrier T4 [12]	RAF No 1 Sqn, Wittering	
XW986	HS Buccaneer S2B	MoD(PE) RAE Farnborough	
XW987	HS Buccaneer S2B	MoD(PE) RAE West Freugh	
XW988	HS Buccaneer S2B	MoD(PE) RAE West Freugh	
XX101	Cushioncraft CC7	International Helicopter Museum, Weston-super-Mare	
XX102	Cushioncraft CC7	Museum of Army Transport, Beverley	
XX105	BAC 1-11/201 (G-ASJD)	MoD(PE) RAE Bedford	
XX108	SEPECAT Jaguar GR1 (G27-313)	MoD(PE) BAe Warton/A&AEE Boscombe Down	
XX109	SEPECAT Jaguar GR1 (8918M)	RAF Coltishall, ground instruction	
XX110	SEPECAT Jaguar GR1 [EP] (8955M)	RAF No 2 SoTT, Cosford	
XX110	SEPECAT Jaguar GR1 Replica (BAPC 169)	RAF No 1 SoTT, Halton	
XX112	SEPECAT Jaguar GR1A [EA]	RAF No 6 Sqn, Coltishall	
XX115	SEPECAT Jaguar GR1 (JI005) (8821M) (fuselage only)	RAF No 1 SoTT, Halton	
XX116	SEPECAT Jaguar GR1A [02] (JI008)	RAF No 226 OCU, Lossiemouth	
XX117	SEPECAT Jaguar GR1A [06] (JI004)	RAF No 226 OCU, Lossiemouth	
XX118	SEPECAT Jaguar GR1 (JI018) (8815M) (fuselage only)	RAF No 1 SoTT, Halton	

Notes	Serial	Type (alternative identity)	Owner, Operator or Location
	XX119	SEPECAT Jaguar GR1 [01] (8898M)	RAF No 226 OCU, Lossiemouth
	XX121	SEPECAT Jaguar GR1 [EQ]	RAF, stored Shawbury
	XX139	SEPECAT Jaguar T2A [C]	RAF No 226 OCU, Lossiemouth
	XX140	SEPECAT Jaguar T2 [D]	RAF, stored Shawbury
	XX141	SEPECAT Jaguar T2A [ET]	RAF 6 Sqn, Coltishall
	XX143	SEPECAT Jaguar T2A [GS] (JI002)	RAF No 54 Sqn, Coltishall
	XX144	SEPECAT Jaguar T2A [I]	RAF No 226 OCU, Lossiemouth
	XX145	SEPECAT Jaguar T2	MoD(PE) ETPS, Boscombe Down
	XX146	SEPECAT Jaguar T2A	RAF, stored Shawbury
	XX150	SEPECAT Jaguar T2A	RAF JMU, Abingdon
	XX154	HS Hawk T1 [1]	MoD(PE) RAE Llanbedr
	XX156	HS Hawk T1	MoD(PE) RAE Bedford
	XX157	HS Hawk T1A	RAF No 2 TWU/63 Sqn, Chivenor
	XX158	HS Hawk T1A	RAF No 2 TWU/63 Sqn, Chivenor
	XX159	HS Hawk T1A	RAF No 1 TWU/234 Sqn, Brawdy
	XX160	HS Hawk T1	MoD(PE) RAE Llanbedr
	XX161	HS Hawk T1	RAF CFS, Valley
	XX162	HS Hawk T1	RAF No 4 FTS, Valley
	XX163	HS Hawk T1	RAF No 4 FTS, Valley
	XX163	HS Hawk T1 Replica (BAPC 152)	RAF Exhibition Flight, Abingdon
	XX164	HS Hawk T1	RAF No 4 FTS, Valley
	XX165	HS Hawk T1	RAF No 4 FTS, Valley
	XX167	HS Hawk T1	RAF No 4 FTS, Valley
	XX168	HS Hawk T1	RAF No 4 FTS, Valley
	XX169	HS Hawk T1	RAF No 4 FTS, Valley
	XX170	HS Hawk T1	RAF CFS, Valley
	XX171	HS Hawk T1	RAF No 4 FTS, Valley
	XX172	HS Hawk T1	RAF CFS, Valley
	XX173	HS Hawk T1	RAF No 4 FTS, Valley
	XX174	HS Hawk T1	RAF No 4 FTS, Valley
	XX175	HS Hawk T1	RAF No 4 FTS, Valley
	XX176	HS Hawk T1	RAF CFS, Valley
	XX177	HS Hawk T1	RAF CFS, Valley
	XX178	HS Hawk T1	RAF No 4 FTS, Valley
	XX179	HS Hawk T1	RAF No 4 FTS, Valley
	XX181	HS Hawk T1	RAF No 1 TWU, Brawdy
	XX182	HS Hawk T1	RAF No 4 FTS, Valley
	XX183	HS Hawk T1	RAF No 4 FTS, Valley
	XX184	HS Hawk T1	RAF CFS, Valley
	XX185	HS Hawk T1	RAF No 4 FTS, Valley
	XX186	HS Hawk T1A	RAF No 2 TWU/63 Sqn, Chivenor
	XX187	HS Hawk T1A	RAF No 1 TWU/79 Sqn, Brawdy
	XX188	HS Hawk T1A	RAF No 1 TWU/234 Sqn, Brawdy
	XX189	HS Hawk T1A [J]	RAF No 2 TWU/151 Sqn, Chivenor
	XX190	HS Hawk T1A	RAF No 1 TWU/234 Sqn, Brawdy
	XX191	HS Hawk T1A	RAF No 1 TWU/79 Sqn, Brawdy
	XX192	HS Hawk T1A	RAF No 1 TWU/79 Sqn, Brawdy
	XX193	HS Hawk T1A	RAF No 1 TWU/234 Sqn, Brawdy
	XX194	HS Hawk T1A	RAF No 1 TWU/234 Sqn, Brawdy
	XX195	HS Hawk T1A	RAF No 2 TWU/63 Sqn, Chivenor
	XX196	HS Hawk T1A	RAF No 1 TWU/234 Sqn, Brawdy
	XX197	HS Hawk T1A (wreck)	*Written off 13 May 1988 at Brawdy*
	XX198	HS Hawk T1A	RAF No 1 TWU/79 Sqn, Brawdy
	XX199	HS Hawk T1A	RAF No 2 TWU/63 Sqn, Chivenor
	XX200	HS Hawk T1A	RAF No 1 TWU/79 Sqn, Brawdy
	XX201	HS Hawk T1A [N]	RAF No 2 TWU/151 Sqn, Chivenor
	XX202	HS Hawk T1A [P]	RAF No 2 TWU/151 Sqn, Chivenor
	XX203	HS Hawk T1A	RAF No 2 TWU/63 Sqn, Chivenor
	XX204	HS Hawk T1A [H]	RAF No 2 TWU/151 Sqn, Chivenor
	XX205	HS Hawk T1A [V]	RAF No 2 TWU/151 Sqn, Chivenor
	XX217	HS Hawk T1A	RAF No 2 TWU/63 Sqn, Chivenor
	XX218	HS Hawk T1A	RAF No 1 TWU/234 Sqn, Brawdy
	XX219	HS Hawk T1A [T]	RAF No 2 TWU/151 Sqn, Chivenor
	XX220	HS Hawk T1A	RAF No 1 TWU/234 Sqn, Brawdy
	XX221	HS Hawk T1A	RAF No 1 TWU/79 Sqn, Brawdy
	XX222	HS Hawk T1A	RAF No 1 TWU/79 Sqn, Brawdy
	XX224	HS Hawk T1	RAF CFS, Valley
	XX225	HS Hawk T1	RAF No 4 FTS, Valley
	XX226	HS Hawk T1	RAF No 4 FTS, Valley
	XX227	HS Hawk T1A	RAF *Red Arrows*, Scampton
	XX228	HS Hawk T1A [Q]	RAF No 2 TWU/151 Sqn, Chivenor

Serial	Type (alternative identity)	Owner, Operator or Location	Notes
XX230	HS Hawk T1A [M]	RAF No 2 TWU/151 Sqn, Chivenor	
XX231	HS Hawk T1	RAF No 4 FTS, Valley	
XX232	HS Hawk T1	RAF No 4 FTS, Valley	
XX233	HS Hawk T1	RAF Red Arrows, Scampton	
XX234	HS Hawk T1	RAF No 4 FTS, Valley	
XX235	HS Hawk T1	RAF No 4 FTS, Valley	
XX236	HS Hawk T1	RAF No 4 FTS, Valley	
XX237	HS Hawk T1	RAF Red Arrows, Scampton	
XX238	HS Hawk T1	RAF CFS, Valley	
XX239	HS Hawk T1	RAF No 4 FTS, Valley	
XX240	HS Hawk T1	RAF No 4 FTS, Valley	
XX242	HS Hawk T1	RAF No 4 FTS, Valley	
XX243	HS Hawk T1A	Crashed 22 January 1988	
XX244	HS Hawk T1	RAF No 4 FTS, Valley	
XX245	HS Hawk T1	RAF No 4 FTS, Valley	
XX246	HS Hawk T1A	RAF No 2 TWU/63 Sqn, Chivenor	
XX247	HS Hawk T1A	RAF No 1 TWU/234 Sqn, Brawdy	
XX248	HS Hawk T1A	RAF No 1 TWU/79 Sqn, Brawdy	
XX249	HS Hawk T1	RAF No 4 FTS, Valley	
XX250	HS Hawk T1	RAF No 4 FTS, Valley	
XX252	HS Hawk T1A	RAF Red Arrows, Scampton	
XX253	HS Hawk T1A	RAF Red Arrows, Scampton	
XX254	HS Hawk T1A	RAF No 2 TWU/63 Sqn, Chivenor	
XX255	HS Hawk T1A	RAF No 2 TWU/63 Sqn, Chivenor	
XX256	HS Hawk T1A	RAF No 2 TWU/63 Sqn, Chivenor	
XX257	HS Hawk T1	RAF Chivenor, BDRT	
XX258	HS Hawk T1A	RAF No 1 TWU/79 Sqn, Brawdy	
XX260	HS Hawk T1A	RAF Red Arrows, Scampton	
XX261	HS Hawk T1A	RAF No 1 TWU/79 Sqn, Brawdy	
XX263	HS Hawk T1A	RAF No 2 TWU/63 Sqn, Chivenor	
XX264	HS Hawk T1A	RAF Red Arrows, Scampton	
XX265	HS Hawk T1A [U]	RAF No 2 TWU/151 Sqn, Chivenor	
XX266	HS Hawk T1A	RAF Red Arrows, Scampton	
XX278	HS Hawk T1A	RAF No 2 TWU/63 Sqn, Chivenor	
XX280	HS Hawk T1A	RAF No 1 TWU/79 Sqn, Brawdy	
XX281	HS Hawk T1A [O]	RAF No 2 TWU/151 Sqn, Chivenor	
XX282	HS Hawk T1A	RAF No 2 TWU/63 Sqn, Chivenor	
XX283	HS Hawk T1A [Z]	RAF No 2 TWU/151 Sqn, Chivenor	
XX284	HS Hawk T1A	RAF No 2 TWU/151 Sqn, Chivenor	
XX285	HS Hawk T1A [R]	RAF No 2 TWU/151 Sqn, Chivenor	
XX286	HS Hawk T1A	RAF No 1 TWU/79 Sqn, Brawdy	
XX287	HS Hawk T1A	RAF No 2 TWU/63 Sqn, Chivenor	
XX288	HS Hawk T1A	RAF No 1 TWU, Brawdy	
XX289	HS Hawk T1A	RAF No 2 TWU/63 Sqn, Chivenor	
XX290	HS Hawk T1	RAF No 4 FTS, Valley	
XX291	HS Hawk T1	RAF No 4 FTS, Valley	
XX292	HS Hawk T1	RAF No 4 FTS, Valley	
XX294	HS Hawk T1	RAF Red Arrows, Scampton	
XX295	HS Hawk T1	RAF No 4 FTS, Valley	
XX296	HS Hawk T1	RAF No 4 FTS, Valley	
XX297	HS Hawk T1A (8933M)	RAF Finningley Fire Section	
XX297	HS Hawk T1 Replica (BAPC171)	RAF Exhibition Flight, Abingdon	
XX299	HS Hawk T1	RAF No 4 FTS, Valley	
XX301	HS Hawk T1A [L]	RAF No 2 TWU/151 Sqn, Chivenor	
XX302	HS Hawk T1A	RAF No 1 TWU/234 Sqn, Brawdy	
XX303	HS Hawk T1A	RAF No 1 TWU/234 Sqn, Brawdy	
XX304	HS Hawk T1A	RAF Red Arrows, Scampton	
XX306	HS Hawk T1A	RAF Red Arrows, Scampton	
XX307	HS Hawk T1	RAF No 4 FTS, Valley	
XX308	HS Hawk T1	RAF Red Arrows, Scampton	
XX309	HS Hawk T1	RAF No 4 FTS, Valley	
XX310	HS Hawk T1	RAF No 4 FTS, Valley	
XX311	HS Hawk T1	RAF CFS, Valley	
XX312	HS Hawk T1	RAF No 1 TWU, Brawdy	
XX313	HS Hawk T1	RAF No 4 FTS, Valley	
XX314	HS Hawk T1 [S]	RAF No 2 TWU/151 Sqn, Chivenor	
XX315	HS Hawk T1A	RAF No 1 TWU/234 Sqn, Brawdy	
XX316	HS Hawk T1A	RAF No 1 TWU/79 Sqn, Brawdy	
XX317	HS Hawk T1A	RAF No 1 TWU/234 Sqn, Brawdy	
XX318	HS Hawk T1A	RAF No 1 TWU/79 Sqn, Brawdy	
XX319	HS Hawk T1A	RAF No 1 TWU/79 Sqn, Brawdy	
XX320	HS Hawk T1A	RAF No 2 TWU/63 Sqn, Chivenor	
XX321	HS Hawk T1A	RAF No 2 TWU/63 Sqn, Chivenor	

Notes	Serial	Type (alternative identity)	Owner, Operator or Location
	XX322	HS Hawk T1A [W]	RAF No 2 TWU/151 Sqn, Chivenor
	XX323	HS Hawk T1A	RAF No 1 TWU/234 Sqn, Brawdy
	XX324	HS Hawk T1A	RAF No 1 TWU/234 Sqn, Brawdy
	XX325	HS Hawk T1A [X]	RAF No 2 TWU/151 Sqn, Chivenor
	XX326	HS Hawk T1A [A]	RAF No 1 TWU/151 Sqn, Chivenor
	XX327	HS Hawk T1A	MoD(PE) RAE Farnborough
	XX329	HS Hawk T1A [C]	RAF No 2 TWU/151 Sqn, Chivenor
	XX330	HS Hawk T1A [D]	RAF No 2 TWU/151 Sqn, Chivenor
	XX331	HS Hawk T1A	RAF No 2 TWU/63 Sqn, Chivenor
	XX332	HS Hawk T1A	RAF No 2 TWU/151 Sqn, Chivenor
	XX334	HS Hawk T1A	RAF No 2 TWU/63 Sqn, Chivenor
	XX335	HS Hawk T1A [I]	RAF No 2 TWU/151 Sqn, Chivenor
	XX337	HS Hawk T1A [K]	RAF No 2 TWU/151 Sqn, Chivenor
	XX338	HS Hawk T1	RAF No 4 FTS, Valley
	XX339	HS Hawk T1A	RAF No 1 TWU/234 Sqn, Brawdy
	XX341	HS Hawk T1 ASTRA [1]	MoD(PE) A&AEE, Boscombe Down
	XX342	HS Hawk T1 [2]	MoD(PE) ETPS, Boscombe Down
	XX343	HS Hawk T1 [3]	MoD(PE) ETPS, Boscombe Down
	XX344	HS Hawk T1 (8847M)	RAF Abingdon, BDRF
	XX345	HS Hawk T1A [Y]	RAF No 2 TWU/151 Sqn, Chivenor
	XX346	HS Hawk T1A	RAF No 2 TWU/63 Sqn, Chivenor
	XX347	HS Hawk T1	RAF No 4 FTS, Valley
	XX348	HS Hawk T1A	RAF No 1 TWU/79 Sqn, Brawdy
	XX349	HS Hawk T1	RAF No 2 TWU/63 Sqn, Chivenor
	XX350	HS Hawk T1A	RAF No 1 TWU/234 Sqn, Brawdy
	XX351	HS Hawk T1A	RAF No 1 TWU/234 Sqn, Brawdy
	XX352	HS Hawk T1A	RAF No 2 TWU/63 Sqn, Chivenor
	XX370	WS Gazelle AH1 [A]	AAC No 658 Sqn, Netheravon
	XX371	WS Gazelle AH1	AAC No 12 Flt, Wildenrath
	XX372	WS Gazelle AH1 [B]	AAC No 658 Sqn, Netheravon
	XX373	WS Gazelle AH1	AAC No 663 Sqn, Soest
	XX375	WS Gazelle AH1	AAC No 658 Sqn, Netheravon
	XX378	WS Gazelle AH1	*Written off 24 February 1982*
	XX379	WS Gazelle AH1 [D]	AAC No 658 Sqn, Netheravon
	XX380	WS Gazelle AH1 [A]	RM 3 CBAS, Yeovilton
	XX381	WS Gazelle AH1	AAC No 2 Flt, Netheravon
	XX382	WS Gazelle HT3 [M]	RAF No 2 FTS, Shawbury
	XX383	WS Gazelle AH1 [E]	AAC No 658 Sqn, Netheravon
	XX384	WS Gazelle AH1	AAC No 661 Sqn, Hildesheim
	XX385	WS Gazelle AH1 [W]	AAC No 653 Sqn, Soest
	XX386	WS Gazelle AH1	AAC No 12 Flt, Wildenrath
	XX387	WS Gazelle AH1	AAC No 661 Sqn, Hildesheim
	XX388	WS Gazelle AH1	AAC No 652 Sqn, Hildesheim
	XX389	WS Gazelle AH1	AAC No 652 Sqn, Hildesheim
	XX391	WS Gazelle HT2 [56/CU]	RN No 705 Sqn, Culdrose
	XX392	WS Gazelle AH1 [W]	AAC No 670 Sqn, Middle Wallop
	XX393	WS Gazelle AH1	AAC No 2 Flt, Netheravon
	XX394	WS Gazelle AH1	AAC No 2 Flt, Netheravon
	XX395	WS Gazelle AH1	AAC No 662 Sqn, Soest
	XX396	WS Gazelle HT3 (8718M) [N]	RAF Exhibition Flight, Henlow
	XX398	WS Gazelle AH1	AAC No 661 Sqn, Hildesheim
	XX399	WS Gazelle AH1	RM, stored Wroughton
	XX403	WS Gazelle AH1 [Y]	AAC No 670 Sqn, Middle Wallop
	XX405	WS Gazelle AH1	AAC No 669 Sqn, Detmold
	XX406	WS Gazelle HT3 [P]	RAF No 2 FTS, Shawbury
	XX407	WS Gazelle AH1	AAC No 661 Sqn, Hildesheim
	XX408	WS Gazelle AH1 (330)	RM 3CBAS, Yeovilton
	XX409	WS Gazelle AH1	AAC No 656 Sqn, Netheravon
	XX410	WS Gazelle HT2 [58/CU]	RN AES, Lee-on-Solent
	XX411	WS Gazelle AH1 [X]	AAC Middle Wallop, BDRT
	XX411	WS Gazelle AH1 (tail only)	FAA Museum, RNAS Yeovilton
	XX412	WS Gazelle AH1 [B]	RM 3 CBAS, Yeovilton
	XX413	WS Gazelle AH1	RM 3 CBAS, Yeovilton
	XX414	WS Gazelle AH1	AAC No 662 Sqn, Soest
	XX416	WS Gazelle AH1	AAC No 664 Sqn, Minden
	XX417	WS Gazelle AH1	AAC No 665 Sqn, Aldergrove
	XX418	WS Gazelle AH1	AAC No 669 Sqn, Minden
	XX419	WS Gazelle AH1	AAC No 661 Sqn, Detmold
	XX431	WS Gazelle HT2 [43/CU]	RN No 705 Sqn, Culdrose
	XX432	WS Gazelle AH1	AAC No 664 Sqn, Minden
	XX433	WS Gazelle AH1	AAC No 665 Sqn, Aldergrove
	XX434	WS Gazelle AH1	RAF Abingdon, BDRF
	XX435	WS Gazelle AH1	AAC No 663 Sqn, Soest
	XX436	WS Gazelle HT2 [39/CU]	RN No 705 Sqn, Culdrose

Serial	Type (alternative identity)	Owner, Operator or Location	Notes
XX437	WS Gazelle AH1	AAC No 663 Sqn, Soest	
XX438	WS Gazelle AH1	AAC No 664 Sqn, Minden	
XX439	WS Gazelle AH1	AAC No 669 Sqn, Hildesheim	
XX440	WS Gazelle AH1 (G-BCHN)	AAC No 665 Sqn, Aldergrove	
XX441	WS Gazelle HT2 [38/CU]	RN No 705 Sqn, Culdrose	
XX442	WS Gazelle AH1	AAC No 664 Sqn, Detmold	
XX443	WS Gazelle AH1	AAC No 663 Sqn, Soest	
XX444	WS Gazelle AH1	AAC No 656 Sqn, Netheravon	
XX445	WS Gazelle AH1	AAC No 669 Sqn, Detmold	
XX446	WS Gazelle HT2 [57/CU]	RN No 705 Sqn, Culdrose	
XX447	WS Gazelle AH1	AAC No 663 Sqn, Soest	
XX448	WS Gazelle AH1	AAC No 659 Sqn, Detmold	
XX449	WS Gazelle AH1	AAC No 669 Sqn, Detmold	
XX450	WS Gazelle AH1 [D]	RM 3 CBAS, Yeovilton	
XX451	WS Gazelle HT2 [58/CU]	RN No 705 Sqn, Culdrose	
XX452	WS Gazelle AH1	AAC Middle Wallop Fire Section	
XX453	WS Gazelle AH1	AAC No 661 Sqn, Detmold	
XX454	WS Gazelle AH1	AAC No 664 Sqn, Detmold	
XX455	WS Gazelle AH1	AAC No 661 Sqn, Hildesheim	
XX456	WS Gazelle AH1	AAC No 669 Sqn, Detmold	
XX457	WS Gazelle AH1 [H]	AAC No 670 Sqn, Middle Wallop	
XX460	WS Gazelle AH1	AAC No 661 Sqn, Hildesheim	
XX462	WS Gazelle AH1	AAC No 652 Sqn, Hildesheim	
XX466	HS Hunter T66B/T7 [830/DD]	RNAS Culdrose, SAH	
XX467	HS Hunter T66B/T7	Air Service Training, Perth	
XX469	WS Lynx HAS2 (G-BNCL) (A2657)	Privately owned, Helicopter Museum of GB	
XX475	SA Jetstream T2 [572/CU] (G-AWVJ/N1036S)	RN 750 Sqn, Culdrose	
XX476	SA Jetstream T2 [561/CU] (G-AXGL/N1037S)	RN No 750 Sqn, Culdrose	
XX477	SA Jetstream T1 (8462M) (G-AXXS)	RAF Finningley — ground instruction	
XX478	SA Jetstream T2 [564/CU] (G-AXXT)	RN No 750 Sqn, Culdrose	
XX479	SA Jetstream T2 [563/CU] (G-AXUR)	RN No 750 Sqn, Culdrose	
XX480	SA Jetstream T2 [565/CU] (G-AXXU)	RN No 750 Sqn, Culdrose	
XX481	SA Jetstream T2 [560/CU] (G-AXUP)	RN No 750 Sqn, Culdrose	
XX482	SA Jetstream T1 [J]	RAF No 6 FTS, Finningley	
XX483	SA Jetstream T2 [562/CU]	RN No 750 Sqn, Culdrose	
XX484	SA Jetstream T2 [566/CU]	RN No 750 Sqn, Culdrose	
XX485	SA Jetstream T2 [567/CU]	RN No 750 Sqn, Culdrose	
XX486	SA Jetstream T2 [569/CU]	RN No 750 Sqn, Culdrose	
XX487	SA Jetstream T2 [568/CU]	RN No 750 Sqn, Culdrose	
XX488	SA Jetstream T2 [571/CU]	RN No 750 Sqn, Culdrose	
XX489	SA Jetstream T2 [575/CU]	RN No 750 Sqn, Culdrose	
XX490	SA Jetstream T2 [570/CU]	RN No 750 Sqn, Culdrose	
XX491	SA Jetstream T1 [K]	RAF No 6 FTS, Finningley	
XX492	SA Jetstream T1 [A]	RAF No 6 FTS, Finningley	
XX493	SA Jetstream T1 [L]	RAF No 6 FTS, Finningley	
XX494	SA Jetstream T1 [B]	RAF No 6 FTS, Finningley	
XX495	SA Jetstream T1 [C]	RAF No 6 FTS, Finningley	
XX496	SA Jetstream T1 [D]	RAF No 6 FTS, Finningley	
XX497	SA Jetstream T1 [E]	RAF No 6 FTS, Finningley	
XX498	SA Jetstream T1 [F]	RAF No 6 FTS, Finningley	
XX499	SA Jetstream T1 [G]	RAF No 6 FTS, Finningley	
XX500	SA Jetstream T1 [H]	RAF No 6 FTS, Finningley	
XX507	HS125 CC2	RAF No 32 Sqn, Northolt	
XX508	HS125 CC2	RAF No 32 Sqn, Northolt	
XX513	SA Bulldog T1 [A]	RAF No 1 FTS/RNEFTS, Topcliffe	
XX515	SA Bulldog T1 [7]	RAF CFS, Scampton	
XX516	SA Bulldog T1 [C]	RAF No 1 FTS/RNEFTS, Topcliffe	
XX517	SA Bulldog T1 [S]	RAF No 1 FTS/RNEFTS, Topcliffe	
XX518	SA Bulldog T1 [Z]	RAF Liverpool UAS, Woodvale	
XX519	SA Bulldog T1 [I]	RAF No 1 FTS/RNEFTS, Topcliffe	
XX520	SA Bulldog T1 [2]	RAF CFS, Scampton	
XX521	SA Bulldog T1 [01]	RAF, East Lowlands UAS, Turnhouse	
XX522	SA Bulldog T1 [E]	RAF No 1 FTS/RNEFTS, Topcliffe	
XX523	SA Bulldog T1 [F]	RAF No 1 FTS/RNEFTS, Topcliffe	
XX524	SA Bulldog T1 [04]	RAF, London UAS, Abingdon	
XX525	SA Bulldog T1 [03]	RAF, East Lowlands UAS, Turnhouse	
XX526	SA Bulldog T1 [C]	RAF, Oxford UAS, Abingdon	

Notes	Serial	Type (alternative identity)	Owner, Operator or Location
	XX527	SA Bulldog T1 [G]	RAF No 1 FTS/RNEFTS, Topcliffe
	XX528	SA Bulldog T1 [D]	RAF, Oxford UAS, Abingdon
	XX529	SA Bulldog T1 [H]	RAF No 1 FTS/RNEFTS, Topcliffe
	XX530	SA Bulldog T1 [12]	CTE, RAF Manston
	XX531	SA Bulldog T1 [B]	RAF No 1 FTS/RNEFTS, Topcliffe
	XX532	SA Bulldog T1 [J]	RAF, Yorkshire UAS, Finningley
	XX533	SA Bulldog T1 [J]	RAF No 1 FTS/RNEFTS, Topcliffe
	XX534	SA Bulldog T1 [04]	RAF, East Lowlands UAS, Turnhouse
	XX535	SA Bulldog T1 [10]	RAF, London UAS, Abingdon
	XX536	SA Bulldog T1 [D]	RAF No 1 FTS/RNEFTS, Topcliffe
	XX537	SA Bulldog T1 [02]	RAF, East Lowlands UAS, Turnhouse
	XX538	SA Bulldog T1 [P]	RAF No 1 FTS/RNEFTS, Topcliffe
	XX539	SA Bulldog T1 [1]	RAF CFS, Scampton
	XX540	SA Bulldog T1 [K]	RAF No 1 FTS/RNEFTS, Topcliffe
	XX541	SA Bulldog T1 [L]	RAF No 1 FTS/RNEFTS, Topcliffe
	XX543	SA Bulldog T1 [F]	RAF, Yorkshire UAS, Finningley
	XX544	SA Bulldog T1 [01]	RAF, London UAS, Abingdon
	XX545	SA Bulldog T1 PAX [02]	RAF, East Lowlands UAS, Turnhouse
	XX546	SA Bulldog T1 [03]	RAF, London UAS, Abingdon
	XX547	SA Bulldog T1 [05]	RAF, London UAS, Abingdon
	XX548	SA Bulldog T1 [06]	RAF, London UAS, Abingdon
	XX549	SA Bulldog T1 [T]	RAF No 1 FTS/RNEFTS, Topcliffe
	XX550	SA Bulldog T1 [Z]	RAF, Northumbria UAS, Leeming
	XX551	SA Bulldog T1 [M]	RAF No 1 FTS/RNEFTS, Topcliffe
	XX552	SA Bulldog T1 [08]	RAF, London UAS, Abingdon
	XX553	SA Bulldog T1 [07]	RAF, London UAS, Abingdon
	XX554	SA Bulldog T1 [09]	RAF, London UAS, Abingdon
	XX555	SA Bulldog T1 [10]	RAF CFS, Scampton
	XX556	SA Bulldog T1 [S]	RAF, East Midlands UAS, Newton
	XX557	SA Bulldog T1 PAX	RAF Topcliffe, ground instruction
	XX558	SA Bulldog T1 [P]	RAF Birmingham UAS, Cosford
	XX559	SA Bulldog T1	RAF, Glasgow & Strathclyde UAS, Glasgow
	XX560	SA Bulldog T1	RAF, Glasgow & Strathclyde UAS, Glasgow
	XX561	SA Bulldog T1 [A]	RAF, Aberdeen, Dundee & St Andrews UAS, Leuchars
	XX562	SA Bulldog T1 [E]	RAF No 13 AEF, Sydenham
	XX611	SA Bulldog T1	RAF, Glasgow & Strathclyde UAS, Glasgow
	XX612	SA Bulldog T1 [05]	RAF, Wales UAS, St Athan
	XX613	SA Bulldog T1 [A]	RAF, Queen's UAS, Sydenham
	XX614	SA Bulldog T1 [1]	RAF, stored Shawbury
	XX615	SA Bulldog T1 [2]	RAF, Manchester UAS, Woodvale
	XX616	SA Bulldog T1 [3]	RAF, Manchester UAS, Woodvale
	XX617	SA Bulldog T1 [4]	RAF, Manchester UAS, Woodvale
	XX619	SA Bulldog T1 [B]	RAF, Yorkshire UAS, Finningley
	XX620	SA Bulldog T1 [C]	RAF, Yorkshire UAS, Finningley
	XX621	SA Bulldog T1 [D]	RAF, Yorkshire UAS, Finningley
	XX622	SA Bulldog T1 [E]	RAF, Yorkshire UAS, Finningley
	XX623	SA Bulldog T1 [M]	RAF, East Midlands UAS, Newton
	XX624	SA Bulldog T1 [G]	RAF, Yorkshire UAS, Finningley
	XX625	SA Bulldog T1 [01]	RAF, Wales UAS, St Athan
	XX626	SA Bulldog T1 [02]	RAF, Wales UAS, St Athan
	XX627	SA Bulldog T1 [03]	RAF, Wales UAS, St Athan
	XX628	SA Bulldog T1 [04]	RAF, Wales UAS, St Athan
	XX629	SA Bulldog T1 [V]	RAF, Northumbria UAS, Leeming
	XX630	SA Bulldog T1 [A]	RAF, Cambridge, under repair
	XX631	SA Bulldog T1 [14]	RAF, Northumbria UAS, Leeming
	XX632	SA Bulldog T1 [D]	RAF, Bristol UAS, Filton
	XX633	SA Bulldog T1 [X]	RAF, Northumbria UAS, Leeming
	XX634	SA Bulldog T1 [C]	RAF, Cambridge UAS, Teversham
	XX635	SA Bulldog T1 (8767M) [S]	RAF St Athan, CTTS
	XX636	SA Bulldog T1 [Y]	RAF, Northumbria UAS, Leeming
	XX637	SA Bulldog T1	RAF, stored Shawbury
	XX638	SA Bulldog T1 [N]	RAF No 1 FTS/RNEFTS, Topcliffe
	XX639	SA Bulldog T1 [02]	RAF, London UAS, Abingdon
	XX640	SA Bulldog T1 [U]	RAF, Queen's UAS, Sydenham
	XX653	SA Bulldog T1 [E]	RAF, Bristol UAS, Filton
	XX654	SA Bulldog T1 [A]	RAF, Bristol UAS, Filton
	XX655	SA Bulldog T1 [B]	RAF, Bristol UAS, Filton
	XX656	SA Bulldog T1 [C]	RAF, Bristol UAS, Filton
	XX657	SA Bulldog T1 [U]	RAF, Cambridge UAS, Teversham
	XX658	SA Bulldog T1 [A]	RAF, Cambridge UAS, Teversham

Serial	Type (alternative identity)	Owner, Operator or Location	Notes
XX659	SA Bulldog T1 [S]	RAF, Cambridge UAS, Teversham	
XX660	SA Bulldog T1 [A]	BAe Prestwick, spares recovery	
XX661	SA Bulldog T1 [B]	RAF, Oxford UAS, Abingdon	
XX663	SA Bulldog T1 [B]	RAF, Aberdeen, Dundee & St Andrews UAS, Leuchars	
XX664	SA Bulldog T1 [05]	RAF, East Lowlands UAS, Turnhouse	
XX665	SA Bulldog T1 [E]	RAF, Aberdeen, Dundee & St Andrews UAS, Leuchars	
XX666	SA Bulldog T1 [V]	RAF No 1 FTSh RNEFTS, Topcliffe	
XX667	SA Bulldog T1 [D]	RAF, Aberdeen, Dundee & St Andrews UAS, Leuchars	
XX668	SA Bulldog T1 [1]	RAF, Manchester UAS, Woodvale	
XX669	SA Bulldog T1 [B]	RAF, Birmingham UAS, Cosford	
XX670	SA Bulldog T1 [C]	RAF, Birmingham UAS, Cosford	
XX671	SA Bulldog T1 [D]	RAF, Birmingham UAS, Cosford	
XX672	SA Bulldog T1 [E]	RAF, Birmingham UAS, Cosford	
XX685	SA Bulldog T1 [L]	RAF, Liverpool UAS, Woodvale	
XX686	SA Bulldog T1 [U]	RAF, Liverpool UAS, Woodvale	
XX687	SA Bulldog T1 [A]	RAF, East Midlands UAS, Newton	
XX688	SA Bulldog T1 [S]	RAF, Liverpool UAS, Woodvale	
XX689	SA Bulldog T1 [3]	RAF CFS, Scampton	
XX690	SA Bulldog T1 [A]	RAF, Yorkshire UAS, Finningley	
XX691	SA Bulldog T1 [H]	RAF, Yorkshire UAS, Finningley	
XX692	SA Bulldog T1 [5]	RAF CFS, Scampton	
XX693	SA Bulldog T1 [4]	RAF CFS, Scampton	
XX694	SA Bulldog T1 [E]	RAF, East Midlands UAS, Newton	
XX695	SA Bulldog T1 [2]	RAF CFS, Scampton	
XX696	SA Bulldog T1 [8]	RAF CFS, Scampton	
XX697	SA Bulldog T1 [Q]	RAF, Queen's UAS, Sydenham	
XX698	SA Bulldog T1 [9]	RAF CFS, Scampton	
XX699	SA Bulldog T1 [Q]	RAF No 1 FTS/RNEFTS, Topcliffe	
XX700	SA Bulldog T1 [R]	RAF No 1 FTS/RNEFTS, Topcliffe	
XX701	SA Bulldog T1 [02]	RAF, Southampton UAS, Lee-on-Solent	
XX702	SA Bulldog T1 [bl]	RAF, Glasgow & Strathclyde UAS, Glasgow	
XX704	SA Bulldog T1 [U]	RAF, East Midlands UAS, Newton	
XX705	SA Bulldog T1 [05]	RAF, Southampton UAS, Lee-on-Solent	
XX706	SA Bulldog T1 [01]	RAF, Southampton UAS, Lee-on-Solent	
XX707	SA Bulldog T1 [04]	RAF, Southampton UAS, Lee-on-Solent	
XX708	SA Bulldog T1 [03]	RAF, Southampton UAS, Lee-on-Solent	
XX709	SA Bulldog T1 [C]	RAF, Aberdeen, Dundee & St Andrews UAS, Leuchars	
XX710	SA Bulldog T1 [5]	RAF, Manchester UAS, Woodvale	
XX711	SA Bulldog T1 [S]	RAF, Queen's UAS, Sydenham	
XX712	SA Bulldog T1 [1]	*Crashed Ainsdale 2 March 1988*	
XX713	SA Bulldog T1 [6]	RAF CFS, Scampton	
XX714	SA Bulldog T1	MoD(PE) BAe Prestwick	
XX719	SEPECAT Jaguar GR1A [EQ]	RAF No 6 Sqn, Coltishall	
XX720	SEPECAT Jaguar GR1A (JI003) [EN]	RAF No 6 Sqn, Coltishall	
XX722	SEPECAT Jaguar GR1 [EF]	RAF, stored Shawbury	
XX723	SEPECAT Jaguar GR1A [05]	RAF No 226 OCU, Lossiemouth	
XX724	SEPECAT Jaguar GR1 [GA]	RAF No 54 Sqn, Coltishall	
XX724	SEPECAT Jaguar GR1 Replica (BAPC150) [GA]	RAF Exhibition Flight, Abingdon	
XX725	SEPECAT Jaguar GR1A [EL] (JI010)	RAF No 6 Sqn, Coltishall	
XX726	SEPECAT Jaguar GR1 [EB] (8947M)	RAF No 1 SoTT, Halton	
XX727	SEPECAT Jaguar GR1 [ER] (8951M)	RAF No 2 SoTT, Cosford	
XX729	SEPECAT Jaguar GR1A (JI012) [07]	RAF No 226 OCU, Lossiemouth	
XX730	SEPECAT Jaguar GR1 [EC] (8952M)	RAF No 2 SoTT, Cosford	
XX733	SEPECAT Jaguar GR1A [EF]	RAF No 6 Sqn, Coltishall	
XX734	SEPECAT Jaguar GR1 (JI014) (8816M)	RAF Coltishall, BDRT	
XX736	SEPECAT Jaguar GR1 (JI013)	BAe Warton, stored	
XX737	SEPECAT Jaguar GR1A [GG] (JI015)	RAF No 54 Sqn, Coltishall	
XX738	SEPECAT Jaguar GR1A [GJ] (JI016)	RAF No 54 Sqn, Coltishall	
XX739	SEPECAT Jaguar GR1 (8902M) [I]	RAF No 1 SoTT, Halton	

Notes	Serial	Type (alternative identity)	Owner, Operator or Location
	XX741	SEPECAT Jaguar GR1A [EJ]	RAF No 6 Sqn, Coltishall
	XX743	SEPECAT Jaguar GR1 [EG] (8949M)	RAF No 1 SoTT, Halton
	XX744	SEPECAT Jaguar GR1 [DJ]	RAF, stored Shawbury
	XX745	SEPECAT Jaguar GR1A [EB]	RAF No 6 Sqn, Coltishall
	XX746	SEPECAT Jaguar GR1A [09] (8895M)	RAF No 1 SoTT, Halton
	XX747	SEPECAT Jaguar GR1 [08] (8903M)	RAF No 1 SoTT, Halton
	XX748	SEPECAT Jaguar GR1A [GD]	RAF No 54 Sqn, Coltishall
	XX751	SEPECAT Jaguar GR1 [10] (8937M)	RAF No 2 SoTT, Cosford
	XX752	SEPECAT Jaguar GR1A	RAF No 54 Sqn, Coltishall
	XX753	SEPECAT Jaguar GR1 [05]	RAF, stored Shawbury
	XX754	SEPECAT Jaguar GR1A [GR]	RAF No 54 Sqn, Coltishall
	XX756	SEPECAT Jaguar GR1 [AM] (8899M)	RAF No 2 SoTT, Cosford
	XX757	SEPECAT Jaguar GR1 [CU] (8948M)	RAF No 1 SoTT, Halton
	XX763	SEPECAT Jaguar GR1 [24]	RAF, stored Shawbury
	XX764	SEPECAT Jaguar GR1 [13]	RAF, stored Shawbury
	XX765	SEPECAT Jaguar ACT	MoD(PE) BAe, stored Warton
	XX766	SEPECAT Jaguar GR1A [GP]	RAF No 54 Sqn, Coltishall
	XX767	SEPECAT Jaguar GR1A [GE]	RAF No 54 Sqn, Coltishall
	XX818	SEPECAT Jaguar GR1 [DE] (8945M)	RAF No 1 SoTT, Halton
	XX819	SEPECAT Jaguar GR1 [CE] (8923M)	RAF No 2 SoTT, Cosford
	XX821	SEPECAT Jaguar GR1 [P] (8896M)	SIF, RAFC Cranwell
	XX824	SEPECAT Jaguar GR1 [AD]	RAF, stored Shawbury
	XX825	SEPECAT Jaguar GR1 [BN]	RAF, stored Shawbury
	XX826	SEPECAT Jaguar GR1 [34]	RAF, stored Shawbury
	XX829	SEPECAT Jaguar T2A [D]	RAF No 226 OCU, Lossiemouth
	XX830	SEPECAT Jaguar T2	MoD(PE) ETPS, Boscombe Down
	XX832	SEPECAT Jaguar T2A [S]	RAF No 226 OCU, Lossiemouth
	XX833	SEPECAT Jaguar T2A [Z]	RAF No 41 Sqn, Coltishall
	XX834	SEPECAT Jaguar T2A [EZ]	Crashed 7 Sep 1988, W. Germany
	XX835	SEPECAT Jaguar T2	MoD(PE) RAE Farnborough
	XX836	SEPECAT Jaguar T2A [ER]	RAF No 6 Sqn, Coltishall
	XX837	SEPECAT Jaguar T2 [Z]	RAF, stored Shawbury
	XX838	SEPECAT Jaguar T2A [X]	RAF No 226 OCU, Lossiemouth
	XX839	SEPECAT Jaguar T2A [Y]	RAF No 226 OCU, Lossiemouth
	XX840	SEPECAT Jaguar T2A [34]	RAF No 2 Sqn, Laarbruch
	XX841	SEPECAT Jaguar T2 [S]	RAF, stored Shawbury
	XX842	SEPECAT Jaguar T2A [EW]	RAF No 6 Sqn, Coltishall
	XX843	SEPECAT Jaguar T2A [GT]	RAF No 54 Sqn, Coltishall
	XX844	SEPECAT Jaguar T2 [F]	Cranfield Institute of Technology
	XX845	SEPECAT Jaguar T2 [AZ]	RAF JMU, Abingdon
	XX846	SEPECAT Jaguar T2A [Y]	RAF No 41 Sqn, Coltishall
	XX847	SEPECAT Jaguar T2 [G]	RAF, stored Shawbury
	XX885	HS Buccaneer S2B	RAF No 208 Sqn, Lossiemouth
	XX886	HS Buccaneer S2B	RAF Honington, WLT instructional use
	XX887	HS Buccaneer S2B	RAF, stored Shawbury
	XX888	HS Buccaneer S2B	RAF, stored Shawbury
	XX889	HS Buccaneer S2B	RAF No 12 Sqn, Lossiemouth
	XX892	HS Buccaneer S2B	BAe Woodford
	XX893	HS Buccaneer S2B	RAF/BAe Woodford
	XX894	HS Buccaneer S2B	BAe Woodford
	XX895	HS Buccaneer S2B	RAF No 12 Sqn, Lossiemouth
	XX896	HS Buccaneer S2B	RAF No 12 Sqn, Lossiemouth
	XX897	HS Buccaneer S2B	MoD(PE) RS&RE, Bedford
	XX899	HS Buccaneer S2B	RAF No 237 OCU, Lossiemouth
	XX900	HS Buccaneer S2B [MS]	RAF No 208 Sqn, Lossiemouth
	XX901	HS Buccaneer S2B	RAF No 237 OCU, Lossiemouth
	XX907	WS Lynx AH1	RAE, stored Farnborough
	XX910	WS Lynx HAS2	RAE, stored Farnborough
	XX914	BAC VC10 srs 1103 (G-ATDJ/8777M) (rear fuselage)	RAF AMS, Brize Norton
	XX919	BAC 1-11/402 (PI-C 1121)	MoD(PE) RAE Farnborough
	XX946	Panavia Tornado (P02) (8883M)	RAF Honington for ground instruction/ Saudi Support Unit
	XX947	Panavia Tornado (P03) (8797M)	RAF Marham for ground instruction

Serial	Type (alternative identity)	Owner, Operator or Location	Notes
XX948	Panavia Tornado (P06) (8879M)	RAF No 2 SoTT, Cosford	
XX955	SEPECAT Jaguar GR1A [GK]	RAF No 54 Sqn, Coltishall	
XX956	SEPECAT Jaguar GR1 [BE] (8950M)	RAF No 1 SoTT, Halton	
XX958	SEPECAT Jaguar GR1 [BK]	RAF, stored Shawbury	
XX959	SEPECAT Jaguar GR1 [CJ] (8953M)	RAF No 2 SoTT, Cosford	
XX962	SEPECAT Jaguar GR1A [EK]	RAF No 6 Sqn, Coltishall	
XX965	SEPECAT Jaguar GR1A [04]	RAF No 226 OCU, Lossiemouth	
XX966	SEPECAT Jaguar GR1A (8904M) [EL]	RAF No 1 SoTT, Halton	
XX967	SEPECAT Jaguar GR1 [AC]	RAF, stored Shawbury	
XX968	SEPECAT Jaguar GR1 [AJ]	RAF, stored Shawbury	
XX969	SEPECAT Jaguar GR1A (8897M) [01]	RAF No 2 SoTT, Cosford	
XX970	SEPECAT Jaguar GR1A [EH]	RAF No 6 Sqn, Coltishall	
XX974	SEPECAT Jaguar GR1A [EG]	RAF No 6 Sqn, Coltishall	
XX975	SEPECAT Jaguar GR1 [07] (8905M)	RAF No 1 SoTT, Halton	
XX976	SEPECAT Jaguar GR1 (8906M) [BD]	RAF No 1 SoTT, Halton	
XX977	SEPECAT Jaguar GR1	RAF, stored Shawbury	
XX979	SEPECAT Jaguar GR1A [JS]	MoD(PE) A&AEE Boscombe Down	
XZ101	SEPECAT Jaguar GR1A [Q]	RAF No 41 Sqn, Coltishall	
XZ103	SEPECAT Jaguar GR1A	RAF No 41 Sqn, Coltishall	
XZ104	SEPECAT Jaguar GR1A [24]	RAF No 2 Sqn, Laarbruch	
XZ106	SEPECAT Jaguar GR1A [26]	RAF No 2 Sqn, Laarbruch	
XZ107	SEPECAT Jaguar GR1A [H]	RAF No 41 Sqn, Coltishall	
XZ108	SEPECAT Jaguar GR1A [28]	RAF No 2 Sqn, Laarbruch	
XZ109	SEPECAT Jaguar GR1A [29]	RAF No 2 Sqn, Laarbruch	
XZ111	SEPECAT Jaguar GR1A [31]	RAF No 2 Sqn, Laarbruch	
XZ112	SEPECAT Jaguar GR1A [32]	RAF No 2 Sqn, Laarbruch	
XZ113	SEPECAT Jaguar GR1A [30]	RAF No 2 Sqn, Laarbruch	
XZ114	SEPECAT Jaguar GR1A [B]	RAF No 41 Sqn, Coltishall	
XZ115	SEPECAT Jaguar GR1A [C]	RAF No 41 Sqn, Coltishall	
XZ117	SEPECAT Jaguar GR1A [E]	RAF No 41 Sqn, Coltishall	
XZ118	SEPECAT Jaguar GR1A [F]	RAF No 41 Sqn, Coltishall	
XZ119	SEPECAT Jaguar GR1A [G]	RAF No 41 Sqn, Coltishall	
XZ129	HS Harrier GR3 [09]	RAF No 1 Sqn, Wittering	
XZ130	HS Harrier GR3 [H]	RAF No 3 Sqn, Gutersloh	
XZ131	HS Harrier GR3	RAF No 1417 Flt, Belize	
XZ132	HS Harrier GR3 [C]	RAF No 4 Sqn, Gutersloh	
XZ133	HS Harrier GR3 [10]	RAF No 1 Sqn, Wittering	
XZ135	HS Harrier GR3 [P] (8848M) (nose only)	RAF Exhibition Flight, Abingdon	
XZ138	HS Harrier GR3 [01]	RAF No 1 Sqn, Wittering	
XZ145	HS Harrier T4 [-]	RAF No 233 OCU, Wittering	
XZ146	HS Harrier T4 [W]	RAF No 233 OCU, Wittering	
XZ147	HS Harrier T4A [S]	RAF No 233 OCU, Wittering	
XZ170	WS Lynx AH7	MoD(PE) Westlands, Yeovil	
XZ171	WS Lynx AH1	MoD(PE) Rolls-Royce, Filton	
XZ172	WS Lynx AH1 [K]	AAC No 671 Sqn, Middle Wallop	
XZ173	WS Lynx AH1	AAC No 651 Sqn, Hildesheim	
XZ174	WS Lynx AH1	AAC No 651 Sqn, Hildesheim	
XZ175	WS Lynx AH1 [A]	AAC No 671 Sqn, Middle Wallop	
XZ176	WS Lynx AH1	AAC No 656 Sqn, Netheravon	
XZ177	WS Lynx AH1	AAC No 652 Sqn, Hildesheim	
XZ178	WS Lynx AH1	AAC No 659 Sqn, Detmold	
XZ179	WS Lynx AH1/5	MoD(PE) ETPS Boscombe Down	
XZ180	WS Lynx AH1	MoD(PE) stored, Wroughton	
XZ181	WS Lynx AH1	AAC Fleetlands	
XZ182	WS Lynx AH1	RM 3 CBAS, Yeovilton	
XZ183	WS Lynx AH1	AAC No 659 Sqn, Detmold	
XZ184	WS Lynx AH1	AAC No 659 Sqn, Detmold	
XZ185	WS Lynx AH1	AAC No 663 Sqn, Soest	
XZ186	WS Lynx AH1	AAC No 655 Sqn, Aldergrove	
XZ187	WS Lynx AH1	AAC No 655 Sqn, Aldergrove	
XZ188	WS Lynx AH1	AAC No 655 Sqn, Aldergrove	
XZ190	WS Lynx AH1	AAC No 651 Sqn, Hildesheim	
XZ191	WS Lynx AH1	AAC No 651 Sqn, Hildesheim	
XZ192	WS Lynx AH1	AAC Fleetlands	
XZ193	WS Lynx AH1	AAC No 656 Sqn, Netheravon	
XZ194	WS Lynx AH1	AAC No 653 Sqn, Soest	

Notes	Serial	Type (alternative identity)	Owner, Operator or Location
	XZ195	WS Lynx AH1	Westlands, Yeovil
	XZ196	WS Lynx AH1 [B]	AAC No 653 Sqn, Soest
	XZ197	WS Lynx AH1	AAC No 665 Sqn, Aldergrove
	XZ198	WS Lynx AH1	AAC No 656 Sqn, Netheravon
	XZ199	WS Lynx AH1 [C]	AAC No 653 Sqn, Soest
	XZ203	WS Lynx AH1 [B]	AAC No 671 Sqn, Middle Wallop
	XZ205	WS Lynx AH1	AAC Fleetlands
	XZ206	WS Lynx AH1	AAC No 657 Sqn, Oakington
	XZ207	WS Lynx AH1	AAC No 655 Sqn, Aldergrove
	XZ208	WS Lynx AH1	AAC No 657 Sqn, Oakington
	XZ209	WS Lynx AH1	AAC No 662 Sqn, Soest
	XZ210	WS Lynx AH1	AAC No 663 Sqn, Soest
	XZ211	WS Lynx AH1	AAC No 659 Sqn, Detmold
	XZ212	WS Lynx AH1	AAC No 656 Sqn, Netheravon
	XZ213	WS Lynx AH1 [TAD213]	AAC AETW, Middle Wallop
	XZ214	WS Lynx AH1	AAC 653 Sqn, Soest
	XZ215	WS Lynx AH1 [T]	RM 3CBAS, Yeovilton
	XZ216	WS Lynx AH1	AAC No 656 Sqn, Netheravon
	XZ217	WS Lynx AH1	AAC No 656 Sqn, Netheravon
	XZ218	WS Lynx AH1	AAC No 665 Sqn, Aldergrove
	XZ219	WS Lynx AH1	AAC No 662 Sqn, Soest
	XZ220	WS Lynx AH1	AAC No 669 Sqn, Detmold
	XZ221	WS Lynx AH1	AAC No 657 Sqn, Oakington
	XZ222	WS Lynx AH1	AAC D&TS, Middle Wallop
	XZ227	WS Lynx HAS3 [472/AM]	RN No 815 Sqn, Portland
	XZ228	WS Lynx HAS3 [405/LN]	RN No 829 Sqn, Portland
	XZ229	WS Lynx HAS3 [406]	RN No 829 Sqn, Portland
	XZ230	WS Lynx HAS3 [443/JP]	RN No 815 Sqn, Portland
	XZ231	WS Lynx HAS3 [417/NM]	RN No 815 Sqn, Portland
	XZ232	WS Lynx HAS3 [335/CF]	RN No 815 Sqn, Portland
	XZ233	WS Lynx HAS3 [435/ED]	RN No 829 Sqn, Portland
	XZ234	WS Lynx HAS3 [301]	RN No 815 Sqn, Portland
	XZ235	WS Lynx HAS3 [605]	RN No 829 Sqn, Portland
	XZ236	WS Lynx HAS8	MoD(PE) Westlands, Yeovil
	XZ237	WS Lynx HAS3 [603]	RN No 829 Sqn, Portland
	XZ238	WS Lynx HAS3 [645]	RN No 702 Sqn, Portland
	XZ239	WS Lynx HAS3 [330/BZ]	RN No 815 Sqn, Portland
	XZ240	WS Lynx HAS3 [344]	RN No 815 Sqn, Portland
	XZ241	WS Lynx HAS3 [604]	RN No 829 Sqn, Portland
	XZ243	WS Lynx HAS3 [635/PO]	*Ditched 10 March 1988*
	XZ244	WS Lynx HAS3 [374/VB]	RN No 829 Sqn, Portland
	XZ245	WS Lynx HAS3 [342]	RN No 829 Sqn, Portland
	XZ246	WS Lynx HAS3 [434/ED]	RN No 829 Sqn, Portland
	XZ248	WS Lynx HAS3 [345/NC]	RN No 815 Sqn, Portland
	XZ249	WS Lynx HAS2	RNEC Manadon for instruction
	XZ250	WS Lynx HAS3 [342]	RN No 829 Sqn, Portland
	XZ252	WS Lynx HAS3 [644]	RN No 702 Sqn, Portland
	XZ254	WS Lynx HAS3 [410/GC]	RN No 815 Sqn, Portland
	XZ255	WS Lynx HAS3 [450/SS]	RN No 829 Sqn, Portland
	XZ256	WS Lynx HAS3	RN MoD(PE) A&AEE, Boscombe Down
	XZ257	WS Lynx HAS3 [634]	RN No 702 Sqn, Portland
	XZ280	BAe Nimrod AEW3	RAF, stored Waddington
	XZ281	BAe Nimrod AEW3	RAF, stored Waddington
	XZ282	BAe Nimrod AEW3	RAF, stored Abingdon
	XZ283	BAe Nimrod AEW3	RAF, stored Waddington
	XZ284	HS Nimrod MR2	RAF No 42 Sqn, St Mawgan
	XZ285	BAe Nimrod AEW3	RAF, stored Abingdon
	XZ286	BAe Nimrod AEW3	RAF, stored Abingdon
	XZ287	BAe Nimrod AEW3	RAF, stored Abingdon
	XZ290	WS Gazelle AH1	AAC, stored Wroughton
	XZ291	WS Gazelle AH1	AAC No 12 Flt, Wildenrath
	XZ292	WS Gazelle AH1	AAC No 664 Sqn, Minden
	XZ294	WS Gazelle AH1	AAC No 664 Sqn, Minden
	XZ295	WS Gazelle AH1	AAC No 12 Flt, Wildenrath
	XZ296	WS Gazelle AH1	AAC No 663 Sqn, Soest
	XZ298	WS Gazelle AH1	AAC No 669 Sqn, Detmold
	XZ299	WS Gazelle AH1	AAC No 657 Sqn, Oakington
	XZ300	WS Gazelle AH1	AAC No 664 Sqn, Minden
	XZ301	WS Gazelle AH1	AAC No 664 Sqn, Minden
	XZ302	WS Gazelle AH1	AAC No 655 Sqn, Aldergrove
	XZ303	WS Gazelle AH1	AAC No 663 Sqn, Soest
	XZ304	WS Gazelle AH1	AAC No 664 Sqn, Minden
	XZ305	WS Gazelle AH1	AAC No 665 Sqn, Aldergrove
	XZ307	WS Gazelle AH1	AAC No 665 Sqn, Aldergrove

Serial	Type (alternative identity)	Owner, Operator or Location	Notes
XZ308	WS Gazelle AH1 [L]	AAC No 670 Sqn, Middle Wallop	
XZ309	WS Gazelle AH1	AAC No 664 Sqn, Minden	
XZ310	WS Gazelle AH1	AAC No 661 Sqn, Hildesheim	
XZ311	WS Gazelle AH1	AAC No 664 Sqn, Minden	
XZ312	WS Gazelle AH1	AAC No 2 Flt, Netheravon	
XZ313	WS Gazelle AH1	*Written off 23 October 1983*	
XZ314	WS Gazelle AH1	AAC No 656 Sqn, Netheravon	
XZ315	WS Gazelle AH1	AAC No 670 Sqn, Middle Wallop	
XZ316	WS Gazelle AH1 [R]	AAC No 670 Sqn, Middle Wallop	
XZ317	WS Gazelle AH1 [Q]	AAC No 670 Sqn, Middle Wallop	
XZ318	WS Gazelle AH1 [A]	AAC No 670 Sqn, Middle Wallop	
XZ319	WS Gazelle AH1 [S]	AAC No 670 Sqn, Middle Wallop	
XZ320	WS Gazelle AH1	MoD(PE) A&AEE, Boscombe Down	
XZ321	WS Gazelle AH1	AAC, stored Wroughton	
XZ322	WS Gazelle AH1 [N]	AAC No 670 Sqn, Middle Wallop	
XZ323	WS Gazelle AH1	AAC, stored Wroughton	
XZ324	WS Gazelle AH1	AAC, stored Wroughton	
XZ325	WS Gazelle AH1	AAC, stored Wroughton	
XZ326	WS Gazelle AH1 [C]	RM, stored Wroughton	
XZ327	WS Gazelle AH1	AAC, stored Wroughton	
XZ328	WS Gazelle AH1	AAC No 657 Sqn, Oakington	
XZ329	WS Gazelle AH1 [J]	AAC No 670 Sqn, Middle Wallop	
XZ330	WS Gazelle AH1	AAC No 663 Sqn, Soest	
XZ331	WS Gazelle AH1	AAC No 657 Sqn, Oakington	
XZ332	WS Gazelle AH1 [O]	AAC No 670 Sqn, Middle Wallop	
XZ333	WS Gazelle AH1 [A]	AAC No 670 Sqn, Middle Wallop	
XZ334	WS Gazelle AH1	AAC No 657 Sqn, Oakington	
XZ335	WS Gazelle AH1	AAC No 3 Flt, Topcliffe	
XZ336	WS Gazelle AH1	AAC No 3 Flt, Topcliffe	
XZ337	WS Gazelle AH1	AAC No 664 Sqn, Detmold	
XZ338	WS Gazelle AH1 [X]	AAC No 670 Sqn, Middle Wallop	
XZ339	WS Gazelle AH1	MoD(PE) Westlands, Weston-super-Mare	
XZ340	WS Gazelle AH1 [T]	AAC No 670 Sqn, Middle Wallop	
XZ341	WS Gazelle AH1	AAC D&TS, Middle Wallop	
XZ342	WS Gazelle AH1 [Z]	AAC No 663 Sqn, Soest	
XZ343	WS Gazelle AH1	AAC No 12 Flt, Wildenrath	
XZ344	WS Gazelle AH1	AAC No 3 Flt, Topcliffe	
XZ345	WS Gazelle AH1	AAC No 3 Flt, Topcliffe	
XZ346	WS Gazelle AH1	MoD(PE) A&AEE, Boscombe Down	
XZ347	WS Gazelle AH1	AAC No 3 Flt, Topcliffe	
XZ348	WS Gazelle AH1	AAC No 2 Flt, Netheravon	
XZ349	WS Gazelle AH1 [M]	AAC No 670 Sqn, Middle Wallop	
XZ355	SEPECAT Jaguar GR1A [J]	RAF No 41 Sqn, Coltishall	
XZ356	SEPECAT Jaguar GR1A [R]	RAF No 41 Sqn, Coltishall	
XZ357	SEPECAT Jaguar GR1A [K]	RAF No 41 Sqn, Coltishall	
XZ358	SEPECAT Jaguar GR1A [L]	RAF No 41 Sqn, Coltishall	
XZ359	SEPECAT Jaguar GR1A [M]	RAF No 41 Sqn, Coltishall	
XZ360	SEPECAT Jaguar GR1A [N]	RAF No 41 Sqn, Coltishall	
XZ361	SEPECAT Jaguar GR1A [25]	RAF No 2 Sqn, Laarbruch	
XZ362	SEPECAT Jaguar GR1A [27]	RAF No 2 Sqn, Laarbruch	
XZ363	SEPECAT Jaguar GR1A [A]	RAF No 41 Sqn, Coltishall	
XZ363	SEPECAT Jaguar GR1A Replica [A] (BAPC 151)	RAF Exhibition Flight, Abingdon	
XZ364	SEPECAT Jaguar GR1A [21]	RAF No 2 Sqn, Laarbruch	
XZ366	SEPECAT Jaguar GR1A [22]	RAF No 2 Sqn, Laarbruch	
XZ367	SEPECAT Jaguar GR1A [20]	RAF No 2 Sqn, Laarbruch	
XZ368	SEPECAT Jaguar GR1 [8900M] [AG]	RAF No 2 SoTT, Cosford	
XZ369	SEPECAT Jaguar GR1A [EE]	RAF No 6 Sqn, Coltishall	
XZ370	SEPECAT Jaguar GR1 [BN]	RAF, stored Shawbury	
XZ371	SEPECAT Jaguar GR1 (8907M) [AP]	RAF No 2 SoTT, Cosford	
XZ372	SEPECAT Jaguar GR1A [ED]	RAF No 6 Sqn, Coltishall	
XZ373	SEPECAT Jaguar GR1A [GF]	RAF No 54 Sqn, Coltishall	
XZ374	SEPECAT Jaguar GR1	RAF, stored Shawbury	
XZ375	SEPECAT Jaguar GR1A [GB]	RAF No 54 Sqn, Coltishall	
XZ377	SEPECAT Jaguar GR1A [GC]	RAF No 54 Sqn, Coltishall	
XZ378	SEPECAT Jaguar GR1A [EP]	RAF No 6 Sqn, Coltishall	
XZ381	SEPECAT Jaguar GR1 [BL]	RAF, stored Shawbury	
XZ382	SEPECAT Jaguar GR1 (8908M) [AE]	RAF No 1 SoTT, Halton	
XZ383	SEPECAT Jaguar GR1 (8901M) [AF]	RAF No 2 SoTT, Cosford	

Notes	Serial	Type (alternative identity)	Owner, Operator or Location
	XZ384	SEPECAT Jaguar GR1 [BC] (8954M)	RAF No 2 SoTT, Cosford
	XZ385	SEPECAT Jaguar GR1A [GM]	RAF No 54 Sqn, Coltishall
	XZ387	SEPECAT Jaguar GR1A	RAF, Coltishall
	XZ389	SEPECAT Jaguar GR1 [BL] (8946M)	RAF No 1 SoTT, Halton
	XZ390	SEPECAT Jaguar GR1A	RAF, stored Shawbury
	XZ391	SEPECAT Jaguar GR1A [GN]	RAF No 54 Sqn, Coltishall
	XZ392	SEPECAT Jaguar GR1A [GQ]	RAF No 54 Sqn, Coltishall
	XZ394	SEPECAT Jaguar GR1A [ES]	RAF No 6 Sqn, Coltishall
	XZ396	SEPECAT Jaguar GR1A [EM]	RAF No 6 Sqn, Coltishall
	XZ398	SEPECAT Jaguar GR1A [D] (JI007)	RAF No 41 Sqn, Coltishall
	XZ399	SEPECAT Jaguar GR1A [03]	RAF No 226 OCU, Lossiemouth
	XZ400	SEPECAT Jaguar GR1A [GH]	RAF No 54 Sqn, Coltishall
	XZ431	HS Buccaneer S2B	RAF No 208 Sqn, Lossiemouth
	XZ432	HS Buccaneer S2B	RAF No 237 OCU, Lossiemouth
	XZ439	BAe Sea Harrier FRS1 [2]	MoD(PE) BAe Dunsfold
	XZ440	BAe Sea Harrier FRS1 [126/L]	RN No 800 Sqn, Yeovilton
	XZ445	BAe Harrier T4A [722]	RN No 899 Sqn, Yeovilton
	XZ451	BAe Sea Harrier FRS1 [123-L]	RN, stored St Athan
	XZ455	BAe Sea Harrier FRS1 [712]	RN No 800 Sqn, Yeovilton
	XZ457	BAe Sea Harrier FRS1 [125-L]	RN No 899 Sqn, Yeovilton
	XZ459	BAe Sea Harrier FRS1 [717]	RN No 899 Sqn, Yeovilton
	XZ460	BAe Sea Harrier FRS1 [719]	RN No 899 Sqn, Yeovilton
	XZ492	BAe Sea Harrier FRS1 [128/L]	RN No 800 Sqn, Yeovilton
	XZ493	BAe Sea Harrier FRS1 [716]	RN No 899 Sqn, Yeovilton
	XZ494	BAe Sea Harrier FRS1 [004/R]	RN No 801 Sqn, Yeovilton
	XZ495	BAe Sea Harrier FRS1 [714]	RN No 899 Sqn, Yeovilton
	XZ497	BAe Sea Harrier FRS1	MoD(PE) BAe Dunsfold
	XZ498	BAe Sea Harrier FRS1 [001/R]	RN No 801 Sqn, Yeovilton
	XZ499	BAe Sea Harrier FRS1 [715]	RN No 899 Sqn, Yeovilton
	XZ550	Slingsby Venture T2	RAF No 642 VGS, Linton-on-Ouse
	XZ551	Slingsby Venture T2	RAF, stored Syerston
	XZ552	Slingsby Venture T2	RAF, stored Syerston
	XZ553	Slingsby Venture T2 [Q]	RAF No 663 VGS, Kinloss
	XZ554	Slingsby Venture T2	RAF No 633 VGS, Cosford
	XZ555	Slingsby Venture T2	RAF ACCGS, Syerston
	XZ556	Slingsby Venture T2 [56]	RAF ACCGS, Syerston
	XZ557	Slingsby Venture T2	RAF No 633 VGS, Cosford
	XZ558	Slingsby Venture T2 [8]	RAF No 624 VGS, Chivenor
	XZ559	Slingsby Venture T2 [3]	RAF No 1 MGSP, Halton
	XZ560	Slingsby Venture T2	RAF Syerston
	XZ561	Slingsby Venture T2 [1]	RAF No 632 VGS, Ternhill
	XZ562	Slingsby Venture T2	RAF ACCGS, Syerston
	XZ563	Slingsby Venture T2	RAF No 635 VGS, Samlesbury
	XZ564	Slingsby Venture T2 [4]	RAF No 663 VGS, Kinloss
	XZ570	WS61 Sea King HAS5 (mod)	MoD(PE) Westlands, Yeovil
	XZ571	WS61 Sea King HAS5 [136]	RN No 826 Sqn, Culdrose
	XZ574	WS61 Sea King HAS5 [506]	RN No 810 Sqn, Culdrose
	XZ575	WS61 Sea King HAS5 [599]	RN No 706 Sqn, Culdrose
	XZ576	WS61 Sea King HAS6 [411]	RN NASU, Culdrose
	XZ577	WS61 Sea King HAS5 [138]	RN No 826 Sqn, Culdrose
	XZ578	WS61 Sea King HAS5 [501]	RN No 810 Sqn, Culdrose
	XZ579	WS61 Sea King HAS5 [017/R]	RN No 820 Sqn, Culdrose
	XZ580	WS61 Sea King HAS5 [595]	RN No 706 Sqn, Culdrose
	XZ581	WS61 Sea King HAS6	MoD(PE) A&AEE/Westland Yeovil
	XZ582	WS61 Sea King HAS5 [264/L]	RN No 814 Sqn, Yeovilton
	XZ585	WS61 Sea King HAR3	RAF No 202 Sqn SAR*
	XZ586	WS61 Sea King HAR3 [S]	RAF No 202 Sqn SAR*
	XZ587	WS61 Sea King HAR3	RAF No 202 Sqn SAR*
	XZ588	WS61 Sea King HAR3	RAF No 202 Sqn SAR*
	XZ589	WS61 Sea King HAR3	RAF No 202 Sqn SAR*
	XZ590	WS61 Sea King HAR3	RAF No 202 Sqn SAR*
	XZ591	WS61 Sea King HAR3 [S]	RAF SKTU, RNAS Culdrose
	XZ592	WS61 Sea King HAR3 [S]	RAF No 78 Sqn, Mount Pleasant, Fl
	XZ593	WS61 Sea King HAR3	RAF No 202 Sqn SAR*
	XZ594	WS61 Sea King HAR3	RAF No 202 Sqn SAR*
	XZ595	WS61 Sea King HAR3	RAF No 202 Sqn SAR*
	XZ596	WS61 Sea King HAR3	RAF No 202 Sqn SAR*
	XZ597	WS61 Sea King HAR3	RAF SKTU, RNAS Culdrose
	XZ598	WS61 Sea King HAR3	RAF No 202 Sqn SAR*
	XZ599	WS61 Sea King HAR3 [S]	RAF No 202 Sqn SAR*
	XZ605	WS Lynx AH1 [X]	RM 3 CBAS, Yeovilton

Serial	Type (alternative identity)	Owner, Operator or Location	Notes
XZ606	WS Lynx AH1	RNAY Fleetlands	
XZ607	WS Lynx AH1	AAC No 669 Sqn, Detmold	
XZ608	WS Lynx AH1	AAC No 659 Sqn, Detmold	
XZ609	WS Lynx AH1	AAC, stored Wroughton	
XZ610	WS Lynx AH1	AAC No 654 Sqn, Detmold	
XZ611	WS Lynx AH1 [H]	AAC No 671 Sqn, Middle Wallop	
XZ612	WS Lynx AH1 [Y]	RM 3 CBAS, Yeovilton	
XZ613	WS Lynx AH1	AAC No 655 Sqn, Aldergrove	
XZ614	WS Lynx AH1	RM 3 CBAS, Yeovilton	
XZ615	WS Lynx AH1	RM 3 CBAS, Yeovilton	
XZ616	WS Lynx AH1	AAC, Fleetlands	
XZ617	WS Lynx AH7 [C]	AAC No 671 Sqn, Middle Wallop	
XZ630	Panavia Tornado (P12)	MoD(PE) BAe Warton	
XZ631	Panavia Tornado GR1T	MoD(PE) BAe Warton	
XZ641	WS Lynx AH7	AAC AETW, Middle Wallop	
XZ642	WS Lynx AH1	AAC No 663 Sqn, Soest	
XZ643	WS Lynx AH1	AAC No 663 Sqn, Soest	
XZ644	WS Lynx AH1	AAC No 657 Sqn, Oakington	
XZ645	WS Lynx AH1	AAC No 669 Sqn, Detmold	
XZ646	WS Lynx AH1	AAC No 654 Sqn, Detmold	
XZ647	WS Lynx AH1	AAC No 659 Sqn, Detmold	
XZ648	WS Lynx AH1 [D]	AAC No 671 Sqn, Middle Wallop	
XZ649	WS Lynx AH1 [L]	AAC No 671 Sqn, Middle Wallop	
XZ650	WS Lynx AH1	AAC No 659 Sqn, Detmold	
XZ651	WS Lynx AH1	AAC No 657 Sqn, Oakington	
XZ652	WS Lynx AH1	AAC No 659 Sqn, Detmold	
XZ653	WS Lynx AH1	AAC No 654 Sqn, Detmold	
XZ654	WS Lynx AH1	AAC No 654 Sqn, Detmold	
XZ655	WS Lynx AH1	AAC No 655 Sqn, Aldergrove	
XZ661	WS Lynx AH1	AAC No 652 Sqn, Hildesheim	
XZ662	WS Lynx AH1	AAC No 652 Sqn, Hildesheim	
XZ663	WS Lynx AH1	AAC No 659 Sqn, Detmold	
XZ664	WS Lynx AH1	AAC No 665 Sqn, Aldergrove	
XZ665	WS Lynx AH1	AAC No 665 Sqn, Aldergrove	
XZ666	WS Lynx AH1	AAC No 665 Sqn, Aldergrove	
XZ667	WS Lynx AH1 [B]	AAC No 653 Sqn, Soest	
XZ668	WS Lynx AH1 [C]	AAC No 663 Sqn, Soest	
XZ669	WS Lynx AH1 [D]	AAC No 663 Sqn, Soest	
XZ670	WS Lynx AH1 [E]	AAC No 663 Sqn, Soest	
XZ671	WS Lynx AH1	AAC, stored Wroughton	
XZ672	WS Lynx AH1	AAC No 659 Sqn, Detmold	
XZ673	WS Lynx AH1 [W]	AAC No 652 Sqn, Hildesheim	
XZ674	WS Lynx AH1	AAC No 652 Sqn, Hildesheim	
XZ675	WS Lynx AH1	AAC No 652 Sqn, Hildesheim	
XZ676	WS Lynx AH1	AAC No 656 Sqn, Netheravon	
XZ677	WS Lynx AH1	AAC No 651 Sqn, Hildesheim	
XZ678	WS Lynx AH1	AAC No 651 Sqn, Hildesheim	
XZ679	WS Lynx AH1	AAC No 651 Sqn, Hildesheim	
XZ680	WS Lynx AH1 [F]	AAC No 671 Sqn, Middle Wallop	
XZ681	WS Lynx AH1	AAC Middle Wallop, BDRT	
XZ689	WS Lynx HAS3 [411/EB]	RN No 815 Sqn, Portland	
XZ690	WS Lynx HAS3 [635/PO]	RN No 702 Sqn, Portland	
XZ691	WS Lynx HAS3 [322/AV]	RN No 815 Sqn, Portland	
XZ692	WS Lynx HAS3 [643]	RN No 702 Sqn, Portland	
XZ693	WS Lynx HAS3 [640]	RN No 702 Sqn, Portland	
XZ694	WS Lynx HAS3 [332]	RN No 815 Sqn, Portland	
XZ695	WS Lynx HAS3 [403/BX]	RN No 829 Sqn, Portland	
XZ696	WS Lynx HAS3 [475/HM]	RN No 815 Sqn, Portland	
XZ697	WS Lynx HAS3 [602]	RN No 829 Sqn, Portland	
XZ698	WS Lynx HAS3	RNAY Fleetlands	
XZ699	WS Lynx HAS3 [300]	RN No 815 Sqn, Portland	
XZ719	WS Lynx HAS3 [374]	RN No 829 Sqn, Portland	
XZ720	WS Lynx HAS3 [331/BZ]	RN No 829 Sqn, Portland	
XZ721	WS Lynx HAS3 [431]	RN No 829 Sqn, Portland	
XZ722	WS Lynx HAS3 [332]	RNAY Fleelands	
XZ723	WS Lynx HAS3 [454/PN]	RN No 829 Sqn, Portland	
XZ724	WS Lynx HAS3	RN No 829 Sqn, Portland	
XZ725	WS Lynx HAS3 [320/AZ]	RN No 815 Sqn, Portland	
XZ726	WS Lynx HAS3 [464/DN]	RN No 829 Sqn, Portland	
XZ727	WS Lynx HAS3 [305/PO]	RN No 815 Sqn, Portland	

Note: *The SAR Wing and SAREW are based at RAF Finningley, with the SKTU at RNAS Culdrose and with No 202 Sqn SAR detached flights: A Flt—RAF Boulmer; B Flt—RAF Brawdy; C Flt—RAF Manston; D Flt—RAF Lossiemouth; E Flt—RAF Leconfield.

Notes	Serial	Type (alternative identity)	Owner, Operator or Location
	XZ728	WS Lynx HAS3 [432/SC]	RN No 829 Sqn, Portland
	XZ729	WS Lynx HAS3 [471/PB]	RN No 829 Sqn, Portland
	XZ730	WS Lynx HAS3 [341/AG]	RN No 815 Sqn, Portland
	XZ731	WS Lynx HAS3 [641]	RN No 702 Sqn, Portland
	XZ732	WS Lynx HAS3 [601]	RN No 829 Sqn, Portland
	XZ733	WS Lynx HAS3 [334/SN]	RN No 815 Sqn, Portland
	XZ734	WS Lynx HAS3 [360/MC]	RN No 815 Sqn, Portland
	XZ735	WS Lynx HAS3 [301]	RN No 815 Sqn, Portland
	XZ736	WS Lynx HAS3 [424/MV]	RN No 829 Sqn, Portland
	XZ916	WS61 Sea King HAS5 [130]	Ditched 13 October 1988 off Plymouth
	XZ918	WS61 Sea King HAS5	RN Fleetlands
	XZ920	WS61 Sea King HAR5 [822]	RN No 771 Sqn, Culdrose
	XZ921	WS61 Sea King HAS5 [593/R]	RN No 706 Sqn, Culdrose
	XZ922	WS61 Sea King HAS5 [500]	RN No 810 Sqn, Culdrose
	XZ930	WS Gazelle HT3 [Q]	RAF No 2 FTS, Shawbury
	XZ931	WS Gazelle HT3 [R]	RAF No 2 FTS, Shawbury
	XZ932	WS Gazelle HT3 [S]	RAF No 2 FTS, Shawbury
	XZ933	WS Gazelle HT3 [T]	RAF No 2 FTS, Shawbury
	XZ934	WS Gazelle HT3 [U]	RAF No 2 FTS, Shawbury
	XZ935	WS Gazelle HT3	RAF No 32 Sqn, Northolt
	XZ936	WS Gazelle HT3	MoD(PE) ETPS Boscombe Down
	XZ937	WS Gazelle HT3 [Y]	RAF No 2 FTS, Shawbury
	XZ938	WS Gazelle HT2 [45/CU]	RN No 705 Sqn, Culdrose
	XZ939	WS Gazelle HT3 [Z]	MoD(PE) ETPS, Boscombe Down
	XZ940	WS Gazelle HT3 [O]	RAF No 2 FTS, Shawbury
	XZ941	WS Gazelle HT3 [B]	RAF No 2 FTS, Shawbury
	XZ942	WS Gazelle HT2 [42/CU]	RN No 705 Sqn, Culdrose
	XZ964	BAe Harrier GR3 [D]	RAF No 1417 Flt, Belize
	XZ965	BAe Harrier GR3 [M]	RAF No 3 Sqn, Gutersloh
	XZ966	BAe Harrier GR3 [K]	RAF No 4 Sqn, Gutersloh
	XZ967	BAe Harrier GR3 [B]	RAF No 3 Sqn, Gutersloh
	XZ968	BAe Harrier GR3 [F]	RAF No 1417 Flt, Belize
	XZ969	BAe Harrier GR3	RAF No 4 Sqn, Gutersloh
	XZ970	BAe Harrier GR3 [R]	RAF No 3 Sqn, Gutersloh
	XZ971	BAe Harrier GR3 [G]	RAF No 1417 Flt, Belize
	XZ987	BAe Harrier GR3 [O]	RAF No 4 Sqn, Gutersloh
	XZ990	BAe Harrier GR3 [A]	RAF No 3 Sqn, Gutersloh
	XZ991	BAe Harrier GR3 [C]	RAF No 3 Sqn, Gutersloh
	XZ993	BAe Harrier GR3 [11]	RAF No 1 Sqn, Wittering
	XZ994	BAe Harrier GR3 [C]	RAF No 233 OCU, Wittering
	XZ995	BAe Harrier GR3 [J]	RAF No 3 Sqn, Gutersloh
	XZ996	BAe Harrier GR3 [X]	RAF No 4 Sqn, Gutersloh
	XZ997	BAe Harrier GR3 [J]	RAF No 233 OCU, Wittering
	XZ998	BAe Harrier GR3 [C]	RAF No 1417 Flt, Belize
	XZ999	BAe Harrier GR3 [H]	RAF No 4 Sqn, Gutersloh
	ZA101	BAe Hawk 100 (G-HAWK/XX155)	BAe Dunsfold
	ZA105	WS61 Sea King HAR3 [S]	RAF No 78 Sqn, Mount Pleasant, Fl
	ZA110	BAe Jetstream T2 [573/CU] (G-AXUO)	RN No 750 Sqn, Culdrose
	ZA111	BAe Jetstream T2 [574/CU] (G-AXFV)	RN No 750 Sqn, Culdrose
	ZA126	WS61 Sea King HAS5 [591/R]	RN No 706 Sqn, Culdrose
	ZA127	WS61 Sea King HAS5 [504]	RN No 810 Sqn, Culdrose
	ZA128	WS61 Sea King HAS5 [598]	RN No 706 Sqn, Culdrose
	ZA129	WS61 Sea King HAS6	RNAY Fleetlands
	ZA130	WS61 Sea King HAS5 [253]	RN No 824 Sqn, Prestwick
	ZA131	WS61 Sea King HAS5 [133]	RN No 826 Sqn, Culdrose
	ZA133	WS61 Sea King HAS6 [254]	RN No 824 Sqn, Prestwick
	ZA134	WS61 Sea King HAS6 [252]	RN No 824 Sqn, Prestwick
	ZA135	WS61 Sea King HAS5 [505]	RN No 810 Sqn, Culdrose
	ZA136	WS61 Sea King HAS6 [251]	RN No 824 Sqn, Prestwick
	ZA137	WS61 Sea King HAS5 [137]	RN No 826 Sqn, Culdrose
	ZA140	BAe VC10 K2 (G-ARVL) [A]	RAF No 101 Sqn, Brize Norton
	ZA141	BAe VC10 K2 (G-ARVG) [B]	RAF No 101 Sqn, Brize Norton
	ZA142	BAe VC10 K2 (G-ARVI) [C]	RAF No 101 Sqn, Brize Norton
	ZA143	BAe VC10 K2 (G-ARVK) [D]	RAF No 101 Sqn, Brize Norton
	ZA144	BAe VC10 K2 (G-ARVC) [E]	RAF No 101 Sqn, Brize Norton
	ZA147	BAe VC10 K3 (5H-MMT) [F]	RAF No 101 Sqn, Brize Norton
	ZA148	BAe VC10 K3 (5Y-ADA) [G]	RAF No 101 Sqn, Brize Norton
	ZA149	BAe VC10 K3 (5X-UVJ) [H]	RAF No 101 Sqn, Brize Norton
	ZA150	BAe VC10 K3 (5H-MOG) [J]	RAF No 101 Sqn, Brize Norton
	ZA166	WS61 Sea King HAS5 [590]	RN No 706 Sqn, Culdrose
	ZA167	WS61 Sea King HAS5 [265/L]	RN No 814 Sqn, Culdrose

Serial	Type (alternative identity)	Owner, Operator or Location	Notes
ZA168	WS61 Sea King HAS5 [271/L]	RN No 814 Sqn, Culdrose	
ZA169	WS61 Sea King HAS5 [587]	RN No 706 Sqn, Culdrose	
ZA170	WS61 Sea King HAS5 [584]	RN No 706 Sqn, Culdrose	
ZA175	BAe Sea Harrier FRS1 [713]	RN No 899 Sqn, Yeovilton	
ZA176	BAe Sea Harrier FRS1 [007/R]	RN No 801 Sqn, Yeovilton	
ZA191	BAe Sea Harrier FRS1 [129/L]	RN No 800 Sqn, Yeovilton	
ZA193	BAe Sea Harrier FRS1 [003/R]	RN No 801 Sqn, Yeovilton	
ZA195	BAe Sea Harrier FRS2	MoD(PE) BAe Dunsfold	
ZA250	BAe Harrier T52 (G-VTOL)	BAe Dunsfold	
ZA254	Panavia Tornado F2	MoD(PE) BAe Warton/A&AEE Boscombe Down	
ZA267	Panavia Tornado F2T	MoD(PE) A&AEE Boscombe Down	
ZA283	Panavia Tornado F2	MoD(PE) BAe Warton/A&AEE Boscombe Down	
ZA291	WS61 Sea King HC4 [VO]	RN No 846 Sqn, Yeovilton	
ZA292	WS61 Sea King HC4 [E]	RN No 845 Sqn, Yeovilton	
ZA293	WS61 Sea King HC4	RN stored, Wroughton	
ZA295	WS61 Sea King HC4 [ZU]	RN No 707 Sqn, Yeovilton	
ZA296	WS61 Sea King HC4 [VK]	RN No 846 Sqn, Yeovilton	
ZA297	WS61 Sea King HC4 [F]	RN No 845 Sqn, Yeovilton	
ZA298	WS61 Sea King HC4 [VN] (G-BJNM)	RN No 846 Sqn, Yeovilton	
ZA299	WS61 Sea King HC4 [ZV]	RN No 707 Sqn, Yeovilton	
ZA310	WS61 Sea King HC4 [VQ]	RN No 846 Sqn, Yeovilton	
ZA312	WS61 Sea King HC4 [ZT]	RN No 707 Sqn, Yeovilton	
ZA313	WS61 Sea King HC4 [VR]	RN No 846 Sqn, Yeovilton	
ZA314	WS61 Sea King HC4 [ZI]	RN No 707 Sqn, Yeovilton	
ZA319	Panavia Tornado GR1T [B-11]	RAF TTTE, Cottesmore	
ZA320	Panavia Tornado GR1T [B-01]	RAF TTTE, Cottesmore	
ZA321	Panavia Tornado GR1 [B-58]	RAF TTTE, Cottesmore	
ZA322	Panavia Tornado GR1	RAF TWCU/45 Sqn, Honington	
ZA323	Panavia Tornado GR1T [B-14]	RAF TTTE, Cottesmore	
ZA324	Panavia Tornado GR1T [B-02]	RAF TTTE, Cottesmore	
ZA325	Panavia Tornado GR1T [B-03]	RAF TTTE, Cottesmore	
ZA326	Panavia Tornado GR1T	MoD(PE) RAE Bedford	
ZA327	Panavia Tornado GR1 [B-51]	RAF TTTE, Cottesmore	
ZA328	Panavia Tornado GR1	MoD(PE) BAe Warton	
ZA329	Panavia Tornado GR1 [B-52]	Crashed 9 August 1988 nr Appleby	
ZA330	Panavia Tornado GR1T [B-08]	RAF TTTE, Cottesmore	
ZA352	Panavia Tornado GR1T [B-04]	RAF TTTE, Cottesmore	
ZA353	Panavia Tornado GR1	RAF Marham	
ZA354	Panavia Tornado GR1	MoD(PE) BAe Warton	
ZA355	Panavia Tornado GR1 [B-54]	RAF TTTE, Cottesmore	
ZA356	Panavia Tornado GR1T [B-07]	RAF TTTE, Cottesmore	
ZA357	Panavia Tornado GR1T [B-05]	RAF TTTE, Cottesmore	
ZA358	Panavia Tornado GR1T [B-06]	RAF TTTE, Cottesmore	
ZA359	Panavia Tornado GR1	RAF No 617 Sqn, Marham	
ZA360	Panavia Tornado GR1 [17]	RAF No 27 Sqn, Marham	
ZA361	Panavia Tornado GR1 [B-57]	RAF TTTE, Cottesmore	
ZA362	Panavia Tornado GR1T [B-09]	RAF TTTE, Cottesmore	
ZA365	Panavia Tornado GR1T [GZ]	RAF No 20 Sqn, Laarbruch	
ZA367	Panavia Tornado GR1T	RAF TWCU/45 Sqn, Honington	
ZA368	Panavia Tornado GR1T	RAF TWCU/45 Sqn, Honington	
ZA369	Panavia Tornado GR1A [GO]	RAF No 20 Sqn, Laarbruch	
ZA370	Panavia Tornado GR1A [15]	RAF No 27 Sqn, Marham	
ZA371	Panavia Tornado GR1 [GF]	RAF No 20 Sqn, Laarbruch	
ZA372	Panavia Tornado GR1A	RAF TWCU/45 Sqn, Honington	
ZA373	Panavia Tornado GR1A [BR-60]	RAF TTTE, Cottesmore	
ZA374	Panavia Tornado GR1	RAF TWCU/45 Sqn, Honington	
ZA375	Panavia Tornado GR1	RAF TWCU/45 Sqn, Honington	
ZA376	Panavia Tornado GR1 [E]	MoD(PE) SAOEU Boscombe Down	
ZA392	Panavia Tornado GR1 [EK]	RAF No 15 Sqn, Laarbruch	
ZA393	Panavia Tornado GR1	RAF TWCU/45 Sqn, Honington	
ZA394	Panavia Tornado GR1A [I]	RAF No 2 Sqn, Laarbruch	
ZA395	Panavia Tornado GR1A [FP]	RAF No 16 Sqn, Laarbruch	
ZA396	Panavia Tornado GR1 [GE]	RAF No 20 Sqn, Laarbruch	
ZA397	Panavia Tornado GR1A [DM]	RAF No 31 Sqn, Bruggen	
ZA398	Panavia Tornado GR1A [DN]	RAF No 31 Sqn, Bruggen	
ZA399	Panavia Tornado GR1 [GA]	RAF No 20 Sqn, Laarbruch	
ZA400	Panavia Tornado GR1A [BM]	RAF No 14 Sqn, Bruggen	
ZA401	Panavia Tornado GR1 [GJ]	RAF No 20 Sqn, Laarbruch	
ZA402	Panavia Tornado GR1	BAe Warton	
ZA403	Panavia Tornado GR1	BAe Warton	
ZA404	Panavia Tornado GR1A	RAF TWCU/45 Sqn, Honington	

Notes	Serial	Type (alternative identity)	Owner, Operator or Location
	ZA405	Panavia Tornado GR1A [BR-62]	RAF TTTE, Cottesmore
	ZA406	Panavia Tornado GR1A [15]	RAF No 27 Sqn, Marham
	ZA407	Panavia Tornado GR1	RAF TWCU/45 Sqn, Honington
	ZA409	Panavia Tornado GR1T	RAF TWCU/45 Sqn, Honington
	ZA410	Panavia Tornado GR1T [EX]	RAF No 15 Sqn, Laarbruch
	ZA411	Panavia Tornado GR1T [GY]	RAF No 20 Sqn, Laarbruch
	ZA412	Panavia Tornado GR1T [GT]	RAF
	ZA446	Panavia Tornado GR1 [EF]	RAF No 15 Sqn, Laarbruch
	ZA447	Panavia Tornado GR1 [EA]	RAF No 15 Sqn, Laarbruch
	ZA448	Panavia Tornado GR1 [EB]	Crashed 30 March 1988, Nellis, USA
	ZA449	Panavia Tornado GR1	BAe Warton
	ZA450	Panavia Tornado GR1 [EC]	RAF No 15 Sqn, Laarbruch
	ZA452	Panavia Tornado GR1 [GK]	RAF No 20 Sqn, Laarbruch
	ZA453	Panavia Tornado GR1 [EG]	RAF No 15 Sqn, Laarbruch
	ZA454	Panavia Tornado GR1 [EH]	RAF No 15 Sqn, Laarbruch
	ZA455	Panavia Tornado GR1 [EJ]	RAF No 15 Sqn, Laarbruch
	ZA456	Panavia Tornado GR1 [GB]	RAF No 20 Sqn, Laarbruch
	ZA457	Panavia Tornado GR1 [AJ]	RAF No 9 Sqn, Bruggen
	ZA458	Panavia Tornado GR1 [FB]	RAF No 16 Sqn, Laarbruch
	ZA459	Panavia Tornado GR1 [EL]	RAF No 15 Sqn, Laarbruch
	ZA460	Panavia Tornado GR1 [FD]	RAF No 16 Sqn, Laarbruch
	ZA461	Panavia Tornado GR1 [AM]	RAF No 9 Sqn, Bruggen
	ZA462	Panavia Tornado GR1 [EM]	RAF No 15 Sqn, Laarbruch
	ZA463	Panavia Tornado GR1 [GL]	RAF No 20 Sqn, Laarbruch
	ZA464	Panavia Tornado GR1 [GM]	RAF No 20 Sqn, Laarbruch
	ZA465	Panavia Tornado GR1 [FK]	RAF No 16 Sqn, Laarbruch
	ZA466	Panavia Tornado GR1 [FH]	RAF No 16 Sqn, Laarbruch
	ZA467	Panavia Tornado GR1 [FF]	RAF No 16 Sqn, Laarbruch
	ZA468	Panavia Tornado GR1 [EN]	RAF No 15 Sqn, Laarbruch
	ZA469	Panavia Tornado GR1 [GD]	RAF No 20 Sqn, Laarbruch
	ZA470	Panavia Tornado GR1 [FL]	RAF No 16 Sqn, Laarbruch
	ZA471	Panavia Tornado GR1 [FJ]	RAF No 16 Sqn, Laarbruch
	ZA472	Panavia Tornado GR1 [EE]	RAF No 15 Sqn, Laarbruch
	ZA473	Panavia Tornado GR1 [FM]	RAF No 16 Sqn, Laarbruch
	ZA474	Panavia Tornado GR1 [FG]	RAF No 16 Sqn, Laarbruch
	ZA475	Panavia Tornado GR1 [FC]	RAF No 16 Sqn, Laarbruch
	ZA490	Panavia Tornado GR1 [GG]	RAF No 20 Sqn, Laarbruch
	ZA491	Panavia Tornado GR1 [GC]	RAF No 20 Sqn, Laarbruch
	ZA492	Panavia Tornado GR1 [FE]	RAF No 16 Sqn, Laarbruch
	ZA494	Panavia Tornado GR1 [15]	RAF Honington, Fire Section
	ZA540	Panavia Tornado GR1T	RAF TWCU/45 Sqn, Honington
	ZA541	Panavia Tornado GR1T	RAF TWCU/45 Sqn, Honington
	ZA542	Panavia Tornado GR1 [04]	RAF No 27 Sqn, Marham
	ZA543	Panavia Tornado GR1	RAF TWCU/45 Sqn, Honington
	ZA544	Panavia Tornado GR1T [BX]	RAF No 14 Sqn, Bruggen
	ZA545	Panavia Tornado GR1	RAF TWCU/45 Sqn, Honington
	ZA546	Panavia Tornado GR1 [05]	RAF No 27 Sqn, Marham
	ZA547	Panavia Tornado GR1 [03]	RAF No 27 Sqn, Marham
	ZA548	Panavia Tornado GR1T [ML]	RAF No 617 Sqn, Marham
	ZA549	Panavia Tornado GR1T [08]	RAF No 27 Sqn, Marham
	ZA550	Panavia Tornado GR1 [16]	RAF No 27 Sqn, Marham
	ZA551	Panavia Tornado GR1T [MT]	RAF No 617 Sqn, Marham
	ZA552	Panavia Tornado GR1T [FZ]	RAF No 16 Sqn, Laarbruch
	ZA553	Panavia Tornado GR1 [01]	RAF No 27 Sqn, Marham
	ZA554	Panavia Tornado GR1 [11]	RAF No 27 Sqn, Marham
	ZA555	Panavia Tornado GR1T (remains)	RAF Honington
	ZA556	Panavia Tornado GR1	RAF TWCU/45 Sqn, Honington
	ZA557	Panavia Tornado GR1 [12]	RAF No 27 Sqn, Marham
	ZA559	Panavia Tornado GR1	RAF TWCU/45 Sqn, Honington
	ZA560	Panavia Tornado GR1	RAF TWCU/45 Sqn, Honington
	ZA561	Panavia Tornado GR1 [02]	RAF No 27 Sqn, Marham
	ZA562	Panavia Tornado GR1T [06]	RAF No 27 Sqn, Marham
	ZA563	Panavia Tornado GR1 [10]	RAF No 27 Sqn, Marham
	ZA564	Panavia Tornado GR1 [14]	RAF No 27 Sqn, Marham
	ZA585	Panavia Tornado GR1 [MG]	RAF No 617 Sqn, Marham
	ZA587	Panavia Tornado GR1	RAF TWCU/45 Sqn, Honington
	ZA588	Panavia Tornado GR1	RAF TWCU/45 Sqn, Honington
	ZA589	Panavia Tornado GR1	RAF TWCU/45 Sqn, Honington
	ZA590	Panavia Tornado GR1	RAF TWCU/45 Sqn, Honington
	ZA591	Panavia Tornado GR1	RAF No 617 Sqn, Marham
	ZA592	Panavia Tornado GR1 [B]	RAF No 617 Sqn, Marham
	ZA593	Panavia Tornado GR1 [MF]	Crashed nr Appleby 9 August 1988
	ZA594	Panavia Tornado GR1T [EY]	RAF No 15 Sqn, Laarbruch
	ZA595	Panavia Tornado GR1T	RAF TWCU/45 Sqn, Honington

Serial	Type (alternative identity)	Owner, Operator or Location	Notes
ZA596	Panavia Tornado GR1	RAF TWCU/45 Sqn, Honington	
ZA597	Panavia Tornado GR1 [M]	RAF/BAe Warton	
ZA598	Panavia Tornado GR1T [MS]	RAF No 617 Sqn, Marham	
ZA599	Panavia Tornado GR1T	RAF TWCU/45 Sqn, Honington	
ZA600	Panavia Tornado GR1 [07]	RAF No 27 Sqn, Marham	
ZA600	Panavia Tornado GR1 Replica (BAPC 155)	RAF Exhibition Flight, Abingdon	
ZA601	Panavia Tornado GR1 [MM]	RAF No 617 Sqn, Marham	
ZA602	Panavia Tornado GR1T [AZ]	RAF No 9 Sqn, Bruggen	
ZA604	Panavia Tornado GR1T	RAF TWCU/45 Sqn, Honington	
ZA606	Panavia Tornado GR1 [09]	RAF No 27 Sqn, Marham	
ZA607	Panavia Tornado GR1 [MP]	RAF No 617 Sqn, Marham	
ZA608	Panavia Tornado GR1	RAF No 617 Sqn, Marham	
ZA609	Panavia Tornado GR1 [MJ]	RAF No 617 Sqn, Marham	
ZA611	Panavia Tornado GR1 [A]	RAF No 617 Sqn, Marham	
ZA612	Panavia Tornado GR1T [CX]	RAF No 17 Sqn, Bruggen	
ZA613	Panavia Tornado GR1 [N]	RAF No 617 Sqn, Marham	
ZA614	Panavia Tornado GR1 [E]	RAF No 617 Sqn, Marham	
ZA625	Slingsby Venture T2 [1]	RAF 616 VGS, Henlow	
ZA626	Slingsby Venture T2 [C]	RAF No 624 VGS, Chivenor	
ZA627	Slingsby Venture T2	RAF 613 VGS, Halton	
ZA628	Slingsby Venture T2 [B]	RAF 637 VGS, Little Rissington	
ZA629	Slingsby Venture T2 [9]	RAF No 664 VGS, Bishops Court, NI	
ZA630	Slingsby Venture T2	RAF 616 VGS, Henlow	
ZA631	Slingsby Venture T2 [1]	RAF ACCGS, Syerston	
ZA632	Slingsby Venture T2 [2]	RAF No 632 VGS, Ternhill	
ZA633	Slingsby Venture T2 [3]	RAF No 616 VGS, Henlow	
ZA634	Slingsby Venture T2 [C]	RAF No 635 VGS, Samlesbury	
ZA652	Slingsby Venture T2	RAF ACCGS, Syerston	
ZA653	Slingsby Venture T2 [3]	RAF No 612 VGS, Benson	
ZA654	Slingsby Venture T2 [D]	RAF, stored Syerston	
ZA655	Slingsby Venture T2 [V]	RAF No 644 VGS, Syerston	
ZA656	Slingsby Venture T2 [6]	RAF Halton	
ZA657	Slingsby Venture T2	RAF No 644 VGS, Syerston	
ZA658	Slingsby Venture T2	RAF ACCGS/644 VGS, Syerston	
ZA659	Slingsby Venture T2	RAF No 642 VGS, Linton-on-Ouse	
ZA660	Slingsby Venture T2 [6]	RAF No 612 VGS, Benson	
ZA661	Slingsby Venture T2 [3]	RAF No 637 VGS, Little Rissington	
ZA662	Slingsby Venture T2 [62]	RAF No 633 VGS, Cosford	
ZA663	Slingsby Venture T2 [3]	RAF ACCGS, Syerston	
ZA664	Slingsby Venture T2 [X]	RAF, stored Syerston	
ZA665	Slingsby Venture T2	RAF No 637 VGS, Little Rissington	
ZA666	Slingsby Venture T2 [6]	RAF No 613 VGS, Halton	
ZA670	B-V Chinook HC1 [BG]	RAF No 18 Sqn, Gutersloh	
ZA671	B-V Chinook HC1 [EO]	RAF No 7 Sqn, Odiham	
ZA672	B-V Chinook HC1 [BH]	Written off 6 May 1988 at Hannover	
ZA673	B-V Chinook HC1 [FF]	RAF No 240 OCU, Odiham	
ZA674	B-V Chinook HC1 [BA]	MoD(PE) A&AEE, Boscombe Down	
ZA675	B-V Chinook HC1 [BB]	RAF No 18 Sqn, Gutersloh	
ZA676	B-V Chinook HC1 [FG]	RAF, stored Wroughton	
ZA677	B-V Chinook HC1 [EU]	RAF No 7 Sqn, Odiham	
ZA678	B-V Chinook HC1 [EZ]	RAF No 7 Sqn, Odiham	
ZA679	B-V Chinook HC1	RAF No 18 Sqn, Gutersloh	
ZA680	B-V Chinook HC1 [T]	RAF No 78 Sqn, Mount Pleasant, FI	
ZA681	B-V Chinook HC1 [ES]	RAF No 7 Sqn, Odiham	
ZA682	B-V Chinook HC1	RAF No 18 Sqn, Gutersloh	
ZA683	B-V Chinook HC1 [EW]	RAF No 7 Sqn, Odiham	
ZA684	B-V Chinook HC1 [EL]	RAF No 7 Sqn, Odiham	
ZA704	B-V Chinook HC1	RAF No 18 Sqn, Gutersloh	
ZA705	B-V Chinook HC1 [EK]	RAF No 7 Sqn, Gutersloh	
ZA707	B-V Chinook HC1 [EV]	RAF No 7 Sqn, Odiham	
ZA708	B-V Chinook HC1	RAF Fleetlands	
ZA709	B-V Chinook HC1 [F]	RAF No 78 Sqn, Mount Pleasant, FI	
ZA710	B-V Chinook HC1 [EY]	RAF No 7 Sqn, Odiham	
ZA711	B-V Chinook HC1 [ET]	RAF No 7 Sqn, Odiham	
ZA712	B-V Chinook HC1 [ER]	RAF No 7 Sqn, Odiham	
ZA713	B-V Chinook HC1 [EN]	RAF No 7 Sqn, Odiham	
ZA714	B-V Chinook HC1 [EX]	RAF No 7 Sqn, Odiham	
ZA717	B-V Chinook HC1 [EM]	RAF No 7 Sqn, Odiham	
ZA718	B-V Chinook HC1 [EQ]	RAF No 7 Sqn, Odiham	
ZA720	B-V Chinook HC1 [EP]	RAF No 7 Sqn, Odiham	
ZA726	WS Gazelle AH1	AAC No 663 Sqn, Soest	
ZA728	WS Gazelle AH1 [E]	RM 3 CBAS, Yeovilton	
ZA729	WS Gazelle AH1	AAC No 661 Sqn, Detmold	

Notes	Serial	Type (alternative identity)	Owner, Operator or Location
	ZA730	WS Gazelle AH1 [F]	RM, stored Wroughton
	ZA731	WS Gazelle AH1 [C]	AAC No 29 Flt, Suffield, Canada
	ZA733	WS Gazelle AH1	AAC No 665 Sqn, Aldergrove
	ZA734	WS Gazelle AH1	AAC No 25 Flt, Belize
	ZA735	WS Gazelle AH1	AAC No 25 Flt, Belize
	ZA736	WS Gazelle AH1 [A]	AAC No 29 Flt, Suffield, Canada
	ZA737	WS Gazelle AH1 [V]	AAC No 670 Sqn, Middle Wallop
	ZA765	WS Gazelle AH1	AAC No 25 Flt, Belize
	ZA766	WS Gazelle AH1	AAC No 663 Sqn, Soest
	ZA767	WS Gazelle AH1	AAC No 25 Flt, Belize
	ZA768	WS Gazelle AH1 [F]	AAC No 670 Sqn, Middle Wallop
	ZA769	WS Gazelle AH1 [K]	AAC No 670 Sqn, Middle Wallop
	ZA771	WS Gazelle AH1 [Z]	AAC No 670 Sqn, Middle Wallop
	ZA772	WS Gazelle AH1	AAC No 656 Sqn, Netheravon
	ZA773	WS Gazelle AH1	AAC No 665 Sqn, Aldergrove
	ZA774	WS Gazelle AH1	AAC No 655 Sqn, Aldergrove
	ZA775	WS Gazelle AH1	AAC No 656 Sqn, Netheravon
	ZA776	WS Gazelle AH1 [F]	RM 3 CBAS, Yeovilton
	ZA777	WS Gazelle AH1	AAC No 661 Sqn, Hildesheim
	ZA801	WS Gazelle HT3 [V]	Scrapped at RAF Abingdon
	ZA802	WS Gazelle HT3 [W]	RAF No 2 FTS, Shawbury
	ZA803	WS Gazelle HT3 [X]	RAF No 2 FTS, Shawbury
	ZA804	WS Gazelle HT3 [I]	RAF No 2 FTS, Shawbury
	ZA934	WS Puma HC1 [FC]	RAF No 240 OCU, Odiham
	ZA935	WS Puma HC1 [CT]	RAF No 33 Sqn, Odiham
	ZA936	WS Puma HC1 [CU]	RAF No 1563 Flt, Belize
	ZA937	WS Puma HC1 [CV]	RAF No 33 Sqn, Odiham
	ZA938	WS Puma HC1 [CW]	RAF No 33 Sqn, Odiham
	ZA939	WS Puma HC1 [CX]	RAF No 1563 Flt, Belize
	ZA940	WS Puma HC1 [CY]	RAF No 33 Sqn, Odiham
	ZA941	WS Puma HC1	MoD(PE) RAE Farnborough
	ZA947	Douglas Dakota C3	MoD(PE) RAE Farnborough
	ZB500	WS Lynx (G-LYNX) (ZA500)	Reverted to G-LYNX
	ZB506	WS61 Sea King Mk 4X	MoD(PE) RAE Bedford
	ZB507	WS61 Sea King Mk 4X	MoD(PE) RAE Farnborough
	ZB600	BAe Harrier T4 [Z]	RAF No 233 OCU, Wittering
	ZB601	BAe Harrier T4 [Y]	RAF No 233 OCU, Wittering
	ZB602	BAe Harrier T4 [R]	RAF No 233 OCU, Wittering
	ZB603	BAe Harrier T4 [Q]	RAF No 233 OCU, Wittering
	ZB604	BAe Harrier T4N [720]	RN No 899 Sqn, Yeovilton
	ZB605	BAe Harrier T4N [721]	RN No 899 Sqn, Yeovilton
	ZB615	SEPECAT Jaguar T2	MoD(PE) IAM Farnborough
	ZB625	WS Gazelle HT3 [N]	RAF No 2 FTS, Shawbury
	ZB626	WS Gazelle HT3 [L]	RAF No 2 FTS, Shawbury
	ZB627	WS Gazelle HT3 [A]	RAF No 2 FTS, Shawbury
	ZB628	WS Gazelle HT3 [V]	RAF No 2 FTS, Shawbury
	ZB629	WS Gazelle HT3	RAF No 32 Sqn, Northolt
	ZB646	WS Gazelle HT2	MoD(PE) RAE Farnborough
	ZB647	WS Gazelle HT2 [CU]	RN, stored Wroughton
	ZB648	WS Gazelle HT2	RN, stored Wroughton
	ZB649	WS Gazelle HT2	RN FONAC, Yeovilton
	ZB665	WS Gazelle AH1	AAC, stored Wroughton
	ZB666	WS Gazelle AH1 [G]	AAC No 670 Sqn, Middle Wallop
	ZB667	WS Gazelle AH1	AAC No 664 Sqn, Detmold
	ZB668	WS Gazelle AH1	AAC No 665 Sqn, Aldergrove
	ZB669	WS Gazelle AH1	AAC No 670 Sqn, Middle Wallop
	ZB670	WS Gazelle AH1	AAC No 665 Sqn, Aldergrove
	ZB671	WS Gazelle AH1 [E]	AAC No 29 Flt, Suffield, Canada
	ZB672	WS Gazelle AH1	AAC No 3 Flt, Topcliffe
	ZB673	WS Gazelle AH1 [P]	AAC No 670 Sqn, Middle Wallop
	ZB674	WS Gazelle AH1	AAC, stored Wroughton
	ZB675	WS Gazelle AH1	AAC, stored Wroughton
	ZB676	WS Gazelle AH1	AAC, stored Wroughton
	ZB677	WS Gazelle AH1	AAC No 661 Sqn, Hildesheim
	ZB678	WS Gazelle AH1	AAC, stored Wroughton
	ZB679	WS Gazelle AH1	RNAY Fleetlands
	ZB680	WS Gazelle AH1 [B]	AAC No 29 Flt, Suffield, Canada
	ZB681	WS Gazelle AH1	AAC No 665 Sqn, Aldergrove
	ZB682	WS Gazelle AH1	AAC No 665 Sqn, Aldergrove
	ZB683	WS Gazelle AH1	AAC No 655 Sqn, Aldergrove
	ZB684	WS Gazelle AH1	AAC No 655 Sqn, Aldergrove
	ZB685	WS Gazelle AH1	AAC No 665 Sqn, Aldergrove
	ZB686	WS Gazelle AH1	AAC No 655 Sqn, Aldergrove

Serial	Type (alternative identity)	Owner, Operator or Location	Notes
ZB687	WS Gazelle AH1	AAC No 655 Sqn, Aldergrove	
ZB688	WS Gazelle AH1	AAC No 670 Sqn, Middle Wallop	
ZB689	WS Gazelle AH1	AAC, stored Wroughton	
ZB690	WS Gazelle AH1	AAC, stored Wroughton	
ZB691	WS Gazelle AH1	AAC, stored Wroughton	
ZB692	WS Gazelle AH1	AAC, stored Wroughton	
ZB693	WS Gazelle AH1	AAC, stored Wroughton	
ZD230	BAC Super VC10 (G-ASGA)	RAF, stored Abingdon	
ZD232	BAC Super VC10 (G-ASGD) (8699M)	RAF Brize Norton Fire Section	
ZD233	BAC Super VC10 (G-ASGE)	FSCTE, RAF Manston	
ZD234	BAC Super VC10 (G-ASGF) (8700M)	Burned at RAF Brize Norton	
ZD235	BAC Super VC10 (G-ASGG)	RAF, stored Abingdon	
ZD239	BAC Super VC10 (G-ASGK)	RAF, stored Abingdon	
ZD240	BAC Super VC10 (G-ASGL)	RAF, stored Abingdon	
ZD241	BAC Super VC10 (G-ASGM)	RAF, stored Abingdon	
ZD243	BAC Super VC10 (G-ASGR)	RAF, stored Abingdon	
ZD249	WS Lynx HAS3	MoD(PE) Westlands, Yeovil	
ZD250	WS Lynx HAS3 [352/SD]	RN No 829 Sqn, Portland	
ZD251	WS Lynx HAS3 [332]	RN No 815 Sqn, Portland	
ZD252	WS Lynx HAS3 [302/PO]	RN No 815 Sqn, Portland	
ZD253	WS Lynx HAS3 [475/HM]	RN No 815 Sqn, Portland	
ZD254	WS Lynx HAS3 [631]	RN No 702 Sqn, Portland	
ZD255	WS Lynx HAS3 [466]	RN No 829 Sqn, Portland	
ZD256	WS Lynx HAS3 [333/BM]	RN No 815 Sqn, Portland	
ZD257	WS Lynx HAS3 [407/YK]	RN No 815 Sqn, Portland	
ZD258	WS Lynx HAS3 [GIB]	RN No 815 Sqn (208 Flt), Gibraltar	
ZD259	WS Lynx HAS3 [323/AB]	RN No 815 Sqn, Portland	
ZD260	WS Lynx HAS3 [303/PO]	RN No 815 Sqn, Portland	
ZD261	WS Lynx HAS3	RNAY, Fleetlands	
ZD262	WS Lynx HAS3 [632]	RN No 702 Sqn, Portland	
ZD263	WS Lynx HAS3 [630]	RN No 702 Sqn, Portland	
ZD264	WS Lynx HAS3 [304]	RN No 815 Sqn, Portland	
ZD265	WS Lynx HAS3 [328]	RN No 829 Sqn, Portland	
ZD266	WS Lynx HAS8	MoD(PE) Westlands, Yeovil	
ZD267	WS Lynx HAS8	MoD(PE) Westlands, Yeovil	
ZD268	WS Lynx HAS8/1 [479]	RN No 829 Sqn, Portland	
ZD272	WS Lynx AH1 [F]	AAC No 663 Sqn, Soest	
ZD273	WS Lynx AH1	AAC No 656 Sqn, Netheravon	
ZD274	WS Lynx AH1	AAC No 656 Sqn, Netheravon	
ZD275	WS Lynx AH1	AAC No 657 Sqn, Oakington	
ZD276	WS Lynx AH1	AAC No 652 Sqn, Hildesheim	
ZD277	WS Lynx AH1	AAC No 657 Sqn, Oakington	
ZD278	WS Lynx AH1	AAC, stored Wroughton	
ZD279	WS Lynx AH1 [L]	AAC No 671 Sqn, Middle Wallop	
ZD280	WS Lynx AH1	AAC No 663 Sqn, Soest	
ZD281	WS Lynx AH1	AAC No 656 Sqn, Netheravon	
ZD282	WS Lynx AH1 [V]	RM 3 CBAS, Yeovilton	
ZD283	WS Lynx AH1	AAC No 671 Sqn, Middle Wallop	
ZD284	WS Lynx AH1 [W]	RM 3 CBAS, Yeovilton	
ZD285	WS Lynx AH5	MoD(PE) RAE Farnborough	
ZD318	BAe Harrier GR5	MoD(PE) BAe Dunsfold	
ZD319	BAe Harrier GR5	MoD(PE) BAe Dunsfold	
ZD320	BAe Harrier GR5	MoD(PE) BAe Dunsfold	
ZD321	BAe Harrier GR5	MoD(PE) A&AEE Boscombe Down/BAe Dunsfold	
ZD322	BAe Harrier GR5 [A]	RAF No 233 OCU, Wittering	
ZD323	BAe Harrier GR5 [C]	RAF No 233 OCU, Wittering	
ZD324	BAe Harrier GR5 [B]	RAF No 233 OCU, Wittering	
ZD326	BAe Harrier GR5	RAF No 1 Sqn, Wittering	
ZD327	BAe Harrier GR5 [D]	RAF No 233 OCU, Wittering	
ZD328	BAe Harrier GR5 [S]	MoD(PE) SAOEU, Boscombe Down	
ZD329	BAe Harrier GR5 [F]	RAF No 233 OCU, Wittering	
ZD330	BAe Harrier GR5 [E]	MoD(PE) SAOEU, Boscombe Down	
ZD345	BAe Harrier GR5 [A]	MoD(PE) SAOEU, Boscombe Down	
ZD346	BAe Harrier GR5 [E]	RAF No 233 OCU, Wittering	
ZD347	BAe Harrier GR5	RAF Wittering	
ZD348	BAe Harrier GR5 [G]	RAF No 233 OCU, Wittering	
ZD349	BAe Harrier GR5 [H]	RAF No 233 OCU, Wittering	
ZD350	BAe Harrier GR5	RAF No 1 Sqn, Wittering	
ZD351	BAe Harrier GR5 [03]	RAF No 1 Sqn, Wittering	
ZD352	BAe Harrier GR5 [U]	MoD(PE) SAOEU, Boscombe Down	

Notes	Serial	Type (alternative identity)	Owner, Operator or Location
	ZD353	BAe Harrier GR5 [06]	RAF No 1 Sqn, Wittering
	ZD354	BAe Harrier GR5 [09]	RAF No 1 Sqn, Wittering
	ZD355	BAe Harrier GR5 [MF]	RAF, ASF Wittering
	ZD375	BAe Harrier GR5	MoD(PE) SAOEU, Boscombe Down
	ZD376	BAe Harrier GR5	RAF
	ZD377	BAe Harrier GR5	RAF
	ZD378	BAe Harrier GR5 [14]	RAF No 1 Sqn, Wittering
	ZD379	BAe Harrier GR5 [15]	RAF No 1 Sqn, Wittering
	ZD380	BAe Harrier GR5 [16]	RAF No 1 Sqn, Wittering
	ZD400	BAe Harrier GR5	RAF
	ZD401	BAe Harrier GR5	RAF
	ZD402	BAe Harrier GR5	RAF
	ZD403	BAe Harrier GR5	RAF
	ZD404	BAe Harrier GR5	RAF
	ZD405	BAe Harrier GR5	RAF
	ZD406	BAe Harrier GR5	RAF
	ZD407	BAe Harrier GR5	RAF
	ZD408	BAe Harrier GR5	RAF
	ZD409	BAe Harrier GR5	RAF
	ZD410	BAe Harrier GR5	RAF
	ZD411	BAe Harrier GR5	RAF
	ZD412	BAe Harrier GR5	RAF
	ZD430	BAe Harrier GR5	RAF
	ZD431	BAe Harrier GR5	RAF
	ZD432	BAe Harrier GR5	RAF
	ZD433	BAe Harrier GR5	RAF
	ZD434	BAe Harrier GR5	RAF
	ZD435	BAe Harrier GR5	RAF
	ZD436	BAe Harrier GR5	RAF
	ZD437	BAe Harrier GR5	RAF
	ZD438	BAe Harrier GR5	RAF
	ZD461	BAe Harrier GR5	RAF
	ZD462	BAe Harrier GR5	RAF
	ZD463	BAe Harrier GR5	RAF
	ZD464	BAe Harrier GR5	RAF
	ZD465	BAe Harrier GR5	RAF
	ZD466	BAe Harrier GR5	RAF
	ZD467	BAe Harrier GR5	RAF
	ZD468	BAe Harrier GR5	RAF
	ZD469	BAe Harrier GR5	RAF
	ZD470	BAe Harrier GR5	RAF
	ZD472	Harrier GR5 Replica [01] (BAPC191)	RAF Exhibition Flight, Abingdon
	ZD476	WS61 Sea King HC4 [ZS]	RN No 707 Sqn, Yeovilton
	ZD477	WS61 Sea King HC4 [VL]	RN No 846 Sqn, Yeovilton
	ZD478	WS61 Sea King HC4 [VM]	RN No 846 Sqn, Yeovilton
	ZD479	WS61 Sea King HC4 [ZW]	RN No 707 Sqn, Yeovilton
	ZD480	WS61 Sea King HC4 [VP]	RN No 846 Sqn, Yeovilton
	ZD485	FMA IA58 Pucara (A-515)	See A-515 Argentine serials
	ZD493	BAC VC10 (G-ARVJ)	RAF Fire Section Brize Norton
	ZD559	WS Lynx AH5	MoD(PE) RAE Bedford
	ZD560	WS Lynx AH7	MoD(PE) ETPS Boscombe Down
	ZD565	WS Lynx HAS3 [633]	RN No 702 Sqn, Portland
	ZD566	WS Lynx HAS3 [637]	RN No 702 Sqn, Portland
	ZD567	WS Lynx HAS3 [636]	RN No 702 Sqn, Portland
	ZD574	B-V Chinook HC1 [FH]	RAF No 240 OCU, Odiham
	ZD575	B-V Chinook HC1	RAF No 240 OCU, Odiham
	ZD576	B-V Chinook HC1 [FG]	RAF No 240 OCU, Odiham
	ZD578	BAe Sea Harrier FRS1	MoD(PE) A&AEE Boscombe Down
	ZD579	BAe Sea Harrier FRS1 [719]	RN No 899 Sqn, Yeovilton
	ZD580	BAe Sea Harrier FRS1	RN No 899 Sqn, Yeovilton
	ZD581	BAe Sea Harrier FRS1 [718]	RN No 899 Sqn, Yeovilton
	ZD582	BAe Sea Harrier FRS1 [127/L]	RN No 800 Sqn, Yeovilton
	ZD607	BAe Sea Harrier FRS1 [006/R]	RN No 801 Sqn, Yeovilton
	ZD608	BAe Sea Harrier FRS1 [710]	RN No 899 Sqn, Yeovilton
	ZD609	BAe Sea Harrier FRS1 [000/R]	RN No 801 Sqn, Yeovilton
	ZD610	BAe Sea Harrier FRS1 [713]	RN No 899 Sqn, Yeovilton
	ZD611	BAe Sea Harrier FRS1	RN AMG, Yeovilton
	ZD612	BAe Sea Harrier FRS1 [002/R]	RN No 801 Sqn, Yeovilton
	ZD613	BAe Sea Harrier FRS1 [710]	RN No 899 Sqn, Yeovilton
	ZD614	BAe Sea Harrier FRS1 [124/L]	RN No 800 Sqn, Yeovilton
	ZD615	BAe Sea Harrier FRS1 [005/R]	RN No 801 Sqn, Yeovilton
	ZD620	BAe 125 CC3	RAF No 32 Sqn, Northolt
	ZD621	BAe 125 CC3	RAF No 32 Sqn, Northolt

Serial	Type (alternative identity)	Owner, Operator or Location	Notes
ZD625	WS61 Sea King HC4 [ZX]	RN No 707 Sqn, Yeovilton	
ZD626	WS61 Sea King HC4 [ZY]	RN No 707 Sqn, Yeovilton	
ZD627	WS61 Sea King HC4 [ZZ]	RN No 707 Sqn, Yeovilton	
ZD630	WS61 Sea King HAS5 [013/R]	RN No 820 Sqn, Culdrose	
ZD631	WS61 Sea King HAS5 [019/R]	RN No 820 Sqn, Culdrose	
ZD633	WS61 Sea King HAS5 [012/R]	RN No 820 Sqn, Culdrose	
ZD634	WS61 Sea King HAS5 [702]	RN No 819 Sqn, Prestwick	
ZD636	WS61 Sea King HAS5 [701]	RN No 819 Sqn, Prestwick	
ZD637	WS61 Sea King HAS5 [704/PW]	RN No 819 Sqn, Prestwick	
ZD643	Schleicher Vanguard TX1 (BGA2884)	RAF No 618 VGS, West Malling	
ZD644	Schleicher Vanguard TX1 (BGA2883)	RAF, stored Dunstable	
ZD645	Schleicher Vanguard TX1 (BGA2885)	RAF ACCGS, Syerston	
ZD646	Schleicher Vanguard TX1 (BGA2886)	RAF ACCGS, Syerston	
ZD647	Schleicher Vanguard TX1 (BGA2887)	RAF, stored Dunstable	
ZD648	Schleicher Vanguard TX1 (BGA2888)	RAF, stored Dunstable	
ZD649	Schleicher Vanguard TX1 (BGA2889)	RAF, stored Syerston	
ZD650	Schleicher Vanguard TX1 (BGA2890)	RAF No 618 VGS, West Malling	
ZD651	Schleicher Vanguard TX1 (BGA2891)	RAF ACCGS, Syerston	
ZD652	Schleicher Vanguard TX1 (BGA2892)	RAF No 618 VGS, West Malling	
ZD657	Schleicher Valiant TX1 (BGA2893)	RAF No 631 VGS, Sealand	
ZD658	Schleicher Valiant TX1 (BGA2894)	RAF ACCGS, Syerston	
ZD659	Schleicher Valiant TX1 (BGA2895)	RAF ACCGS, Syerston	
ZD660	Schleicher Valiant TX1 (BGA2896)	RAF No 645 VGS, Catterick	
ZD661	Schleicher Valiant TX1 (BGA2897)	RAF, stored Syerston	
ZD667	BAe Harrier GR3 [U]	RAF No 4 Sqn, Gutersloh	
ZD668	BAe Harrier GR3 [J]	RAF No 4 Sqn, Gutersloh	
ZD669	BAe Harrier GR3 [I]	RAF No 4 Sqn, Gutersloh	
ZD670	BAe Harrier GR3 [W]	RAF No 4 Sqn, Gutersloh	
ZD703	BAe 125 CC3	RAF No 32 Sqn, Northolt	
ZD704	BAe 125 CC3	RAF No 32 Sqn, Northolt	
ZD707	Panavia Tornado GR1 [BK]	RAF No 14 Sqn, Bruggen	
ZD708	Panavia Tornado GR1	BAe Warton	
ZD709	Panavia Tornado GR1 [AD]	RAF No 9 Sqn, Bruggen	
ZD710	Panavia Tornado GR1 [BJ]	RAF No 14 Sqn, Bruggen	
ZD711	Panavia Tornado GR1T [DY]	RAF No 31 Sqn, Bruggen	
ZD712	Panavia Tornado GR1T [BY]	RAF No 14 Sqn, Bruggen	
ZD713	Panavia Tornado GR1T	RAF TWCU/45 Sqn, Honington	
ZD714	Panavia Tornado GR1 [BE]	RAF No 14 Sqn, Bruggen	
ZD715	Panavia Tornado GR1 [DB]	RAF No 31 Sqn, Bruggen	
ZD716	Panavia Tornado GR1 [O]	MoD(PE) SAOEU Boscombe Down	
ZD717	Panavia Tornado GR1 [CD]	RAF No 17 Sqn, Bruggen	
ZD718	Panavia Tornado GR1 [BH]	RAF No 14 Sqn, Bruggen	
ZD719	Panavia Tornado GR1 [AD]	RAF No 9 Sqn, Bruggen	
ZD720	Panavia Tornado GR1 [CK]	RAF No 17 Sqn, Bruggen	
ZD739	Panavia Tornado GR1 [AC]	RAF No 9 Sqn, Bruggen	
ZD740	Panavia Tornado GR1 [DA]	RAF No 31 Sqn, Bruggen	
ZD741	Panavia Tornado GR1T [AY]	RAF No 9 Sqn, Bruggen	
ZD742	Panavia Tornado GR1T [CY]	RAF No 17 Sqn, Bruggen	
ZD743	Panavia Tornado GR1T	RAF TWCU/45 Sqn, Honington	
ZD744	Panavia Tornado GR1 [BD]	RAF No 14 Sqn, Bruggen	
ZD745	Panavia Tornado GR1 [AB]	RAF No 9 Sqn, Bruggen	
ZD746	Panavia Tornado GR1 [DJ]	RAF No 31 Sqn, Bruggen	
ZD747	Panavia Tornado GR1 [DK]	RAF No 31 Sqn, Bruggen	
ZD748	Panavia Tornado GR1 [DG]	RAF No 31 Sqn, Bruggen	
ZD749	Panavia Tornado GR1 [U]	MoD(PE) SAOEU Boscombe Down	
ZD788	Panavia Tornado GR1 [CB]	RAF No 17 Sqn, Bruggen	
ZD789	Panavia Tornado GR1 [CE]	RAF No 17 Sqn, Bruggen	
ZD790	Panavia Tornado GR1 [DL]	RAF No 31 Sqn, Bruggen	
ZD791	Panavia Tornado GR1 [BG]	RAF No 14 Sqn, Bruggen	

Notes	Serial	Type (alternative identity)	Owner, Operator or Location
	ZD792	Panavia Tornado GR1 [CF]	RAF No 17 Sqn, Bruggen
	ZD793	Panavia Tornado GR1 [CA]	RAF No 17 Sqn, Bruggen
	ZD808	Panavia Tornado GR1 [CJ]	Written off 10 May 1988 in W. Germany
	ZD809	Panavia Tornado GR1 [AA]	RAF No 9 Sqn, Bruggen
	ZD810	Panavia Tornado GR1 [CG]	RAF No 17 Sqn, Bruggen
	ZD811	Panavia Tornado GR1 [DF]	RAF No 31 Sqn, Bruggen
	ZD812	Panavia Tornado GR1T [FV]	RAF No 16 Sqn, Laarbruch
	ZD842	Panavia Tornado GR1T	RAF TWCU/45 Sqn, Honington
	ZD843	Panavia Tornado GR1 [DH]	RAF No 31 Sqn, Bruggen
	ZD844	Panavia Tornado GR1 [DE]	RAF No 31 Sqn, Bruggen
	ZD845	Panavia Tornado GR1 [BA]	RAF No 14 Sqn, Bruggen
	ZD846	Panavia Tornado GR1 [BL]	RAF No 14 Sqn, Bruggen
	ZD847	Panavia Tornado GR1 [CH]	RAF No 17 Sqn, Bruggen
	ZD848	Panavia Tornado GR1 [BC]	RAF No 14 Sqn, Bruggen
	ZD849	Panavia Tornado GR1 [CC]	RAF No 17 Sqn, Bruggen
	ZD850	Panavia Tornado GR1 [CL]	RAF No 17 Sqn, Bruggen
	ZD851	Panavia Tornado GR1 [DC]	RAF No 31 Sqn, Bruggen
	ZD890	Panavia Tornado GR1 [AE]	RAF No 9 Sqn, Bruggen
	ZD891	Panavia Tornado GR1 [BB]	Crashed 13 January 1989, W. Germany
	ZD892	Panavia Tornado GR1 [AF]	RAF No 9 Sqn, Bruggen
	ZD893	Panavia Tornado GR1 [AG]	RAF No 9 Sqn, Bruggen
	ZD895	Panavia Tornado GR1 [BF]	RAF No 14 Sqn, Bruggen
	ZD899	Panavia Tornado F2T	MoD(PE) BAe Warton
	ZD900	Panavia Tornado F2T	MoD(PE) A&AEE, Boscombe Down
	ZD901	Panavia Tornado F2T [AB]	RAF, stored St Athan
	ZD902	Panavia Tornado F2T	MoD(PE) RAE Farnborough
	ZD903	Panavia Tornado F2T [AB]	RAF, stored St Athan
	ZD904	Panavia Tornado F2T [AE]	RAF, stored At Athan
	ZD905	Panavia Tornado F2 [AV]	RAF, stored St Athan
	ZD906	Panavia Tornado F2 [AN]	RAF, stored St Athan
	ZD932	Panavia Tornado F2 [AM]	RAF, stored St Athan
	ZD933	Panavia Tornado F2 [AO]	RAF, stored St Athan
	ZD934	Panavia Tornado F2T [AD]	RAF, stored St Athan
	ZD935	Panavia Tornado F2T	MoD(PE) ETPS, Boscombe Down
	ZD936	Panavia Tornado F2 [AP]	RAF, stored St Athan
	ZD937	Panavia Tornado F2 [AQ]	RAF, stored St Athan
	ZD938	Panavia Tornado F2 [AR]	RAF, stored St Athan
	ZD939	Panavia Tornado F2	RAF, stored St Athan
	ZD940	Panavia Tornado F2	RAF, stored St Athan
	ZD941	Panavia Tornado F2 [AU]	RAF, stored St Athan
	ZD948	Lockheed TriStar KC1 (G-BFCA)	RAF No 216 Sqn, Brize Norton
	ZD949	Lockheed TriStar K1 (G-BFCB)	RAF No 216 Sqn, Brize Norton
	ZD950	Lockheed TriStar KC1 (G-BFCC)	RAF No 216 Sqn, Brize Norton
	ZD951	Lockheed TriStar K1 (G-BFCD)	RAF No 216 Sqn, Brize Norton
	ZD952	Lockheed TriStar KC1 (G-BFCE)	RAF No 216 Sqn, Brize Norton
	ZD953	Lockheed TriStar KC1 (G-BFCF)	RAF No 216 Sqn, Brize Norton
	ZD974	Schempp-Hirth Janus C (BGA2875)	RAF ACCGS, Syerston
	ZD975	Schempp-Hirth Janus C (BGA2876)	RAF ACCGS, Syerston
	ZD980	B-V Chinook HC1	RAF No 18 Sqn, Gutersloh
	ZD981	B-V Chinook HC1 [BD]	RAF No 18 Sqn, Gutersloh
	ZD982	B-V Chinook HC1 [FI]	RAF No 240 OCU, Odiham
	ZD983	B-V Chinook HC1 [BF]	RAF No 18 Sqn, Gutersloh
	ZD984	B-V Chinook HC1 [BE]	RAF No 18 Sqn, Gutersloh
	ZD990	BAe Harrier T4 [T]	RAF No 233 OCU, Wittering
	ZD991	BAe Harrier T4 [S]	RAF No 4 Sqn, Gutersloh
	ZD992	BAe Harrier T4 [P]	RAF No 233 OCU, Wittering
	ZD993	BAe Harrier T4 [U]	RAF No 233 OCU, Wittering
	ZD996	Panavia Tornado GR1A [AK]	RAF No 9 Sqn, Bruggen
	ZE116	Panavia Tornado GR1A [AL]	RAF No 9 Sqn, Bruggen
	ZE154	Panavia Tornado F3T [AK]	RAF No 229 OCU/65 Sqn, Coningsby
	ZE155	Panavia Tornado F3	MoD(PE) A&AEE, Boscombe Down
	ZE156	Panavia Tornado F3 [AV]	RAF, stored At Athan
	ZE157	Panavia Tornado F3T [AH]	RAF, stored St Athan
	ZE158	Panavia Tornado F3 [AP]	RAF, stored St Athan
	ZE159	Panavia Tornado F3 [AW]	RAF, stored St Athan
	ZE160	Panavia Tornado F3T [AG]	RAF, stored St Athan
	ZE161	Panavia Tornado F3 [DX]	RAF No 11 Sqn, Leeming
	ZE162	Panavia Tornado F3	RAF, stored St Athan
	ZE163	Panavia Tornado F3T [AL]	RAF No 229 OCU/65 Sqn, Coningsby
	ZE164	Panavia Tornado F3 [AU]	RAF, stored St Athan
	ZE165	Panavia Tornado F3 [AZ]	RAF, stored St Athan

Serial	Type (alternative identity)	Owner, Operator or Location	Notes
ZE166	Panavia Tornado F3T [AI]	RAF, stored St Athan	
ZE167	Panavia Tornado F3 [AR]	RAF, stored St Athan	
ZE168	Panavia Tornado F3 [AO]	RAF, stored St Athan	
ZE199	Panavia Tornado F3T [AJ]	RAF, stored St Athan	
ZE200	Panavia Tornado F3 [CJ]	RAF, No 5 Sqn, Coningsby	
ZE201	Panavia Tornado F3 [AQ]	RAF, stored Coningsby	
ZE202	Panavia Tornado F3T [AH]	RAF No 229 OCU/65 Sqn, Coningsby	
ZE203	Panavia Tornado F3 [AO]	RAF No 229 OCU/65 Sqn, Coningsby	
ZE204	Panavia Tornado F3	RAF No 229 OCU/65 Sqn, Coningsby	
ZE205	Panavia Tornado F3T [AA]	RAF No 229 OCU/65 Sqn, Coningsby	
ZE206	Panavia Tornado F3 [BF]	RAF No 229 OCU/Sqn, Coningsby	
ZE207	Panavia Tornado F3 [BJ]	RAF No 29 Sqn, Coningsby	
ZE208	Panavia Tornado F3T [BR]	RAF No 29 Sqn, Coningsby	
ZE209	Panavia Tornado F3 [AS]	RAF No 229 OCU/65 Sqn, Coningsby	
ZE210	Panavia Tornado F3 [AW]	RAF No 229 OCU/65 Sqn, Coningsby	
ZE250	Panavia Tornado F3T [AF]	RAF No 229 OCU/65 Sqn, Coningsby	
ZE251	Panavia Tornado F3 [AX]	RAF No 229 OCU/65 Sqn, Coningsby	
ZE252	Panavia Tornado F3 [AY]	RAF No 229 OCU/65 Sqn, Coningsby	
ZE253	Panavia Tornado F3T [AB]	RAF No 229 OCU/65 Sqn, Coningsby	
ZE254	Panavia Tornado F3 [BG]	RAF No 29 Sqn, Coningsby	
ZE255	Panavia Tornado F3 [BH]	RAF No 29 Sqn, Coningsby	
ZE256	Panavia Tornado F3T	RAF No 229 OCU/65 Sqn, Coningsby	
ZE257	Panavia Tornado F3 [BD]	RAF No 29 Sqn, Coningsby	
ZE258	Panavia Tornado F3 [BE]	RAF No 29 Sqn, Coningsby	
ZE287	Panavia Tornado F3T [AE]	RAF No 229 OCU/65 Sqn, Coningsby	
ZE288	Panavia Tornado F3 [BI]	RAF No 29 Sqn, Coningsby	
ZE289	Panavia Tornado F3 [BA]	RAF No 29 Sqn, Coningsby	
ZE290	Panavia Tornado F3T [AD]	RAF No 229 OCU/65 Sqn, Coningsby	
ZE291	Panavia Tornado F3 [AZ]	RAF No 229 OCU/65 Sqn, Coningsby	
ZE292	Panavia Tornado F3T [AC]	RAF No 229 OCU/65 Sqn, Coningsby	
ZE293	Panavia Tornado F3 [AQ]	RAF No 229 OCU/65 Sqn, Coningsby	
ZE294	Panavia Tornado F3 [AR]	RAF No 229 OCU/65 Sqn, Coningsby	
ZE295	Panavia Tornado F3T [AM]	RAF No 229 OCU/65 Sqn, Coningsby	
ZE296	Panavia Tornado F3 [BB]	RAF No 29 Sqn, Coningsby	
ZE338	Panavia Tornado F3	RAF No 229 OCU/65 Sqn, Coningsby	
ZE339	Panavia Tornado F3T [AG]	RAF No 229 OCU/65 Sqn, Coningsby	
ZE340	Panavia Tornado F3 [BC]	RAF No 29 Sqn, Coningsby	
ZE341	Panavia Tornado F3 [BK]	RAF No 29 Sqn, Coningsby	
ZE342	Panavia Tornado F3T [AI]	RAF No 229 OCU/65 Sqn, Coningsby	
ZE343	McD Phantom F-4J(UK) [T]	RAF No 74 Sqn, Wattisham	
ZE350	McD Phantom F-4J(UK) [I]	RAF No 74 Sqn, Wattisham	
ZE351	McD Phantom F-4J(UK) [G]	RAF No 74 Sqn, Wattisham	
ZE352	McD Phantom F-4J(UK) [E]	RAF No 74 Sqn, Wattisham	
ZE353	McD Phantom F-4J(UK) [R]	RAF No 74 Sqn, Wattisham	
ZE354	McD Phantom F-4J(UK) [S]	RAF No 74 Sqn, Wattisham	
ZE355	McD Phantom F-4J(UK) [Q]	RAF No 74 Sqn, Wattisham	
ZE356	McD Phantom F-4J(UK) [N]	RAF No 74 Sqn, Wattisham	
ZE357	McD Phantom F-4J(UK) [J]	RAF No 74 Sqn, Wattisham	
ZE359	McD Phantom F-4J(UK) [O]	RAF No 74 Sqn, Wattisham	
ZE360	McD Phantom F-4J(UK) [P]	RAF No 74 Sqn, Wattisham	
ZE361	McD Phantom F-4J(UK) [V]	RAF No 74 Sqn, Wattisham	
ZE362	McD Phantom F-4J(UK) [W]	RAF No 74 Sqn, Wattisham	
ZE363	McD Phantom F-4J(UK) [Z]	RAF No 74 Sqn, Wattisham	
ZE364	WS61 Sea King HAR3	RAF No 74 Sqn, Wattisham	
ZE368	WS61 Sea King HAR3	RAF No 202 Sqn SAR*	
ZE369	WS61 Sea King HAR3	RAF No 202 Sqn SAR*	
ZE370	WS Lynx AH5	RAF No 202 Sqn SAR*	
ZE375	WS Lynx AH7	MoD(PE) Rolls-Royce, Filton	
ZE376	WS Lynx AH7	MoD(PE) Westlands, Yeovil	
ZE377	WS Lynx AH7	AAC AETW, Middle Wallop	
ZE378	WS Lynx AH7	AAC MoD(PE) Westlands, Yeovil	
ZE379	WS Lynx AH7	AAC No 665 Sqn, Aldergrove	
ZE380	WS Lynx AH7	AAC Wroughton	
ZE381	WS Lynx AH7	AAC No 665 Sqn, Aldergrove	
ZE382	WS Lynx AH7	AAC Fleetlands	
ZE383	BAe 125 CC3	AAC Wroughton	
ZE395	BAe 125 CC3	RAF No 32 Sqn, Northolt	
ZE396	Agusta A109A (AE-334)	RAF No 32 Sqn, Northolt	
ZE410	Agusta A109A (AE-331)	AAC 7 Regt HQ Flt, Netheravon	
ZE411	Agusta A109A	AAC 7 Regt HQ Flt, Netheravon	
ZE412	Agusta A109A	AAC 7 Regt HQ Flt, Netheravon	
ZE413	WS61 Sea King HAS5 [502]	AAC 7 Regt HQ Flt, Netheravon	
ZE418	WS61 Sea King HAS5 [014/R]	RN No 810 Sqn, Culdrose	
ZE419		RN No 820 Sqn, Culdrose	

Notes	Serial	Type (alternative identity)	Owner, Operator or Location
	ZE420	WS61 Sea King HAS5 [010/R]	RN No 820 Sqn, Culdrose
	ZE421	WS61 Sea King HAS5 [581]	RN No 706 Sqn, Culdrose
	ZE422	WS61 Sea King HAS5 [270/L]	RN No 814 Sqn, Culdrose
	ZE425	WS61 Sea King HC4 [A]	RN No 845 Sqn, Yeovilton
	ZE426	WS61 Sea King HC4 [B]	RN No 845 Sqn, Yeovilton
	ZE427	WS61 Sea King HC4 [YC]	RN No 845 Sqn, Yeovilton
	ZE428	WS61 Sea King HC4 [D]	RN No 845 Sqn, Yeovilton
	ZE432	BAC 1-11/479 (DQ-FBV)	MoD(PE) ETPS Boscombe Down
	ZE433	BAC 1-11/479 (DQ-FBQ)	MoD(PE) RAE Bedford
	ZE438	BAe Jetstream T3 [576]	RN No 750 Sqn, Culdrose
	ZE439	BAe Jetstream T3 [577]	RN No 750 Sqn, Culdrose
	ZE440	BAe Jetstream T3 [578]	RN No 750 Sqn, Culdrose
	ZE441	BAe Jetstream T3 [579]	RN No 750 Sqn, Culdrose
	ZE477	WS Lynx 3	MoD(PE) Westlands, Yeovil
	ZE495	Grob Viking T1 (BGA3000)	RAF No 662 VGS, Arbroath
	ZE496	Grob Viking T1 (BGA3001)	RAF ACCGS, Syerston
	ZE497	Grob Viking T1 (BGA3002)	RAF, stored Syerston
	ZE498	Grob Viking T1 (BGA3003)	RAF, stored Syerston
	ZE499	Grob Viking T1 (BGA3004)	RAF, stored Syerston
	ZE500	Grob Viking T1 (BGA3005)	RAF, stored Syerston
	ZE501	Grob Viking T1 (BGA3006)	RAF ACCGS, Syerston
	ZE502	Grob Viking T1 (BGA3007)	RAF No 645 VGS, Catterick
	ZE503	Grob Viking T1 (BGA3008)	RAF No 625 VGS, South Cerney
	ZE504	Grob Viking T1 (BGA3009)	RAF No 645 VGS, Catterick
	ZE520	Grob Viking T1 (BGA3010)	RAF No 645 VGS, Catterick
	ZE521	Grob Viking T1 (BGA3011)	RAF No 662 VGS, Arbroath
	ZE522	Grob Viking T1 (BGA3012)	RAF No 622 VGS, Upavon
	ZE523	Grob Viking T1 (BGA3013)	RAF No 631 VGS, Sealand
	ZE524	Grob Viking T1 (BGA3014)	RAF No 611 VGS, Swanton Morley
	ZE525	Grob Viking T1 (BGA3015)	RAF No 626 VGS, Predannack
	ZE526	Grob Viking T1 (BGA3016)	RAF ACCGS, Syerston
	ZE527	Grob Viking T1 (BGA3017)	RAF No 611 VGS, Swanton Morley
	ZE528	Grob Viking T1 (BGA3018)	RAF No 631 VGS, Sealand
	ZE529	Grob Viking T1 (BGA3019)	RAF ACCGS, Syerston
	ZE530	Grob Viking T1 (BGA3020)	RAF No 645 VGS, Catterick
	ZE531	Grob Viking T1 (BGA3021)	RAF No 631, VGS, Sealand
	ZE532	Grob Viking T1 (BGA3022)	RAF, ACCGS Syerston
	ZE533	Grob Viking T1 (BGA3023)	RAF No 622 VGS, Upavon
	ZE534	Grob Viking T1 (BGA3024)	RAF No 662 VGS, Arbroath
	ZE550	Grob Viking T1 (BGA3025)	RAF No 622 VGS, Upavon
	ZE551	Grob Viking T1 (BGA3026)	RAF No 611 VGS, Swanton Morley
	ZE552	Grob Viking T1 (BGA3027)	RAF No 662 VGS, Arbroath
	ZE553	Grob Viking T1 (BGA3028)	RAF, stored Syerston
	ZE554	Grob Viking T1 (BGA3029)	RAF No 631 VGS, Sealand
	ZE555	Grob Viking T1 (BGA3030)	RAF No 631 VGS, Sealand
	ZE556	Grob Viking T1 (BGA3031)	RAF No 631 VGS, Sealand
	ZE557	Grob Viking T1 (BGA3032)	RAF No 661 VGS, Kirknewton
	ZE558	Grob Viking T1 (BGA3033)	RAF No 634 VGS, St Athan
	ZE559	Grob Viking T1 (BGA3034)	RAF No 661 VGS, Kirknewton
	ZE560	Grob Viking T1 (BGA3035)	RAF No 611 VGS, Swanton Morley
	ZE561	Grob Viking T1 (BGA3036)	RAF No 661 VGS, Kirknewton
	ZE562	Grob Viking T1 (BGA3037)	RAF No 631 VGS, Sealand
	ZE563	Grob Viking T1 (BGA3038)	RAF No 661 VGS, Kirknewton
	ZE564	Grob Viking T1 (BGA3039)	RAF No 661 VGS, Kirknewton
	ZE584	Grob Viking T1 (BGA3040)	RAF No 662 VGS, Arbroath
	ZE585	Grob Viking T1 (BGA3041)	RAF ACCGS, Syerston
	ZE586	Grob Viking T1 (BGA3042)	RAF No 625 VGS, South Cerney
	ZE587	Grob Viking T1 (BGA3043)	RAF No 622 VGS, Upavon
	ZE588	Grob Viking T1 (BGA3044)	RAF No 614 VGS, Wethersfield
	ZE589	Grob Viking T1 (BGA3045)	RAF No 634 VGS, St Athan
	ZE590	Grob Viking T1 (BGA3046)	RAF No 622 VGS, Upavon
	ZE591	Grob Viking T1 (BGA3047)	RAF ACCGS, Systerton
	ZE592	Grob Viking T1 (BGA3048)	RAF Halton
	ZE593	Grob Viking T1 (BGA3049)	RAF No 614 VGS, Wethersfield
	ZE594	Grob Viking T1 (BGA3050)	RAF No 662 VGS, Arbroath
	ZE595	Grob Viking T1 (BGA3051)	RAF No 625 VGS, South Cerney
	ZE600	Grob Viking T1 (BGA3052)	RAF, stored Syerston
	ZE601	Grob Viking T1 (BGA3053)	RAF ACCGS, Syerston
	ZE602	Grob Viking T1 (BGA3054)	RAF No 617 VGS, Manston
	ZE603	Grob Viking T1 (BGA3055)	RAF No 618 VGS, West Malling
	ZE604	Grob Viking T1 (BGA3056)	RAF, stored Syerston
	ZE605	Grob Viking T1 (BGA3057)	RAF No 618 VGS, West Malling
	ZE606	Grob Viking T1 (BGA3058)	RAF No 626 VGS, Predannack
	ZE607	Grob Viking T1 (BGA3059)	RAF No 636 VGS, Swansea

Serial	Type (alternative identity)	Owner, Operator or Location	Notes
ZE608	Grob Viking T1 (BGA3060)	RAF No 625 VGS, South Cerney	
ZE609	Grob Viking T1 (BGA3061)	RAF No 622 VGS, Upavon	
ZE610	Grob Viking T1 (BGA3062)	RAF No 621 VGS, Weston-super-Mare	
ZE611	Grob Viking T1 (BGA3063)	RAF No 621 VGS, Weston-super-Mare	
ZE612	Grob Viking T1 (BGA3064)	RAF No 621 VGS, Weston-super-Mare	
ZE613	Grob Viking T1 (BGA3065)	RAF No 621 VGS, Weston-super-Mare	
ZE614	Grob Viking T1 (BGA3066)	RAF No 621 VGS, Weston-super-Mare	
ZE625	Grob Viking T1 (BGA3067)	RAF No 643 VGS, Scampton	
ZE626	Grob Viking T1 (BGA3068)	RAF ACCGS, Syerston	
ZE627	Grob Viking T1 (BGA3069)	RAF ACCGS, Syerston	
ZE628	Grob Viking T1 (BGA3070)	RAF No 643 VGS, Scampton	
ZE629	Grob Viking T1 (BGA3071)	RAF No 615 VGS, Kenley	
ZE630	Grob Viking T1 (BGA3072)	RAF No 636 VGS, Swansea	
ZE631	Grob Viking T1 (BGA3073)	RAF No 643 VGS, Scampton	
ZE632	Grob Viking T1 (BGA3074)	RAF No 614 VGS, Weathersfield	
ZE633	Grob Viking T1 (BGA3075)	RAF No 615 VGS, Kenley	
ZE634	Grob Viking T1 (BGA3076)	RAF, stored Syerston	
ZE635	Grob Viking T1 (BGA3077)	RAFC AEF Cranwell	
ZE636	Grob Viking T1 (BGA3078)	RAF Halton	
ZE637	Grob Viking T1 (BGA3079)	RAF No 614 VGS, Wethersfield	
ZE650	Grob Viking T1 (BGA3080)	RAF No 618 VGS, West Malling	
ZE651	Grob Viking T1 (BGA3081)	RAF No 618 VGS, West Malling	
ZE652	Grob Viking T1 (BGA3082)	RAF No 614 VGS, Wethersfield	
ZE653	Grob Viking T1 (BGA3083)	RAF No 615 VGS, Kenley	
ZE654	Grob Viking T1 (BGA3084)	RAF No 618 VGS, West Malling	
ZE655	Grob Viking T1 (BGA3085)	RAF No 618 VGS, West Malling	
ZE656	Grob Viking T1 (BGA3086)	RAF No 617 VGS, Manston	
ZE657	Grob Viking T1 (BGA3087)	RAF No 618 VGS, West Malling	
ZE658	Grob Viking T1 (BGA3088)	RAF No 615 VGS, Kenley	
ZE659	Grob Viking T1 (BGA3089)	RAF No 615 VGS, Kenley	
ZE677	Grob Viking T1 (BGA3090)	RAF No 615 VGS, Kenley	
ZE678	Grob Viking T1 (BGA3091)	RAF No 615 VGS, Kenley	
ZE679	Grob Viking T1 (BGA3092)	RAF No 615 VGS, Kenley	
ZE680	Grob Viking T1 (BGA3093)	RAF No 617 VGS, Manston	
ZE681	Grob Viking T1 (BGA3094)	RAF No 615 VGS, Kenley	
ZE682	Grob Viking T1 (BGA3095)	RAF No 643 VGS, Scampton	
ZE683	Grob Viking T1 (BGA3096)	RAF No 617 VGS, Manston	
ZE684	Grob Viking T1 (BGA3097)	RAF ACCGS, Syerston	
ZE685	Grob Viking T1 (BGA3098)	RAF No 617 VGS, Manston	
ZE686	Grob Viking T1 (BGA3099)	MoD(PE), Slingsby, Kirkbymoorside	
ZE690	BAe Sea Harrier FRS1	RN, stored St Athan	
ZE691	BAe Sea Harrier FRS1	RN, stored St Athan	
ZE692	BAe Sea Harrier FRS1	RN, stored St Athan	
ZE693	BAe Sea Harrier FRS1	RN, stored St Athan	
ZE694	BAe Sea Harrier FRS1	RN, stored St Athan	
ZE695	BAe Sea Harrier FRS1	RN, stored St Athan	
ZE696	BAe Sea Harrier FRS1	RN No 800 Sqn, Yeovilton	
ZE697	BAe Sea Harrier FRS1 [122/L]	RN No 800 Sqn, Yeovilton	
ZE698	BAe Sea Harrier FRS1	RN, stored St Athan	
ZE700	BAe 146 CC2	RAF Queen's Flight, Benson	
ZE701	BAe 146 CC2	RAF Queen's Flight, Benson	
ZE704	Lockheed TriStar K2 (N508PA)	RAF No 216 Sqn, Brize Norton	
ZE705	Lockheed TriStar K2 (N509PA)	RAF No 216 Sqn, Brize Norton	
ZE706	Lockheed TriStar K2 (N503PA)	MoD(PE) Marshalls, Cambridge	
ZE728	Panavia Tornado F3T [BS]	RAF No 29 Sqn, Coningsby	
ZE729	Panavia Tornado F3	RAF OEU, Coningsby	
ZE730	Panavia Tornado F3	RAF OEU, Coningsby	
ZE731	Panavia Tornado F3	RAF OEU, Coningsby	
ZE732	Panavia Tornado F3 [CH]	RAF No 5 Sqn, Coningsby	
ZE733	Panavia Tornado F3 [CI]	RAF, stored Coningsby	
ZE734	Panavia Tornado F3 [CJ]	RAF No 5 Sqn, Coningsby	
ZE735	Panavia Tornado F3T [CT]	RAF No 5 Sqn, Coningsby	
ZE736	Panavia Tornado F3 [CK]	RAF No 5 Sqn, Coningsby	
ZE737	Panavia Tornado F3 [CE]	RAF No 5 Sqn, Coningsby	
ZE755	Panavia Tornado F3 [CG]	RAF No 5 Sqn, Coningsby	
ZE756	Panavia Tornado F3	MoD(PE), BAe Warton	
ZE757	Panavia Tornado F3	MoD(PE), BAe Warton	
ZE758	Panavia Tornado F3 [CB]	RAF No 5 Sqn, Coningsby	
ZE759	Panavia Tornado F3T [AN]	RAF No 229 OCU/65 Sqn, Coningsby	
ZE760	Panavia Tornado F3 [CF]	RAF No 5 Sqn, Coningsby	
ZE761	Panavia Tornado F3 [CC]	RAF No 5 Sqn, Coningsby	
ZE762	Panavia Tornado F3 [CA]	RAF No 5 Sqn, Coningsby	
ZE763	Panavia Tornado F3 [CD]	RAF No 5 Sqn, Coningsby	
ZE764	Panavia Tornado F3 [DH]	RAF No 11 Sqn, Leeming	

Notes	Serial	Type (alternative identity)	Owner, Operator or Location
	ZE785	Panavia Tornado F3 [DA]	RAF No 11 Sqn, Leeming
	ZE786	Panavia Tornado F3T [DT]	RAF No 11 Sqn, Leeming
	ZE787	Panavia Tornado F3 [DB]	RAF No 11 Sqn, Leeming
	ZE788	Panavia Tornado F3 [DC]	RAF No 11 Sqn, Leeming
	ZE789	Panavia Tornado F3 [DD]	RAF No 11 Sqn, Leeming
	ZE790	Panavia Tornado F3 [DE]	RAF No 11 Sqn, Leeming
	ZE791	Panavia Tornado F3 [DF]	RAF No 11 Sqn, Leeming
	ZE792	Panavia Tornado F3 [DG]	RAF No 11 Sqn, Leeming
	ZE793	Panavia Tornado F3T [DZ]	RAF No 11 Sqn, Leeming
	ZE794	Panavia Tornado F3 [DI]	RAF No 11 Sqn, Leeming
	ZE808	Panavia Tornado F3 [DJ]	RAF No 11 Sqn, Leeming
	ZE809	Panavia Tornado F3 [EZ]	RAF No 23 Sqn, Leeming
	ZE810	Panavia Tornado F3 [EN]	RAF No 23 Sqn, Leeming
	ZE811	Panavia Tornado F3 [EB]	RAF No 23 Sqn, Leeming
	ZE812	Panavia Tornado F3 [EA]	RAF No 23 Sqn, Leeming
	ZE830	Panavia Tornado F3T	RAF No 23 Sqn, Leeming
	ZE831	Panavia Tornado F3	RAF No 23 Sqn, Leeming
	ZE832	Panavia Tornado F3 [ ]	RAF No 23 Sqn, Leeming
	ZE833	Panavia Tornado F3	RAF No 23 Sqn, Leeming
	ZE834	Panavia Tornado F3	RAF No 23 Sqn, Leeming
	ZE835	Panavia Tornado F3	RAF No 23 Sqn, Leeming
	ZE836	Panavia Tornado F3	RAF No 23 Sqn, Leeming
	ZE837	Panavia Tornado F3T	RAF No 23 Sqn, Leeming
	ZE838	Panavia Tornado F3	RAF
	ZE839	Panavia Tornado F3	RAF No 23 Sqn, Leeming
	ZE858	Panavia Tornado F3	RAF No 23 Sqn, Leeming
	ZE859	Panavia Tornado F3	RAF
	ZE860	Panavia Tornado F3	RAF
	ZE861	Panavia Tornado F3	RAF
	ZE862	Panavia Tornado F3T	RAF
	ZE882	Panavia Tornado F3	RAF
	ZE883	Panavia Tornado F3	RAF
	ZE884	Panavia Tornado F3	RAF
	ZE885	Panavia Tornado F3	RAF
	ZE886	Panavia Tornado F3	RAF
	ZE887	Panavia Tornado F3	RAF
	ZE888	Panavia Tornado F3T	RAF
	ZE889	Panavia Tornado F3	RAF
	ZE890	Panavia Tornado F3	RAF
	ZE891	Panavia Tornado F3	RAF
	ZE905	Panavia Tornado F3	RAF
	ZE906	Panavia Tornado F3	RAF
	ZE907	Panavia Tornado F3	RAF
	ZE908	Panavia Tornado F3T	RAF
	ZE909	Panavia Tornado F3	RAF
	ZE910	Panavia Tornado F3	RAF
	ZE911	Panavia Tornado F3	RAF
	ZE912	Panavia Tornado F3	RAF
	ZE913	Panavia Tornado F3	RAF
	ZE914	Panavia Tornado F3	RAF
	ZE934	Panavia Tornado F3T	RAF
	ZE935	Panavia Tornado F3	RAF
	ZE936	Panavia Tornado F3	RAF
	ZE937	Panavia Tornado F3	RAF
	ZE938	Panavia Tornado F3	RAF
	ZE939	Panavia Tornado F3	RAF
	ZE940	Panavia Tornado F3	RAF
	ZE941	Panavia Tornado F3T	RAF
	ZE942	Panavia Tornado F3	RAF
	ZE943	Panavia Tornado F3	RAF
	ZE960	Panavia Tornado F3	RAF
	ZE961	Panavia Tornado F3	RAF
	ZE962	Panavia Tornado F3	RAF
	ZE963	Panavia Tornado F3	RAF
	ZE964	Panavia Tornado F3T	RAF
	ZE965	Panavia Tornado F3	RAF
	ZE966	Panavia Tornado F3	RAF
	ZE967	Panavia Tornado F3	RAF
	ZE968	Panavia Tornado F3	RAF
	ZE969	Panavia Tornado F3	RAF
	ZE982	Panavia Tornado F3	RAF
	ZE983	Panavia Tornado F3	RAF
	ZF115	WS61 Sea King Mk 4	MoD(PE) ETPS, Boscombe Down

Serial	Type (alternative identity)	Owner, Operator or Location	Notes
ZF116	WS61 Sea King HC4	MoD(PE) A&AEE, Boscombe Down	
ZF117	WS61 Sea King HC4 [G]	RN No 845 Sqn, Yeovilton	
ZF118	WS61 Sea King HC4 [H]	RN No 845 Sqn, Yeovilton	
ZF119	WS61 Sea King HC4 [VJ]	RN No 846 Sqn, Yeovilton	
ZF120	WS61 Sea King HC4 [620]	RN No 772 Sqn, Portland	
ZF121	WS61 Sea King HC4 [621]	RN No 772 Sqn, Portland	
ZF122	WS61 Sea King HC4 [622]	RN No 772 Sqn, Portland	
ZF123	WS61 Sea King HC4 [623]	RN No 772 Sqn, Portland	
ZF124	WS61 Sea King HC4 [624]	RN No 772 Sqn, Portland	
ZF130	BAe 125-600B (G-BLUW)	MoD(PE) BAe Dunsfold	
ZF135	Shorts Tucano T1	RAF CFS, Scampton	
ZF136	Shorts Tucano T1	MoD(PE) A&AEE, Boscombe Down	
ZF137	Shorts Tucano T1	MoD(PE) A&AEE, Boscombe Down	
ZF138	Shorts Tucano T1	RAF TDCS, Scampton	
ZF139	Shorts Tucano T1	RAF TDCS, Scampton	
ZF140	Shorts Tucano T1	RAF TDCS, Scampton	
ZF141	Shorts Tucano T1	RAF TDCS, Scampton	
ZF142	Shorts Tucano T1	RAF TDCS, Scampton	
ZF143	Shorts Tucano T1	RAF TDCS, Scampton	
ZF144	Shorts Tucano T1	RAF	
ZF145	Shorts Tucano T1	RAF	
ZF1	Shorts Tucano T1	RAF	
ZF1	Shorts Tucano T1	RAF	
ZF1	Shorts Tucano T1	RAF	
ZF1	Shorts Tucano T1	RAF	
ZF1	Shorts Tucano T1	RAF	
ZF1	Shorts Tucano T1	RAF	
ZF1	Shorts Tucano T1	RAF	
ZF1	Shorts Tucano T1	RAF	
ZF1	Shorts Tucano T1	RAF	
ZF1	Shorts Tucano T1	RAF	
ZF1	Shorts Tucano T1	RAF	
ZF444	BN2A Islander (G-WOTG)	RAF Parachute Association, Weston-on-the-Green	
ZF520	Piper PA-31 Navajo Chieftain (N35823/G-BLZK)	MoD(PE) RAE Farnborough	
ZF521	Piper PA-31 Navajo Chieftain (N27509)	MoD(PE) RAE Farnborough	
ZF522	Piper PA-31 Navajo Chieftain (N4261A/G-RNAV/N27728)	MoD(PE) RAE Farnborough	
ZF526	WS61 Sea King Mk 42B [W]	For Indian Navy as IN513	
ZF534	BAe EAP	BAe Warton	
ZF537	WS Lynx AH7	AAC, stored Wroughton	
ZF538	WS Lynx AH7	AAC Fleetlands	
ZF539	WS Lynx AH7	AAC Fleetlands	
ZF540	WS Lynx AH7	AAC D&TS, Middle Wallop	
ZF557	WS Lynx HA53	RN, stored Wroughton	
ZF558	WS Lynx HA53	RN A&AEE Boscombe Down	
ZF559	WS Lynx HA53	RN, stored Wroughton	
ZF560	WS Lynx HA53	RN, stored Wroughton	
ZF561	WS Lynx HA53	RN, stored Wroughton	
ZF562	WS Lynx HA53	RN, stored Portland	
ZF563	WS Lynx HA53	RN, stored Wroughton	
ZF573	BN2T Islander (G-SRAY)	MoD(PE), Bembridge	
ZF577	BAC Lightning F53	Haydon Baillie Aircraft & Naval Museum	
ZF578	BAC Lightning F53	Wales Aircraft Museum, Cardiff Airport	
ZF579	BAC Lightning F53	Haydon Baillie Aircraft & Naval Museum	
ZF580	BAC Lightning F53	BAe Samlesbury Gate	
ZF581	BAC Lightning F53	Haydon Baillie Aircraft & Naval Museum	
ZF582	BAC Lightning F53	Haydon Baillie Aircraft & Naval Museum	
ZF583	BAC Lightning F53	Solway Aviation Society, Carlisle	
ZF584	BAC Lightning F53	Ferranti, Edinburgh	
ZF585	BAC Lightning F53	Haydon Baillie Aircraft & Naval Museum	
ZF586	BAC Lightning F53	Haydon Baillie Aircraft & Naval Museum	
ZF587	BAC Lightning F53	Haydon Baillie Aircraft & Naval Museum	
ZF588	BAC Lightning F53	East Midlands Aero Park	
ZF589	BAC Lightning F53	Haydon Baillie Aircraft & Naval Museum	
ZF590	BAC Lightning F53	Haydon Baillie Aircraft & Naval Museum	
ZF591	BAC Lightning F53	Haydon Baillie Aircraft & Naval Museum	
ZF592	BAC Lightning F53	Haydon Baillie Aircraft & Naval Museum	
ZF593	BAC Lightning F53		
ZF594	BAC Lightning F53	Haydon Baillie Aircraft & Naval Museum	
ZF595	BAC Lightning T55		
ZF596	BAC Lightning T55	Haydon Baillie Aircraft & Naval Museum	
ZF597	BAC Lightning T55	Haydon Baillie Aircraft & Naval Museum	

Notes	Serial	Type (alternative identity)	Owner, Operator or Location
	ZF598	BAC Lightning T55 (713)	Midland Air Museum, Coventry
	ZF622	Piper Navajo Chieftain (N3548Y)	MoD(PE) A&AEE Boscombe Down
	ZF641	WS/Agusta EH-101 [PP1]	MoD(PE) EHI, Milan
	ZF644	WS EH-101 Merlin [PP4]	MoD(PE) Westlands, Yeovil
	ZF649	WS EH-101 Merlin [PP5]	MoD(PE) Westlands, Yeovil
	ZG101	WS EH-101 (mock-up) [GB]	Westlands/Agusta, Yeovil
	ZG887	WS Lynx Mk 88	*To West German Navy as 83+15*
	ZG388	WS Lynx Mk 88	*To West German Navy as 83+16*
	ZG389	WS Lynx Mk 88	*To West German Navy as 83+17*
	ZG468	WS70 Blackhawk	Westland Helicopters, Yeovil
	ZG601	WS61 Sea King Mk 42B [W]	*To Indian Navy IN515*
	ZG602	WS61 Sea King Mk 42B [W]	*For Indian Navy IN514*
	ZG603	WS61 Sea King Mk 42B [W]	*For Indian Navy as IN516*
	ZG604	WS61 Sea King Mk 42B [W]	*To Indian Navy as IN517*
	ZG605	WS61 Sea King Mk 42B [W]	*For Indian Navy as IN518*
	ZG606	WS61 Sea King Mk 42B [W]	*For Indian Navy as IN519*
	ZG607	WS61 Sea King Mk 42B [W]	*To Indian Navy as IN520*
	ZG608	WS61 Sea King Mk 42B [W]	*For Indian Navy as IN521*
	ZG609	WS61 Sea King Mk 42B [W]	*For Indian Navy as IN522*
	ZG610	WS61 Sea King Mk 42B [W]	*For Indian Navy as IN523*
	ZG611	WS61 Sea King Mk 42B [W]	*For Indian Navy as IN524*
	ZG621	BAC 167 Strikemaster (G-BIDB)	*To Ecuador AF T-59*
	ZG622	BAC 167 Strikemaster (G-BIHZ)	*To Ecuador AF T-60*
	ZG623	BAC 167 Strikemaster	*To Ecuador AF T-61*
	ZG624	BAC 167 Strikemaster	*To Ecuador AF FAE373*
	ZG625	BAC 167 Strikemaster	*To Ecuador AF FAE374*
	ZG626	BAC 167 Strikemaster	*To Ecuador AF FAE375*
	ZG805	BAC 167 Strikemaster	*To OJ-1 Botswana Defence Force*
	ZG806	BAC 167 Strikemaster	*To OJ-2 Botswana Defence Force*
	ZG807	BAC 167 Strikemaster	*To OJ-5 Botswana Defence Force*
	ZG808	BAC 167 Strikemaster	*To OJ-6 Botswana Defence Force*
	ZG809	BAC 167 Strikemaster	*To OJ-7 Botswana Defence Force*
	ZG810	BAC 167 Strikemaster	*To OJ-3 Botswana Defence Force*
	ZG811	BAC 167 Strikemaster	*To OJ-8 Botswana Defence Force*
	ZG812	BAC 167 Strikemaster	*To OJ-9 Botswana Defence Force*
	ZG813	BAC 167 Strikemaster	*To OJ-4 Botswana Defence Force*
	ZG844	PBN 2T Turbine Defender (G-BLNE)	AL.1 AAC Middle Wallop
	ZG845	PBN 2T Turbine Defender (G-BLNT)	AL.1 AAC Middle Wallop
	ZG846	PBN 2T Turbine Defender (G-BLNU)	AL.1 AAC Middle Wallop
	ZG847	PBN 2T Turbine Defender (G-BLNV)	AL.1 AAC Middle Wallop
	ZG848	PBN 2T Turbine Defender (G-BLNY)	AL.1 AAC Middle Wallop
	ZG879	Powerchute Raider Mk 1	MoD(PE) RAE Farnborough
	ZG884	WS Lynx AH9	MoD(PE) for AAC
	ZG885	WS Lynx AH9	MoD(PE) for AAC
	ZG886	WS Lynx AH9	MoD(PE) for AAC
	ZG887	WS Lynx AH9	MoD(PE) for AAC
	ZG888	WS Lynx AH9	MoD(PE) for AAC
	ZG889	WS Lynx AH9	MoD(PE) for AAC
	ZG914	WS Lynx AH9	MoD(PE) for AAC
	ZG915	WS Lynx AH9	MoD(PE) for AAC
	ZG916	WS Lynx AH9	MoD(PE) for AAC
	ZG917	WS Lynx AH9	MoD(PE) for AAC
	ZG918	WS Lynx AH9	MoD(PE) for AAC
	ZG919	WS Lynx AH9	MoD(PE) for AAC
	ZG920	WS Lynx AH9	MoD(PE) for AAC
	ZG921	WS Lynx AH9	MoD(PE) for AAC
	ZG922	WS Lynx AH9	MoD(PE) for AAC
	ZG923	WS Lynx AH9	MoD(PE) for AAC
	ZH100	Boeing Sentry AEW1	MoD(PE) for RAF
	ZH101	Boeing Sentry AEW1	MoD(PE) for RAF
	ZH102	Boeing Sentry AEW1	MoD(PE) for RAF
	ZH103	Boeing Sentry AEW1	MoD(PE) for RAF
	ZH104	Boeing Sentry AEW1	MoD(PE) for RAF
	ZH105	Boeing Sentry AEW1	MoD(PE) for RAF
	ZH106	Boeing Sentry AEW1	MoD(PE) for RAF
	ZH200	BAe Hawk 200	MoD(PE), BAe Warton

RAF Maintenance Command/ Support Command 'M' number cross-reference

1764M/K4972	7473M/XE946	7739M/XA801	7932M/WZ744	8055BM/XM404
2365M/K6038	7491M/WT569	7741M/VZ477	7933M/XR220	8056M/XG337
4354M/BL614	7496M/WT612	7750M/*WK864*	7937M/WS843	8057M/XR243
5377M/EP120	7499M/WT555	(WL168)	7938M/XH903	8060M/WW397
5405M/LF738	7510M/WT694	7751M/WL131	7939M/XD596	8062M/XR669
5466M/*BN230*	7525M/WT619	7755M/WG760	7940M/XL764	8063M/WT536
(LF751)	7530M/WT648	7758M/PM651	7949M/XF974	8070M/EP120
5690M/MK356	7532M/WT651	7759M/PK664	7955M/XH767	8071M/TE476
5718M/BM597	7533M/WT680	7761M/XH318	7957M/XF545	8072M/PK624
5758M/DG202	7543M/WN901	7762M/XE670	7959M/WS774	8073M/TB252
6457M/ML427	7544M/WN904	7770M/WT746	7960M/WS726	8074M/TE392
6490M/LA255	7548M/PS915	7796M/WJ676	7961M/WS739	8075M/RW382
6850M/TE184	7554M/FS890	7805M/TW117	7964M/WS760	8076M/XM386
6944M/RW386	7564M/XE982	7806M/TA639	7965M/WS792	8077M/XN594
6946M/RW388	7570M/XD674	7809M/XA699	7967M/*WS844*	8078M/XM351
6948M/DE673	7582M/*WP180*	7816M/WG763	(WS788)	8079M/XN492
6960M/MT847	(WP190)	7817M/TX214	7969M/WS840	8080M/XM480
7000M/TE392	7583M/WP185	7822M/XP248	7970M/WP907	8081M/XM468
7001M/TE356	7602M/WE600	7825M/WK991	7971M/XK699	8082M/XM409
7008M/EE549	7604M/*XD429*	7827M/XA917	7972M/XH764	8083M/XM367
7014M/N6720	(XD542)	7829M/XH992	7973M/WS807	8084M/XM369
7015M/NL985	7605M/WS692	7839M/WV781	7976M/XK418	8085M/XM467
7035M/*K2567*	7606M/WV562	7840M/XK482	7979M/XM529	8086M/TB752
(DE306)	7607M/TJ138	7841M/WV703	7980M/XM561	8087M/XN925
7060M/VF301	7615M/WV679	7847M/WV276	7982M/XH892	8088M/XN602
7090M/EE531	7616M/WW388	7849M/XF319	7983M/XD506	8092M/WK654
7118M/LA198	7618M/WW442	7851M/WZ706	7986M/WG777	8094M/WT520
7119M/LA226	7621M/WV686	7852M/XG506	7988M/XL149	8101M/WH984
7150M/PK683	7622M/WV606	7854M/XM191	7990M/XD452	8102M/WT486
7151M/VT229	7625M/WD356	7855M/XK416	7997M/XG452	8103M/WR985
7154M/WB188	7630M/VZ304	7859M/XP283	7998M/*WM515*	8106M/WR982
7174M/VX272	7631M/VX185	7860M/XL738	(XD515)	8108M/WV703
7175M/VV106	7641M/XA634	7862M/XR246	8005M/WG768	8113M/WV753
7200M/VT812	7645M/WD293	7864M/XP244	8007M/XF990	8114M/WL798
7241M/TE311	7646M/VX461	7865M/TX226	8009M/XG518	8117M/WR974
7243M/TE462	7648M/XF785	7866M/XH278	8010M/XG547	8118M/*WZ475*
7244M/TB382	7656M/WJ573	7867M/XH980	8011M/XV269	(WZ549)
7245M/RW382	7663M/XA571	7868M/WZ736	8012M/VS562	8119M/WR971
7246M/TD248	7673M/WV332	7869M/WK935	8016M/XT677	8121M/XM474
7256M/TB752	7688M/WW421	7870M/XM556	8017M/XL762	8122M/XD613
7257M/TB752	7693M/WV483	7872M/*WZ826*	8018M/XN344	8128M/WH775
7279M/TB752	7696M/WV493	(XD826)	8019M/WZ869	8130M/WH798
7281M/TB252	7697M/WV495	7881M/WD413	8020M/WB847	8131M/WT507
7285M/VV119	7698M/WV499	7882M/XD525	8021M/XL824	8133M/WT518
7288M/PK724	7700M/WV544	7883M/XT150	8022M/XN341	8139M/XJ582
7293M/RW393	7703M/WG725	7887M/XD375	8023M/XD463	8140M/XJ571
7323M/VV217	7704M/TW536	7890M/XD453	8025M/XH124	8141M/XN688
7325M/R5868	7705M/WL505	7891M/XM693	8027M/XM555	8142M/XJ560
7362M/*475081*	7706M/WB584	7894M/XD818	8032M/XH837	8143M/XN691
(VP546)	7709M/WT933	7895M/WF784	8033M/XD382	8147M/XR526
7416M/WN907	7711M/PS915	7896M/XA900	8034M/XL703	8151M/WV795
7421M/WT600	7712M/WK281	7898M/XP854	8040M/XR493	8153M/WV903
7422M/WT684	7715M/XK724	7899M/XG540	8041M/XF690	8154M/WV908
7428M/WK198	7716M/WS776	7900M/WA576	8043M/XF836	8155M/WV797
7432M/WZ724	7717M/XA549	7902M/WZ550	8046M/XL770	8156M/XE339
7435M/WE539	7718M/WA577	7906M/WH132	8049M/WE168	8158M/XE369
7443M/WX853	7719M/WK277	7917M/WA591	8050M/XG329	8159M/XD528
7451M/TE476	7722M/XA571	7920M/WL360	8051M/XN929	8160M/XD622
7458M/WX905	7729M/WB758	7923M/XT133	8052M/WH166	8161M/XE993
7464M/XA564	7734M/XD536	7928M/XE849	8054AM/XM410	8162M/WM913
7467M/WP978	7736M/WZ559	7930M/WH301	8054BM/XM417	8163M/XP919
7470M/XA553	7737M/XD602	7931M/RD253	8055AM/XM402	8164M/*WN105*
				(WF299)

8165M/WH791	8371M/XA847	8473M/*WP180*	8586M/XE643	8679M/XF526
8169M/WH364	8372M/K8042	(WP190)	8587M/XP677	8680M/XF527
8171M/XJ607	8373M/P2617	8475M/360043	8588M/XR681	8681M/XG164
8172M/XJ609	8375M/NX611	(PJ376)	8589M/XR700	8682M/XP404
8173M/XN685	8376M/RF398	8477M/4101	8590M/XM191	8683M/WJ870
8174M/WZ576	8377M/R9125	(DG200)	8591M/XA813	8684M/XJ634
8176M/WH791	8378M/*T9707*	8478M/10639	8595M/XH278	8685M/XF516
8177M/WM224	8379M/DG590	(RN228)	8598M/WP270	8686M/XG158
8179M/XN928	8380M/Z7197	8479M/730301	8602M/*PF179*	8687M/XJ639
8180M/XN930	8382M/VR930	(AX772)	(XR541)	8689M/WK144
8182M/XN953	8383M/K9942	8432M/112372	8603M/XR951	8691M/WT518
8183M/*XN972*	8384M/X4590	(VK893)	8604M/XS104	8693M/WH863
(XN962)	8385M/N5912	8483M/420430	8606M/XP530	8695M/WJ817
8184M/WT520	8386M/NV778	8487M/J-1172	8607M/XP538	8696M/WH773
8186M/WH977	8387M/T6296	8488M/WL627	8608M/XP540	8697M/WJ825
8187M/WH791	8388M/XL993	8489M/XN816	8609M/XR953	8699M/ZD232
8188M/XG327	8389M/VX573	8490M/WH703	8610M/XL502	8700M/ZD234
8189M/WD646	8390M/SL542	8491M/WJ880	8611M/WF128	8701M/XP352
8190M/XJ918	8392M/SL674	8492M/WJ872	8612M/XD182	8702M/XG196
8192M/XR658	8393M/KK987	8493M/XR571	8613M/XJ724	8703M/VW453
8194M/XK862	8394M/WG422	8494M/XP557	8615M/XP532	8704M/XN643
8196M/XE920	8395M/WF408	8495M/XR672	8616M/XP541	8705M/XT281
8197M/WT346	8396M/XK740	8498M/XR670	8617M/XM709	8706M/XF383
8198M/WT339	8398M/WR967	8499M/XP357	8618M/XP504	8708M/XF509
8203M/XD377	8399M/WR539	8501M/XP640	8619M/XP511	8709M/XG209
8205M/XN819	8401M/XP686	8502M/XP686	8620M/XP534	8710M/XG274
8206M/WG419	8402M/XN769	8503M/XS451	8621M/XR538	8711M/XG290
8207M/WD318	8403M/XK531	8505M/XL384	8622M/XR980	8712M/XF439
8208M/WG303	8406M/XP831	8506M/XR704	8623M/XR998	8713M/XG225
8209M/WG418	8407M/XP585	8507M/XS215	8624M/XS102	8714M/XK149
8210M/WG471	8408M/XS186	8508M/XS218	8625M/XS105	8715M/*XF445*
8211M/WK570	8409M/XS209	8509M/XT141	8626M/XS109	(XG264)
8212M/WK587	8410M/XR662	8510M/XP567	8627M/XP558	8716M/XV155
8213M/WK626	8412M/XM147	8511M/WT305	8628M/XJ380	8718M/XX396
8214M/WP264	8413M/XM192	8513M/XN724	8630M/WG362	8719M/XT257
8215M/WP869	8414M/XM173	8514M/XS176	8631M/XR574	8721M/XP354
8216M/WP927	8417M/XM144	8515M/WH869	8632M/XP533	8722M/WJ640
8217M/WZ866	8418M/XM178	8516M/XR643	8634M/WP314	8723M/XL567
8222M/XJ604	8422M/XM169	8517M/XA932	8635M/XP514	8724M/XW923
8224M/XN699	8427M/XM172	8538M/XN781	8637M/XR991	8726M/XP299
8226M/XP921	8428M/XH593	8546M/XN728	8638M/XS101	8727M/XR486
8229M/XM355	8429M/XH592	8548M/WT507	8639M/XS107	8728M/WT532
8230M/XM362	8431M/XR651	8549M/WT534	8640M/XR977	8729M/WJ815
8231M/XM375	8434M/XM411	8550M/XT595	8641M/XR987	8730M/XD186
8232M/XM381	8435M/XN512	8551M/XN774	8642M/XR537	8731M/XP361
8233M/XM408	8436M/XN554	8554M/TG511	8643M/WJ867	8732M/XJ729
8234M/XN458	8437M/WG362	8556M/XN855	8645M/XD163	8733M/XL318
8235M/XN549	8439M/WZ846	8559M/XN467	8646M/XK969	8734M/XM657
8236M/XP573	8440M/WD935	8560M/XR569	8647M/XP338	8735M/WJ681
8237M/XS179	8441M/XR107	8561M/XS100	8648M/XK526	8736M/XF375
8238M/XS180	8442M/XP411	8562M/XS110	8650M/XP333	8738M/*XF519*
8239M/XS210	8444M/XP400	8564M/XN387	8652M/WH794	(XJ695)
8344M/WH960	8445M/XK968	8565M/*XF979*	8653M/XS120	8739M/XH170
8345M/XG540	8447M/XP359	(E-408)	8654M/XL898	8740M/WE173
8346M/XN734	8453M/XP745	8566M/XV279	8655M/XN126	8741M/XW329
8350M/WH840	8454M/XP442	8567M/WL738	8656M/XP405	8743M/WD790
8352M/XN632	8455M/XP444	8568M/XP503	8657M/VZ634	8745M/XL392
8355M/*KG374*	8457M/XS871	8569M/XR535	8661M/XJ727	8746M/XH171
(KN645)	8458M/XP672	8570M/XR954	8662M/XR458	8747M/WJ629
8357M/WK576	8459M/XR650	8571M/XR984	8664M/WJ603	8749M/XH537
8359M/WF825	8460M/XP680	8572M/XM706	8666M/XE793	8751M/XT255
8360M/WP863	8462M/XX477	8573M/XM708	8667M/WP972	8752M/XR509
8361M/WB670	8463M/XP355	8575M/XP542	8668M/WJ821	8753M/WL795
8362M/WG477	8465M/W1048	8576M/XP502	8670M/XL384	8754M/XG882
8363M/WG463	8466M/L-866	8577M/XP532	8671M/XJ435	8755M/*WH699*
8364M/WG464	8467M/WP912	8578M/XR534	8672M/XP351	(WJ637)
8365M/XK421	8468M/	8579M/XR140	8673M/XD165	8756M/XL427
8366M/XG454	MM5701 (BT474)	8580M/XP516	8674M/XP395	8757M/XM656
8367M/XG474	8470M/584219	8581M/WJ775	8676M/XL577	8760M/XL386
8368M/XF926	(PN999)	8582M/XE874	8677M/*XF519*	8762M/WH740
8369M/WE139	8472M/120227	8584M/WH903	(XJ695)	8763M/WH665
8370M/N1671	(VH513)	8585M/XE670	8678M/XE656	8764M/XP344

8767M/XX635	8814M/XM927	8857M/XW544	8897M/XX969	8935M/XR713
8768M/A-522	8815M/XX118	8858M/XW541	8898M/XX119	8937M/XX751
8769M/A-528	8816M/XX734	8859M/XW545	8899M/XX756	8938M/WV746
8770M/XL623	8817M/XN652	8860M/XW549	8900M/XZ368	8939M/XP741
8771M/XM602	8819M/XS479	8861M/XW528	8901M/XZ383	8940M/XR716
8772M/WR960	8820M/VP952	8862M/XN473	8902M/XV339	8941M/
8773M/XV156	8821M/XX115	8863M/XG154	8903M/XX747	8942M/XN185
8774M/XV338	8822M/VP957	8864M/WJ678	8904M/XX966	8943M/XE799
8777M/XV914	8823M/VP965	8865M/XN641	8905M/XX975	8944M/WZ791
8778M/XM598	8824M/VP971	8866M/XL609	8906M/XX976	8945M/XX818
8779M/XM607	8825M/WB530	8867M/XK532	8907M/XZ731	8946M/XZ389
8780M/WK102	8826M/XV638	8868M/WH775	8908M/XZ382	8947M/XX726
8781M/WE982	8828M/XS587	8869M/WH957	8909M/XV784	8948M/XX757
8782M/XH136	8829M/XE653	8870M/WH964	8910M/XL160	8949M/XX743
8783M/XW272	8830M/XF515	8871M/WJ565	8911M/XH673	8950M/XX956
8784M/VP976	8831M/XG160	8873M/XR453	8912M/XL189	8951M/XX727
8785M/XS642	8832M/XG172	8874M/XE597	8913M/XT857	8952M/XX730
8786M/XN495	8833M/XL569	8875M/XE624	8914M/WH844	8953M/XX959
8789M/XK970	8834M/XL572	8876M/*VM791*	8915M/XH132	8954M/XZ384
8790M/XK986	8835M/XL576	(XA312)	8916M/XL163	8955M/XX110
8791M/XP329	8836M/XL592	8877M/XP159	8917M/XM372	8956M/
8792M/XP345	8837M/XL617	8879M/XX948	8918M/XX109	8957M/
8793M/XP346	8838M/*34037*	8880M/XF435	8919M/XT486	8958M/
8794M/XP398	(429356)	8881M/XG254	8920M/XT469	8959M/
8795M/VP958	8839M/XG194	8882M/XR396	8921M/XT466	8960M/
8796M/XK943	8840M/XG252	8883M/XX946	8923M/XX819	8961M/
8797M/XX947	8844M/XJ676	8884M/VX275	8924M/XP701	8962M/XR727
8799M/WV787	8845M/XS572	8885M/XW922	8925M/XP706	8963M/
8800M/XG226	8846M/XE673	8886M/XA243	8926M/XP749	8964M/
8801M/XS650	8847M/XX344	8887M/WK162	8927M/XP750	8965M/
8802M/XJ608	8848M/XZ135	8888M/XA231	8928M/XP751	8966M/
8805M/XT772	8850M/XV436	8889M/XN239	8929M/XP764	8967M/
8806M/XP140	8852M/XV337	8890M/WT532	8930M/XR720	8968M/
8807M/XL587	8853M/XT277	8892M/XL618	8931M/XV779	8969M/
8810M/XJ825	8854M/XV154	8894M/XT669	8932M/XR718	8970M/
8811M/XL445	8855M/XT284	8895M/XX746	8933M/XX297	
8813M/VT260	8856M/XT274	8896M/XX821	8934M/XR749	

RN Engineering 'A' airframe number cross-reference

A646/SX300	A2538/XJ393	A2611/XJ575	A2645/WF225	A2673/WF122
A680/DE373	A2539/XG831	A2612/XN650	A2646/XK988	A2674/WF125
A696/SX300	A2540/WN464	A2614/XN314	A2647/XS463	A2675/XS881
A2001/*P4139*	A2542/XA862	A2616/XN651	A2648/XS125	A2678/XR955
(HS618)	A2543/XA870	A2618/XP116	A2649/XS869	A2679/XP535
A2054/SX300	A2556/XE327	A2619/XS695	A2650/XP160	A2680/XP157
A2055/SX336	A2557/WV798	A2620/XN650	A2651/XG596	A2682/XM845
A2127/DE373	A2571/XG577	A2621/XJ584	A2653/XK943	A2683/XS878
A2439/WF219	A2572/XJ402	A2622/XJ602	A2654/XN302	A2684/XP151
A2472/XA508	A2574/XD332	A2623/XN697	A2655/XN953	A2685/XS886
A2483/WF259	A2575/XG574	A2624/XN692	A2657/XX469	A2686/XS873
A2503/WM994	A2576/WV198	A2625/XL846	A2658/XP984	A2687/XS877
A2509/*WN105*	A2577/XB480	A2626/XL847	A2659/XV669	A2688/XP158
(WF299)	A2579/XN332	A2627/XN967	A2660/WV908	A2689/XM874
A2510/WM913	A2580/XE369	A2628/XP558	A2661/WV795	A2690/XS887
A2511/*WM983*	A2581/XK532	A2629/XM667	A2662/*WN105*	A2691/XS868
(XE489)	A2597/XS509	A2630/XL853	(WF299)	A2692/XM917
A2517/WM961	A2598/XJ482	A2632/WV903	A2663/XN309	A2693/XM843
A2522/WM993	A2600/XN934	A2633/XE369	A2664/XV644	A2694/XS865
A2525/XN334	A2602/XN925	A2635/XE339	A2666/XS339	A2695/XS876
A2526/WV911	A2603/XK911	A2637/WV797	A2667/XP226	A2696/XS882
A2527/XP107	A2605/XN308	A2639/XN650	A2668/XS885	A2697/XS870
A2530/WM969	A2607/XK944	A2640/XP155	A2669/XP149	A2699/XS570
A2531/WG718	A2608/XA459	A2642/XL836	A2670/XS128	A2700/XP930
A2532/WV826	A2609/XM329	A2643/*XN297*	A2671/XS867	A2701/XL500
A2534/XE368	A2610/XN647	(XN311)	A2672/XS537	A2702/XS545

RN Engineering cross-reference

A2703/XT441	A2715/	A2724/	A2733/	A2742/
A2705/XS866	A2716/	A2725/	A2734/	A2743/
A2706/XM868	A2717/	A2726/	A2735/	A2744/
A2707/XS122	A2718/	A2727/	A2736/	A2745/
A2709/XR991	A2719/	A2728/	A2737/	A2746/
A2710/	A2720/	A2729/	A2738/	A2747/
A2712/XN359	A2721/	A2730/	A2739/	A2748/
A2713/XN386	A2722/XT757	A2731/	A2740/	A2749/
A2714/XL880	A2723/XT487	A2732/	A2741/	A2750/

RAF Gliding and Soaring Association Markings

Notes	Identity	Type, Previous Identity and Competition Number	Club and Location
	R1	Schempp-Hirth Janus C (BGA 2723)	Cranwell GC, RAF Cranwell
	R2	Schempp-Hirth Janus C	RAFG&SA Centre, RAF Bicester
	R3	Schleicher ASK-13	RAFG&SA Centre, RAF Bicester
	R4	Schleicher ASK-13	Anglia GC, RAF Wattisham
	R5	Schleicher Ka-7	Four Counties GC, RAF Syerston
	R7	Schleicher ASK-13	Clevelands GC, RAF Dishforth
	R8	Grob G102 Astir CS (OY-XGE)	RAFG&SA Centre, RAF Bicester
	R9	Schempp-Hirth Janus B	Four Counties GC, RAF Syerston
	R10	Schempp-Hirth Discus B [R10]	RAFG&SA Centre, RAF Bicester
	R11	Schempp-Hirth Discus	Chilterns GC, RAF Halton
	R15	Schleicher Ka-7	Bannerdown GC, RAF Hullavington
	R16	Schempp-Hirth Ventus [16]	RAFG&SA Centre, RAF Bicester
	R18	Schleicher ASW-19 [R18]	Fenlands GC, RAF Marham
	R20	Schleicher ASK-21	Bannerdown GC, RAF Hullavington
	R21	Schleicher ASK-21	RAFG&SA Centre, RAF Bicester
	R22	Schleicher ASK-21	Wrekin GC, RAF Cosford
	R25	Schleicher ASK-21	Fulmar GC, RAF Kinloss
	R26	Schempp-Hirth Nimbus 3 [26]	RAFG&SA Centre, RAF Bicester
	R27	Schempp-Hirth Ventus [27]	RAFG&SA Centre, RAF Bicester
	R29	Schleicher Ka-7	Humber GC, RAF Scampton
	R30	Glaser-Dirks DG-300 [R30]	Humber GC, RAF Scampton
	R32	Schleicher ASK-18	Fulmar GC, RAF Kinloss
	R33	Schleicher ASK-18	RAFG&SA Centre, RAF Bicester
	R34	Schleicher ASK-21	Bannerdown GC, RAF Hullavington
	R36	Schleicher ASK-18	Four Counties GC, RAF Syerston
	R37	Schleicher ASK-13	Wrekin GC, RAF Cosford
	R40	Schleicher ASK-21	RAFG&SA Centre, RAF Bicester
	R41	Schleicher ASK-13	Chilterns GC, RAF Halton
	R42	Schleicher K-8b	Anglia GC, RAF Wattisham
	R43	Schleicher ASK-18	Wrekin GC, RAF Cosford
	R44	Schleicher K-8b	RAFG&SA Centre, RAF Bicester
	R45	Schleicher K-8b	Fulmar GC, RAF Kinloss
	R46	Schleicher ASK-13	Fenlands GC, RAF Marham
	R47	Schleicher K-8b	Cranwell GC, RAF Cranwell
	R49	Schleicher ASK-18	Bannerdown GC, RAF Hullavington
	R50	Grob G103 Acro	RAFG&SA Centre, RAF Bicester
	R52	Grob G103A Twin II Acro	Four Counties GC, RAF Syerston
	R57	Grob G102 Astir	Four Counties GC, RAF Syerston
	R58	Grob G103a Twin Astir Acro (BGA 2873)	Four Counties GC, RAF Syerston
	R60	Grob G102 Astir	Clevelands GC, RAF Dishforth
	R63	Grob G102 Astir	Humber GC, RAF Scampton
	R66	Grob G102 Astir	Cranwell GC, RAF Cranwell
	R67	Grob G102 Astir	Anglia GC, RAF Wattisham
	R68	Grob G102 Astir	Wrekin GC, RAF Cosford
	R69	Grob G102 Astir	Fenlands GC, RAF Marham
	R75	Schleicher K-8b	Fenlands GC, RAF Marham
	R77	Grob G102 Astir	RAFG&SA Centre, RAF Bicester
	R78	Grob G102 Astir	Bannerdown GC, RAF Hullavington
	R82	Grob G102 Astir	Fulmar GC, RAF Kinloss
	R83	Schleicher ASK-13	Four Counties GC, RAF Syerston
	R84	Grob G102 Astir	Chilterns GC, RAF Halton
	R85	Schleicher K-8b	Fenlands GC, RAF Marham
	R86	Schleicher ASK-13	Fenlands GC, RAF Marham

Identity	Type, Previous Identity and Competition Number	Club and Location	Notes
R87	Schempp-Hirth Ventus [87]	Four Counties GC, RAF Syerston	
R88	Schleicher ASK-13	Humber GC, RAF Scampton	
R95	Schleicher K-8b	Clevelands GC, RAF Dishforth	
R96	Schleicher K-8b	Chilterns GC, RAF Halton	
R98	Schleicher K-8b	Humber GC, RAF Scampton	
232	Rolladen-Schneider LS4 [232]	Cranwell GC, RAF Cranwell	

RN Gliding and Soaring Association Markings

N1	Eiri PiK-20D (BGA 2537/786)	Portsmouth Naval GC, RNAS Lee-on-Solent	
N11	Schleicher K-8B (BGA 2142)	Portsmouth Naval GC, RNAS Lee-on-Solent	
N12	Grob G102 Astir II (BGA 2630)	Portsmouth Naval GC, RNAS Lee-on-Solent	
N13	SZD-30 Pirat (BGA 2031)	Portsmouth Naval GC, RNAS Lee-on-Solent	
N14	Slingsby T50 Skylark 4 (BGA 1239/103)	Portsmouth Naval GC, RNAS Lee-on-Solent	
N21	Slingsby T21B Sedbergh (BGA 673)	Portsmouth Naval GC, RNAS Lee-on-Solent	
N22	Omnipol L-13 Blanik (BGA 2407)	Portsmouth Naval GC, RNAS Lee-on-Solent	
N23	Slingsby T49B Capstan (BGA 1196)	Portsmouth Naval GC, RNAS Lee-on-Solent	
N27	Schleicher Ka-7 (BGA 1157)	Portsmouth Naval GC, RNAS Lee-on-Solent	
N29	Schleicher ASK-13 (BGA 3254)	Portsmouth Naval GC, RNAS Lee-on-Solent	
N31	Slingsby T.49B Capstan (BGA 1134)	Heron GC, RNAS Yeovilton	
N32	LET L-13 Blanik (BGA 2066)	Heron GC, RNAS Yeovilton	
N33	Schempp-Hirth H.S.7 Mini-Nimbus (BGA 2353)	Heron GC, RNAS Yeovilton	
N34	Grob G.102 Astir (BGA 2289) [480]	Heron GC, RNAS Yeovilton	
N35	Grob G.103 Twin Astir (BGA 3191)	Heron GC, RNAS Yeovilton	
N38		Heron GC, RNAS Yeovilton	
N51	Centrair 101A Pegase (BGA 2987/EVM)	Seahawk GC, RNAS Culdrose	
N52	SZD-30 Pirat II (BGA 1551/CHG)	Seahawk GC, RNAS Culdrose	
N53	LET L-13 Blanik (BGA 2263/DPC)	Seahawk GC, RNAS Culdrose	
N54	Slingsby T.49B Capstan (BGA 1360/BZG)	Seahawk GC, RNAS Culdrose	
N55	Slingsby T.49B Capstan (BGA 1118/BPD)	Seahawk GC, RNAS Culdrose	

Army Gliding and Soaring Association Markings

AGA 1	Rolladen-Schneider LS4 [412]	Wyvern GC, RAF Upavon	
AGA 2	Schempp-Hirth HS7 Mini-Nimbus C (BGA2553/ EBK) [52]	Kestrel GC, RAF Odiham	
AGA 3	Schempp-Hirth Cirrus 75 [A7]	Kestrel GC, RAF Odiham	
AGA 6	Grob G102 Astir CS [212]	Wyvern GC, RAF Upavon	
AGA 8	Schleicher ASK-21 [EKG]	Wyvern GC, RAF Upavon	
AGA 9	Schleicher ASK-23 [A6]	Wyvern GC, RAF Upavon	
AGA 11	Schleicher ASK-21 [A3]	Kestrel GC, RAF Odiham	
AGA 14	Schleicher ASK-13 [A2]	Wyvern GC, RAF Upavon	
AGA 15	Schleicher ASK-13 [A1]	Kestrel GC, RAF Odiham	

Gliding Association Markings

Notes	Identity	Type, Previous Identity and Competition Number	Club and Location
	AGA 16	Schleicher ASK-18 [35]	Kestrel GC, RAF Odiham
	AGA 18	Schleicher ASK-23 [A5]	Kestrel GC, RAF Odiham
	AGA	Schempp-Hirth Discus [12]	Wyvern GC, RAF Upavon

RN Landing Platform and Shore Station Code-letters

Alpha-Numeric Sequence

Notes	Sqn code	Deck letters	Name and Pennant Number	Type/task
	323	AB	HMS *Ambuscade* (F172)	Type 21
	430	AC	HMS *Achilles* (F12)	Leander
	455	AE	HMS *Ariadne* (F72)	Leander
	341	AG	HMS *Avenger* (F185)	Type 21
	327	AL	HMS *Alacrity* (F174)	Type 21
	472	AM	HMS *Andromeda* (F57)	Leander
	470	AP	HMS *Apollo* (F70)	Leander
	426	AR	HMS *Arethusa* (F38)	Leander
		AS	RFA *Argus* (A135)	Aviation Training ship
	466	AT	HMS *Argonaut* (F56)	Leander
	322	AV	HMS *Active* (F171)	Type 21
	326	AW	HMS *Arrow* (F173)	Type 21
	320	AZ	HMS *Amazon* (F169)	Type 21
	328	BA	HMS *Brave* (F94)	Type 22
	—	BD	RFA *Sir Bedivere* (L3004)	Landing ship
	—	BE	RFA *Blue Rover* (A270)	Fleet tanker
	333	BM	HMS *Birmingham* (D86)	Type 42
	334	BS	HMS *Bristol* (D23)	Type 82
	342	BT	HMS *Brilliant* (F90)	Type 22
	—	BV	HMS *Black Rover* (A273)	Fleet tanker
	346/7	BW	HMS *Broadsword* (F88)	Type 22
	403	BX	HMS *Battleaxe* (F89)	Type 22
	330	BZ	HMS *Brazen* (F91)	Type 22
	335	CF	HMS *Cardiff* (D108)	Type 42
	—	CH	HMS *Challenger* (K07)	Seabed ops
	463	CP	HMS *Cleopatra* (F28)	Leander
	—	CU	RNAS Culdrose (HMS *Seahawk*)	
	—	CW	HMS *Cornwall* (F99)	Type 22
	431	CY	HMS *Charybdis* (F75)	Leander
	—	DC	HMS *Dumbarton Castle* (P268)	Fishery protection
	—	DG	RFA *Diligence* (A132)	Maintenance
	464	DN	HMS *Danae* (F47)	Leander
	411	EB	HMS *Edinburgh* (D97)	Type 42
	434/5	ED	HMS *Endurance* (A171)	Ice Patrol
	—	EN	RFA *Engadine* (K08)	Helicopter support
	433	EU	HMS *Euryalus* (F15)	Leander
	420	EX	HMS *Exeter* (D89)	Type 42
	342	FA	RFA *Fort Austin* (A386)	Support ship
	343	FG	RFA *Fort Grange* (A385)	Support ship
	—	FL	RNAY Fleetlands	
	—	FS	HMS *Fearless* (L10)	Assault
	410	GC	HMS *Gloucester* (D96)	Type 42
	—	GN	RFA *Green Rover* (A268)	Fleet tanker
	—	GR	RFA *Sir Geraint* (L3027)	Landing ship
	—	GV	RFA *Gold Rover* (A271)	Fleet tanker
	344	GW	HMS *Glasgow* (D88)	Type 42
	—	GY	RFA *Grey Rover* (A269)	Fleet tanker
	416	HL	HMS *Hecla* (A133)	Hecla
	414	HT	HMS *Hecate* (A137)	Hecla
	—	ID	HMS *Intrepid* (L11)	Assault
	465	JO	HMS *Juno* (F52)	Leander
	443	JP	HMS *Jupiter* (F60)	Leander
	—	L	HMS *Illustrious* (R06)	Carrier
	—	LC	HMS *Leeds Castle* (P258)	Fishery protection
	—	LN	RFA *Sir Lancelot* (L3029)	Landing ship
	405	LO	HMS *London* (F95)	Type 22

94

Sqn code	Deck letters	Name and Pennant Number	Type/task	Notes
332	LP	HMS *Liverpool* (D92)	Type 42	
—	LS	RNAS Lee-on-Solent (HMS *Daedalus*)		
360	MC	HMS *Manchester* (D95)	Type 42	
424	MV	HMS *Minerva* (F45)	Leander	
—	N	HMS *Invincible* (R05)	Carrier	
345	NC	HMS *Newcastle* (D87)	Type 42	
417	NM	HMS *Nottingham* (D91)	Type 42	
347	OD	RFA *Olmeda* (A124)	Fleet tanker	
347	ON	RFA *Olna* (A123)	Fleet tanker	
347	OW	RFA *Olwen* (A122)	Fleet tanker	
471	PB	HMS *Phoebe* (F42)	Leander	
445	PLY	HMS *Plymouth* (F126)	Type 12	
454	PN	HMS *Penelope* (F127)	Leander	
—	PO	RNAS Portland (HMS *Osprey*)		
—	PV	RFA *Sir Percival* (L3036)	Landing ship	
—	PW	Prestwick Airport (HMS *Gannet*)		
—	R	HMS *Ark Royal* (R09)	Carrier	
436	RG	RFA *Regent* (A486)	Support ship	
462	RO	HMS *Rothesay* (F107)	Type 12	
437	RS	RFA *Resource* (A480)	Support ship	
432	SC	HMS *Scylla* (F71)	Leander	
337	SD	HMS *Sheffield* (F96)	Type 23	
334	SN	HMS *Southampton* (D90)	Type 42	
450	SS	HMS *Sirius* (F40)	Leander	
—	TM	RFA *Sir Tristram* (L3505)	Landing ship	
347	TS	RFA *Tidespring* (A75)	Fleet tanker	
375	VB	HMS *Beaver* (F93)	Type 22	
—	VL	RNAS Yeovilton (HMS *Heron*)		
—	WU	RNAY Wroughton		
376	XB	HMS *Boxer* (F92)	Type 22	
407	YK	HMS *York* (D98)	Type 42	
		HMS *Coventry* (F98)	Type 22	
		RFA *Oakleaf*	Fleet tanker	No pad
		RFA *Orangeleaf*	Fleet tanker	No pad
		HMS *Norfolk*	Type 23	
		HMS *Argyll*	Type 23	
		HMS *Lancaster*	Type 23	
		HMS *Marlborough*	Type 23	
		HMS *Campbeltown* (F86)	Type 22	
		HMS *Chatham* (F87)	Type 22	
		RFA *Sir Galahad*	Landing ship	

Ships' Numeric Code — Deck Letters Analysis

	0	1	2	3	4	5	6	7	8
32	AZ	GIB	AV	AB			AW	AL	BA
33	BZ		LP	BM	BS SN	CF		SD OD	
34		AG	BT FA	FG	GW	NC	BW	ON OW TS BW	
36	MC								
37						VB	XB		
40			BX	BX		LO		YK	
41	GC	EB			HT		HL	NM	PO
42	EX				MV		AR		
43	AC	CY	SC	EU	ED	ED	RG	RS	
44				JP		PLY			
45	SS				PN	AE			
46			RO	CP	DN	JO	AT		
47	AP	PB	AM						

A Guide to the Location of Operational Bases in the UK

This section is to assist the reader to locate the places in the United Kingdom where operational military aircraft are based. The term 'aircraft' also includes helicopters and gliders.

The alphabetical order listing gives each location in relation to its county and to its nearest classified road(s) ('by' means adjoining; 'of' means proximate to), together with its approximate direction and mileage from the centre of a nearby major town or city.

Some civil airports are included where active military units are also based, but **excluded** are MoD sites with non-operational aircraft (eg 'gate guardians'), the bases of privately-owned civil aircraft which wear military markings, and museums.

User	Base name	County	Location	Distance/direction from (town)
RAE	Aberporth	Dyfed	N of A487	6m ENE of Cardigan
RAF	Abingdon	Oxfordshire	W by B4017, W of A34	5m SSW of Oxford
USAF	Alconbury	Cambridgeshire	E by A1/A14	4m NW of Huntingdon
RAF	Aldergrove/Belfast Airport	Northern Ireland	W by A26	13m W of Belfast
RAF	Arbroath	Tayside	E of A933	2m NW of Arbroath
RAF	Benson	Oxfordshire	E by A423	1m NE of Wallingford
USAF	Bentwaters	Suffolk	E of A1152/B1069	14m NE of Ipswich
RAF	Bicester	Oxfordshire	E by A421	13m NNE of Oxford
RAF	Binbrook	Lincolnshire	W of B1203	10m SSW of Grimsby
A&AEE	Boscombe Down	Wiltshire	S by A303, W of A338	6m N of Salisbury
RAF	Boulmer	Northumberland	E of B1339	4m E of Alnwick
RAF	Brawdy	Dyfed	N of A487	9m NW of Haverfordwest
RAF	Brize Norton	Oxfordshire	W of A4095	5m SW of Witney
RAF	Catterick	Yorkshire North	E by A1	7m WNW of Northallerton
RAF	Chivenor	Devon	S of A361	4m WNW of Barnstaple
RAF	Church Fenton	Yorkshire North	S of B1223	7m WNW of Selby
RAF	Coltishall	Norfolk	W of B1150	9m NNE of Norwich
RAF	Coningsby	Lincolnshire	S of A153, W by B1192	10m NW of Boston
RAF	Cosford	Shropshire	W of A41, N of A464	9m WNW of Wolverhampton
RAF	Cottesmore	Leicestershire	W of A1	9m NW of Stamford
RAF	Cranwell	Lincolnshire	N by A17, S by B1429	5m WNW of Sleaford
RNAS	Culdrose	Cornwall	E by A3083	1m SE of Helston
RAF	Dishforth	Yorkshire North	E by A1	4m E of Ripon
BAe	Dunsfold	Surrey	W of A281, S of B2130	9m S of Guildford
RAF	Exeter Airport	Devon	S by A30	4m ENE of Exeter
USAF	Fairford	Gloucestershire	S of A417	9m ESE of Cirencester
RAE	Farnborough	Hampshire	W of A325, N of A323	2m W of Farnborough
RAF/ BAe	Filton	Avon	E by M5 jn 17, W by A38	4m N of Bristol
RAF	Finningley	Yorkshire South	W of A614, S of B1396	6m ESE of Doncaster
RNAY	Fleetlands	Hampshire	E by A32	2m SE of Fareham
RAF	Glasgow Airport/ Abbotsinch	Strathclyde	N by M8 jn 28	7m W of city
USAF	Greenham Common	Berkshire	N of A339	2m SE of Newbury

The Shuttleworth Collection at Old Warden operates Bristol Fighter D8096. *PRM*

Westland Lysander V9281 is now owned by Wessex Aviation & Transport and is based at Henstridge. *PRM*

Auster AOP5 G-APAF is painted in its former military colours as TW511. *PRM*

WT722 is one of the FRADU Hunter T8Cs operated by Flight Refuelling at RNAS Yeovilton.   *PRM*

Arnold Glass has six ex-RAF Lightnings at Cranfield, including this F6 XS899. *PRM*

No 771 NAS has re-equipped with Sea King HAR5s including XV647. *PRM*

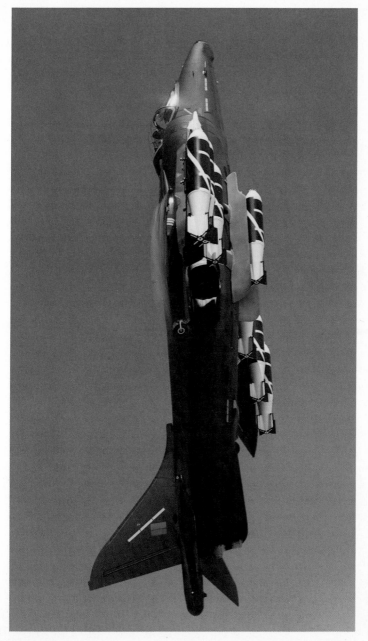

Harrier GR5 ZD346. *British Aerospace*

A Brawdy-based Hawk T1A XX351 from No 1TWU/234 Sqn. *PRM*

A Venture T2 XZ558 of No 624 VGS at RAF Chivenor. *PRM*

No 229 OCU Tornado F3 ZE251 with the 'shadow' markings of No 65 Sqn. *PRM*

Two-seat Sk-35X Draken AT-154 flown by No 725 Sqn, RDAF from Karup. *PRM*

Dassault-Breguet's prototype Rafale. *PRM*

Spanish AF CASA 101 Aviojet 79-18 operated by Esc 79.   *PRM*

Transall 50+61 of LTG63 West German AF. *PRM*

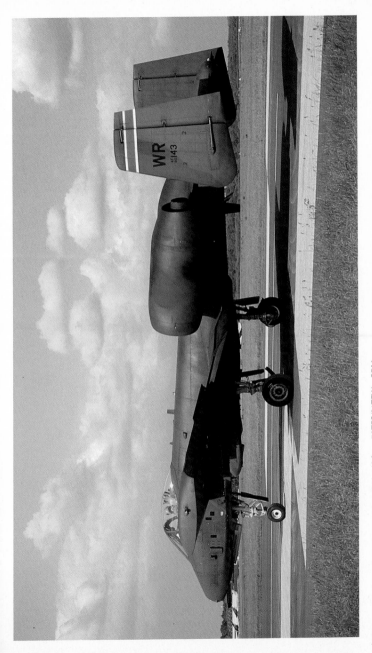

Woodbridge-based A-10A Thunderbolt II 80-143 from 78TFS/81TFW. *PRM*

20 TFW General Dynamics F-111E 68-037 flies from RAF Upper Heyford. *PRM*

User	Base name	County	Location	Distance/direction from (town)
RAF	Halton	Buckinghamshire	N of A4011, S of B4544	4m ESE of Aylesbury
RAF	Henlow	Bedfordshire	E of A600, W of A6001	1m SW of Henlow
RAF	Honington	Suffolk	E of A134, W of A1088	6m S of Thetford
RAF	Hullavington	Wiltshire	W of A429	1m N of M4 jn 17
RAF	Kemble	Gloucestershire	NW of A429, S of A433	4m SW of Cirencester
RAF	Kenley	Greater London	W of A22	1m W of Warlingham
RAF	Kinloss	Grampian	E of B9011, N of B9089	3m NE of Forres
RAF	Kirknewton	Lothian	E by B7031, N by A70	8m SW of Edinburgh
USAF	Lakenheath	Suffolk	W by A1065	8m W of Thetford
RAF	Leconfield	Humberside	E of A164	3m N of Beverley
RNAS	Lee-on-Solent	Hampshire	S by B3334	3m S of Fareham
RAF	Leeming	Yorkshire North	E of A1	5m SW of Northallerton
RAF	Leuchars	Fife	E of A919	7m SE of Dundee
RAF	Linton-on-Ouse	Yorkshire North	E of B6265	10m NW of York
RAF	Little Rissington	Gloucestershire	W of A429	6m NNW of Burford
RAE	Llanbedr	Gwynedd	W of A496	7m NNW of Barmouth
RAF	Lossiemouth	Grampian	W of B9135, S of B9040	4m N of Elgin
RAF	Lyneham	Wiltshire	W of A3102, S of A420	10m WSW of Swindon
RAE	Machrihanish	Strathclyde	W of A83	3m W of Campbeltown
RAF	Manston	Kent	N by A253	3m W of Ramsgate
RAF	Marham	Norfolk	N by A1122	6m W of Swaffham
AAC	Middle Wallop	Hampshire	S by A343	6m SW of Andover
USAF	Mildenhall	Suffolk	S by A1101	9m NNE of Newmarket
AAC	Netheravon	Wiltshire	E of A345	5m N of Amesbury
RAF	Newton	Nottinghamshire	N of A52, W of A46	7m E of Nottingham
RAF	Northolt	Greater London	N by A40	3m E of M40 jn 1
AAC	Oakington	Cambridgeshire	E of B1050, N of A604	6m NW of Cambridge
RAF	Odiham	Hampshire	E of A32	2m S of M3 jn 5
RAF	Plymouth Airport/ Roborough	Devon	E by A386	4m NNE of Plymouth
RNAS	Portland	Dorset	E by A354	3m S of Weymouth
RNAS	Predannack	Cornwall	W by A3083	7m S of Helston
RNAS	Prestwick Airport	Strathclyde	E by A79	3m N of Ayr
RAF	St Athan	Glamorgan South	N of B4270	13m WSW of Cardiff
RAF	St Mawgan/ Newquay Airport	Cornwall	N of A3059	4m ENE of Newquay
RAF	Samlesbury	Lancashire	N by A677, S by A59	5m E of Preston
RAF	Scampton	Lincolnshire	W by A15	6m N of Lincoln
USAF	Sculthorpe	Norfolk	N by A148, E by B1454	4m W of Fakenham
RAF	Sealand	Clwyd	W by A550	6m WNW of Chester
RAF	Shawbury	Shropshire	W of B5063	7m NNE of Shrewsbury
RAF	South Cerney	Gloucestershire	W by A419	3m SE of Cirencester
RAF	Swanton Morley	Norfolk	W of B1147	4m NNE of Dereham
RAF	Swansea Airport/ Fairwood Common	Glamorgan West	W by A4118	6m W of Swansea
RAF	Swinderby	Lincolnshire	S by A46	9m SW of Lincoln
RAF	Sydenham/Belfast Harbour-City Airport	Northern Ireland	W by A2	E of city

UK Operational Bases

User	Base name	County	Location	Distance/direction from (town)
RAF	Syerston	Nottinghamshire	W of A46	5m SW of Newark
RAF	Ternhill	Shropshire	W by A41	3m SW of Market Drayton
RAF	Teversham/ Cambridge Airport	Cambridgeshire	S by A1303	2m E of Cambridge
RAE	Thurleigh	Bedfordshire	E of A6, W of B660	7m N of Bedford
AAC	Topcliffe	Yorkshire North	E of A167, W of A168	3m SW of Thirsk
RAF	Turnhouse/ Edinburgh Airport	Lothian	N of A8	6m W of Edinburgh
RAF	Upavon	Wiltshire	S by A342	14m WNW of Andover
USAF	Upper Heyford	Oxfordshire	N of B4030, W of A43	12m N of Oxford
RAF	Valley	Gwynedd	S of A5 on Anglesey	5m SE of Holyhead
RAF	Waddington	Lincolnshire	E by A607, W by A15	5m S of Lincoln
BAe	Warton	Lancashire	S by A584	8m SE of Blackpool
RAF	Wattisham	Suffolk	N of B10786	5m SSW of Stowmarket
RAE	West Freugh	Dumfries & Galloway	S by A757, W by A715	5m SE of Stranraer
RAF	West Malling	Kent	E of A228	5m W of Maidstone
RAF	Weston-on-the-Green	Oxfordshire	E by A43	9m N of Oxford
RAF	Weston-super-Mare	Avon	W by A371	1m E of Weston-super-Mare
RAF	Wethersfield	Essex	E of B1053	7m NNW of Braintree
RAF	Wittering	Northamptonshire	W by A1, N of A47	3m S of Stamford
USAF	Woodbridge	Suffolk	S of B1084	11m ENE of Ipswich
RAF	Woodvale	Merseyside	W of A565	5m SSW of Southport
RAF	Wroughton	Wiltshire	E of A361	4m SSW of Swindon
RAF	Wyton	Cambridgeshire	E of A141, N of B1090	3m NE of Huntingdon
WS	Yeovil	Somerset	N of A30, S of A3088	1m W of Yeovil
RNAS	Yeovilton	Somerset	S by B3151, S of A303	5m N of Yeovil

RN Code-Squadron-Base-Aircraft Cross-check

Code Numbers	Deck/Base Letters	Unit	Location	Aircraft Type(s)
000 – 005	R	801 Sqn	Yeovilton	Sea Harrier FRS1
010 – 020	R	820 Sqn	Culdrose	Sea King HAS5
122 – 128	L	800 Sqn	Yeovilton	Sea Harrier FRS1
130 – 139	—	826 Sqn	Culdrose	Sea King HAS5
180 – 187	—	849 Sqn	Culdrose	Sea King AEW2A
251 – 254	—	824 Sqn	Prestwick	Sea King HAS5
264 – 274	L	814 Sqn	Culdrose	Sea King HAS5
300 – 306	PO	815 Sqn	Portland	Lynx HAS2/HAS3
320 – 479	*	815/829 Sqns	Portland	Lynx HAS2/HAS3
500 – 510	—	810 Sqn	Culdrose	Sea King HAS5
538 – 559	CU	705 Sqn	Culdrose	Gazelle HT2
560 – 575	CU	750 Sqn	Culdrose	Jetstream T2
576 – 579	—	750 Sqn	Culdrose	Jetstream T3
580 – 599	—	706 Sqn	Culdrose	Sea King HAS5
600 – 605	PO	829 Sqn	Portland	Lynx HAS2/HAS3
606 – 612	PO	829 Sqn	Portland	Lynx HAS2/HAS3
620 – 628	PO	772 Sqn	Portland	Sea King HC4
630 – 638	PO	702 Sqn	Portland	Lynx HAS2/HAS3
640 – 648	PO	702 Sqn	Portland	Lynx HAS2/HAS3
701 – 707	PW	819 Sqn	Prestwick	Sea King HAS5

*See foregoing separate ships' Deck Letter Analysis

Code Numbers	Deck/Base Letters	Unit	Location	Aircraft Type(s)
710 – 716	VL	899 Sqn	Yeovilton	Sea Harrier FRS1
717-718, 723	VL	899 Sqn	Yeovilton	Harrier T4N
719 – 720	VL	899 Sqn	Yeovilton	Hunter T8M
721-722	VL	899 Sqn	Yeovilton	Sea Harrier FRS1
738-739	VL	Station Flt	Yeovilton	Chipmunk T10
816 – 817	—	771 Sqn	Culdrose	Chipmunk T10
820 – 826	CU	771 Sqn	Culdrose	Sea King HAR5
830 – 838	VL	FRADU	Yeovilton	Hunter GA11
840 – 848	VL	FRADU	Yeovilton	Canberra TT18
860 – 868	VL	FRADU	Yeovilton	Hunter GA11
869 – 880	VL	FRADU	Yeovilton	Hunter T7/T8
901 – 912	—	FGF	Plymouth	Chipmunk T10

British-based Historic Aircraft in Overseas Markings

Some 'Historic' aircraft carry the markings of overseas air arms and can be seen in the UK, mainly preserved in museums and collections or taking part in air shows.

Serial	Type (alternative identity)	Owner, Operator or Location	Notes
Argentina			
A-515	FMA IA58 Pucara (ZD485)	RAF Cosford Aerospace Museum	
A-517	FMA IA58 Pucara (G-BLRP)	Privately owned, Channel Islands	
A-522	FMA IA58 Pucara (8768M)	FAA Museum, RNAS Yeovilton	
A-528	FMA IA58 Pucara (8769M)	Museum of Army Flying, Middle Wallop	
A-533	FMA IA58 Pucara (ZD486)	Museum of Army Flying, Middle Wallop	
A-549	FMA IA58 Pucara (ZD487)	Imperial War Museum, Duxford	
AE-406	Bell UH-1H	Museum of Army Flying, Middle Wallop	
AE-409	Bell UH-1H [656]	Museum of Army Flying, Middle Wallop	
AE-422	Bell UH-1H	FAA Museum, RNAS Yeovilton	
AE-520	Vertol CH-47C Chinook	RAF, stored Wroughton	
PA-12	SA330L Puma HC1 (ZE449)	Westlands, Sherborne	
0729	Beech T-34C Turbo Mentor [1-A-411]	FAA Museum, RNAS Yeovilton	
0767	Macchi MB339AA [4-A-116]	FAA Museum, RNAS Yeovilton	
Australia			
A2-4	Supermarine Seagull V (VH-ALB)	RAF Museum, Hendon	
A16-199	Lockheed Hudson IV (G-BEOX) (FH174) [SF-R]	RAF Museum, Hendon	
A17-48	DH Tiger Moth (N48DH)	Privately owned, Staverton	
Belgium			
FT-36	Lockheed T-33A	Dumfries & Galloway Aviation Museum, Tinwald Downs	
FT-37	Lockheed T-33A	RAF Alconbury	
HD-75	Hanriot HD1 (OO-APJ/G-AFDX/N75)	RAF Museum, Hendon	
Chad			
126912	AD-4N Skyraider [22-DJ]	Privately owned, North Weald	
Canada			
671	DHC Chipmunk T10 (G-BNZC)	British Aerial Museum, Duxford	
920	VS Stranraer (CF-BXO) [Q-N]	RAF Museum, Hendon	
5481	Hawker Hurricane	Privately owned, Sandown	
5424	Hawker Hurricane II (G-HURI)	Privately owned, Duxford	
9059	Bristol Bolingbroke IVT	Privately owned, Portsmouth	
9893	Bristol Bolingbroke IVT	Imperial War Museum store	
9940	Bristol Bolingbroke IVT	Royal Scottish Museum of Flight, East Fortune	
10201	Bristol Bolingbroke IVT	British Aerial Museum, Duxford	
18393	Avro Canada CF-100 (G-BCYK)	Imperial War Museum, Duxford	
20385	CCF T-6J Harvard IV (G-BGPB)	Harvard Formation Team, North Weald	

Historic Aircraft

Notes	Serial	Type (alternative identity)	Owner, Operator or Location
	Denmark		
	E-402	Hawker Hunter F51	Lovaux, Hurn
	E-407	Hawker Hunter F51	Privately owned, Lutterworth
	E-419	Hawker Hunter F51	North East Aircraft Museum, Usworth
	E-421	Hawker Hunter F51	Brooklands College of Technology, Surrey
	E-423	Hawker Hunter F51	Second World War Aircraft Preservation Society, Lasham
	E-424	Hawker Hunter F51	South Yorkshire Aviation Society, Firbeck
	E-425	Hawker Hunter F51	Midland Air Museum, Coventry
	E-427	Hawker Hunter F51 (G-9-447)	BAe OTD, Brough
	E-430	Hawker Hunter F51	Privately owned, Charlwood, Surrey
	ET-273	Hawker Hunter T7	Lovaux, Macclesfield
	L866	Consolidated Catalina (8466M)	RAF Cosford Aerospace Museum
	R-756	Lockheed F-104G	Midland Air Museum, Coventry
	Egypt		
	705	Yak 18 (G-OYAK)	Privately owned, Earls Colne
	Eire		
	177	Percival Provost T51 (G-BLIW)	Privately owned, Shoreham
	178	Percival Provost T51 (G-BKOS)	Privately owned, Coombe Bissett
	Finland		
	VI-3	Valtion Viima (G-BAAY)	Privately owned, White Waltham
	France		
	9	Dassault Mystère IVA [004]	RAF Bentwaters
	16	Dassault Mystère IVA	RAF Lakenheath
	19	Deperdussin Replica (BAPC136)	Leisure Sport, Thorpe Park
	25	Dassault Mystère IVA	RAF Woodbridge
	36	Dassault Mystère IVA [EABDR 8]	RAF Upper Heyford BDRT
	37	Nord 3400 [MAB]	Privately owned, Coventry
	39	Nord 3400 [MOC]	Privately owned, Coventry
	45	SNCAN Stampe SV4C (G-BHFG)	Privately owned, Enstone
	46	Dassault Mystère IVA [EABDR 9]	RAF Upper Heyford
	50	Dassault Mystère IVA	RAF Woodbridge
	57	Dassault Mystère IVA [8-MT]	Imperial War Museum, Duxford
	59	Dassault Mystère IVA [314-TH]	Wales Aircraft Museum, Cardiff
	65	Nord 3202 (G-BMBF)	Privately owned, Stamford
	68	Nord 3400 [MHA]	Privately owned, Coventry
	70	Dassault Mystère IVA [8-NV]	Midland Air Museum, Coventry
	75	Dassault Mystère IVA [11]	RAF Lakenheath
	79	Dassault Mystère IVA [8-NB]	Norfolk & Suffolk Aviation Museum, Flixton
	83	Dassault Mystère IVA [8-MS]	Newark Air Museum, Winthorpe
	84	Dassault Mystère IVA [8-NF]	Robertsbridge Aviation Society, Headcorn
	85	Dassault Mystère IVA	Privately owned, Bruntingthorpe
	97	Dassault Mystère IVA [10]	RAF Molesworth
	99	Dassault Mystère IVA	RAF Lakenheath
	101	Dassault Mystère IVA [8-MN]	Bomber County Aviation Museum, Hemswell
	103	Nord Norecrin (G-BHXJ)	Privately owned, Booker
	104	Dassault Mystère IVA	RAF Bentwaters
	113	Dassault Mystère IVA	RAF Lakenheath
	120	SNCAN Stampe SV4C (G-AZGC)	Privately owned, Booker
	121	Dassault Mystère IVA [8-MY]	City of Norwich Aviation Museum
	121	Nord 3400 [MJA]	Privately owned, Coventry
	126	Dassault Mystère IVA	RAF Lakenheath
	127	Dassault Mystère IVA [EABDR 7]	RAF Upper Heyford
	129	Dassault Mystère IVA [EABDR 6]	RAF Upper Heyford
	133	Dassault Mystère IVA	RAF Woodbridge
	145	Dassault Mystère IVA	RAF Lakenheath
	146	Dassualt Mystère IVA [8-MC]	North East Aircraft Museum, Usworth
	241	Dassault Mystère IVA [2]	RAF Lakenheath
	276	Dassault Mystère IVA	RAF Woodbridge
	285	Dassault Mystère IVA	RAF Lakenheath
	300	Dassault Mystère IVA [5]	RAF Lakenheath
	309	Dassault Mystère IVA [8]	RAF Lakenheath
	318	Dassault Mystère IVA [8-NY]	Dumfries & Galloway Aviation Museum, Tinwald Downs

Serial	Type (alternative identity)	Owner, Operator or Location	Notes
319	Dassault Mystère IVA [8-ND]	Rebel Air Museum, Earls Colne	
1076	Morane MS230 (G-AVEB)	Privately owned, Booker	
3398	Spad XIII Replica (G-BFYO) [2]	FAA Museum, RNAS Yeovilton	
19252	Lockheed T-33A [314-UY]	Tangmere Military Av Museum	
133722	Vought F4U-7 Corsair (NX1337A) [15F-22]	Privately owned, Duxford/Sutton Bridge	
42163	NA F-100D Super Sabre [11-YG]	Dumfries & Galloway Aviation Museum, Tinwald Downs	
42165	NA F-100D Super Sabre [11-ML]	Imperial War Museum, Duxford	
42204	NA F-100D Super Sabre [11-MQ]	RAF Alconbury	
54433	Lockheed T-33A [WD]	Norfolk & Suffolk Aviation Museum, Flixton	
63938	NA F-100F Super Sabre [11-MU]	Lashenden Air Warfare Museum, Headcorn	
S4523	Spad S-VII (N4727V)	Imperial War Museum, Lambeth	
Germany			
C19/18	Albatros Replica (BAPC 118)	Privately owned, North Weald	
D5397/17	Albatros D.VA Replica (G-BFXL)	FAA Museum, RNAS Yeovilton	
1Z+NK	Amiot AAC1 (6316)	Imperial War Museum, Duxford	
BU+CK	CASA 1-131E Jungmann (G-BUCK)	Privately owned, White Waltham	
6J+PR	CASA 2111D (G-AWHB)	Aces High Ltd, North Weald	
N7+AA	CASA 352L (G-BFHF)	Privately owned, Coventry	
A1+BT	CZL Super Aero (G-APRR)	Privately owned, Elstree	
HD5-1	Dornier Do24T-3 [58-1]	RAF Museum, Hendon	
475081	Fieseler Fi156C Storch (VP546/7362M)	RAF St Athan Historic Aircraft Collection	
28368	Flettner Fl282V Kolibri	Midland Air Museum, Coventry	
100143	Focke-Achgelis Fa330	Imperial War Museum, Duxford	
100502	Focke-Achgelis Fa330	Lincolnshire Aviation Museum, East Kirkby	
100509	Focke-Achgelis Fa330	Science Museum, stored South Kensington	
100545	Focke-Achgelis Fa330	Torbay Aircraft Museum, Paignton	
100549	Focke-Achgelis Fa330	Greater Manchester Museum of Science and Industry	
8	Focke Wulf FW190 Replica (G-WULF)	Privately owned, Elstree	
7334	Focke Wulf FW190 Replica (G-SYFW) [2+1]	Privately owned, Guernsey	
584219/38	Focke Wulf FW190F-8/U1 (PN999/8470M)	RAF St Athan Historic Aircraft Collection	
733682	Focke Wulf FW190A-8/R6	Imperial War Museum, Duxford	
4253/18	Fokker D.VII (G-BFPL)	Privately owned, Duxford	
5125/18	Fokker D.VII Replica (BAPC 110)	Leisure Sport, Thorpe Park	
8417/18	Fokker D.VII	RAF Museum store	
102/18	Fokker Dr.1 Dreidekker Replica (BAPC 88)	FAA Museum, RNAS Yeovilton	
150/17	Fokker Dr.1 Dreidekker Replica (BAPC 139)	Leisure Sport, Thorpe Park	
152/17	Fokker Dr.1 Dreidekker Replica (G-ATJM)	Privately owned, North Weald	
425/17	Fokker Dr.1 Dreidekker Replica (BAPC 133)	Torbay Aircraft Museum, Paignton	
425/17	Fokker Dr.1 Dreidekker Replica (G-BEFR)	Privately owned, Dunkeswell (summer) FAA Museum, Yeovilton (winter)	
422/15	Fokker EIII replica (G-AVJO)	Privately owned, Booker	
75	Hanriot HD-1 (G-AFDX)	RAF Museum, Hendon	
22912	Hansa Brandenburg W.29 Replica (BAPC 138)	Leisure Sport, Thorpe Park	
701152	Heinkel He111H-23 (8471M) [NT+SL]	RAF Museum, Hendon	
120227	Heinkel He162A Salamander (VH513/8472M) [2]	RAF St Athan Historic Aircraft Collection	
120235	Heinkel He162A Salamander	Imperial War Museum, Duxford	
+14	Hispano HA1112 (C4K-235/G-BJZZ/G-HUNN)	Privately owned, Thruxton	
494083	Junkers Ju87D-3 (8474M) [RI+JK]	RAF Museum, Hendon	
360043	Junkers Ju88R-1 (PJ876/8475M) [D5+EV]	RAF Museum, Hendon	
22+57	Lockheed F104G Starfighter	Bomber County Aviation Museum, Laceby	
7198/18	LVG C.VI (G-AANJ)	Shuttleworth Collection, Old Warden	

Historic Aircraft

Notes	Serial	Type (alternative identity)	Owner, Operator or Location
	6	Messerschmitt Bf109 Replica (BAPC74)	Torbay Aircraft Museum
	14	Messerschmitt Bf109 Replica (BAPC67)	Midland Air Museum, Coventry
	1190	Messerschmitt Bf109E-3	Privately owned, Hurn
	1480	Messerschmitt Bf109 [6]	Kent Battle of Britain Museum, Hawkinge
	4101	Messerschmitt Bf109E-3 (DG200/8477M) [12]	RAF Museum, Hendon
	10639	Messerschmitt Bf109G-6 (RN228/8478M)	Privately owned, RAF Benson
	730301	Messerschmitt Bf110G-4 (AX772/8479M) [D5+RL]	RAF Museum, Hendon
	191316	Messerschmitt Me163B Komet	Science Museum, South Kensington
	191614	Messerschmitt Me163B Komet (8481M)	RAF Cosford Aerospace Museum
	191659	Messerschmitt Me163B Komet [15]	Royal Scottish Museum of Flight, East Fortune
	191660	Messerschmitt Me163B Komet [3]	Imperial War Museum, Duxford
	112372	Messerschmitt Me262A-1 (VK893/8482M) [9K-XK]	RAF St Athan Historic Aircraft Collection
	420430	Messerschmitt Me410A-1/U2 (8483M) [3U+CC]	RAF St Athan Historic Aircraft Collection
	7A+WN	Morane-Saulnier MS500 (G-AZMH)	Privately owned, Chalmington, Dorset
	FI+S	Morane-Saulnier MS505 (G-BIRW) Criquet	Royal Scottish Museum of Flight, East Fortune
	17	Nord 1002 (G-ATBG)	Privately owned, Sutton Bridge
	14	Pilatus P-2 (J-108/G-BJAX)	Privately owned, Andrewsfield
	16+RF	Pilatus P-2 (U-110/G-PTWO)	Privately owned, Duxford
	Greece		
	52-6541	Republic F-84F Thunderflash	North East Aircraft Museum, Usworth
	51-6151	Canadair F-86D Sabre (really 51-6171)	North East Aircraft Museum, Usworth
	India		
	Q497	EE Canberra T4 (WH847)	BAe Warton Fire Service
	Iraq		
	333	DH Vampire T55 (pod only)	Military Aircraft Preservation Group, Hadfield, Derbys
	Israel		
	28	NA P-51D Mustang	Privately owned, Fowlmere, Cambs
	41	NA P-51D Mustang	Privately owned, N. Yorkshire
	Italy		
	MM5701	Fiat CR42 (BT474/8468M) [13-95]	RAF Museum, Hendon
	MM53211	Fiat G.46-4 (BAPC 79)	Privately owned, Lympne
	MM53432	NA T-6D [RM-11]	Privately owned, South Wales
	MM53692	CCF T-6G Texan	RAeS Medway Branch, Rochester
	MM53795	CCF Harvard IV (G-BJST) [SC-66]	Privately owned, RAF Kemble
	MM53796	CCF Harvard IV [SC-52]	Privately owned, RAF Kemble
	MM54099	CCF T-6G Harvard [RR-56]	Privately owned, Rochester
	Japan		
		Kawasaki Ki46-111 (8484M)	RAF St Athan Hist A/C Roll
	24	Kawasaki Ki100-1B (8476M)	RAF St Athan Historic Aircraft Collection
	Morocco		
	92	MH1521 Broussard (G-BJGW)	Privately owned, Duxford
	Netherlands		
	E-15	Fokker S-11 Instructor (G-BIYU)	Privately owned, Chessington
	E31	Fokker S-11 Instructor (G-BEPV)	Strathallan A/C Collection
	R-163	Piper L-21B Super Cub (G-BIRH)	Privately owned, Lee-on-Solent
	204/V	Lockheed SP-2H Neptune	RAF Cosford Aerospace Museum
	N-202	Hunter F6 (nose only) [10]	Pinewood Studios, Elstree
	N-250	Hunter F6 (nose only) [G-9-185]	Science Museum, South Kensington
	New Zealand		
	NZ5628	Vought F4U-4B Corsair (N240CA)	Privately owned, Duxford

Serial	Type (alternative identity)	Owner, Operator or Location	Notes
Norway			
56321	Saab S91B Safir (G-BKPY) [U-AB]	Newark Air Museum, Winthorpe	
Poland			
1120	MiG-15	RAF Museum, Hendon	
1420	MiG-15 (G-BMZF)	FAA Museum, RNAS Yeovilton	
Portugal			
1513	NA Harvard II	Privately owned, Cranfield	
3460	Dornier 27 (G-BMFG)	Privately owned, Booker	
3497	Dornier 27 (G-BMFH)	Booker	
Qatar			
QA10	Hunter FGA 78	Lovaux, Bournemouth	
QA11	Hunter FGA 78	Lovaux, Bournemouth	
Russia			
53	Bell RP-63C Kingcobra (N62822/44-4393)	Privately owned, Duxford	
South Africa			
6130	Lockheed Ventura II (AJ469)	RAF Museum Store, Henlow	
Spain			
EM-01	DH60G Moth (G-AAOR) [30-03]	Privately owned, Shoreham	
HD5-1	Dornier Do24T-3 [58-1]	RAF Museum, Hendon	
T2-124	Messerschmitt Bf-109K [FE-124]	Warbirds of GB, Bitteswell	
C4E-88	Messerschmitt Bf-109E	Tangmere Military Aviation Museum	
Sweden			
29640	Saab J-29F [20-08]	Midland Air Museum, Coventry	
35075	Saab J-35J Draken [40]	Imperial War Museum, Duxford	
Switzerland			
C-499	EKW C3605	Privately owned, Booker	
U-142	Pilatus P-2 (G-BONE)	Privately owned, Southend	
U-143	Pilatus P-2 (G-CJCI)	Privately owned, Micheldever	
J-1008	DH Vampire FB6	Mosquito Aircraft Museum, London Colney	
J-1172	DH Vampire FB6 (8487M)	Greater Manchester Museum of Science and Industry	
J-1605	DH Venom FB50 (G-BLID)	Privately owned, Duxford	
J-1614	DH Venom FB50 (G-BLIE)	Privately owned, Glasgow	
J-1632	DH Venom FB50 (G-VNOM)	Privately owned, Cranfield	
J-1704	DH Venom FB54	RAF Cosford Aerospace Museum	
J-1758	DH Venom FB54 (G-BLSD/N203DM)	Aces High Ltd, North Weald	
USA			
01534	Northrop F-5E Tiger II (Replica)	RAF Alconbury on display	
0-17899	Convair VT-29B	Imperial War Museum, Duxford	
100884	Douglas C-47A Dakota 3 (G-DAKS)	Privately owned, North Weald	
11042	Wolf WII Replica (G-BMZX) [7]	Privately owned, Neath, W. Glam	
11083	Wolf WII Replica (G-BNAI) [5]	Privately owned, Carmarthen	
111989	Cessna L-19A Bird Dog (N33600)	Museum of Army Flying, Middle Wallop	
115042	NA T-6G Texan (G-BGHU) [TA-042]	Privately owned, Headcorn	
115302	Piper L-18C Super Cub (G-BJTP) [TP]	Privately owned, Winterbourne, Bristol	
121714	Grumman F8F-2P Bearcat (NX700H) [S/100]	Privately owned, Duxford	
122095	Grumman F8F-1B Bearcat	The Fighter Collection, Duxford	
13064	NA P-47D Thunderbolt	RAF Museum store, Cardington	
1411	Grumman Widgeon (N444M)	Privately owned, Biggin Hill	
14286	Lockheed T-33A [WK]	Imperial War Museum, Duxford	
14419	Lockheed T-33A	Midland Air Museum, Coventry	
140547	NA T-28C Trojan (N2800Q)	Privately owned, Duxford	
146289	NA T-28C Trojan (N99153)	Norfolk & Suffolk Aviation Museum, Flixton	
14700	NA T-6G Texan	Privately owned, Coventry	
150225	Westland Wessex (G-AWOX) [123]	Privately owned, Hurn	
151632	NA TB-25N Mitchell (NL9494Z) (really 430925)	Privately owned, Coventry	
153008	McD F-4N Phantom	RAF Alconbury, BDRT	

Historic Aircraft

Notes	Serial	Type (alternative identity)	Owner, Operator or Location
	155848	McD F-4S Phantom (WT-11/ VMFA-232]	FAA Museum, RNAS Yeovilton
	159233	AV-8A Harrier [CG-03] (VMA-231)	FAA Museum, RNAS Yeovilton
164	Beech C-45 (G-BKGL) (really RCAF 5193)		British Aerial Museum, Duxford
	16718	Lockheed T-33A [314-UJ]	City of Norwich Aviation Museum
	16769	Lockheed T-33A	RAF Mildenhall Fire Section
	17473	Lockheed T-33A	RAF Cosford Aerospace Museum
	17657	Douglas A-26K Invader (FY64) (nose only)	Booker Air Museum
18-2001	Piper L-18C Super Cub (G-BIZV) (really 52-2401)		Privately owned, White Waltham
	19036	Lockheed T-33A	Newark Air Museum, Winthorpe
226671	Republic P-47D Thunderbolt [MX-X] (NX47DD)		Privately owned, Duxford
231965	Boeing B-17G (F-BDRS) [IY-GS] (really 44-83735)		Imperial War Museum, Duxford
236800	Piper L-4A Cub (G-BHPK) [44-A] (really 42-38410)		Privately owned, Tibenham
	24198	Lockheed VC-140B Jetstar	RAF Mildenhall, BDRT
243809	Waco CG-4A Hadrian (BAPC 185)		Museum of Army Flying, Middle Wallop
	24434	Republic F-105G Thunderchief (PY62) [LN]	RAF Lakenheath, BDRT
	24535	Kaman HH-43F Huskie	Midland Air Museum, Coventry
26	Boeing-Stearman N2S (G-BAVO)		Privately owned, Liverpool
2807	NA T-6G Texan (G-BHTH) [V-103]		Privately owned, Kidlington
	29261	Calver Cadet (G-CDET)	Privately owned, Booker
	29963	Lockheed T-33A	Wales Aircraft Museum, Cardiff
	315509	Douglas C-47A (G-BHUB)	Imperial War Museum, Duxford
329417	Piper L-4A Cub (G-BDHK) (really 42-38400)		Privately owned, Coleford
	329471	Piper L-4H Cub (G-BGXA) [44-F]	Privately owned, Martley, Worcs
	329601	Piper L-4H Cub (G-AXHR) [D-44]	Privately owned, Nayland
	329854	Piper L-4H Cub (G-BMKC) [72-A]	Privately owned, Booker
	329934	Piper L-4H Cub (G-BCPH) [72-B]	Privately owned, Booker
	330485	Piper L-4H Cub (G-AJES) [44-C]	Privately owned, Dunkeswell
34037	NA TB-25N Mitchell (N9115Z/ 8838M) (really 429366)		RAF Museum, Hendon
	37699	McD F-4C Phantom (FY63)	RAF Fairford, BDRT
	40707	McD F-4C Phantom (FY64)	RAF Mildenhall Fire Section
413048	Piper L-4J Cub (G-BCXJ) [39-E] (really 44-80752)		Privately owned, Compton Abbas
41386	Thomas-Morse S4 Scout Replica (G-MJTD)		Privately owned, Hitchin
	414151	NA P51D Mustang (NL314BG [HO-M]	Warbirds of GB, Biggin Hill
	42157	NA F-100D Super Sabre [UH]	North East Aviation Museum, Usworth
	42174	NA F-100D Super Sabre [UH]	Midland Air Museum, Coventry
	42196	NA F-100D Super Sabre [LT]	Norfolk & Suffolk Aviation Museum, Flixton
	42212	NA F-100D Super Sabre [LN]	RAF Sculthorpe, gate
	42223	NA F-100D Super Sabre	Newark Air Museum, Winthorpe
	431171	NA B-25J Mitchell (N7614C)	Imperial War Museum, Duxford
44	Piper PA-18-95 Super Cub (G-BJLH) [K-33]		Privately owned, Felthorpe
	430823	B-25J Mitchell (N1042B) [69]	Aces High Ltd, North Weald
	44-83184	Fairchild 24R Argus III [7] (G-RGUS)	Privately owned, Tongham
	454467	Piper J-3C-65 Cub (G-BILI)	Privately owned, Bristol
	454537	Piper L-4J Cub (G-BFDL) [44-J]	Privately owned, Meppershall
	461748	Boeing B-29A Superfortress (G-BHDK) [Y]	Imperial War Museum, Duxford
463221	NA P-51D Mustang (N51JJ) (really 473149) [G4-S]		Privately owned, Duxford
	472028	NA P-51D Mustang (41 IAF)	Privately owned, Teesside
	472216	NA P-51D Mustang (G-BIXL) [HO-M]	Privately owned, North Weald
472258	NA P-51D Mustang (really 473979) [WZ-I]		Imperial War Museum, Duxford
	472773	NA P-51D Mustang (RL-F] (G-SUSY)	Privately owned, Micheldever
	473415	NA P-51D Mustang (N6526D)	RAF Museum, Hendon
	473877	NA P-51D Mustang (N167F) [B6-S]	Privately owned, Duxford
	479609	Piper L-4H Cub (G-BHXY) [PR]	Privately owned, Pen-y-Parc, Clwyd
	479766	Piper L-4H Cub (G-BKHG)	Privately owned, Goldcliff, Mon
	480015	Piper L-4H Cub (G-AKIB)	Privately owned, Bodmin
	480133	Piper L-4J Cub (G-BDCD) [44-B]	Privately owned, Slinfold

Serial	Type (alternative identity)	Owner, Operator or Location	Notes
480321	Piper L-4J Cub (G-FRAN) [44-H]	Privately owned, Stapleford	
480480	Piper L-4J Cub (G-BECN) [44-E]	Privately owned, Milden	
480594	Piper L-4J Cub (G-BEDJ)	Privately owned, Ashford Hill	
483009	NA AT-6D Texan (really 244450)	Epping Museum, North Weald	
483868	Boeing B-17G Fortress (N5237V) [A-N]	RAF Museum, Hendon	
485784	Boeing B-17G (G-BEDF) [K-G]	Privately owned, Duxford	
511371	NA P-51D Mustang (NL1051S) [VF-S]	Privately owned, Southend	
51-15227	NA T-6G Harvard (G-BKRA) [10]	Privately owned, Staverton	
51-15673	Piper L-18C Super Cub (G-CUBI)	Privately owned, Felixkirk	
540	Piper L-4H Cub (G-BCNX) (really 43-29877)	Privately owned, Monewden	
54137	CCF Harvard IV (G-CTKL) [69]	Privately owned, Dunkeswell	
542447	Piper L-21B Super Cub (G-SCUB)	Privately owned, Anwick	
542457	Piper L-21B Super Cub (G-LION/R-167)	Privately owned, Nayland	
542474	Piper L-21B Super Cub (G-PCUB/R-184)	Privately owned, Shoreham	
54439	Lockheed T-33A	North East Aviation Museum, Usworth	
5547	Lockheed T-33A (really 19036)	Newark Air Museum, Winthorpe	
588	CAC-18 Mustang 23 (G-HAEC) [CH-V]	Privately owned, Duxford	
60312	McDonnell F-101F Voodoo [AR]	RAF Alconbury, BDRT	
60689	Boeing B-52D Stratofortress	Imperial War Museum, Duxford	
607327	Piper L-21B Super Cub [09-L] (G-ARAO)	Privately owned, Lambley	
612414	Boeing CH-47A Chinook	RAF Odiham, instructional use	
63000	NA F-100D Super Sabre (really 42160)	Wales Aircraft Museum, Cardiff	
63319	NA F-100D Super Sabre (really 42269) [319-FW]	RAF Lakenheath, at gate	
63-414	McD F-4C Phantom (37414)	RAF Woodbridge BDRT	
63-419	McD F-4C Phantom (37419)	RAF Alconbury BDRT	
63-428	Republic F-105G Thunderchief [JB] (really 24428)	RAF Upper Heyford BDRT	
63-449	McD F-4C Phantom (37449) [SA]	RAF Upper Heyford BDRT	
63-471	McD F-4C Phantom (37471) [LN]	RAF Lakenheath BDRT	
63-610	McD F-4C Phantom (37610)	RAF Lakenheath BDRT	
64-707	McD F-4C Phantom (40707)	RAF Mildenhall BDRT	
66692	Lockheed U2CT	RAF Alconbury, BDRT	
6771	Republic F-84F Thunderstreak (really 52-7133) (ex-FU-6)	RAF Museum/RAeS Medway Branch, Rochester	
68-060	GD F111E (pod)	Dumfries & Galloway Aviation Museum, Tinwald Downs	
70270	McDonnell F-101B Voodoo	RAF Woodbridge	
70-494	Republic F-105G Thunderchief [LN] (really 24434)	RAF Lakenheath, BDRT	
7797	Aeronca L-16A (G-BFAF)	Privately owned, Finmere	
80260	McDonnell F-101B Voodoo	RAF Bentwaters	
82062	DHC U-6A Beaver	Midland Air Museum, Coventry	
88297	Goodyear FG-1D Corsair (N8297) [29]	Privately owned, Duxford	
897	Aeronca 11AC Chief (G-BJEV)	Privately owned, Little Gransden	
91007	Lockheed T-33A (G-TJET) (really 51-8566) [TR-007]	Privately owned, Cranfield	
985	Boeing A75N-1 Stearman (G-ERIX) (really 4Z-16930)	Privately owned, Sutton Bridge	
Yugoslavia			
13064	Republic P-47D Thunderbolt	RAF Museum Restoration Centre, Cardington	

Irish Army Air Corps Military Aircraft Markings

Notes	Serial	Type (alternative identity)	Owner, operator and location
	34	Miles Magister	Irish Aviation Museum Store, Castlemoate House, Dublin
	141	Avro Anson	Irish Aviation Museum Store, Castlemoate House, Dublin
	164	DH Chipmunk T20	Engineering Wing, Baldonnel (stored)
	168	DH Chipmunk T20	Training Wing, Gormanston (stored)
	172	DH Chipmunk T20	Training Wing, Gormanston (stored)
	173	DH Chipmunk T20	South East Aviation Enthusiasts, Waterford
	176	DH Dove 4	South East Aviation Enthusiasts, Waterford
	181	Percival Provost T51	Baldonnel, Fire Section
	183	Percival Provost T51	Irish Aviation Museum Store, Castlemoate House, Dublin
	184	Percival Provost T51	South East Aviation Enthusiasts, Waterford
	187	DH Vampire T55	Aviation Society of Ireland, stored, Waterford
	189	Percival Provost T51	Baldonnel, Fire Section
	191	DH Vampire T55	Irish Aviation Museum Store, Castlemoate House, Dublin
	192	DH Vampire T55	South East Aviation Enthusiasts, Waterford
	193	DH Vampire T55	Baldonnel Fire Section
	195	Sud Alouette III	No 1 Support Wing, Baldonnel
	196	Sud Alouette III	No 1 Support Wing, Baldonnel
	197	Sud Alouette III	No 1 Support Wing, Baldonnel
	198	DH Vampire T11 (XE977)	On display, Baldonnel
	199	DH Chipmunk T22	Training Wing store, Gormanston
	202	Sud Alouette III	No 1 Support Wing, Baldonnel
	203	Cessna FR172H	No 2 Support Wing, Gormanston
	205	Cessna FR172H	No 2 Support Wing, Gormanston
	206	Cessna FR172H	No 2 Support Wing, Gormanston
	207	Cessna FR172H	No 2 Support Wing, Gormanston
	208	Cessna FR172H	No 2 Support Wing, Gormanston
	209	Cessna FR172H	No 2 Support Wing, Gormanston
	210	Cessna FR172H	No 2 Support Wing, Gormanston
	211	Sud Alouette III	No 1 Support Wing, Baldonnel
	212	Sud Alouette III	No 1 Support Wing, Baldonnel
	213	Sud Alouette III	No 1 Support Wing, Baldonnel
	214	Sud Alouette III	No 1 Support Wing, Baldonnel
	215	Fouga Super Magister	No 1 Support Wing, Baldonnel
	216	Fouga Super Magister	No 1 Support Wing, Baldonnel
	217	Fouga Super Magister	No 1 Support Wing, Baldonnel
	218	Fouga Super Magister	No 1 Support Wing, Baldonnel
	219	Fouga Super Magister	No 1 Support Wing, Baldonnel
	220	Fouga Super Magister	No 1 Support Wing, Baldonnel
	221	Fouga Super Magister [3-KE]	Engineering Wing, Baldonnel
	222	SIAI SF-260W Warrior	Training Wing, Baldonnel
	223	SIAI SF-260W Warrior	Training Wing, Baldonnel
	225	SIAI SF-260W Warrior	Training Wing, Baldonnel
	226	SIAI SF-260W Warrior	Training Wing, Baldonnel
	227	SIAI SF-260W Warrior	Training Wing, Baldonnel
	228	SIAI SF-260W Warrior	Training Wing, Baldonnel
	229	SIAI SF-260W Warrior	Training Wing, Baldonnel
	230	SIAI SF-260W Warrior	Training Wing, Baldonnel
	231	SIAI SF-260W Warrior	Training Wing, Baldonnel
	232	Beech King Air 200 (EI-BCY)	Transport & Training Squadron, Baldonnel
	233	SIAI SF-260MC	Engineering Wing, Baldonnel (stored)
	234	Beech King Air 200 (EI-BFJ)	Transport & Training Squadron, Baldonnel
	235	SIAI SF-260W Warrior	Training Wing, Baldonnel

Serial	Type (alternative identity)	Owner, Operator or Location	Notes
237	Aerospatiale Gazelle	Advanced Flying Training School, Baldonnel	
238	HS125/700B	Transport & Training Squadron, Baldonnel	
240	Beech King Air 200	Transport & Training Squadron, Baldonnel	
241	Aerospatiale Gazelle	Advanced Flying Training School, Baldonnel	
243	Cessna FR172P	No 2 Support Wing, Gormanston	
244	SA365F Dauphin II	No 3 Support Wing, Baldonnel	
245	SA365F Dauphin II	No 3 Support Wing, Baldonnel	
246	SA365F Dauphin II	No 3 Support Wing, Baldonnel	
247	SA365F Dauphin II	No 3 Support Wing, Baldonnel	
248	SA365F Dauphin II	No 3 Support Wing, Baldonnel	

Overseas Military Aircraft Markings

Aircraft included in this section are a selection of those likely to be seen visiting UK civil and military airfields on transport flights, exchange visits, exercises and for air shows. It is not a comprehensive list of *all* aircraft operated by the air arms concerned.

Serial	Serial	Serial
AUSTRALIA	A97-180	1106/F
Royal Australian Air Force	A97-181	1107/G
Boeing 707-338C	A97-189	1108/H
33 Sqn, Canberra	A97-190	1109/I
A20-623		1110/J
A20-624	**Lockheed**	
A20-627	**P-3C Orion**	**Saab 105ÖE**
A20-629	Edinburgh, NSW	**(green)**
	10 Sqn*	II Staffel, Linz
Boeing 707-368C	11 Sqn †	1111/A
33 Sqn, Canberra	A9-656†	1112/B
A20-103	A9-657†	1114/D
A20-261	A9-658†	1116/F
	A9-659†	1117/G
Lockheed	A9-660†	1119/I
C-130H Hercules	A9-661†	1120/J
36 Sqn, Richmond	A9-662†	
A97-001	A9-663†	**Saab 105ÖE (red)**
A97-002	A9-664†	II Staffel, Graz
A97-003	A9-665†	1122/B
A97-004	A9-751*	1123/C
A97-005	A9-752*	1124/D
A97-006	A9-753*	1125/E
A97-007	A9-754*	1126/F
A97-008	A9-755*	1127/G
A97-009	A9-756*	1128/H
A97-010	A9-757*	1129/I
A97-011	A9-758*	1130/J
A97-012	A9-759*	
	A9-760*	**Saab 105ÖE (blue)**
Lockheed		I Staffel, Zeltweg
C130E Hercules	**AUSTRIA**	1131/A
37 Sqn, Richmond	**Oesterreichische**	1132/B
A97-159	**Luftstreitkrafte**	1133/C
A97-160	**Saab 105ÖE**	1134/D
A97-167	**(yellow)**	1135/E
A97-168	I Staffel, Linz	1136/F
A97-171	1101/A	1137/G
A97-172	1102/B	1139/I
A97-177	1104/D	1140/J
A97-178	1105/E	

Overseas Serials

**Short SC7
Skyvan 3M**
Flachenstaffel, Tullin
5S-TA
5S-TB

**BELGIUM
Force Aerienne Belge/
Belgische Luchtmacht
D-BD Alpha Jet**
7/11 Smaldeel, 9 Wing,
Brustem

AT01	
AT02	
AT03	
AT05	
AT06	
AT08	
AT09	
AT10	
AT11	
AT12	
AT13	
AT14	
AT15	
AT16	
AT17	
AT18	
AT19	
AT20	
AT21	
AT22	
AT23	
AT24	
AT25	
AT26	
AT27	
AT28	
AT29	
AT30	
AT31	
AT32	
AT33	

**Dassault Mirage
5BA**
1 Flight, Bierset 8/42
Smaldeel, Bierset

BA01	1 Flt
BA03	8 Sm
BA04	
BA08	8 Sm
BA10	1 Flt
BA11	1 Flt
BA15	8 Sm
BA16	
BA17	1 Flt
BA18	1 Flt
BA20	1 Flt
BA21	8 Sm
BA22	
BA23	8 Sm
BA26	1 Flt
BA27	8 Sm
BA30	8 Sm
BA31	1 Flt
BA33	1 Flt
BA37	1 Flt
BA39	
BA42	8 Sm
BA43	
BA44	1 Flt
BA45	8 Sm

BA46	1 Flt
BA48	8 Sm
BA50	8 Sm
BA52	8 Sm
BA53	
BA54	1 Flt
BA56	
BA57	
BA59	
BA60	8 Sm
BA62	

**Dassault Mirage
5BD**
1 Flight, Bierset 8/42
Smaldeel, Bierset

BD01	8 Sm
BD03	8 Sm
BD04	42 Sm
BD08	42 Sm
BD09	1 Flt
BD10	8 Sm
BD11	8 Sm
BD12	8 Sm
BD13	1 Flt
BD14	8 Sm
BD15	

**Dassault Mirage
5BR**
42 Smaldeel, Bierset

BR03	42 Sm
BR04	42 Sm
BR07	42 Sm
BR08	42 Sm
BR09	42 Sm
BR10	42 Sm
BR12	42 Sm
BR13	42 Sm
BR14	42 Sm
BR15	42 Sm
BR16	42 Sm
BR17	42 Sm
BR19	42 Sm
BR21	42 Sm
BR22	42 Sm
BR23	42 Sm
BR24	42 Sm
BR25	42 Sm
BR26	42 Sm
BR27	42 Sm

Boeing 727-29C
21 Smaldeel, Melsbroek
CB01
CB02

**Swearingen
Merlin IIIA**
21 Smaldeel, Melsbroek
CF01
CF02
CF04
CF05
CF06

**Lockheed
C-130H Hercules**
20 Smaldeel, Melsbroek
CH01
CH02
CH03
CH04

CH05	
CH06	
CH07	
CH08	
CH09	
CH10	
CH11	
CH12	

**Dassault
Falcon 20E**
21 Smaldeel, Melsbroek
CM01
CM02

Fouga CM170 Magister
1/3 Wing, Bierset
9 Wing, Brustem
10 Wing, Kleine-Brogel
VVS, Beauvechain

MT3	9W
MT13	3W
MT14	9W
MT23	3W
MT26	3W
MT29	10W
MT30	VVS
MT31	9W
MT33	9W
MT34	9W
MT36	9W
MT40	10W
MT42	10W
MT44	VVS
MT46	1W
MT48	VVS
MT49	3W

**Hawker-Siddeley
HS748 Srs 2A**
21 Smaldeel, Melsbroek
CS01
CS02
CS03

**General Dynamics
F-16A**
349/350 Smaldeel, Bevekom
(1 Wg);
OCS, Bevekom;
2/23/31 Smaldeel, Kleine
Brogel (10 Wg)

FA01	349 Sm
FA02	350 Sm
FA03	349 Sm
FA04	350 Sm
FA05	349 Sm
FA09	349 Sm
FA10	349 Sm
FA12	350 Sm
FA16	349 Sm
FA17	349 Sm
FA18	350 Sm
FA19	350 Sm
FA20	349 Sm
FA21	349 Sm
FA22	350 Sm
FA23	350 Sm
FA25	350 Sm
FA26	349 Sm
FA27	349 Sm
FA28	350 Sm
FA30	350 Sm

Serial		Serial		Serial	
FA31	349 Sm	FA113		ST06	
FA32	350 Sm	FA114		ST09	
FA34	349 Sm	FA115		ST11	
FA36	350 Sm	FA116		ST12	
FA37	349 Sm	FA117		ST15	
FA38	350 Sm	FA118		ST16	
FA39	350 Sm	FA119		ST17	
FA40	349 Sm	FA120		ST18	
FA43	349 Sm	FA121		ST19	
FA44	350 Sm	FA122		ST20	
FA45	349 Sm	FA123		ST21	
FA46	349 Sm	FA124		ST22	
FA47	349 Sm	FA125		ST23	
FA48	350 Sm	FA126		ST24	
FA49	349 Sm	FA127		ST25	
FA50	350 Sm	FA128		ST26	
FA51	350 Sm	FA129		ST27	
FA53	350 Sm	FA130		ST29	
FA54	350 Sm	FA131		ST30	
FA55	349 Sm	FA132		ST31	
FA56	31 Sm	FA133		ST32	
FA57	23 Sm	FA134		ST33	
FA58	31 Sm	FA135		ST34	
FA60	31 Sm	FA136		ST35	
FA61	23 Sm			ST36	
FA64	31 Sm	**General Dynamics**			
FA65	23 Sm	**F-16B**		**Belgische Landmacht**	
FA66	31 Sm	349/350 Smaldeel, Bevekom		**Britten-Norman BN-2A**	
FA67	23 Sm	(1 Wg);		**Islander**	
FA68	31 Sm	OCS, Bevekom;		*15/16 Smaldeel, Brasschaat	
FA69	23 Sm	2/23/31 Smaldeel, Kleine		†SvHLV, Brasschaat	
FA70	31 Sm	Brogel (10 Wg)		B01/LA*	
FA71	23 Sm	FB01	OCS	B02/LB*	
FA72	31 Sm	FB02	350 Sm	B03/LC*	
FA73	23 Sm	FB03	350 Sm	B04/LD†	
FA74	31 Sm	FB04	OCS	B05/LE†	
FA75	23 Sm	FB05	OCS	B06/LF†	
FA76	31 Sm	FB06	OCS	B07/LG†	
FA77	23 Sm	FB07	349 Sm	B08/LH†	
FA78	31 Sm	FB08	OCS	B09/LI*	
FA80	31 Sm	FB09	OCS	B10/LJ†	
FA81	23 Sm	FB10	OCS	B11/LK†	
FA82	31 Sm	FB11	349 Sm	B12/LL†	
FA83	23 Sm	FB12	OCS		
FA84	31 Sm	FB13	10 Wg	**Sud Alouette II**	
FA85	23 Sm	FB14	23 Sm	16 Sm, Butzweilerhof	
FA86	31 Sm	FB15	10 Wg	17 Sm, Werl	
FA87	23 Sm	FB17	349 Sm	18 Sm, Merzbruck	
FA88	31 Sm	FB18	23 Sm	†SvHLV, Brasschaat	
FA89	23 Sm	FB19	31 Sm	A04	16 Sm
FA90	31 Sm	FB20	10 Wg	A05	†
FA91	23 Sm	FB21		A08	18 Sm
FA92	31 Sm	FB22		A09	17 Sm
FA93	23 Sm	FB23		A11	†
FA94	31 Sm	FB24		A12	17 Sm
FA95	23 Sm			A13	18 Sm
FA96	2 Sm			A14	16 Sm
FA97	2 Sm	**Westland Sea**		A15	17 Sm
FA98	2 Sm	**King Mk48**		A16	17 Sm
FA99	2 Sm	40 Smaldeel, Koksijde		A18	16 Sm
FA100	2 Sm	RS01		A22	†
FA101	2 Sm	RS02		A23	18 Sm
FA102	2 Sm	RS03		A24	†
FA103	2 Sm	RS04		A25	16 Sm
FA104	2 Sm	RS05		A26	†
FA105	2 Sm			A27	18 Sm
FA106	2 Sm			A29	18 Sm
FA107		**Siai Marchetti**		A31	†
FA108		**SF.260MB**		A32	18 Sm
FA109		Ecole de Pilotage		A34	17 Sm
FA110		Elementaire, (5 Sm)		A35	†
FA111		Gossoncourt		A37	17 Sm
FA112		ST02		A38	17 Sm
		ST03			
		ST04			

Overseas Serials

Serial	Serial	Serial
A40 17Sm	C-130 2464	**Lockheed**
A41 †	C-130 2465	**C-130E Hercules**
A42 18 Sm	C-130 2466	426 Sqn, Trenton
A43 †	C-130 2467	429 Sqn, Winnipeg
A44 †		435 Sqn, Edmonton
A45 18 Sm	**Lockheed**	436 Sqn, Trenton
A46 17 Sm	**RC-130E Hercules**	130305
A47 18 Sm	6 GAV 1 Esq Recife	130306
A48 17 Sm	C-130 2459	130307
A49 16 Sm		130308
A50 16 Sm		130310
A53 †		130311
A54 †	**CANADA**	130313
A55 †	**Canadian Forces**	130314
A56 16 Sm	**McDonnell Douglas**	130315
A57 16 Sm	**CF-18A Hornet**	130316
A59 17 Sm	1st CAD, Sollingen	130317
A61 17 Sm	West Germany	130318
A62 17 Sm	188728	130319
A63 †	188729	130320
A64 16 Sm	188730	130321
A65 18 Sm	188731	130322
A66 †	188732	130323
A67 16 Sm	188733	130324
A68 17 Sm	188734	130325
A69 †	188735	130326
A70 18 Sm	188736	130327
A72 †	188738	130328
A73 †	188739	
A74 16 Sm	188740	**Lockheed**
A75 18 Sm	188741	**C-130H Hercules**
A76 18 Sm	188742	130332
A77 †	188743	130333
A78 16 Sm	188744	130334
A79 16 Sm	188745	130335
A80 18 Sm	188746	130336
A81 †	188747	130337
A90 †	188748	
A92 †	188749	**Canadair CT-133**
A93 †	188750	**Silver Star**
A94 †	188751	GTTF, Sollingen
A95 †	188752	West Germany
	188753	133052
Belgische Zeemacht	188754	133094
Sud Alouette III	188755	133345
40 Smaldeel, Koksijde	188756	133450
M1 (OT-ZPA)	188757	133542
M2 (OT-ZPB)	188758	
M3 (OT-ZPC)	188759	**Bell CH-136 Kiowa**
	188760	444 Sqn, Lahr, West
BRAZIL	188761	Germany
Forca Aerea Brazileira	188762	136224
Lockheed	188763	136225
C-130E Hercules	188764	136226
1 GT 2 Esq Afonsos	188765	136227
C-130 2451	188766	136228
C-130 2453	188767	136229
C-130 2454	188768	136230
C-130 2455	188769	136231
C-130 2456	188770	136232
C-130 2458	188796	136233
C-130 2460		136234
		136236
Lockheed	**McDonnell Douglas**	136237
KC-130H Hercules	**CF-18B Hornet**	
1 GT 1 Esq Afonsos	1st CAD, Sollingen, West	**Boeing CC-137**
C-130 2461	Germany	**(B.707-374C)**
C-130 2462	188918	437 Sqn, Ottawa
	188922	13701
Lockheed	188923	13702
C-130H Hercules	188926	13703
1 GT 1 Esq Afonsos	188927	13704
C-130 2463	188928	13705

Serial	Serial	Serial

Lockheed
CP-140 Aurora
404/405/415 Sqns,
Greenwood; 407 Sqn,
Comox
140101
140102
140103
140104
140105
140106
140107
140108
140109
140110
140111
140112
140113
140114
140115
140116
140117
140118

DHC CC-142
Dash 8
412 Sqn, Lahr West Germany
142801
142802

Canadair CC-144
Challenger
412 Sqn, Lahr
West Germany
144601
144602
144605
144606
144608
144609
144610
144613
144614
144615
144616

CHILE
Fuerza Aérea de Chile
Lockheed
C-130H Hercules
Grupo 10, Santiago
995
996

DENMARK
Kongelige Danske
Flyvevaabnet
Saab A-35XD
Draken
Eskadrille 725, Karup
A001
A002
A004
A005
A006
A007
A008
A009
A010
A011
A012
A014
A017

A018
A019
A020

Saab S-35XD
Draken
Eskadrille 729, Karup
AR102
AR104
AR105
AR106
AR107
AR108
AR109
AR110
AR111
AR112
AR113
AR114
AR115
AR116
AR117
AR118
AR119
AR120

Saab Sk-35XD
Draken
*Eskadrille 725, Karup
†Eskadrille 729, Karup
AT151†
AT152†
AT153*
AT154*
AT155†
AT156*
AT157*
AT158*
AT160*

Lockheed
C-130H Hercules
Eskadrille 721, Vaerlose
B678
B679
B680

General Dynamics
F-16A
Eskadrille 723, Aalborg;
Eskadrille 726, Aalborg;
Eskadrille 727, Skrydstrup;
Eskadrille 730, Skrydstrup
E004
E005
E006
E007
E008
E016
E017
E018

E174	Esk 730
E176	Esk 730
E177	Esk 730
E178	Esk 727
E180	Esk 730
E181	Esk 727
E182	Esk 723
E183	Esk 723
E184	Esk 723
E187	Esk 727
E188	Esk 730
E189	Esk 726

E190	Esk 723
E191	Esk 730
E192	Esk 730
E193	Esk 723
E194	Esk 730
E195	Esk 723
E196	Esk 723
E197	Esk 723
E198	Esk 726
E199	Esk 727
E200	Esk 726
E202	Esk 727
E203	Esk 727
E596	Esk 723
E597	Esk 730
E598	Esk 727
E599	Esk 726
E600	Esk 723
E601	Esk 730
E602	Esk 723
E603	Esk 723
E604	Esk 723
E605	Esk 730
E606	Esk 730
E607	Esk 726
E608	Esk 723
E609	Esk 730
E610	Esk 727
E611	Esk 727

General Dynamics
F-16B

ET022	Esk 727
ET197	Esk 727
ET198	Esk 723
ET199	Esk 726
ET204	Esk 727
ET205	Esk 730
ET206	Esk 727
ET207	Esk 730
ET208	Esk 727
ET210	Esk 726
ET612	Esk 730
ET613	Esk 727
ET614	Esk 726
ET615	Esk 727

Grumman
Gulfstream III
Eskadrille 721, Vaerlose
F249
F313
F330

Saab 17
Supporter
*Flyveskolen, Avno (FLSK);
†Haerens Flyvetjaeneste
(Danish Army), Vandel;
‡Eskadrille 721, Vaerlose

T401	Aalborg Stn Flt
T402	Skystrup Stn Flt
T403	Karup Stn Flt
T404	Karup Stn Flt
T405	Karup Stn Flt
T407	Karup Stn Flt
T408	‡
T409	‡
T410	†
T411	†
T412	†
T413	†
T414	†

Overseas Serials

Serial	Serial	Serial
T415 †	**EGYPT**	41 315-VN
T417 †	**Al Quwwat al-Jawwiya**	42 315-VO
T418 †	**Ilmisriya**	43 315-VP
T419 ‡	**Lockheed**	44 315-VQ
T420 *	**C-130H Hercules**	45 315-VR
T421 *	16 Sqn, Cairo West	46 315-VS
T422 *	1271/SU-BAB	47 315-VT
T423 *	1272/SU-BAC	48 315-VU
T425 *	1273/SU-BAD	49 315-VV
T426 *	1274/SU-BAE	50 315-VW
T427 *	1275/SU-BAF	51 2-BD
T428 *	1277/SU-BAI	52 315-VX
T429 Aalborg Stn Flt	1278/SU-BAJ	53 315-VY
T430 *	1279/SU-BAK	54 315-VZ
T431 *	1280/SU-BAL	56 315-WA
T432 *	1281/SU-BAM	57 2-BC
	1282/SU-BAN	58 315-WB
	1283/SU-BAP	59 2-BE
Sikorsky S-61A	1284/SU-BAQ	60 315-WC
Eskadrille 722, Vaerlose	1285/SU-BAR	61 315-WD
U240	1286/SU-BAS	62 315-WE
U275	1287/SU-BAT	63 315-WF
U276	1288/SU-BAU	64 315-WG
U277	1289/SU-BAV	65 315-WH
U278	1290/SU-BEW	66 315-WI
U279	1291/SU-BEX	67 315-WJ
U280	1292/SU-BEY	68 315-WK
U481		69 315-WL
	FRANCE	70 315-WM
	Armee de l'Air	71 315-WN
Sovaernets	**Aerospatiale TB-30**	72 315-WO
Flyvetjaeneste	**Epsilon**	73 315-WP
(Navy)	GE315, Cognac	74 315-WQ
Westland Lynx	1 315-UA	75 315-WR
HAS80	2 315-UB	76 315-WS
Eskadrille 722, Vaerlose	3 FZ	77 315-WT
S035	4 315-UC	78 315-WU
S134	5 315-UD	79 315-WV
S142	6 315-UE	80 315-WW
S170	7 315-UF	81 315-WX
S175	8 315-UG	82 315-WY
S181	9 315-UH	83 315-WZ
S191	10 315-UI	84 315-XA
S249	11 315-UJ	85 315-XB
S256	12 315-UK	86 315-XC
	13 315-UL	87 315-XD
	14 315-UM	88 315-XE
Haerens	15 315-UN	89 315-XF
Flyvetjaeneste	16 315-UO	90 315-XG
(Army)	17 315-UP	91 315-XH
Hughes 500M	18 315-UQ	92 315-XI
Vandel	19 315-UR	93 315-XJ
H201	20 315-US	94 315-XK
H202	21 315-UT	95 315-XL
H203	22 315-UU	96 315-XM
H205	23 315-UV	97 315-XN
H206	24 315-UW	98 315-XO
H207	25 315-UX	99 315-XP
H209	26 315-UY	100 315-XQ
H210	27 315-UZ	101 315-XR
H211	28 315-VA	102 315-XS
H212	29 315-VB	103 315-XT
H213	30 315-VC	104 315-XU
H244	31 315-VD	105 315-XV
H245	32 315-VE	106 315-XW
H246	33 315-VF	107 315-XX
	34 315-VG	108 315-XY
	35 315-VH	109 315-XZ
	36 315-VI	110 315-YA
ECUADOR	37 315-VJ	111 315-YB
Lockheed	38 315-VK	112 315-YC
C-130H Hercules	39 315-VL (CEV)	113 315-YD
FAE-812	40 315-VM	114 315-YE
FAE-893		

113

FURTHER READING
FROM IAN ALLAN

abc BRITISH AIRPORTS (3rd edition)   *A. J. Wright*
A guide to Britain's airports with full details on facilities and operations.
7¼"×4¾" 112pp paperback **£3.95**

abc CIVIL AIRCRAFT MARKINGS 1989   *A. J. Wright*
The handy reference guide for the spotter.
7¼"×4¾" c304pp inc colour paperback **£3.75**

abc EUROPEAN AIRPORTS   *A. J. Wright*
Alan Wright describes the major airports of Western Europe.
7¼"×4¾" 96pp paperback **£4.95**

Aircraft Illustrated Special:
AIR TRAFFIC CONTROL   *G. Duke*
Further information upon the fascinating subject of air traffic control.
11¼"×8¼" 48pp paperback **£3.95**

BRITISH AIRWAYS   *G. Endres*
A graphic account of 'The World's Favourite Airline'.
11½"×8½" 112pp inc colour **£15.95**

CIVIL AIRLINER RECOGNITION   *P. R. March*
A handbook describing the major civil airliners of the world. Illustrated in colour throughout.
7¼"×4¾" 128pp inc colour paperback **£5.95**

Classic Civil Aircraft 1:
LOCKHEED CONSTELLATION   *K. Wixey*
To many the Lockheed Constellation was the most aesthetically pleasing civil aircraft ever built. Find out why in the first volume of the new 'Classic Civil Aircraft' series.
9¼"×6¾" 112pp **£9.95**

'MODERN CIVIL AIRCRAFT' SERIES
These illustrated volumes trace the development and operational history of recent airliners.
1: **VICKERS VC-10** *M. Hedley* **£2.95**
2: **CONCORDE** *P. Birtles* **£5.95**
5: **BAC 1-11** *M. Hardy* **£4.95**
6: **BOEING 757/767** *P. Birtles* **£5.95**
7: **McDONNELL DOUGLAS DC-10** *A. J. Wright* **£5.95**
8: **TRISTAR** *P. Birtles* **£6.95**

All: 9¼"×6¾" 80pp/96pp paperback

114

Serial		Serial		Serial		
115	315-YF	**Cessna 411**		E68	8-NP	2/8
116	315-YG	CEV		E69	8-NH	2/8
117	315-YH	6	AD	E70		
118	315-YI	8	AE	E72	314-LF	
119	315-YJ	185	AC	E73	314-TP	
120	315-YK	248	AB	E74	8-NC	2/8
121	315-YL			E75	314-UF	
122	315-YM			E76	8	/8
123	315-YN			E77	8-NA	2/8
124	315-YO	**D-BD Alpha Jet**		E79		
125	315-YP	*Patrouille de		E80	(CEV)	
126	315-YQ	France		E81	8-NK	2/8
127	315-YR	EC 1/8, EC 2/8 Cazaux;		E82	8-NX	2/8
128	315-YS	GE 314, Tours; CEAM (330),		E83	8-NS	2/8
129	315-YT	Mont de Marsan		E84		
130	315-YU	01		E85		
131	315-YV	02	F-ZWRU	E86	314-LN	
132	315-YW	E1	8-NP	2/8	E87	314-LL
133	315-YX	E3	330-BR		E88	
134	315-YY	E4	314-LP		E89	314-TG
135	315-YZ	E5	330-BT		E90	
136	315-ZA	E7	314-LB		E91	
137	315-ZB	E8	314-TD		E92	314-TB
138	315-ZC	E9	8-NN	2/8	E93	8-NT	2/8
139	315-ZD	E10	8-MM	1/8	E94	314-TE
130	315-ZE	E11	8-MP	1/8	E95	8-MO	1/8
141	315-ZF	E12	8-NO	2/8	E96	8-NN	2/8
142	315-ZG	E13	314-LH		E97	314-LE
143	315-ZH	E14	GIRD 312		E98	314-LX
144	315-ZI	E15	314-TK†		E99	8-MW	1/8
145	315-ZJ	E17			E100	CEV
146	315-ZK	E18	314-LM		E101	8-NG	2/8
147	315-ZL	E19	8-MK	1/8	E102	8-ME	1/8
148	315-ZM	E20	314-LO		E103	314-TO
149	315-ZN	E21	8-NR	2/8	E104	314-LC
150	315-ZO	E22	314-LQ		E105	314-TF
		E23	314-UB		E106	314-LV
		E24	8-MA	1/8	E107	F-TERK*
Boeing C-135FR		E25	314-LT		E108	314-UD
ERV 93, Avord, Istres and		E26	314-TI		E109	314-LK
Mont de Marsan		E27	8-MU	1/8	E110	8-MH	1/8
470	93-CA	E28	8-MI	1/8	E112	8-NQ	2/8
471	93-CB	E29	8-MF	1/8	E113	
472	93-CC	E30	314-LD		E114	8-MJ	1/8
474	93-CE	E31	314-UE		E115	
475	93-CF	E32	314-LY		E116	8-NI	2/8
735	93-CG	E33	8-NU	2/8	E117	314-TZ
736	CH	E34			E118	314-TM
737	CI	E35	314-LI		E119	314-TR
738	93-CJ	E36	314-TC		E120	314-TJ
739	93-CK	E37			E121	8-NK	2/8
740	CL	E38			E122	
		E39	314-TS		E123	314-LJ
Cessna 310		E40	8-MD	1/8	E124	8-MC	1/8
CEV		E41			E125	314-TN
045	AU	E42			E126	314-TQ
046	AV	E43			E127	314-LW
185	AU	E44	(CEV)		E128	314-TX
186	BI	E45			E129	8-NB	2/8
0187	BJ	E46			E130	8-MT	1/8
188	BK	E47	8-ND	2/8	E131	314-TY
190	BL	E48	8-NZ	2/8	E132	314-TL
192	BM	E49	314-TR		E133	8-NU	2/8
193	BG	E50			E134	8-NE	2/8
0194	BH	E51	F-TERA* (5)		E135	314-TK
242	AW	E55	F-TERE* (5)		E136	
244	AX	E58	F-TERH* (2)		E137	
820	CL	E61	F-TERJ* (8)		E138	
981	BF	E63	F-TERL* (0)		E139	8-MM	1/8
		E64	314-TT		E140	
Cessna 404		E65	314-TU		E141	8-MQ	1/8
692	DX	E66	314-TV		E142	8-MB	1/8
815	DY	E67	8-MR	1/8	E143	314-TX

Serial		
E144	314-LA	
E145	8-NM	2/8
E146	8-MG	1/8
E147		
E148	8-NJ	2/8
E149	8-MD	1/8
E150	8-NF	2/8
E151		
E152	314-TA	
E153	314-TM	
E154	8-MA	1/8
E155	F-TERF* (6)	
E156	F-TERG* (9)	
E157	314-UC	
E158	314-LR	
E159		
E160	314-LZ	
E161	8-MN	1/8
E162		
E163	314-LS	
E164	8-MS	
E165	314-UA	
E166		
E167	8-MV	1/8
E168	8-NP	2/8
E169	314-LG	
E170	F-TERM* (8)	
E171	F-TERN* (7)	
E172	F-TERO* (4)	
E173	F-TERP* (1)	
E174	F-TERQ* (7)	
E175	314-LU	
E176	8-ML	1/8

Dassault Falcon 20
CEV
SIET 98/120, Cazaux
*ET.60, Villacoublay
†ET.65, Villacoublay
‡CIFAS 328, Bordeaux
CITAC-339, Luxeuil

1	CV (CEV)	
22	CS (CEV)	
49	(SIET 98/120)	
79	CT (CEV)	
86	CG (CEV)	
93	*	
104	CW (CEV)	
115	339-WL	
124	CC (CEV)	
131	CD (CEV)	
138	CR (CEV)	
145	CU (CEV)	
167	*	
182	JA‡	
188	CX (CEV)	
238	M*	
260	†	
263	(CEV)	
268	*	
291	P†	
309	U*	
375	(CEV)	
422	L†	
451	339-WN	
463	339-WM	
483	339-WO	

Dassault Falcon 50
| 5 | FI ET.60 | |
| 78 | FJ ET.60 | |

Serial		

Dassault Falcon 900
ET.60, Villaccublay
| 2 | FP | |

Dassault Mirage IVA/IVP*
EB 1/91, Mont-de-Marsan;
EB 2/91, Cazaux;
EB 1/94 Istres;
CIFAS 328 Bordeaux-Merignac

1	AP	
2	AA	
4	AC	
5	AD	
6	AE	
7	AF	
8/01*	AG	
9	AH	
11	AJ CIFAS 328	
12	AK	
13*	AL	
14	AM	
15	AN	
16	AO	
18	AQ	
19	AR	
20	AS	
21	AT	
23	AV	
24	AW	
25*	AX	
26/02*	AY	
27	AZ	
29	BB	
31	BD	
32	BE	
34	BG	
36*	BI	1/91
37	BJ	
39	BL	
42	BO	
43	BP	
44	BQ	
45	BR CIFAS 328	
46	BS	
47	BT	
48*	BU	
49*	BV CIFAS 328	
51*	BX	
52*	BY	1/91
53*	BZ	
54*	CA	1/91
55*	CB	
56*	CC	
57*	CD	
59*	CF	
61*	CH	2/91
62*	CI	2/91

Dassault Mirage F.1C
EC 5, Orange;
EC 12, Cambrai;
EC 30, Rheims; CEAM (330)
Mont de Marsan

2	5-AG	3/5
3	12-YJ	1/2
4	330-AM	
5		
8		
9	12-YQ	1/12
10	12-KG	3/12
12	12-ZG	2/12

Serial		
14	12-YG	1/12
15	5-ON	2/5
16	5-NN	1/5
17		
18		
19	12-YK	1/12
20	5-OB	2/5
21		
22		
23	12-KD	3/12
24	12-YF	1/12
25	5-OK	2/5
26		
27	30-FB	3/30
29	5-AW	3/5
30	5-AA	3/5
31	12-ZA	2/12
32	5-AU	3/5
33		
35		
36	12-ZB	2/12
37	12-YB	1/12
38	5-AN	3/5
39	12-KA	3/12
40	12-ZJ	2/12
41		
42	5-OC	2/5
43	12-ZD	2/12
44		
47	5-OQ	2/5
48	30-SO	1/30
49		
50	30-SA	1/30
52		
54	30-FO	3/30
55	12-KM	3/12
60		
62	12-ZL	2/12
63		
64		
67	12-KB	3/12
68	12-YL	1/12
69	5-AS	3/5
70		
71	12-KJ	3/12
72	12-KC	3/12
73	12-KP	3/12
74	5-AF	3/5
75	12-KO	3-12
76	12-ZH	2/12
77		
78	12-ZF	2/12
79	12-YM	1/12
80		
81	30-LS	4/20
82		
83	12-YE	1/12
84	12-YO	1/12
85	12-ZQ	2/12
87	30-LR	4/30
90	12-YN	1/12
100	30-MQ	2/30
101	5-AP	3/5
102		
103	30-LQ	4/30
201	30-FM	3/30
202	30-FF	3/30
203	5-NC	1/5
205	5-NL	1/5
206	5-OA	2/5
207	30-SM	1/30
208	5-AV	3/5
210	30-SE	1/30

Serial			Serial			Serial		
211	30-SR	1/30	602			03		(CEV)
213	12-ZR	2/12	603	33-NR	2/33	04		
214	5-OG	2/5	604	33-NK	2/33	1		(CEV)
216	30-SG	1/30	605	33-NF	2/33	2		
217			606	33-TM	3/33	3	330-AV	
218	5-OM	2/5	607	33-CP	1/33	4	330-AW	
219	12-KI	3/12	608	33-TN	3/33	5	330-AS	
220	5-OP	2/5	609	33-TP	3/33	6	330-AY	
221	30-MP	2/30	610	33-CH	1/33	8	2-EC	1/2
223	12-YA	1/12	611	33-CA	1/33	9	2-ED	1/2
224	30-HI	2/30	612	33-NJ	2/33	10	2-LB	3/2
225	30-FL	3/30	613	33-CE	1/33	11	2-EF	1/2
226	30-HE	2/30	614	33-CQ	1/33	12	2-EH	1/2
227	30-SI	1/30	615	33-TA	3/33	13	2-EI	1/2
228	5-OH	2/5	616	33-NG	2/33	14	2-FN	2/2
229	12-YD	1/12	617	33-NO	2/33	15	2-EK	1/2
230	12-YC	1/12	618	330-AA		16	2-EL	1/2
231	30-MA	2/30	619	330-AC		17	2-EM	1/2
232	30-MJ	2/30	620	33-CJ	1/33	18	2-EN	1/2
233			622	33-CR	1/33	19	2-LA	3/2
234	30-SN	1/30	623	33-CM	1/33	20	2-LE	3/2
235			624	33-NE	2/33	21	2-LF	3/2
236	5-NJ	1/5	625			22	2-LG	3/2
237	30-SP	1/30	626	33-NA	2/33	23	2-EA	1/2
238	12-KF	3/12	627	33-NI	2/33	24	2-FM	2/2
239	30-SD	1/30	628	33-TT	3/33	25	2-LK	3/2
240	12-YP	1/12	629	33-CG	1/33	27	2-LM	3/2
241	30-SA	1/30	630	33-NL	2/33	28	2-LN	3/2
242	30-MF	2/30	631	33-CF	1/33	29	2-LO	3/2
243	30-LL	4/30	632	33-CD	1/33	30	2-EO	1/2
244	30-MG	2/30	633	33-NN	2/33	31	2-LP	3/2
245			634	33-TS	3/33	32	2-EP	1/2
246	30-SK	1/30	635	33-TH	3/33	33	2-LQ	3/2
247	5-NI	1/5	636	33-TL	3/33	34	2-LI	3/2
248	12-KQ	3/12	637	330-AB		35		
249	30-SQ	1/30	638	330-AE		36		
251	12-ZP	2/12	640	33-CB	1/33	37	2-LC	3/2
252	30-MB	2/30	641			38	330-AT	
253	30-LM	4/30	642	33-TC	3/33	39	330-AH	
254	12-ZM	2/12	643	33-CO	1/33	40	330-AI	
255	30-MJ	2/30	644	33-NS	2/33	41	5-NB	1/5
256	30-MK	2/30	645	33-TD	3/33	42	5-NS	1/5
257	12-YI	1/12	646	33-NH	2/33	43	5-ND	1/5
258	30-LN	4/30	647	33-TR	3/33	44	5-NE	1/5
259	30-SC	1/30	648	33-CC	1/33	45	5-NF	1/5
260			649	33-TQ	3/33	46	5-NL	1/5
261	12-ZI	2/12	650	33-CN	1/33	47	5-NH	1/5
262	12-ZE	2/12	651	33-NB	2/33	48		
264	12-KN	3/12	652	33-CK	1/33	49		
265	30-LO	4/30	653			50		
267	5-NM	1/5	654	33-TF	3/33	51		
268	5-OO	2/5	655	33-NN	2/33	52		
270	5-NR	1/5	656			53		
271	30-MM	2/30	657			54		
272	12-YH	1/12	658	33-NT	2/33	55		
273	12-ZN	2/12	659	33-NC	2/33	56		
274	5-OF	2/5	660	33-CI	1/33	57		
275			661			58		
277			662	33-CL	1/33	59		
278	5-OE	2/5	664	33-TU	3/33	60		
279	5-NK	1/5	665			61		
280	30-SF	1/30	666			62		
281	30-MR	2/30	667			63		
282	30-SO	1/30	668	33-CL	1/33	64		
283	12-ZO	2/12	669			65		
			670			66		
						67		
						68		
						69		
						70		

Dassault Mirage F.1CR
ER 33 Strasbourg; CEAM Mont de Marsan; EAA601 Chateaudun (330), Mont de Marsan; CEV, Istres
601 (CEV)

Dassault Mirage 2000C
EC 1/2, ECT 2/2, EC 3/2, Dijon; EC 5, Orange; CEAM (330), Mont de Marsan
01

Serial			Serial			Serial		

Dassault Mirage 2000B
CEAM, Mont de Marsan (330);
ECT 2/2, Dijon;
EC 3/2, Dijon

501	2-EQ	(CEV)
502	330-AZ	
503	330-AX	
504	2-FA	2/2
505	2-FB	2/2
506	2-FC	2/2
507	2-FD	2/2
508	2-FE	2/2
509	2-FF	2/2
510	2-FG	2/2
511	2-FH	2/2
512	2-FI	2/2
513	2-FJ	2/2
514	2-FK	2/2
515	330-AN	
516	5-NT	1/5
517	5-NO	1/5
518		
519		
520		
521		
522		
523		
524		
525		

Dassault Rafale
01	AMD-BA

DHC6 Twin Otter
CEAM Mont de Marsan
*ET 65 Villacoublay;
†GAM 56 Evreux

292	OW†
298	OY†
300	OZ†
603	65-CY*
683	65-CT*
730	65-CA*
742	65-CB*
743	65-CZ*
745	330-IG
786	
790	

Douglas DC8F
*EE.51 Evreux
†ET3/60 Charles de Galle

45570	F-RAFE*
45819	F-RAFC†
45820	F-RAFA†
46013	F-RAFG†
46063	F-RAFD†
46130	F-RAFF†

Embraer Xingu
* GE 319 Avord;
† ETE 43 Bordeaux;
‡ETE 44 Aix-en-Provence
CJTAC339, Luxeuil, CEAM, Mont de Marsan

054	YX
064	YY*
072	YA*
073	YB*
075	YC*
076	YD*
078	YE‡

080	YF*	
082	IA(CEAM)	
084	YH*	
086	YI*	
089	YJ*	
091	YK*	
092	YL*	
095	YM*	
096	YN*	
098	YO*	
099	YP*	
101	IB (CEAM)	
102	YS	
103	YT*	
105	YU*	
107	YV*	
108	339-WY	
111	YQ*	

Lockheed C-130H Hercules
*C-130H-30 Hercules
ET-2/61, Orleans

5113	61-PA
5114	61-PB
5119	61-PC
5140	61-PD
5142*	61-PE
5144*	61-PF
5150*	
5151*	
5152*	
5153*	

Morane Saulnier Paris
ETE 41 Metz;
ETE 43 Bordeaux;
ETE 44 Aix-en-Provence;
ET 65 Villacoublay; CEAM (330) Mont de Marsan

1	330-DB	
19	41-AR	
23	65-LA	
24	65-LW	
25	41-AP	
26	65-LN	
27		
29	65-LC	
30	65-LI	
34	43-BB	
35	43-BC	
36	43-BD	
38	41-AS	
44		
45	65-LE	
51		
53	DD	
54	65-LK	
56	65-LV	
57	65-LP	
58	65-LB	
59	330-DO	
60	41-AT	
61	65-LY	
62	65-LV	
65	65-LF	
68	NB	(CEV)
70		
71		
73	65-LF	
75	65-LZ	
77	DE	(GE 314)

78		
79	NL	(CEV)
80	65-LT	
81	65-LL	
83	NC	(CEV)
91	65-LU	
92	330-DA	
93	65-LD	
94	3R-DF	
95		
97	65-LH	
100	NG	(CEV)
113	NI	(CEV)
114	NJ	(CEV)
115	OV	(CEV)
116	ON	(CEV)
117	AZ	(CEV)
118	NQ	(CEV)
119	NL	(CEV)

Nord 262 Fregate
†EdC 70 Chateaudun;
*ET 65 Villacoublay;
ETE 41 Metz;
ETE 44, Aix-en-Provence;
GE 316 Toulouse;
CEAM (330) Mont de Marsan;
CEV, Istres

01	DM	(CEV)
3	OH	(CEV)
55	MH	(CEV)
58	MJ	(CEV)
64	AA*	
66	AB*	
67	MI	(CEV)
68	AC*	
76	316-DA	
77	AK*	
78	AF*	
80	AW*	
81	AH	(ETE.41)
83	316-DB	
86	316-DD	
87	316-DC	
88	AL*	(ETE.41)
89	330-IR	
91	AT*	
92	316-DE	
93	MB†	
94	41-AU	(ETE-41)
95	AR*	
105	AE*	
106	MA†	
107	AX*	
108	AG*	
109	AM*	
110	AS*	(ETE 44)

Transall C-160
Transall C-160H†
EE 54, Evreux (C160H);
ET 61 Orleans (C160A/F);
ET 64 Evreux (C160NG)

A02	61-ZB	
A04	61-BI	(CEV)
A06	61-MI	
F1	61-MA	
F2	61-MB	
F3	61-MC	
F4	61-MD	
F5	61-ME	
F11	61-MF	

Serial			Serial			Serial		
F12	61-MG		**SEPECAT**			A87	11-RX	3/11
F13	61-MH		**Jaguar A**			A88	11-RI	3/11
F15	61-MJ		EC 3 Nancy; EC 1/7, 2/7, 3/7			A89	11-MM	2/11
F16	61-MK		St Dizier; EC 4/7 Istres;			A90	11-MR	2/11
F17	61-ML		EC 1/11, 2/11, 3/11 Toul;			A91	11-YG	4/11
F18	61-MM		EC 4/11 Bordeaux;			A92	11-RS	3/11
F42	61-MN		CEAM (330) Mont de Marsan			A93	11-MV	2/11
F43	61-MO		A1	11-EQ	1/11	A95	11-MQ	2/11
F44	61-MP		A2	11-MD	2/11	A96	11-RC	3/11
F45	61-MQ		A3		(CEV)	A97	11-RG	3/11
F46	61-MR		A5	7-PF	2/7	A98	11-MT	2/11
F48	61-MT		A7	7-PR	2/7	A99	11-EI	1/11
F49	61-MU		A8	11-EB	1/11	A100	11-MP	2/11
F51	61-MW		A9	11-MS	2/11	A101	11-RK	3/11
F52	61-MX		A10	11-EC	1/11	A103	11-MA	2/11
F53	61-MY		A11	3-XA	3/3	A104		
F54	61-MZ		A12	11-YH	4/11	A107	11-ER	1/11
F55	61-ZC		A13	7-PD	2/7	A108		
F86	61-ZD		A14			A110		
F87	61-ZE		A15			A112	11-MO	2/11
F88	61-ZF		A16	7-HN	1/7	A113	11-MW	2/11
F89	61-ZG		A17	7-HE	1/7	A115		
F90	61-ZH		A19	7-II	3/7	A117	11-MH	2/11
F91	61-ZI		A21	7-IA	3/7	A118	11-YI	4/11
F92	61-ZJ		A22	7-HC	1/7	A119	11-RO	3/11
F93	61-ZK		A23	7-NJ	4/7	A120		
F94	61-ZL		A24	7-HH	3/7	A121	11-YN	4/11
F95	61-ZM		A25	7-IB	3/7	A122	11-EA	1/11
F96	61-ZN		A26	7-HQ	1/7	A123	11-MG	2/11
F97	61-ZO		A27	7-IQ	3/7	A124	11-YE	4/11
F98	61-ZP		A28	3-XC	3/3	A126	11-YC	4/11
F99	61-ZQ		A29	7-HA	1/7	A127	11-EH	1/11
F100	61-ZR		A31	7-NR	4/7	A128	11-MF	2/11
F153	61-ZS		A32	7-NL	4/7	A129	11-EE	1/11
F154	61-ZT		A33	7-IH	3/7	A130	11-MC	2/11
F155	61-ZU		A34	7-IL	3/7	A131		(CEV)
F157	61-ZW		A35	7-HG	1/7	A133	11-EF	1/11
F158	61-ZX		A36	7-IE	3/7	A135	11-RJ	3/11
F159	61-ZY		A37			A136		
F160	61-ZZ		A38	7-IC	3/7	A137	11-EJ	1/11
F201	64-GA		A39	7-IP	3/7	A138	11-YF	4/11
F202	64-GB		A40			A139	11-RW	3/11
F203	64-GC		A41	7-ND	4/7	A140	11-EL	1/11
F204	64-GD		A43	7-NF	4/7	A141	11-YO	4/11
F205	64-GE		A44	7-ID	3/7	A142		
F206	64-GF		A46	7-HF	1/7	A144	11-RM	3/11
F207	64-GG		A47	7-HP	1/7	A145	11-RN	3/11
F208	64-GH		A48	7-NH	4/7	A146		
F210	64-GJ		A49	7-IM	3/7	A148	11-YD	4/11
F211	64-GK		A50	11-YM	4/11	A149	11-EK	1/11
F212	64-GL		A53	7-HK	1/7	A150	11-YK	4/11
F213	64-GM		A54	7-HM	1/7	A151	11-EU	1/11
F214	64-GN		A55			A152	330-AG	
F215	64-GO		A56	7-IK	3/7	A153	11-RB	3/11
F216†	F-ZJUP		A58	7-NM	4/7	A154	11-YN	4/11
F217	64-GQ		A59			A156		
F218	64-GR		A60			A157	11-EN	1/11
F219	64-GS		A61	7-IF	3/7	A158		
F220†	F-ZJUS		A64	7-NE	4/7	A159		
F221†	F-ZJUU		A65	7-IO	3/7	A160	(CEAM)	(CEV)
F222	64-GV		A66	7-NC	4/7			
F223	64-GW		A67	7-NB	4/7	**SEPECAT Jaguar E**		
F224	64-GX		A70	7-NI	4/7	E1		(CEV)
F225	64-GY		A72	7-HJ	1/7	E2	7-PH	2/7
F226	64-GZ		A73			E3	7-PN	2/7
F227	64-GP		A74	7-NA	4/7	E4		
F228†	F-ZJUY		A75	11-RH	3/11	E5	7-IJ	3/7
F229†	F-ZJUC		A76	7-HL	1/7	E6	11-ME	2/11
F230†	F-ZJUA		A79	7-NP	4/7	E7	7-PI	2/7
F231†	F-ZJUB		A80	7-IN	3/7	E8	7-PP	2/7
F232†			A82	11-YB	4/11	E9	7-PQ	2/7
			A83	11-YL	4/11	E10		
			A84	11-YJ	4/11	E11	7-PL	2/7

Overseas Serials

E12	7-NK	4/7
E13	11-YY	4/11
E15	7-PJ	2/7
E16	7-HI	1/7
E17		
E18	7-NG	4/7
E19	11-MB	2/11
E20	11-RV	3/11
E21		
E22	7-PC	2/7
E23	11-EV	1/11
E24	7-NK	4/7
E25	7-PE	2/7
E27	11-MA	2/11
E28	7-PK	2/7
E29		
E30	7-PO	2/7
E31	11-RF	3/11
E32		
E33		
E35		
E36	7-4B	1/7
E37	11-MK	2/11
E38	7-PM	2/7
E39	11-YZ	4/11
E40	11-EG	1/11

Aeronavale/Marine
Aerospatiale SA.321G
Super
Frelon
32 F, Lanveoc;
33 F, San Mandrier

101	(32F)
102	(32F)
105	(33F)
106	(32F)
118	(32F)
120	(32F)
122	(32F)
134	(32F)
137	(32F)
141	(32F)
144	(32F)
148	(33F)
149	(32F)
150	(33F)
160	(32F)
162	(32F)
163	(33F)
164	(32F)
165	(32F)

Breguet 1050
Alizé
4F, Lann Bihoue;
6F, Nimes-Garons;
ES 20, Frejus;
ES 59, Hyeres

11	(4F)
12	(4F)
16	(59S)
17	(4F)
22	(6F)
24	(59S)
25	(4F)
26	(59S)
28	
30	(6F)
31	(59S)
33	(4F)
36	(4F)
41	(59S)

43	(4F)
47	(6F)
48	(4F)
50	(59S)
51	(6F)
52	(4F)
53	(6F)
55	(59S)
56	(59S)
59	(6F)
60	(4F)
64	(6F)
65	(6F)
67	(59S)
68	(6F)
73	(6F)
76	(59S)
87	(59S)

Breguet 1150
Atlantic
*21F/22F, Nimes-Garons;
†23F/24F, Lann Bihoue

03*	
04*	
1*	
2*	
5†	
7†	
9	
11*	
13*	
15*	
17†	
21†	
23†	
24†	
25†	
27†	
31*	
35*	
37*	
38*	
41†	
44†	
45†	
47†	
48†	
49*	
50†	
51*	
52*	
53*	
54†	
55†	
56*	
57†	
61*	
65†	
66†	
67*	
68†	
ANG.01	CEV
ANG.02	CEV
ANG.03	CEV
ANG.04	CEV

Dassault
Etendard IVM
*16F, Landivisiau;
†ES 59, Hyeres

1†
3†

5†
7*
9*
11†
13†
14†
15†
16†
21*
22*
26†
29†
30†
32*
34†
36†
37†
40†
41†
42†
51†
52†
53†
56†
57†
59†
60*

Dassault
Etendard IVP/IVMP*
16F Landivisiau

101
107
108
109
114
115
117
118
120
153*
162*
163*
166*

Dassault Super
Etendard
*11F, Landivisiau;
†14F, Landivisiau;
‡17F, Hyeres

1†
2†
3‡
4‡
5‡
6†
7*
8*
9*
10*
11*
12*
13†
14‡
15†
16†
17†
18†
19‡
20
21
23‡
24*

Serial	Serial	Serial
25*	68 (52S)	60 (56S)
26‡	69 (52S)	61 (2S)
27	70 (52S)	62 (3S)
28†	71 (52S)	63 (2S)
29†	74 (52S)	65 (2S)
30‡	77 (11S)	69 (56S)
31†	79 (52S)	70 (3S)
32†	81 (52S)	71 (2S)
33‡	83 (11S)	72 (56S)
34	85 (52S)	73 (56S)
35*	87 (52S)	75 (2S)
37*	90 (52S)	79 (2S)
38*		100 (56S)
39	**LTV F-8E (FN)**	102 (11S)
40*	**Crusader**	104 (11S)
41†	12F, Landivisiau	
42	1	**Piper Navajo**
43†	2	ES 2, Lann Bihoue; ES 3,
44†	3	Hyeres
45*	4	ES 11, Le Bourget
46‡	5	ES 20 Frejus
47†	6	227 (2S)
48‡	7	232 (2S)
49†	8	903 (3S)
50†	10	904 (3S)
51	11	906 (3S)
52†	12	912 (3S)
53†	17	914 (3S)
54†	18	916 (3S)
55*	19	925 (2S)
57‡	23	927 (20S)
59‡	27	929 (2S)
60†	28	931 (2S)
61*	29	
62*	30	**Westland Lynx**
63*	31	**HAS2 (FN)*;**
64*	33	**HAS4 (FN)†**
65‡	34	31F, San Mandrier;
66†	35	34F, Lanveoc;
68‡	37	35F, Lanveoc; ES 20
69*	39	St Raphael
71*	40	260* (20S)
	41	262* (35F)
Dassault Falcon		263* (34F)
10(MER)		264* (34F)
†ES3 Hyeres;	**Morane Saulnier**	265*
*ES 57 Landivisiau	**Paris**	266* (34F)
32*	ES 57, Landivisiau	267*
101*	32	268*
129*	33	269 (34F)
133*	40	270* (34F)
143†	41	271* (35F)
185†	42	272* (20S)
	46	273* (34F)
Dassault Falcon	47	274* (34F)
Guardian	85	275* (34F)
†ES 9 Noumea;	87	276* (34F)
*ES 12 Papeete	88	278* (34F)
CEPA, Istres		621* (34F)
48*	**Nord 262 Fregate**	622* (34F)
65†	ES 2, Lann Bihoue;	623* (34F)
72*	ES 3, Hyeres;	624* (34F)
77†	ES 11, Le Bourget;	625* (34F)
80 (CEPA)	ES 55, Aspretto;	626* (34F)
	ES 56, Nimes-Garons	627* (35F)
Embraer Xingu	16 (2S)	8001† (20S)
ES 11, Le Bourget;	28 (2S)	8002† (34F)
ES 20, Frejus;	43 (56S)	8003† (31F)
ES 52, Lann Bihoue;	45 (56S)	8004† (35F)
55	46 (56S)	8005† (31F)
65 (52S)	51 (56S)	8006† (34F)
66 (52S)	52 (56S)	8007† (34F)
67 (52S)	53 (56S)	8008† (34F)
	59 (2S)	

Overseas Serials

Serial

809† (31F)
810† (31F)
811† (31F)
812† (34F)
813† (31F)
814† (34F)

GREECE
Elliniki Aeroporia
Lockheed
C-130H Hercules
356 Mira, Elefsis
741
742
743
744
745
746
747
748
749
750
751
752

ISRAEL
Heyl ha'avir
Lockheed
C-130H Hercules
4X-FBA/102
4X-FBB/106
4X-FBC/309

Lockheed
C-130E Hercules
4X-FBD/420
4X-FBE/304
4X-FBF/301
4X-FBG/310
4X-FBH/312
4X-FBI/314
4X-FBK/318
4X-FBL/313
4X-FBM/316
4X-FBN/307
4X-FBO/203
4X-FBP/208

Lockeed
C-130H Hercules
4X-FBS/427
4X-FBT/435
4X-FBU/448
4X-FBW/436
4X-FBX/428

Lockheed
KC-130H Hercules
4X-FBY/522
4X-FBZ/545

ITALY
Aeronautica Militare Italiano
Aeritalia G222
*46 Brigata Aerea, Pisa
†14°Stormo, Practica di Mare;
‡RSV, Practica di Mare; 15° Stormo
MM62101‡ RS-36
MM62102* 46-20
MM62103* 46-37

Serial

MM62104* 46-91
MM62105* 46-82
MM62107†
MM62108* 46-30
MM62109* 46-96
MM62110* 46-81
MM62111* 46-83
MM62112* 46-85
MM62113* 46-34
MM62114* 46-80
MM62115* 46-22
MM62116* 46-35
MM62117* 46-25
MM62118* 46-24
MM62119* 46-21
MM62120* 46-90
MM62121* 46-86
MM62122* 46-23
MM62123* 46-28
MM62124* 46-88
MM62125* 46-87
MM62126* 46-26
MM62127* 46-27
MM62128‡ RS-34
MM62129* RS-29
MM62130* 46-31
MM62132* 46-32
MM62133* 46-96
MM62134* 46-33
MM62143* 46-36
MM62144* 46-98
MM62145 15-50
MM62146 15-51
MM62147 15-52

Aeritalia G222TCM
MM62103‡ RS-35
MM62135* 46-94
MM62136* 46-97
MM62137* 46-95
MM62138†

Aeritalia G222RM
14° Stormo, Practica di Mare
MM62139 14-20
MM62140 14-21
MM62141 14-22
MM62142 14-

Aermacchi MB339
*Frecce Tricolori; 61ª Brigata Aerea, Lecce; ‡14° Stormo, Practica di Mare RSV, Practica di Mare
MM54438† 61-93
MM54439* 13
MM54440† 00
MM54441 61-71
MM54442 RS-45
MM54443† 61-50
MM54445 RS-49
MM54446† 61-01
MM54447† 61-02
MM54448† 61-03
MM54449† 61-04
MM54450‡ 14-30
MM54451‡ 61-86
MM54452‡
MM54453† 61-05
MM54454† 61-73
MM54455† 61-07
MM54456† 61-10
MM54457† 61-11

Serial

MM54458† 61-12
MM54459† 61-13
MM54460† 14
MM54461† 61-15
MM54462† 61-16
MM54463† 61-17
MM54464† 20
MM54465† 21
MM54467† 61-23
MM54468† 24
MM54469† 61-25
MM54470† 61-26
MM54471† 27
MM54472† 61-30
MM54473* 7
MM54475* 3
MM54476* 1
MM54477* 4
MM54478* 5
MM54479* 9
MM54480* 8
MM54482* 10
MM54483* 8
MM54484* 2
MM54485* 1
MM54486* 5
MM54487‡ 14-31
MM54488† 61-32
MM54489† 33
MM54490† 61-34
MM54491† 61-35
MM54492† 36
MM54493† 61-37
MM54494† 61-40
MM54495† 41
MM54496† 61-42
MM54497† 61-43
MM54498† 61-44
MM54499† 45
MM54500† 46
MM54501† 61-47
MM54503† 61-51
MM54504† 52
MM54505† 61-53
MM54506† 61-54
MM54507† 61-55
MM54508† 61-56
MM54509† 61-57
MM54510† 60
MM54511† 61
MM54512† 61-62
MM54513† 61-63
MM54514† 64
MM54515† 61-65
MM54516† 66
MM54517† 61-67
MM54518† 61-70
MM54532 61-71
MM54533† 61-72
MM54534† 61-73
MM54535† 61-74
MM54536* 9
MM54537* 0
MM54538† 61-75
MM54539† 61-76
MM54540† 61-77
MM54541 RS-43
MM54542† 61-81
MM54543† 61-82
MM54544† 61-83
MM54545† 61-84
MM54546† 61-85
MM54547† 61-87

Serial	
MM54548†	61-90
MM54549†	61-91
MM54550†	61-92
MM54551*	6

Dassault Falcon 50
31° Stormo, Roma Ciampino

MM62020	
MM62021	

Grumman Gulfstream III
31° Stormo, Roma Ciampino

MM62022	
MM62025	

**Lockheed
C-130H Hercules**
46 Brigata Aerea, Pisa

MM61988	46-02
MM61989	46-03
MM61990	46-04
MM61991	46-05
MM61992	46-06
MM61993	46-07
MM61994	46-08
MM61995	46-09
MM61997	46-11
MM61998	46-12
MM61999	46-13
MM62001	46-15

**McDonnell Douglas
DC9-32**
31° Stormo, Roma Ciampino

MM62012	
MM62013	

Panavia Tornado
*TTTE RAF Cottesmore
6° Stormo, Ghedi
36° Stormo, Gioia del Colle
RSV, Practica di Mare

MM586	
MM7001	RS-01
MM7002	I-92
MM7003*	I-93
MM7004	I-90
MM7005	I-91
MM7006	6-03
MM7007	I-94
MM7008	6-02
MM7009	6-04
MM7010	6-06
MM7011	6-10
MM7012	6-11
MM7013	6-05
MM7014	6-12
MM7015	6-01
MM7016	6-23
MM7017	6-14
MM7018	6-24
MM7019	6-22
MM7020	6-21
MM7021	6-30
MM7022	6-26
MM7023	6-27
MM7024	6-25
MM7025	6-31
MM7026	6-33
MM7027	6-32
MM7028	6-34
MM7029	6-07
MM7030	6-36

Serial	
MM7031	6-37
MM7033	6-42
MM7034	6-41
MM7035	36-30
MM7036	36-31
MM7037	
MM7038	36-33
MM7039	6-52
MM7040	36-35
MM7041	6-43
MM7042	6-47
MM7043	36-36
MM7044	6-44
MM7046	36-34
MM7047	36-37
MM7048	
MM7049	36-40
MM7050	36-44
MM7051	6-12
MM7052	36-41
MM7053	36-45
MM7054	6-46
MM7055	36-47
MM7056	36-52
MM7057	36-54
MM7058	
MM7059	6-45
MM7060	
MM7061	
MM7062	6-53
MM7063	
MM7064	6-54
MM7065	6-55
MM7066	36-32
MM7067	RS-24
MM7068	36-46
MM7069	6-61
MM7070	6-62
MM7071	6-63
MM7072	6-64
MM7073	
MM7074	
MM7075	
MM7076	
MM7077	6-65
MM7078	6-66
MM7079	
MM7080	6-67
MM7081	RS-01
MM7082	RS-02
MM7083	6-70
MM7084	36-42
MM7085	
MM7086	
MM7087	
MM7088	
MM55000*	I-42
MM55001*	I-40
MM55002	I-41
MM55003*	I-43
MM55004*	I-44
MM55005	6-13
MM55006	6-15
MM55007	6-51
MM55008	6-20
MM55009	6-16
MM55010	6-50
MM55011	36-55

**Piaggio-Douglas PD-808;
†PD-808-GE;
*PD-808-RM; ‡PD-808-TA**
14° Stormo, Treviso-San

Serial	
Angelo; 31° Stormo, Roma-Ciampino	
RSV, Practica di Mare	
MM577‡	RS-37
MM578‡	RS-38
MM61948	(31)
MM61949	(31)
MM61950	14-50
MM61951	(31)
MM61952†	(14)
MM61953‡	(31)
MM61954†	14-52
MM61955†	(14)
MM61956‡	14-51
MM61957‡	RS-39
MM61958†	(14)
MM61959†	(14)
MM61960†	(14)
MM61961†	(14)
MM61962†	(14)
MM61963†	(14)
MM62014*	14-53
MM62015*	(14)
MM62016*	14-55
MM62017*	(14)

**JORDAN
Al Quwwat Al-Jawwiya
Alamalakiya Al-Urduniya
Lockheed
C-130B Hercules**
3 Sqn, Amman

340	
341	

**Lockheed
C-130H Hercules**
3 Sqn, Amman

344	
345	
346	
347	

**KUWAIT
Kuwait Air Force
McDonnell Douglas
DC9-32**

KAF 320	
KAF 321	

**Lockheed
L100-30 Hercules**

KAF 322	
KAF 323	
KAF 324	
KAF 325	

**LUXEMBOURG
NATO Boeing E-3A**
NAEWF, Geilenkirchen

LX-N90442	
LX-N90443	
LX-N90444	
LX-N90445	
LX-N90446	
LX-N90447	
LX-N90448	
LX-N90449	
LX-N90450	
LX-N90451	
LX-N90452	
LX-N90453	
LX-N90454	

Overseas Serials

Serial		Serial		Serial	
LX-N90455		J140	315 Sqn	J267*	323 Sqn
LX-N90456		J141	315 Sqn	J268*	323 Sqn
LX-N90457		J142	315 Sqn	J269*	322 Sqn
LX-N90458		J143	315 Sqn	J270*	323 Sqn
LX-N90459		J144	313 Sqn	J358	315 Sqn
		J145	315 Sqn	J359	313 Sqn
Boeing 707-329C		J146	315 Sqn	J360	315 Sqn
NAEWF, Geilenkirchen		J192	311 Sqn	J361	313 Sqn
LX-N19996		J193	311 Sqn	J362	315 Sqn
LX-N20198		J194	311 Sqn	J363	313 Sqn
LX-N20199		J195	315 Sqn	J364	313 Sqn
		J196	311 Sqn	J365	313 Sqn
NETHERLANDS		J197	311 Sqn	J366	313 Sqn
Koninklijke Luchmacht		J198	311 Sqn	J367	313 Sqn
Fokker F-27-100		J199	315 Sqn	J368*	313 Sqn
Friendship		J200	315 Sqn	J369*	313 Sqn
334 Sqn, Soesterberg		J201	315 Sqn	J508	
C-1		J202	315 Sqn	J509	
C-2		J203	315 Sqn	J510	
C-3		J204	315 Sqn	J511	
		J205	315 Sqn	J512	
Fokker F-27-300M		J206	315 Sqn	J513	
Troopship		J207	315 Sqn	J514	
334 Sqn, Soesterberg		J208*	315 Sqn	J515*	
C-4		J209*	315 Sqn	J516*	
C-5		J210*	315 Sqn	J616	311 Sqn
C-6		J211*	315 Sqn	J617	311 Sqn
C-7		J212	323 Sqn	J618	311 Sqn
C-8		J213	323 Sqn	J619	311 Sqn
C-9		J214	323 Sqn	J620	311 Sqn
C-10		J215	322 Sqn	J622	311 Sqn
C-11		J218	322 Sqn	J623	311 Sqn
C-12		J219	322 Sqn	J624	311 Sqn
		J220	322 Sqn	J627	306 Sqn
F-27-200MPA		J221	322 Sqn	J628	306 Sqn
336 Sqn, Hato		J222	322 Sqn	J630	306 Sqn
M-1		J223	322 Sqn	J631	306 Sqn
M-2		J226	322 Sqn	J632	306 Sqn
		J228	322 Sqn	J633	306 Sqn
General Dynamics		J229	322 Sqn	J635	306 Sqn
F-16A/F16B*		J230	322 Sqn	J636	306 Sqn
306 Sqn, Volkel; 311 Sqn,		J231	323 Sqn	J637	306 Sqn
Volkel; 312 Sqn, Volkel;		J232	323 Sqn	J638	306 Sqn
313 Sqn, Twente; 315 Sqn,		J234	323 Sqn	J640	306 Sqn
Twente;		J235	323 Sqn	J641	306 Sqn
322 Sqn, Leeuwarden;		J236	323 Sqn	J642	306 Sqn
323 Sqn, Leeuwarden		J238	322 Sqn	J643	306 Sqn
J001		J239	322 Sqn	J644	306 Sqn
J002		J240	322 Sqn	J645	306 Sqn
J003		J241	322 Sqn	J646	306 Sqn
J004		J242	322 Sqn	J647	306 Sqn
J005		J243	322 Sqn	J648	306 Sqn
J006		J245	323 Sqn	J649*	306 Sqn
J054	313 Sqn	J246	323 Sqn	J650*	312 Sqn
J055	313 Sqn	J247	323 Sqn	J651*	312 Sqn
J056	313 Sqn	J248	323 Sqn	J652*	311 Sqn
J057	313 Sqn	J249	323 Sqn	J653*	306 Sqn
J058		J250	323 Sqn	J654*	311 Sqn
J059		J251	322 Sqn	J655*	306 Sqn
J060		J253	323 Sqn	J656*	312 Sqn
J061		J254	323 Sqn	J657*	311 Sqn
J062		J255	323 Sqn	J864	312 Sqn
J063		J256	323 Sqn	J866	312 Sqn
J064*	313 Sqn	J257	322 Sqn	J867	312 Sqn
J065*		J258	311 Sqn	J868	312 Sqn
J066*		J259*	323 Sqn	J869	312 Sqn
J067*		J260*	322 Sqn	J870	312 Sqn
J068*		J261*	322 Sqn	J871	312 Sqn
J135	315 Sqn	J262*	323 Sqn	J872	312 Sqn
J136	315 Sqn	J263*	323 Sqn	J873	312 Sqn
J137	315 Sqn	J264*	322 Sqn	J874	312 Sqn
J138	315 Sqn	J265*	323 Sqn	J875	312 Sqn
J139	315 Sqn	J266*	323 Sqn	J876	312 Sqn

Serial	Serial	Serial
J877 312 Sqn	A209	302
J878 312 Sqn	A217	303
J879 312 Sqn	A218	304
J880 312 Sqn	A226	305
J881 312 Sqn	A227	306
J882* 312 Sqn	A235	307
J884* 312 Sqn	A246	308
J885* 315 Sqn	A247	309
	A253	310
Northrop NF-5A	A254	311
314 Sqn, Gilze-Rijen	A260	312
316 Sqn, Gilze-Rijen	A261	
K3001 316 Sqn	A266	**Westland Lynx**
K3004 316 Sqn	A267	*UH14A (7 Sqn)
K3005	A275	†SH14B (860 Sqn)
K3012 314 Sqn	A281	‡SH14C (860 Sqn)
K3014 314 Sqn	A292	De Kooij
K3016 314 Sqn	A293	260* K
K3017 316 Sqn	A301	261* K
K3019 316 Sqn	A302	262* K
K3021 314 Sqn	A307	264* K
K3023 314 Sqn	A315	265* K
K3024 314 Sqn	A319	266† K
K3025 316 Sqn	A324	267† K
K3031 316 Sqn	A336	268† K
K3033 314 Sqn	A342	269† K
K3036 314 Sqn	A343	270†
K3039 316 Sqn	A350*	271†
K3041 316 Sqn	A351*	272† K
K3042 314 Sqn	A366	273† PH
K3044 314 Sqn	A374	274†
K3046 314 Sqn	A383	276‡
K3047 316 Sqn	A390*	277‡
K3049 314 Sqn	A391	278‡ K
K3051 314 Sqn	A398	279‡
K3052 314 Sqn	A399	280‡ EV
K3054 314 Sqn	A406	281‡
K3055 314 Sqn	A407	282‡
K3058 316 Sqn	A414	283‡ K
K3061 316 Sqn	A451	
K3062 316 Sqn	A452	**NEW ZEALAND**
K3066 316 Sqn	A453	**Royal New Zealand Air Force**
K3067 314 Sqn	A464	**Boeing 727-22C**
K3069 314 Sqn	A465*	40 Sqn, Whenuapai
K3073 314 Sqn	A470	NZ7271
	A471	NZ7272
Northrop NF-5B	A482	
314 Sqn, Gilze-Rijen	A483	**Lockheed**
316 Sqn, Gilze-Rijen	A488	**C-130H Hercules**
K4001 316 Sqn	A489	40 Sqn, Whenuapai
K4005 316 Sqn	A494	NZ7001
K4006 316 Sqn	A495	NZ7002
K4007 316 Sqn	A499*	NZ7003
K4009 316 Sqn	A500	NZ7004
K4013 316 Sqn	A514	NZ7005
K4014 314 Sqn	A515	
K4015 316 Sqn	A521	**Lockheed**
K4016 316 Sqn	A522	**P-3K Orion**
K4017 314 Sqn	A528	5 Sqn, Whenuapai
K4019 314 Sqn	A529	NZ4201
K4021 314 Sqn	A535	NZ4202
K4024 316 Sqn	A536	NZ4203
K4025 316 Sqn	A542	NZ4204
K4026 316 Sqn	A549	NZ4205
K4027 314 Sqn	A550	NZ4206
K4029 316 Sqn		
	Marine Luchtvaart Dienst	**NIGERIA**
Sud Alouette III	**Lockheed**	**Federal Nigerian Air Force**
*Grasshoppers	**P-3C Orion**	**Lockheed**
298 Sqn, Soesterberg;	320 Sqn, Valkenburg and	**C-130H Hercules**
300 Sqn, Deelen	Keflavik	Lagos
A177	300	NAF-910
A208	301	NAF-911

125

Serial		Serial		Serial
NAF-912		675	331 Skv	908
NAF-913		676	331 Skv	909
NAF-914		677	332 Skv	
NAF-915		678	331 Skv	**Westland**
NAF-917		679	331 Skv	**Sea King Mk43**
NAF-918†		680	331 Skv	330 Skv, Bodø
NAF-918 (NAF 916)		681	331 Skv	060
		682	331 Skv	062
NORWAY		683	331 Skv	066
Kongelige Norske		685	331 Skv	070
Luftforsvaret		687	334 Skv	071
Dassault		3688	331 Skv	072
Falcon 20 ECM		689*	331 Skv	073
335 Skv, Gardermoen		690*	332 Skv	074
041		691*	334 Skv	189
053		692*	334 Skv	
0125		693*	332 Skv	**Westland Lynx**
				Mk86
General Dynamics		**Lockheed**		337 Skv
F-16A/*F-16B		**C-130H Hercules**		207
331 Skv, Bodø; 332 Skv,		335 Skv, Gardermoen		216
Rygge; 334 Skv, Bodø;		952		228
338 Skv, Orland		953		232
272	332 Skv	954		237
273	332 Skv	955		
274	332 Skv	956		**OMAN**
275	332 Skv	957		**Al Quwwat Al Jawwiya al**
276	332 Skv			**Saltanat Oman**
277	332 Skv	**Lockheed**		**BAC 1-11**
278	332 Skv	**P-3B Orion**		**srs 485GD**
279	332 Skv	333 Skv, Andøya		4 Sqn, Seeb
281	332 Skv	576		551
282	332 Skv	583		552
284	332 Skv	599		553
285	332 Skv	600		
286	332 Skv	601		**Lockheed**
287	338 Skv	602		**C-130H Hercules**
288	338 Skv	603		4 Sqn, Seeb
289	338 Skv			501
290	338 Skv	**Northrop F-5A**		502
291	338 Skv	336 Skv, Rygge; 338 Skv,		503
292	338 Skv	Orland		
293	338 Skv	128	336 Skv	**Short Skyvan 3M**
294	338 Skv	130	336 Skv	2 Sqn, Seeb
295	338 Skv	131	336 Skv	901
296	338 Skv	132	336 Skv	902
297	338 Skv	133	336 Skv	903
298	338 Skv	134	336 Skv	904
299	332 Skv	207	336 Skv	905
300	334 Skv	208	336 Skv	906
302*	332 Skv	210	336 Skv	907
303*	332 Skv	215	336 Skv	908
304*	332 Skv	220	336 Skv	910
305*	332 Skv	222	336 Skv	911
306*	332 Skv	225	336 Skv	912
307*	338 Skv	895	336 Skv	913
658	334 Skv	896	336 Skv	914
659	334 Skv	898	336 Skv	915
660	334 Skv	902	336 Skv	916
661	334 Skv			
662	334 Skv	**Northrop F-5B**		**PORTUGAL**
663	334 Skv	336 Skv, Rygge		**Forca Aerea Portuguesa**
664	334 Skv	135		**Cessna T-37C**
665	334 Skv	136		102 Esq, Sintra
666	334 Skv	241		2401
667	331 Skv	242		2402
668	331 Skv	243		2403
669	331 Skv	244		2404
670	331 Skv	387		2406
671	331 Skv	594		2407
672	331 Skv	595		2410
673	331 Skv	906		2411
674	331 Skv	907		2412

Serial		Serial		Serial	
2414		*1610	C-130E	E.25-22	79-22
2415		*1611	C-130E	E.25-23	79-23
2417		*1612	C-130H	E.25-24	79-24
2418		*1613	C-130H	E.25-25	79-25
2419		*1614	C-130H	E.25-26	79-26
2420		*1615	C-130H	E.25-27	79-27
2421		*1616	KC-130H	E.25-28	79-28
2422		*1617	KC-130H	E.25-29	79-29
2423		*1618	C-130H	E.25-30	79-30
2424		*1619	C-130H	E.25-31	79-31
2425		*1621	KC-130H	E.25-32	74-01
2426				E.25-33	74-02
2427		**Lockheed Jetstar**		E.25-34	79-34
2428		1 Sqn, Riyadh		E.25-35	74-03
2429		101		E.25-36	79-36
2430		102		E.25-37	74-04

Lockheed
C-130H Hercules
501 Esq, Lisbon/Montijo
6801
6802
6803
6804
6805

Falcon 20C
504 Esq, Lisbon/Montijo
8101
8102
8103

SAUDI ARABIA
Al Quwwat Al-Jawwiya
as Sa'udiya
Grumman Gulfstream III
1 Sqn, Riyadh
103
107

Lockheed
C-130 Hercules †1 Sqn,
Riyadh
‡4 Sqn, Jeddah
*16 Sqn, Jeddah

†	112	VC-130H
‡	451	C-130E
‡	452	C-130E
‡	455	C-130E
‡	456	KC-130H
‡	457	KC-130H
‡	458	KC-130H
‡	459	KC-130H
‡	460	C-130H
‡	461	C-130H
‡	462	C-130H
‡	463	C-130H
‡	464	C-130H
‡	465	C-130H
‡	466	C-130H
‡	467	C-130H
‡	468	C-130H
‡	469	C-130H
‡	470	C-130H
*	1601	C-130H
*	1602	C-130H
*	1603	C-130H
*	1604	C-130H
*	1605	C-130H
*	1606	C-130E
*	1607	C-130E
*	1608	C-130E
*	1609	C-130E

SINGAPORE
Republic of Singapore Air Force
Lockheed
C-130B Hercules
122 Sqn, Changi
720
721
724
725

Lockheed
C-130H Hercules
122 Sqn, Changi
730
731
732
733

Lockheed KC-130H Hercules
122 Sqn, Changi
734
745

SPAIN
Ejercito del Aire
Boeing 707-381B
Ala 45, Madrid

| T.17-1 | 45-10 |
| T.17-2 | 45-11 |

CASA 101 Aviojet
Grupo 44, Torrejon
411/412 Esc, (Ala41) Matacan
793 Esc, (Ala 79), San Javier

E.25-01	79-01
E.25-03	79-03
XE.25.04	44-06
E.25-05	79-05
E.25-06	79-06
E.25-07	79-07
E.25-08	79-08
E.25-09	79-09
E.25-10	79-10
E.25-11	79-11
E.25-12	79-12
E.25-13	79-13
E.25-14	79-14
E.25-15	79-15
E.25-16	79-16
E.25-17	79-17
E.25-18	79-18
E.25-19	79-19
E.25-20	79-20
E.25-21	79-21
E.25-38	79-38
E.25-39	74-05
E.25-40	74-06
E.25-41	79-41
E.25-42	79-42
E.25-43	79-43
E.25-44	79-44
E.25-45	79-45
E.25-46	79-46
E.25-47	79-47
E.25-48	79-48
E.25-49	79-49
E.25-50	79-40
E.25-51	74-07
E.25-52	74-08
E.25-53	74-09
E.25-54	74-10
E.25-55	411-08
E.25-56	74-11
E.25-57	74-12
E.25-58	
E.25-59	74-13
E.25-60	74-14
E.25-61	74-15
E.25-62	74-16
E.25-63	74-17
E.25-64	74-18
E.25-65	74-19
E.25-66	74-20
E.25-67	74-21
E.25-68	74-22
E.25-69	74-23
E.25-70	74-24
E.25-71	74-25
E.25-72	74-26
E.25-73	74-27
E.25-74	74-28
E.25-75	74-29
E.25-76	74-30
E.25-77	74-31
E.25-78	79-02
E.25-79	74-32
E.25-80	74-33
E.25-81	74-34
E.25-83	74-35
E.25-84	79-04
E.25-85	74-36
E.25-86	74-37
E.25-87	74-38
E.25-88	74-39

Overseas Serials

Serial		Serial		Serial	

CASA 212 Aviocar
212 (XT.12),
212A (T.12B),
212B (TR.12A),
212D (TE.12B),
212E (T.12C).
351/352 Esc (Ala35), Getafe;
403 Esc Cuatro Vientos;
406 Esc Torrejon;
408 Esc, Getafe;
461 Esc Gando, Las Palmas;
721 Esc (Grupo 72),
Alcantarilla;
Grupo 74 Esc Matacan;
792 Esc (Ala79), San Javier.

XT.12-1	406-11
TR.12A-3	403-01
TR.12A-4	403-02
TR.12A-5	403-03
TR.12A-6	403-04
TR.12A-7	403-05
TE.12B-8	79-93
T.12B-9	79-91
T.12B-10	79-92
T.12B-12	35-01
T.12B-13	74-70
T.12B-14	46-30
T.12B-15	35-02
T.12B-16	744-16
T.12B-17	35-03
T.12B-18	46-13
T.12B-19	46-32
T.12B-20	35-04
T.12B-21	35-05
T.12B-22	35-06
T.12B-23	72-01
T.12B-24	35-07
T.12B-25	744-25
T.12B-26	72-02
T.12B-27	46-33
T.12B-28	72-03
T.12B-29	352-29
T.12B-30	744-30
T.12B-31	46-34
T.12B-33	72-04
T.12B-34	744-34
T.12B-35	46-35
T.12B-36	35-09
T.12B-37	72-05
T.12B-38	35-10
T.12B-39	745-39
T.12B-40	79-93
T.12B-41	79-94
T.12C-42	744-42
T.12C-43	46-50
T.12C-44	35-50
T.12B-46	745-46
T.12B-47	72-06
T.12B-48	35-11
T.12B-49	46-36
T.12B-50	745-50
T.12B-51	44-51
T.12B-52	72-07
T.12B-53	35-12
T.12B-54	35-13
T.12B-55	46-37
T.12B-56	745-56
T.12B-57	72-08
T.12B-58	46-38
T.12C-59	35-51
T.12C-60	35-52
T.12C-61	35-53
T.12B-63	35-14

T.12B-64	46-39
T.12B-65	74-80
T.12B-66	72-09
T.12B-67	745-67
T.12B-68	35-15
T.12B-69	35-16
T.12B-70	35-17
T.12B-71	35-18
TR.12D-72	408-01
TR.12D-73	408-02
TR.12D-74	408-03

Dassault Falcon 20
Grupo 45, Madrid

T.11-1	45-04
TM.11-2	45-03
TM.11-3	45-02
TM.11-4	45-01
T.11-5	45-05

Dassault Falcon 50
452 Esc (Ala45), Madrid

T.16-1	45-20

Dassault Falcon 900
452 Esc, Madrid

T.18-1	45-40

Douglas DC8-52
401 Esc (Ala 45), Madrid

T.15-1	45-30

Fokker F.27M
Friendship
400MPA
802 Esc, Gando

D.2-01
D.2-02
D.2-03

Lockheed
C-130 Hercules/
C-130H-30+
311 Esc/312 Esc (Ala31),
Zaragoza

TL.10-1	31-01
T.10-2	31-02
T.10-3	31-03
T.10-4	31-04
T.10-8	31-05
T.10-9	31-06
T.10-10	31-07

Lockheed
KC-130H Hercules
312 Esc (Ala31), Zaragoza

TK.10-5	31-50
TK.10-6	31-51
TK.10-7	31-52
TK.10-11	31-53
TK.10-12	31-54

SUDAN
Silakh Al Jawwiya as
Sudaniya
Lockheed
C-130H Hercules

1100
1101
1102
1103
1104
1105

SWEDEN
Kungliga Svenska Flygvapnet
Lockheed
C-130E Hercules
F7, Satenäs

84001	841
84002	842

Lockheed
C-130H Hercules
F7, Satenäs

84003	843
84004	844
84005	845
84006	846
84007	847
84008	848

Swearingen
Metro III

88002	882
88003	883

Vertol 107-II-4
*F15, Soderhamm
†F21, Lulea
‡F17 Ronneby

04451	91*
04452	92‡
04453	93‡
04454	94†
04455	95*
04456	96
04457	97‡
04458	98‡
04459	99‡
04460	90

Marine Flygtjanst
Vertol 107-II-5
1HKP Div, Berga

04061	61
04063	63
04064	64

Kawasaki-Vertol
KV.107-II
*1 HKPDiv, Berga
†2 HKPDiv, Säve

*04065	65
†04067	67
*04068	68
*04069	69
†04070	70
*04071	71
†04072	72

SWITZERLAND
Schweizerische Flugwaffe
Beech E-50
Twin Bonanza
Transport Corps, Dubendorf

A-711
A-712
A-713

THAILAND
Royal Thai Air Force
Douglas DC.8-62AF

60109
60110
60112 (HS-TGQ)

Serial	Serial	Serial

TURKEY
Turk Hava Kuvvetleri
  Transall C.160D
  221 Filo, Erkilet

019	12-019
020	12-020
021	12-021
022	12-022
023	12-023
024	12-024
026	12-026
027	12-027
028	12-028
029	12-029
030	12-030
031	12-031
032	12-032
033	12-033
034	12-034
035	12-035
036	12-036
037	12-037
038	12-038
039	12-039
040	12-040

Lockheed
C-130E Hercules
  222 Filo, Erkilet

00991	12-991
01468	12-468
01947	12-947
13186	12-186
13187	12-187
13188	12-188
13189	12-189
17949	12-949

UNITED ARAB EMIRATES
United Arab Emirates Air
Force
Abu Dhabi
Lockheed
C-130H Hercules
1211
1212
1213
1214

Lockheed
L.100-30 Hercules
Dubai
311
312

WEST GERMANY
Luftwaffe
  Boeing 707-307C
FBS-BMVg, Köln-Bonn
10+01
10+02
10+03
10+04

Canadair CL601
Challenger
FBS-BMVg, Köln-Bonn
12+01
12+02
12+03
12+04
12+05
12+06
12+07

HFB 320 Hansa Jet
*FBS-BMVg, Köln-Bonn;
†JBG32 Lechfeld;
‡WTD-61, Ingolstadt
16+04‡
16+21†
16+23†
16+24†
16+25†
16+26†
16+27†
16+28†

VFW 614
FBS-BMVg, Köln-Bonn
17+01
17+02
17+03

McD RF-4E
Phantom
AKG 51, Bremgarten;
AKG 52, Leck;
TSLw 1, Kaufbeuren;
WTD 61, Ingolstadt

35+01	WTD 61
35+02	AKG 52
35+03	AKG 51
35+04	AKG 51
35+05	AKG 52
35+06	AKG 51
35+07	AKG 51
35+08	AKG 51
35+09	AKG 52
35+10	AKG 52
35+11	AKG 51
35+12	AKG 51
35+13	AKG 52
35+14	AKG 52
35+17	AKG 52
35+18	AKG 52
35+19	AKG 51
35+20	AKG 52
35+21	AKG 52
35+22	AKG 51
35+24	AKG 52
35+25	AKG 51
35+26	AKG 52
35+28	AKG 51
35+29	AKG 51
35+31	AKG 52
35+32	AKG 52
35+33	AKG 51
35+34	AKG 51
35+35	AKG 51
35+36	AKG 52
35+37	AKG 52
35+38	AKG 51
35+39	AKG 52
35+40	AKG 51
35+41	AKG 52
35+42	AKG 52
35+43	AKG 52
35+44	AKG 51
35+46	AKG 51
35+48	AKG 51
35+49	AKG 51
35+50	AKG 51
35+51	AKG 51
35+52	AKG 52
35+53	AKG 52
35+54	AKG 52
35+56	AKG 51

35+57	AKG 51
35+58	AKG 51
35+59	AKG 51
35+60	AKG 52
35+61	AKG 51
35+62	TsLw 1
35+63	AKG 51
35+64	AKG 51
35+65	AKG 52
35+66	AKG 52
35+67	AKG 52
35+68	AKG 51
35+69	AKG 52
35+71	AKG 51
35+72	AKG 52
35+73	AKG 51
35+74	AKG 52
35+75	AKG 51
35+76	AKG 52
35+77	AKG 52
35+78	AKG 51
35+79	AKG 52
35+82	AKG 51
35+83	WTD 61
35+84	AKG 52
35+85	AKG 52
35+86	AKG 51
35+87	AKG 52
35+88	AKG 51

McD F-4F Phantom
JBG 35, Pferdsfeld;
JBG 36, Hopsten;
JG 71, Wittmundhaven;
JG 74, Neuburg;
TsLw 1, Kaufbeuren;
WTD 61, Ingolstadt

37+01	JBG 36
37+03	JG 71
37+04	TsLw 1
37+05	JG 74
37+06	JG 71
37+07	JBG 36
37+08	JG 71
37+09	JBG 35
37+10	JG 71
37+11	JG 74
37+12	JBG 36
37+13	JBG 35
37+14	TsLw 1
37+15	WTD-61
37+16	WTD-61
37+17	JBG 36
37+18	JBG 35
37+19	JG 71
37+20	JG 74
37+21	JBG 36
37+22	JBG 35
37+23	JG 71
37+24	JG 74
37+25	JBG 36
37+26	JBG 35
37+28	JG 74
37+29	JBG 36
37+30	JBG 35
37+31	JG 71
37+32	JG 74
37+33	JBG 36
37+34	JBG 35
37+35	JG 71
37+36	JG 74
37+37	JBG 36
37+38	JBG 35

Overseas Serials

Serial		Serial		Serial	
37+39	JG 71	38+25	JBG 36	40+22	JBG 41
37+40	JG 74	38+26	JBG 35	40+23	JBG 49
37+41	JBG 36	38+27	JG 71	40+24	JBG 43
37+42	JBG 35	38+28	JG 74	40+25	JBG 49
37+43	JG 71	38+29	JBG 36	40+26	JBG 41
37+44	JG 74	38+30	JBG 35	40+27	JBG 43
37+45	JBG 36	38+31	JG 71	40+28	JBG 41
37+46	JBG 35	38+32	JG 74	40+29	JBG 49
37+47	JG 71	38+33	JBG 36	40+30	JBG 49
37+48	JG 74	38+34	JBG 35	40+31	JBG 43
37+49	JBG 36	38+36	JG 74	40+32	JBG 43
37+50	JBG 35	38+37	JBG 36	40+33	JBG 41
37+51	JG 71	38+38	JBG 35	40+34	JBG 41
37+52	JG 74	38+39	JG 71	40+35	JBG 49
37+53	JBG 36	38+40	JG 74	40+36	JBG 43
37+54	JBG 35	38+42	JBG 35	40+37	JBG 49
37+55	JG 71	38+43	JG 71	40+38	JBG 43
37+56	JG 74	38+44	JG 74	40+39	JBG 41
37+57	JBG 36	38+45	JBG 36	40+40	JBG 49
37+58	JBG 35	38+46	JBG 35	40+41	JBG 41
37+60	JG 74	38+47	JG 71	40+42	JBG 44
37+61	JG 71	38+48	JG 74	40+43	JBG 43
37+63	JG 71	38+49	JBG 36	40+44	JBG 43
37+64	JG 74	38+50	JBG 35	40+45	JBG 41
37+65	JBG 36	38+51	JG 71	40+46	JBG 43
37+66	JBG 35	38+52	JG 74	40+47	JBG 49
37+67	JG 71	38+53	JBG 36	40+48	JBG 43
37+69	JBG 36	38+54	JBG 35	40+49	JBG 49
37+70	JBG 35	38+55	JG 71	40+50	JBG 43
37+71	JG 71	38+56	JG 74	40+51	JBG 41
37+73	JBG 36	38+57	JBG 36	40+52	JBG 44
37+75	JG 71	38+58	JBG 35	40+53	JBG 44
37+76	JG 74	38+59	JG 71	40+54	JBG 43
37+77	JBG 36	38+60	JG 74	40+56	WTD-61
37+78	JBG 35	38+61	JG 71	40+57	JBG 43
37+79	JBG 36	38+62	JBG 35	40+58	JBG 43
37+81	JBG 36	38+63	JG 71	40+59	TsLw3
37+82	JBG 35	38+64	JG 74	40+60	JBG 41
37+83	JG 71	38+66	JG 71	40+61	JBG 43
37+84	JG 74	38+67	JG 71	40+62	JBG 41
37+85	JBG 36	38+68	JG 74	40+63	JBG 41
37+86	JG 71	38+69	JBG 36	40+64	JBG 49
37+88	JG 74	38+70	JBG 35	40+65	JBG 49
37+89	JBG 36	38+72	JG 74	40+66	JBG 44
37+90	JBG 36	38+73	JBG 36	40+67	JBG 49
37+91	WTD 61	38+74	JBG 35	40+68	JBG 41
37+92	JG 74	38+75	JBG 35	40+69	JBG 43
37+93	JBG 36			40+70	JBG 41
37+94	JBG 35	**D-BD Alpha Jet**		40+71	JBG 44
37+96	JG 74	JBG 41, Husum;		40+72	JBG 43
37+97	JBG 36	JBG 43, Oldenburg;		40+73	JBG 49
37+98	JBG 35	JBG 44, Beja (Portugal);		40+74	JBG 41
38+00	JG 74	JBG 44, Fürstenfeldbruck;		40+75	JBG 43
38+01	JBG 36	WTD 61, Ingolstadt		40+76	JBG 49
38+02	JBG 35	40+01	WTD 61	40+77	JBG 49
38+03	JG 71	40+02	WTD 61	40+78	TsLw 3
38+04	JG 74	40+03	JBG 49	40+79	JBG 43
38+05	JBG 36	40+04	JBG 43	40+80	JBG 43
38+06	JBG 35	40+05	JBG 49	40+81	JBG 41
38+07	JG 71	40+06	JBG 49	40+82	JBG 49
38+08	JG 74	40+07	JBG 49	40+84	JBG 49
38+09	JBG 36	40+08	JBG 44	40+85	JBG 49
38+10	JBG 35	40+09	JBG 41	40+86	JBG 44
38+11	JG 71	40+11	JBG 43	40+87	JBG 43
38+12	JG 74	40+12	JBG 49	40+88	JBG 41
38+13	JBG 36	40+13	JBG 43	40+89	JBG 41
38+14	JBG 35	40+14	JBG 43	40+90	JBG 49
38+16	JG 74	40+15	JBG 41	40+91	JBG 49
38+17	JBG 36	40+16	JBG 41	40+92	JBG 43
38+18	JBG 35	40+17	JBG 49	40+93	JBG 49
38+20	JG 74	40+18	JBG 49	40+94	JBG 44
38+21	JBG 36	40+20	JBG 43	40+95	JBG 43
38+24	JG 74	40+21	JBG 41	40+96	JBG 49

Serial		Serial		Serial	
40+97	JBG 44	41+71	JBG 41	43+59	MFG 1
40+98	JBG 44	41+72	JBG 41	43+60	MFG 1
40+99	JBG 41	41+73	JBG 41	43+61	MFG 1
41+00	JBG 43	41+74	JBG 41	43+62	MFG 1
41+01	JBG 43	41+75	JBG 41	43+63	MFG 1
41+02	JBG 41			43+64	MFG 1
41+03	JBG 41	**Panavia Tornado**		43+65	MFG 1
41+04	JBG 49	**Strike/Trainer*/ECR†**		43+66	MFG 1
41+05	JBG 43	†TTTE RAF		43+67	MFG 1
41+06	JBG 41	Cottesmore;		43+68	MFG 1
41+07	JBG 44	JBG 31, Nörvenich;		43+69	MFG 1
41+08	JBG 44	JBG 32, Lechfeld;		43+70	MFG 1
41+09	JBG 49	JBG 34, Memmingen;		43+71	MFG 1
41+10	JBG 49	JBG 33, Büchel;		43+72	MFG 1
41+11	JBG 49	JBG 38, Jever;		43+73	MFG 1
41+12	JBG 43	MBB, Manching;		43+74	MFG 1
41+13	JBG 43	MFG1, Schleswig;		43+75	MFG 1
41+14	JBG 41	MFG2, Eggebek;		43+76	MFG 1
41+15	JBG 41	TsLw1, Kaufbueren;		43+77	MFG 1
41+16	JBG 44	WTD61, Ingolstadt		43+78	MFG 1
41+17	JBG 44	*43+01	G-20†	43+79	MFG 1
41+18	JBG 43	*43+02	G-21†	43+80	MFG 1
41+19	JBG 44	*43+03	G-22†	43+81	MFG 1
41+20	JBG 41	*43+04	G-23†	43+82	MFG 1
41+21	JBG 41	*43+05	G-24†	43+83	MFG 1
41+22	JBG 44	*43+06	G-25†	43+84	MFG 1
41+23	JBG 49	*43+07	G-26†	43+85	MFG 1
41+24	JBG 41	*43+08	G-27†	43+86	MFG 1
41+25	JBG 49	*43+09	G-28†	43+87	MFG 1
41+26	JBG 49	*43+10	G-29†	43+88	MFG 1
41+27	JBG 43	*43+11	G-30†	43+89	MFG 1
41+28	JBG 43	43+12	G-70†	*43+90	JBG 38
41+29	JBG 43	43+13	G-71†	*43+91	JBG 38
41+30	JBG 44	43+14	G-72†	*43+92	JBG 31
41+31	JBG 41	*43+15	G-31†	*43+94	JBG 31
41+32	JBG 41	*43+16	G-32†	43+95	JBG 32
41+33	JBG 41	*43+17	G-33†	43+96	JBG 31
41+34	JBG 43	43+18	G-77†	*43+97	JBG 31
41+35	JBG 49	43+19	JBG-31	43+98	JBG 38
41+36	JBG 49	43+20	G-73†	43+99	JBG 31
41+37	JBG 49	*43+22	JBG 38	44+00	JBG 31
41+38	JBG 49	*43+23	G-34†	*44+01	JBG 38
41+39	JBG 43	43+25	G-75†	44+02	JBG 31
41+40	JBG 43	43+26	G-76†	44+03	JBG 31
41+41	JBG 41	43+27	MFG 1	44+04	JBG 31
41+42	JBG 49	43+28	JBG 38	*44+05	JBG 38
41+43	JBG 43	*43+29	JBG 31	44+06	JBG 31
41+44	JBG 49	43+30	JBG 38	44+07	JBG 31
41+45	JBG 49	*43+31	JBG-31	44+08	JBG 38
41+46	JBG 49	43+32	JBG 38	44+09	JBG 31
41+47	JBG 41	*43+33	JBG 38	*44+10	JBG 38
41+48	JBG 41	43+34	JBG 38	44+11	JBG 31
41+49	JBG 49	*43+35	JBG-34	44+12	JBG 31
41+50	JBG 49	43+36	JBG 38	44+13	JBG 38
41+51	JBG 43	*43+37	G-37†	44+14	JBG 31
41+52	JBG 44	43+38	JBG 38	*44+15	JBG 38
41+53	JBG 41	43+40	JBG 38	44+16	JBG 38
41+54	JBG 41	43+41	JBG 31	44+17	JBG 38
41+55	JBG 49	*43+42	MFG 1	44+18	JBG 31
41+56	JBG 49	*43+43	MFG 1	44+19	JBG 38
41+57	JBG 43	*43+44	MFG 1	*44+20	JBG 38
41+58	JBG 43	*43+45	MFG 1	44+21	JBG 31
41+59	JBG 41	43+46	MFG 1	44+22	JBG 31
41+60	JBG 41	43+47	MFG 1	44+23	JBG 31
41+61	JBG 49	43+48	MFG 1	44+24	JBG 38
41+62	JBG 49	43+50	MFG 1	*44+25	JBG 38
41+63	JBG 43	43+52	MFG 1	44+26	JBG 31
41+64	JBG 43	43+53	MFG 1	44+27	JBG 31
41+65	JBG 41	43+54	MFG 1	44+28	JBG 31
41+66	JBG 41	43+55	MFG 1	44+29	JBG 31
41+67	JBG 49	43+56	MFG 1	44+30	JBG 31
41+68	JBG 49	43+57	MFG 1	44+31	JBG 31
41+70	JBG 43	43+58	MFG 1	44+32	JBG 31
				44+33	JBG 31

Overseas Serials

Serial		Serial		Serial	
44+34	JBG 31	45+11	JBG 33	45+85	JBG 34
44+35	JBG 31	*45+12	MFG 2	45+86	JBG 34
*44+36	JBG 32	*45+13	MFG 2	45+87	JBG 34
*44+37	JBG 32	*45+14	MFG 2	45+88	JBG 34
*44+38	JBG 32	*45+15	MFG 2	45+89	
*44+39	JBG 32	*45+16	MFG 2	45+90	JBG 34
44+40	JBG 31	45+17	JBG 33	45+91	JBG 34
44+41	JBG 31	45+18	JBG 33	45+92	JBG 34
44+42	JBG 32	45+19	JBG 33	45+93	JBG 34
44+43	JBG 32	45+20	JBG 33	45+94	JBG 34
44+44	JBG 31	45+21	JBG 33	45+95	JBG 34
44+46	JBG 32	45+22	JBG 33	45+96	JBG 34
44+48	JBG 31	45+23	JBG 33	45+97	JBG 34
44+49	JBG 31	45+24	JBG 33	45+98	
44+50	JBG 32	45+25	JBG 33	*45+99	JBG 34
44+51	JBG 32	45+26	MFG 2	46+00	JBG 34
44+52	JBG 31	45+27	MFG 2	46+01	
44+53	JBG 32	45+28	MFG 2	46+02	
44+54	JBG 32	45+29	MFG 2	46+03	
44+55	JBG 32	45+30	MFG 2	*46+04	
44+56	JBG 32	45+31	MFG 2	*46+05	
44+57	JBG 32	45+32	MFG 2	*46+06	
44+58	JBG 32	45+33	MFG 2	46+07	
44+59	JBG 32	45+34	MFG 2	46+08	
44+60	JBG 32	45+35	MFG 2	46+09	
44+61	JBG 32	45+36	MFG 2	46+10	
44+62	JBG 32	45+37	MFG 2	46+11	
44+63	JBG 32	45+38	MFG 2	46+12	
44+64	JBG 32	45+39	MFG 2	46+13	
44+65	JBG 32	45+40	MFG 2	46+14	
44+66	JBG 32	45+41	MFG 2	46+15	
44+67	JBG 32	45+42	MFG 2	46+16	
44+68	JBG 32	45+43	MFG 2	46+17	
44+69	JBG 32	45+44	MFG 2	46+18	
44+70	JBG 32	45+45	MFG 2	46+19	
44+71	JBG 32	45+46	MFG 2	46+20	
*44+72	JBG 33	45+47	MFG 2	46+21	
*44+73	JBG 33	45+48	MFG 2	46+22	
*44+74	JBG 33	45+49	MFG 2		
*44+75	JBG 33	45+50	MFG 2		
44+76	JBG 32	45+51	MFG 2	**Transall C-160**	
44+77	JBG 32	45+52	MFG 2	LTG 61, Landsberg; LTG 62,	
44+78	JBG 32	45+53	MFG 2	Wunstorf; LTG 63, Hohn	
44+79	JBG 32	45+54	MFG 2	WTD61 Ingolstadt	
44+80	JBG 32	45+55	MFG 2	50+06	LTG 63
44+81	JBG 32	45+56	MFG 2	50+07	LTG 61
44+82	JBG 32	45+57	MFG 2	50+08	LTG 61
44+83	JBG 32	45+58	JBG 34	50+09	LTG 62
44+84	JBG 32	45+59	MFG 2	50+10	LTG 62
44+85	JBG 32	*45+60	JBG 34	50+17	LTG 62
44+86	JBG 33	*45+61	JBG 34	50+29	LTG 62
44+87	JBG 33	*45+62	JBG 34	50+33	LTG 63
44+88	JBG 33	*45+63	JBG 34	50+34	LTG 62
44+89	JBG 33	45+64	TsLw 1	50+35	LTG 62
44+90	TsLw1	45+65	MFG 2	50+36	LTG 62
44+91	JBG 31	45+66	MFG 2	50+37	LTG 62
44+92	JBG 33	45+67	MFG 2	50+38	LTG 62
44+94	JBG 33	45+68	MFG 2	50+39	LTG 63
44+95	JBG 33	45+69	MFG 2	50+40	LTG 61
44+96	JBG 33	*45+70	JBG 34	50+41	LTG 63
44+97	JBG 33	45+71	MFG 2	50+42	LTG 63
44+98	JBG 33	45+72	MFG 2	50+43	LTG 61
44+99	JBG 33	*45+73	JBG 34	50+44	LTG 61
45+00	JBG 33	45+74	MFG 2	50+45	LTG 63
45+01	JBG 33	45+75		50+46	LTG 62
45+02	JBG 33	45+76	JBG 34	50+47	LTG 61
45+03	JBG 33	*45+77	JBG 34	50+48	TsLw 3
45+04	JBG 33	45+78	JBG 34	50+49	LTG 61
45+05	JBG 33	45+79	JBG 34	50+50	LTG 63
45+06	JBG 33	45+80	JBG 34	50+51	LTG 61
45+07	JBG 33	45+81	JBG 34	50+52	LTG 62
45+08	JBG 33	45+82	JBG 34	50+53	LTG 62
45+09	JBG 33	45+83	JBG 34	50+54	LTG 63
45+10	JBG 33	45+84	JBG 34	50+55	LTG 62
				50+56	LTG 63

Serial		Serial		Serial	
50+57	LTG 61	58+26	LTG 63	59+23*	MFG5
50+58	LTG 63	58+28	JBG 35	59+24*	MFG5
50+59	LTG 63	58+29	LTG 62	59+25*	MFG5
50+60	LTG 62	58+30	LTG 62		
50+61	LTG 63	58+32	JG 74	**Dornier Do228**	
50+62	LTG 61	58+34	LTG 62	FBS-BMVg Köln	
50+64	LTG 61	58+36	LTG 62	98+78	
50+65	LTG 62	58+37	LTD 62		
50+66	LTG 61	58+38	LTG 62	**Breguet**	
50+67	LTG 63	58+39	LTG 62	**1151 Atlantic**	
50+68	LTG 61	58+46	LTG 62	MFG3 Nordholz	
50+69	LTG 63	58+47	JG 74	61+01	
50+70	WTD 61	58+49	JBG 49	61+02	
50+71	LTG 63	58+50	JBG 34	61+03	
50+72	LTG 61	58+52	JBG 32	61+04	
50+73	LTG 62	58+53	JBG 32	61+05	
50+74	LTG 61	58+54	AKG 51	61+06	
50+75	WTD 61	58+55	JBG 32	61+07	
50+76	LTG 63	58+58	JBG 33	61+08	
50+77	LTG 63	58+59	JBG 34	61+09	
50+78	LTG 62	58+60	AKG 52	61+10	
50+79	LTG 63	58+61	JBG 34	61+11	
50+81	LTG 62	58+62	JBG 36	61+12	
50+82	LTG 63	58+65	JG 71	61+13	
50+83	LTG 62	58+66	JBG 38	61+14	
50+84	LTG 63	58+67	JBG 38	61+15	
50+85	LTG 61	58+68	LTG 62	61+16	
50+86	LTG 61	58+69	LTG 62	61+17	
50+87	LTG 63	58+70	LTG 62	61+19	
50+88	LTG 61	58+71	LTG 61	61+20	
50+89	LTG 62	58+72	AKG 51		
50+90	LTG 63	58+73	JBG 31		
50+91	LTG 61	58+74	JBG 41	**Westland**	
50+92	LTG 61	58+76	JBG 41	**Lynx Mk88**	
50+93	LTG 61	58+77	JBG 49	MFG 3 Nordholz	
50+94	LTG 62	58+78	JBG 31	83+01	
50+95	LTG 63	58+79	LTG 62	83+02	
50+96	LTG 61	58+80	JBG 33	83+03	
50+97	LTG 62	58+81	LTG 62	83+04	
50+98	LTG 61	58+82	LTG 62	83+05	
50+99	LTG 61	58+83	LTG 62	83+06	
51+00	LTG 62	58+84	JBG 43	83+07	
51+01	LTG 62	58+85	JG 74	83+08	
51+02	LTG 63	58+86	JBG 49	83+09	
51+03	LTG 62	58+87	JBG 49	83+10	
51+04	LTG 61	58+89	JBG 49	83+11	
51+05	LTG 62	58+90	JBG 49	83+12	
51+06	LTG 63	58+92	JBG 36	83+13	
51+07	LTG 62	58+94	JBG 35	83+14	
51+08	LTG 63	58+98	AKG 52	83+15	
51+09	LTG 63	58+99	JG 71	83+16	
51+10	LTG 61	59+00	FBS-BMVg	83+17	
51+11	LTG 62	59+01	FBS-BMVg	83+18	
51+12	LTG 63	59+02	FBS-BMVg	83+19	
51+13	LTG 61	59+03	FBS-BMVg		
51+14	LTG 63	59+04	FBS-BMVg	**Westland Sea**	
51+15	LTG 61	59+05	FBS-BMVg	**King HAS.41**	
		59+06*	MFG5	MFG 5, Kiel-Holtenau	
Dornier Do.28D-2		59+07*	MFG5	89+50	
Skyservant		59+08*	MFG5	89+51	
LTG61, Landsberg;		59+09*	MFG5	89+52*	
LTG 62, Wunstorf;		59+10*	MFG5	89+53	
LTG 63, Hohn;		59+11*	MFG5	89+54	
WTD 61, Ingolstadt;		59+12*	MFG5	89+55	
FBS-BMVg, Köln-Bonn		59+13*	MFG5	89+56	
MFG 5, Kiel-Holtenau		59+14*	MFG5	89+57	
58+05	WTD 61	59+15*	MFG5	89+58	
58+08	LTG 62	59+16*	MFG5	89+59	
58+09	LTG 62	59+17*	MFG5	89+60	
58+14	LTG 62	59+18*	MFG5	89+61	
58+15	JBG 31	59+19*	MFG5	89+62	
58+18	LTG 63	59+20*	MFG5	89+63	
58+20	JBG 31	59+21*	MFG5	89+65	
58+23	LTG	59+22*	MFG5	89+66	
				89+67	

Overseas Serials

Serial		Serial		Serial	
89+68		84+26	35	84+70	15
89+69		84+27	35	84+71	15
89+70		84+28	35	84+72	15
89+71		84+29	35	84+73	15
		84+30	35	84+74	15
English Electric Canberra		84+31	35	84+75	15
B2		84+32	35	84+76	15
MGA, Manching		84+33	35	84+77	15
99+34		84+34	35	84+78	15
99+35		84+35	35	84+79	15
		84+36	35	84+80	15
Heeresfliegertruppe		84+37	35	84+82	15
Sikorsky/VFW CH-53G		84+38	35	84+83	15
HFlgRgt-15, Rheine-Bentlage		84+39	35	84+84	15
HFlgRgt-25, Laupheim		84+40	25	84+85	15
HFlgRgt-35, Mendig		84+41	HFWS	84+86	15
HFWS, Bückeberg		84+42	25	84+87	15
WTD 61, Ingolstadt		84+43	25	84+88	15
84+01	WTD 61	84+44	25	84+89	15
84+02	WTD 61	84+45	25	84+90	15
84+03	15	84+46	25	84+91	15
84+04	35	84+47	25	84+92	35
84+05	35	84+48	25	84+93	35
84+06	35	84+49	HFWS	84+94	35
84+07	HFWS	84+50	25	84+95	25
84+08	35	84+51	25	84+96	25
84+09	25	84+52	25	84+97	25
84+10	25	84+53	25	84+98	15
84+11	HFWS	84+54	25	84+99	15
84+12	15	84+55	25	85+00	15
84+13	HFWS	84+56	25	85+01	35
84+14	HFWS	84+57	25	85+02	35
84+15	HFWS	84+58	25	85+03	35
84+16	HFWS	84+59	25	85+04	25
84+17	25	84+60	25	85+05	25
84+18	HFWS	84+62	25	85+06	25
84+19	HFWS	84+63	25	85+07	15
84+20	15	84+64	25	85+08	15
84+21	HFWS	84+65	35	85+09	15
84+22	35	84+66	35	85+10	35
84+23	35	84+67	35	85+11	25
84+24	35	84+68	15	85+12	15
84+25	35	84+69	15		

US Military Aircraft Markings

All USAF aircraft have been allocated a fiscal year (FY) number since 1921.
Individual aircraft are given a serial according to the fiscal year in which they
are ordered. The numbers commence at 0001 and are prefixed with the year
of allocation. For example F-111E 68-0001 was the first aircraft ordered in
1968. The fiscal year (FY) serial is carried on the technical bloc which is
usually stencilled on the left-hand side of the aircraft just below the cockpit.
The number displayed on the fin is a corruption of the FY serial. Most tactical
aircraft carry the fiscal year in small figures followed by the last three digits of
the serial in large figures. For example F-111F 70-2362 carries 70362 on its
tail. Large transport and tanker aircraft such as C-130s and KC-135s usually
display a five-figure number commencing with the last digit of the
appropriate fiscal year and four figures of the production number. An
example of this is EC-135H 61-0282 which displays 10282 on its fin. Aircraft of
more than 10 years vintage which might duplicate a five-figure number of a
more modern type in service, are prefixed 0-.

USN serials follow a straightforward numerical sequence which
commenced, for the present series, with the allocation of 00001 to an SB2C
Helldiver by the Bureau of Aeronautics in 1940. Numbers in the 163000 series
are presently being issued. They are usually carried in full on the rear
fuselage of the aircraft and displayed either as a four- or five-figure sequence
or in full on the fin.

UK based USAF Aircraft

The following aircraft are normally based in the UK. They are listed in
numerical order of type with individual aircraft in serial number order, as
depicted on the aircraft. The number in brackets is either the alternative
presentation of the five-figure number commencing with the last digit of the
fiscal year, or the fiscal year where a five-figure serial is presented on the
aircraft. Where it is possible to identify the allocation of aircraft to individual
squadrons by means of colours carried on fin or cockpit edge, this is also
provided.

Serial	Notes	Serial			Notes
		91TFS blue (bl) Woodbridge			
Lockheed TR-1A		92TFS yellow (y) Bentwaters			
95RS/17RW, RAF Alconbury		509TFS grey (gy) Alconbury			
		510TFS purple (pr) Bentwaters			
FY80		511TFS black (bk) Alconbury			
01077		79-217	(90217) r	WR	
01078		79-218	(90218) y	WR	
01079		79-219	(90219) bk	AR	
01081		79-220	(90220) gy	AR	
01083		79-221	(90221) pr	WR	
01085		79-224	(90224) gy	AR	
01086		79-225	(90225) bl	WR	
01088		80-143	(00143) r	WR	
01092		80-144	(00144) gy	AR	
01093		80-145	(00145) r	WR	
01094		80-146	(00146) bk	AR	
		80-147	(00147) pr	WR	
Fairchild A-10A Thunderbolt II		80-155	(00155) pr	WR	
AR: 10 TFW;		80-156	(00156) bk	AR	
WR: 81TFW:		80-157	(00157) bk	AR	
78TFS red (r) Woodbridge					

Notes	Serial		
	80-158	(00158) bl	WR
	80-159	(00159) y	WR
	80-160	(00160) pr	WR
	80-167	(00167) r	WR
	80-168	(00168) y	WR
	80-169	(00169) pr	WR
	80-170	(00170) gy	AR
	80-171	(00171) bl	WR
	80-172	(00172) bk	AR
	80-179	(00179) r	WR
	80-180	(00180) bl	WR
	80-181	(00181) m	WR
	80-183	(00183) pr	WR
	80-184	(00184) bk	AR
	80-192	(00192) y	
	80-194	(00194) gy	AR
	80-195	(00195) pr	WR
	80-196	(00196) bk	AR
	80-203	(00203) r	WR
	80-204	(00204) bl	WR
	80-205	(00205) bl	WR
	80-206	(00206) y	WR
	80-207	(00207) y	WR
	80-208	(00208) gy	AR
	80-215	(00215) pr	WR
	80-216	(00216) pr	WR
	80-217	(00217) y	WR
	80-218	(00218) gy	AR
	80-219	(00219) gy	AR
	80-220	(00220) bl	WR
	80-227	(00227) gy	AR
	80-228	(00228) pr	WR
	80-229	(00229) bk	AR
	80-230	(00230) bk	AR
	80-231	(00231) gy	AR
	80-232	(00232) bl	WR
	80-233	(00233) r	WR
	80-234	(00234) bl	WR
	80-235	(00235) r	WR
	80-236	(00236) r	WR
	80-237	(00237) bk	AR
	80-270	(00270) r	WR
	80-271	(00271) bl	WR
	80-272	(00272) y	WR
	80-273	(00273) gy	AR
	80-274	(00274) pr	WR
	80-275	(00275) bk	AR
	80-276	(00276) y	WR
	80-277	(00277) bk	AR
	80-278	(00278) r	WR
	80-279	(00279) pr	WR
	80-280	(00280) bl	WR
	80-281	(00281) y	WR
	81-939	(10939) gy	AR
	81-940	(10940) bk	AR
	81-941	(10941) r	WR
	81-942	(10942) bl	WR
	81-943	(10943) y	WR
	81-944	(10944) pr	WR
	81-947	(10947) gy	AR
	81-948	(10948) gy	AR
	81-949	(10949) gy	AR
	81-950	(10950) r	WR
	81-951	(10951) bl	WR
	81-952	(10952) pr	WR
	81-953	(10953) gy	AR
	81-954	(10954) y	WR
	81-955	(10955) m	AR
	81-956	(10956) bl	WR
	81-957	(10957) y	WR
	81-960	(10960) r	WR
	81-961	(10961) r	WR
	81-962	(10962) bl	WR
	81-963	(10963) y	WR

Notes	Serial		
	81-964	(10964) gy	AR
	81-965	(10965) pr	WR
	81-966	(10966) pr	WR
	81-967	(10967) bk	AR
	81-976	(10976) bl	WR
	81-977	(10977) y	WR
	81-978	(10978) r	
	81-979	(10979) bk/gy	AR
	81-980	(10980) pr	WR
	819-81	(10981) m	
	81-982	(10982) bl	WR
	81-983	(10983) bl	WR
	81-984	(10984) r	WR
	81-985	(10985) y	WR
	81-986	(10986) bk	AR
	81-987	(10987) gy	AR
	81-988	(10988) pr	WR
	81-990	(10990) gy	AR
	819-91	(10991) bl	
	81-992	(10992) y	WR
	82-646	(20646) pr	WR
	82-647	(20647) bk	AR
	82-649	(20649) bl	WR
	82-650	(20650) pr	WR
	82-654	(20654) r	WR
	82-655	(20655) bl	WR
	82-656	(20656) y	WR
	82-657	(20657) gy	AR
	82-658	(20658) r	WR
	82-659	(20659) bk	WR

**General Dynamics
F-16C/‡F-16D**
WR: 527 AS/81TFW
RAF Bentwaters

85-453	(51453)	[02]
85-459	(51459)	[527th]
85-473	(51473)	
85-	(51	)
85-479	(51479)	[01]
86-209	(60209)	[03]
86-216	(60216)	[12]
86-224	(60224)	
86-227	(60227)	[14]
86-229	(60229)	[04]
86-231	(60231)	[13]
86-237	(60237)	[16]
86-248	(60248)	
86-249	(60249)	
86-254	(60254)	[11]
86-297	(60297)	
86-	(60	)
86-	(60	)
86-	(60	)
86-	(60	)
86-	(60	)
86-	(60	)
86-	(60	)

Sikorsky HH-53B
39SOW: 21 SOS
RAF Woodbridge

14429 (FY66)

Sikorsky CH-53C
39SOW: 21SOS
RAF Woodbridge

01625 (FY70)
10924 (FY68)
10928 (FY68)

Serial	Notes	Serial	Notes

Sikorsky MH-53J
39SOW: 21 SOS
RAF Woodbridge

14431 (FY66)
8284 (FY68)
10930 (FY68)
5796 (FY69)

Lockheed SR-71A Blackbird
9SRW/99 SRS
No 4 Det, RAF Mildenhall

Two aircraft on detachment —
see *USAF* (*US*) section serials.

General Dynamics EF-111A Raven
UH: RAF Upper Heyford
66ECIO/42ECS grey

66-015 (60015)
66-016 (60016)
66-019 (60019)
66-030 (60030)
66-031 (60031)
66-033 (60033)
66-037 (60037)
66-039 (60039)
66-041 (60041)
660-42 (70034)
66-055 (60055)
66-056 (60056)
66-057 (60057)
67-032 (70032)
67-035 (70035)
67-041 (70041)
67-052 (70052)

General Dynamics F-111E
UH: 20TFW, RAF Upper Heyford
55TFS blue/white (bl)
77TFS red (r)
79TFS yellow/black (y)

67-119 (70119) bl
67-120 (70120) m
67-121 (70121) bl
67-122 (70122) y
67-123 (70123) y
68-001 (80001) r
68-002 (80002) y
68-004 (80004) bl
68-005 (80005) bl
68-006 (80006) bl
68-007 (80007) r
68-009 (80009) r
68-010 (80010) y
68-011 (80011) r
68-013 (80013) y
68-014 (80014) bl
68-015 (80015) bl
68-016 (80016) bl
68-017 (80017) r
680-20 TFW (80020) m
68-021 (80021) r
68-022 (80022) y
68-023 (80023) y
68-025 (80025) bl
68-026 (80026) bl
68-027 (80027) r
68-028 (80028) r
68-029 (80029) r
68-030 (80030) y
68-031 (80031) r
68-032 (80032) y

68-033 (80033) y
68-034 (80034) bl
68-035 (80035) bl
68-036 (80036) bl
68-037 (80037) r
68-038 (80038) r
68-039 (80039) r
68-040 (80040) y
68-041 (80041) r
68-043 (80043) y
68-044 (80044) bl
68-046 (80046) bl
68-047 (80047) r
68-048 (80048) r
68-049 (80049) r
68-050 (80050) y
68-051 (80051) r
68-052 (80052) y
68-053 (80053) y
68-054 (80054) bl
680-55 TFS (80055) bl
68-056 (80056) bl
68-059 (80059) r
68-061 (80061) r
68-062 (80062) y
68-063 (80063) y
68-064 (80064) bl
68-065 (80065) bl
68-066 (80066) bl
68-067 (80067) r
68-068 (80068) r
68-069 (80069) r
68-071 (80071) r
68-072 (80072) y
68-073 (80073) y
68-074 (80074) bl
68-075 (80075) bl
68-076 (80076) bl
680-77 AMU (80077) r
68-078 (80078) r
680-79 AMU (80079) y
680-80 AMU (80080) y
68-082 (80082) y
68-083 (80083) y
68-084 (80084) y

General Dynamics F-111F
LN: 48TFW, RAF Lakenheath
492 TFS blue (bl)
493 TFS yellow (y)
494 TFS red (r)
495 TFS green (gn)

70-362 (02362) gn
70-363 (02363) gn
70-364 (02364) bl
70-365 (02365) bl
70-368 (02368) bl
70-369 (02369) gn
70-370 (02370) bl
70-371 (02371) y
70-372 (02372) gn
70-373 (02373) bl
70-374 (02374) y
70-376 (02376) r
70-378 (02378) bl
70-379 (02379) bl
70-381 (02381) r
70-382 (02382) bl
70-383 (02383) bl
70-384 (02384) y
70-386 (02386) r
70-387 (02387) gn
70-390 (02390) gn

USAF (UK based)

Notes	Serial			Notes	Serial		
	70-391	(02391) gn			73-708	(30708) gn	
	70-392	(02392) gn			73-710	(30710) r	
	70-394	(02394) bl			73-711	(30711) r	
	70-396	(02396) y			73-712	(30712) r	
	70-397	(02397) r			73-713	(30713) gn	
	70-398	(02398) y			73-715	(30715) r	
	70-399	(02399) bl			74-177	(40177) bl	
	70-401	(02401) r			74-178	(40178) gn	
	70-402	(02402) gn			74-180	(40180) bl	
	70-403	(02403) bl			74-181	(40181) bl	
	70-404	(02404) y			74-182	(40182) y	
	70-405	(02405) r			74-183	(40183) gn	
	70-406	(02406) bl			74-184	(40184) r	
	70-408	(02408) r			74-185	(40185) r	
	70-409	(02409) r					

Lockheed C-130E/H Hercules
RAF Mildenhall
Continuous presence of
two-month deployments
of 16 aircraft from
314TAW, 317TAW or
463TAW — see USAF
(US) Section serials

	70-411	(02411) bl
	70-412	(02412) y
	70-413	(02413) bl
	70-414	(02414) gn
	70-415	(02415) y
	70-416	(02416) r
	70-417	(02417) y
	70-419	(02419) gn
	71-883	(10883) y
	71-884	(10884) gn
	71-885	(10885) bl
	71-886	(10886) bl
	71-887	(10887) y
	71-888	(10888) bl
	71-889	(10889) y
	71-890	(10890) y
	71-891	(10891) y
	71-892	(10892) y
	71-893	(10893) bl
	71-894	(10894) gn
	72-442	(21442) bl
	72-443	(21443) r
	72-444	(21444) r
	72-445	(21445) bl
	72-446	(21446) gn
	72-448	(21448) multi
	72-449	(21449) y
	72-450	(21450) y
	72-451	(21451) y
	72-452	(21452) y
	73-707	(30707) r

Lockheed C-130 Hercules
67SOS/39 SOW, RAF
Woodbridge
14865 (FY64) HC-130H
60217 (FY66) HC-130P
60220 (FY66) HC-130P
60223 (FY66) HC-130P
95820 (FY69) HC-130N
95823 (FY69) HC-130N
95826 (FY69) HC-130N
95827 (FY69) HC-130N
95831 (FY69) HC-130N

Boeing EC-135H
513ACCW/10 ACCS, RAF Mildenhall
FY61
10282 EC-135H
10285 EC-135H
10286 EC-135H
10291 EC-135H

European based USAF Aircraft

These aircraft are normally based in Western Europe with the USAFE. They are shown in numerical order of type designation, with individual aircraft in serial number order as carried on the aircraft. An alternative five-figure presentation of the serial is shown in brackets where appropriate. Fiscal year (FY) details are also provided if necessary. The unit allocation and operating bases are given for most aircraft.

Serial		Serial		Serial	
Bell UH-1N		**McDonnell Douglas**		68-576	[26 TRW]
58 MAS Ramstein		**RF-4C Phantom**		68-580	(80580)
		ZR: 26TRW/Zweibrucken		68-583	(80583)
FY69		38TRS green/white		68-589	(80589)
96606		68-554	(80554)	69-359	(90359)
96607		68-555	(80555)	69-369	(90369)
96608		68-557	(80557)	69-370	(90370)
96609*		68-561	(80561)	69-380	(90380)
96615		68-565	(80565)	69-382	(90382)
96619*		68-567	(80567)	69-383	(90383)

Serial	
71-251	(10251)
71-254	(10254)
71-259	(10259)
72-152	(20152)
72-153	(20153)

McDonnell Douglas F-4G Phantom
SP: 52TFW
Spangdahlem
23 TFS blue/white (bl)
81 TFS yellow/black (y)
480 TFS red/white (r)

69-202	(97202)	m
69-209	(97209)	y
69-210	(97210)	r
69-212	(97212)	bl
69-228	(97228)	bl
69-232	(97232)	r
69-234	(97234)	r
69-236	(97236)	r
69-237	(90237)	y
69-241	(90241)	bl
69-242	(90242)	bl
69-245	(90245)	bl
69-247	(90247)	y
69-248	(90248) [480TFS]	r
69-250	(90250)	r
69-253	(90253)	r
69-255	(90255)	bl
69-258	(90258)	y
69-259	(90259)	bl
69-262	(97262)	bl
69-263	(97263)	y
69-268	(97268) [7081AMD]	y
69-269	(90269)	r
69-270	(90270)	bl
69-270	(97270)	r
69-274	(90274)	r
69-285	(90285)	y
69-286	(90286)	y
69-291	(97291)	bl
69-293	(97293)	y
69-295	(97295)	y
69-546	(97546)	bl
69-556	(97556)	y
69-558	(97558)	r
69-566	(97566)	bl
69-571	(97571)	bl
69-579	(97579)	r
69-582	(97582)	m
69-587	(97587)	y

McDonnell Douglas C-9A Nightingale *VIP
435TAW/55AAS Rhein Main
(†Chievres)

FY71
10875
10876*†
10878*
10879
10880
10881
10882*

Fairchild A-10A Thunderbolt II
AR: 10TFW: RAF Alconbury
WR: 81 TFW: RAF Woodbridge/ Bentwaters/Forward Operating Locations (FOL) in West Germany:
Det 1 Sembach AB WR
Det 2 WGAF Leipheim WR
Det 3 WGAF Ahlhorn AR
Det 4 WGAF Norvenich WR
At each, eight aircraft on rotation from the six UK-based Squadrons at RAF Alconbury and Woodbridge/Bentwaters — see USAF/UK-based section.

Beech C-12
(*58 MAS Ramstein
†7005ABS Stuttgart
‡JUSMG Torrejon
**MAAG Athens
§MAAG, Ankara
‡‡JUSMG Turkey
£MAAG Dhahran)

Serial		
22549	(FY76)†	C-12C
22550	(FY76)†	C-12C
31212	(FY83)‡	C-12A
31216	(FY73)§	C-12A
31218	(FY73)**	C-12A
40161	(FY84)*	C-12F
40162	(FY84)*	C-12F
40163	(FY84)*	C-12F
40164	(FY84)*	C-12F
40165	(FY84)*	C-12F
40166	(FY84)*	C-12F
60170	(FY70)£	C-12A
60173	(FY70)§	C-12A

McDonnell Douglas F-15C/‡F-15D Eagle
CR: 32TFS Soesterberg
orange/green (or)
BT: 36TFW Bitburg
22TFS red (r)
53TFS yellow/black (y)
525TFS blue (bl)
IS: 57FIS Keflavik
black/white (bk)

79-004	(90004)‡	CR	or
79-005	(90005)‡	CR	or
79-006	(90006)‡	BT	bl
79-007	(90007)‡	BT	bl
79-008	(90008)‡	BT	bl
79-010	(90010)‡	BT	r
79-011	(90011)‡	BT	r
79-012	(90012)‡	BT	r
79-015	(90015)	CR	or
79-016	(90016)	CR	or
79-017	(90017)	CR	or
79-018	(90018)	CR	or
79-019	(90019)	CR	or
79-020	(90020)	CR	or
79-021	(90021)	CR	or
79-022	(90022)	BT	r
79-023	(90023)	CR	or
79-024	(90024)	CR	or
79-025	(90025)	BT	bl
79-026	(90026)	CR	or
79-027	(90027)	CR	or
79-028	(90028)	CR	or
79-029	(90029)	CR	or
79-030	(90030)	CR	or
79-031	(90031)	CR	or
790-32TFS	(90032)	CR	or
79-033	(90033)	CR	or
79-034	(90034)	CR	or
79-035	(90035)	BT	bl
790-36TFW	(90036)	BT	m
79-037	(90037)	BT	bl
79-038	(90038)	BT	bl
79-039	(90039)	BT	bl
79-043	(90043)	BT	bl
79-045	(90045)	BT	bl
79-046	(90046)	BT	bl
79-047	(90047)	BT	bl
79-048	(90048)	BT	y
79-051	(90051)	BT	
79-052	(90052)	BT	r
79-055	(90055)	BT	bl
79-057	(90057)	BT	r
79-058	(90058)	BT	bl
79-060	(90060)	BT	r
79-062	(90062)	BT	bl
79-063	(90063)	BT	r
79-064	(90064)	BT	r
79-066	(90066)	BT	y
79-067	(90067)	BT	r
79-068	(90068)	BT	r
79-069	(90069)	BT	y
79-070	(90070)	BT	y
79-072	(90072)	BT	r
79-073	(90073)	BT	bl
79-074	(90074)	BT	r
79-076	(90076)	BT	y
79-077	(90077)	BT	bl
79-078	(90078)	BT	y
79-079	(90079)	BT	r
80-003	(00003)	BT	r
80-004	(00004)	BT	r
80-005	(00005)	BT	
80-006	(00006)	BT	r
80-009	(00009)	BT	r
80-010	(00010)	BT	r
80-011	(00011)	BT	bl
80-012	(00012)	BT	bl
80-013	(00013)	BT	bl
80-014	(00014)	BT	bl
80-015	(00015)	BT	bl
80-017	(00017)	BT	bl
80-019	(00019)	BT	bl
80-020	(00020)	BT	bl
80-021	(00021)	BT	r
80-022	(00022)	BT	r
80-023	(00023)	BT	r
80-024	(00024)	BT	bl
80-026	(00026)	BT	r
80-028	(00028)	BT	bl
80-029	(00029)	BT	bl
80-031	(00031)	BT	r
80-033	(00033) (A.F. Iceland)		
80-034	(00034)	IS	bk
80-035	(00035)	IS	bk
80-038	(00038)	IS	bk
80-039	(00039)	IS	bk
80-040	(00040)	IS	bk
80-041	(00041)	IS	bk
80-042	(00042)	IS	bk
80-043	(00043)	IS	bk
80-044	(00044)	IS	bk
80-045	(00045)	IS	bk
80-046	(00046)	IS	bk
80-047	(00047)	IS	bk
80-048	(00048)	IS	bk
80-049	(00049)	IS	bk
80-050	(00050)	IS	bk
80-052	(00052)	IS	bk
80-056	(00056)‡	IS	bk
80-057	(00057)‡	IS	bk
81-045	(10045)	CR	or
81-046	(10046)	CR	or
81-047	(10047)	CR	or

USAF (EUR based)

Serial			
81-048	(10048)	CR	or
81-049	(10049)	CR	or
81-065	(10065)‡	CR	or
84-001	(40001)	BT	y
84-002	(40002)	BT	y
84-003	(40003)	BT	y
84-004	(40004)	BT	y
84-005	(40005)	BT	y
84-006	(40006)	BT	y
84-007	(40007)	BT	y
84-008	(40008)	BT	y
84-009	(40009)	BT	m
84-010	(40010)	BT	y
84-014	(40014)	BT	y
84-015	(40015)	BT	y
84-016	(40016)	BT	y
84-017	(40017)	BT	y
84-019	(40019)	BT	y
84-020	(40020)	BT	y
84-021	(40021)	BT	y
84-022	(40022)	BT	y
84-024	(40024)	BT	y
84-025	(40025)	BT	y
84-026	(40026)	BT	y
84-043	(40043)‡	BT	y
84-044	(40044)‡	BT	y

**General Dynamics
F-16C/‡F-16D**
HR: 50TFW Hahn
  10TFS blue/yellow (bl)
  313TFS orange (or)
  496TFS yellow (y)
RS: 86TFW Ramstein
  512TFS green/black (gn)
  526TFS red/black (r)
SP: 52TFW Spangdahlem
  23TFS blue/white (bl)
  81TFS yellow/black (y)
  480TFS red/white (r)
TJ: 104TFW Torrejon
  612TFS blue/white (bl)
  613TFS yellow/black (y)
  614TFS red/black (r)

84-238	(41238)	HR	bl
842-50TFW	(41250)	HR	m
84-263	(41263)	HR	y
84-264	(41264)	HR	y
84-266	(41266)	HR	y
84-271	(41271)	HR	y
84-274	(41274)	HR	br
84-275	(41275)	HR	bl
84-278	(41278)	HR	bl
84-279	(41279)	HR	or
84-282	(41282)	HR	bl
84-283	(41283)	HR	or
84-284	(41284)	HR	y
84-287	(41287)	HR	or
84-288	(41288)	HR	or
84-289	(41289)	HR	y
84-290	(41290)	HR	bl
84-291	(41291)	HR	y
84-292	(41292)	HR	or
84-293	(41293)	HR	y
84-294	(41294)	HR	or
84-295	(41295)	HR	bl
84-296	(41296)	HR	y
[496TFS]			
84-297	(41297)	HR	y
84-298	(41298)	HR	y
84-299	(41299)	HR	y
84-300	(41300)	HR	bl
84-301	(41301)	HR	or

Serial			
84-302	(41302)	HR	or
84-303	(41303)	HR	or
84-304	(41304)	HR	y
84-305	(41305)	HR	y
84-306	(41306)	HR	y
84-307	(41307)	HR	y
84-308	(41308)	HR	or
84-309	(41309)	HR	or
84-310TFS	(41310)	HR	bl
84-311	(41311)	HR	or
84-313TFS	(41313)	HR	or
84-315	(41315)	HR	y
84-316	(41316)	HR	or
84-317	(41317)	HR	y
84-318	(41318)	HR	y
84-324	(41324)‡	HR	or
84-325	(41325)‡	HR	y
84-326	(41326)‡	HR	y
84-327	(41327)‡	HR	or
84-328	(41328)‡	HR	bl
84-331	(41331)‡	HR	bl
84-374	(41374)	HR	bl
84-375	(41375)	HR	or
84-376	(41376)	HR	bl
84-382	(41382)	HR	bl
84-383	(41383)	HR	or
84-384	(41384)	HR	or
84-385	(41385)	HR	bl
84-386	(41386)	HR	y
84-387	(41387)	HR	bl
84-388	(41388)	HR	bl
84-390	(41390)	HR	bl
84-391	(41391)	HR	y
84-392	(41392)	HR	bl
84-393	(41393)	HR	or
84-394	(41394)	HR	or
85-398	(51398)	RS	gn
85-400	(51400)	RS	gn
85-402	(51402)	RS	r
85-403	(51403)	HR	bl
85-404	(51404)	HR	y
85-405	(51405)	HR	y
85-406	(51406)	HR	y
85-407	(51407)	HR	bl
85-408	(51408)	RS	r
85-409	(51409)	HR	bl
85-410	(51410)	RS	r
85-411	(51411)	HR	bl
85-412	(51412)	RS	gn
85-413	(51413)	HR	or
85-415	(51415)	HR	bl
85-416	(51416)	HR	bl
85-417	(51417)	HR	or
85-418	(51418)	HR	bl
85-422	(51422)	RS	r
85-426	(51426)	[526 TFS]	
85-428	(51428)	RS	gn
85-434	(51434)	RS	r
85-436	(51436)	RS	gn
85-438	(51438)	RS	gn
85-440	(51440)	RS	gn
85-442	(51442)	RS	r
85-444	(51444)	RS	r
85-446	(51446)	RS	r
85-448	(51448)	RS	r
85-449	(51449)	RS	r
85-450	(51450)	RS	r
85-451	(51451)	RS	r
85-454	(51454)	RS	gn
85-455	(51455)	RS	gn
85-456	(51456)	RS	gn

Serial			
85-457	(51457)	RS	m
[86TFW]			
85-458	(51458)	RS	gn
85-459	(51459)	RS	gn
85-460	(51460)	RS	r
85-461	(51461)	RS	r
85-464	(51464)	[86TFW]	
85-465	(51465)	RS	r
85-466	(51466)	RS	gn
85-467	(51467)	RS	gn
85-468	(51468)	RS	gn
85-469	(51469)	RS	gn
85-470	(51470)	[512TFS]	
85-471	(51471)	RS	gn
85-472	(51472)	RS	gn
85-474	(51474)	RS	gn
85-475	(51475)	RS	r
85-476	(51476)	RS	r
85-477	(51477)	RS	r
85-478	(51478)	RS	gn
85-480	(51480)	RS	gn
85-481	(51481)	RS	gn
85-484	(51484)	RS	r
85-485	(51485)	RS	gn
85-486TFW	(51486)	RS	gn
85-509	(51509)‡	RS	gn
85-511	(51511)‡	RS	r
85-546	(51546)	RS	r
85-552	(51552)	SP	m
85-572	(51572)‡	SP	m
86-042	(60042)‡	SP	m
86-043	(60043)‡	SP	multi
86-044	(60044)‡	TJ	bl
86-047	(60047)‡	TJ	r
86-049	(60049)‡	TJ	y
86-050	(60050)‡	TJ	gr
86-219	(60219)	SP	r
86-222	(60222)	SP	r
862-23TFS	(60223)	SP	bl
86-225	(60225)	SP	r
86-226	(60226)	SP	r
86-228	(60228)	SP	r
86-230	(60230)	SP	y
86-232	(60232)	SP	bl
86-236	(60236)	TJ	bl
86-242	(60242)	SP	bl
86-243	(60243)	SP	bl
86-244	(60244)	SP	bl
86-245	(60245)	SP	v
86-246	(60246)	SP	bl
86-253	(60253)	SP	y
86-255	(60255)	SP	r
86-258	(60258)	SP	y
86-259	(60259)	SP	r
86-260	(20260)	SP	
86-261	(60261)	SP	y
86-262	(60262)	SP	y
86-263	(60263)	SP	y
86-270	(60270)	SP	y
86-287	(60287)	SP	m
86-288	(60288)	SP	y
86-289	(60289)	TJ	bl
86-302	(60302)	TJ	bl
86-303	(60303)	TJ	bl
86-308	(60308)	TJ	bl
86-311	(60311)	TJ	bl
86-312	(60312)	TJ	bl
86-313	(60313)	TJ	bl
86-315	(60315)	TJ	bl
86-316 AF	(60316)	TJ	bl
86-321	(60321)	TJ	

Serial				Serial		Serial	

Serial			
86-324	(60324)	TJ	bl
86-325	(60325)	TJ	bl
86-326	(60326)	TJ	bl
86-327	(60327)	TJ	bl
86-328	(60328)	TJ	bl
86-329	(60329)	TJ	bl
86-330	(60330)	TJ	bl
86-333	(60333)	TJ	
86-338	(60338)	TJ	bl
86-339	(60339)	TJ	bl
86-340	(60340)	TJ	bl
86-341	(60341)	TJ	
86-342	(60342)	TJ	y
86-344	(60344)	TJ	y
86-345	(60345)	TJ	y
86-346	(60346)	TJ	y
86-347	(60347)	TJ	y
86-348	(60348)	TJ	y
86-349	(60349)	TJ	y
86-350	(60350)	TJ	bl
86-358	(60358)	SP	bl
86-360	(60360)	TJ	bl
86-361	(60361)	TJ	y
86-362	(60362)	TJ	y
86-363	(60363)	TJ	y
86-364	(60364)	TJ	y
86-365	(60365)	TJ	bl
86-366	(60366)	TJ	y
86-367	(60367)	TJ	bl
86-368	(60368)	TJ	y
86-369	(60369)	TJ	y
86-370	(60370)	TJ	y
86-371	(60371)	TJ	
87-217	(70217)	TJ	y
87-218	(70218)	TJ	y
87-219	(70219)	TJ	y
87-220	(70220)	TJ	y
87-221	(70221)	614TFS	
87-222	(70222)	TJ	y
87-223	(70223)	TJ	r
87-224	(70224)	TJ	r
87-225	(70225)	TJ	r
87-226	(70226)	TJ	r
87-227	(70227)	TJ	r
87-228	(70228)	TJ	r
87-229	(70229)	TJ	r
87-230	(70230)	TJ	r
87-233	(70233)	TJ	
87-237	(70237)	TJ	r
87-238	(70238)	TJ	r
87-239	(70239)	TJ	r
87-240	(70240)	TJ	r
87-241	(70241)	TJ	r
87-242	(70242)	TJ	r
87-243	(70243)	TJ	r
87-244	(70244)	TJ	r
87-245	(70245)	TJ	r
87-246	(70246)	TJ	r
87-247	(70247)	TJ	r
87-257	(70257)	SP	bl
87-258	(70258)	TJ	r
87-259	(70259)	TJ	r
87-260	(70260)	SP	r
87-2	(702	)	
87-2	(702	)	
87-2	(702	)	
87-2	(702	)	
87-2	(702	)	
87-2	(702	)	
87-2	(702	)	
87-268	(70268)	SP	bl
87-2	(702	)	
87-270	(70270)	SP	bl

Serial		
87-2	(702	)
87-2	(702	)
87-2	(702	)
87-2	(702	)
87-2	(702	)
87-2	(702	)
87-2	(702	)
87-2	(702	)

Grumman C-20A Gulfstream III
58 MAS, Ramstein

FY83
30500
30501
30502

Gates C-21A Learjet
*58MAS Ramstein
†7005ABS Stuttgart
‡HQ/USEUCOM

FY84
40081†
40082†
40083†
40084*
40085*
40086*

Shorts C-23A Sherpa
322MAW/10MAS
  Zweibrucken

FY83
30512 *Zweibrucken*
30513 *Ramstein*

FY84
40458 *Sembach*
40459 *Spangdahlem*
40460 *Hahn*
40461 *Rhein Main*
40462 *Mildenhall/
  Lakenheath*
40463 *Bitburg*
40464 *Zaragosa*
40465 *Alconbury*
40466 *Bentwaters/Woodbridge*
40467 *Upper Heyford*
40468 *Greenham Common*
40469 *Soesterberg*
40470 *Torrejon*
40471 *Wiesbaden*
40472 *Incirlik*
40473 *Florennes*

North American T-39A Sabre
375AAW Rhein
  Main
24453 (FY62)

Sikorsky CH-53C
--SOS/39 SOW Sembach
01626 (FY70)
01630 (FY70)
10932 (FY68)

Lockheed C-130E Hercules
435TAW Rhein Main: 37TAS;
*7405 OS

01260	(FY70)
01264	(FY70)
01271	(FY70)
01274	(FY70)
10935	(FY68)
10938	(FY68)
10943	(FY68)
10947	(FY68)
17681	(FY64)
18240	(FY64)
21819	(FY62)*
21822	(FY62)*
21828	(FY62)*
37814	(FY63)
37885	(FY63)
40502	(FY64)
40527	(FY64)
40550	(FY64)
96566	(FY69)
96582	(FY69)
96583	(FY69)

Lockheed EC-130H Hercules
SB: 66ECW/43 ECS, Sembach

FY73
31583
31584
31585
31588
31590
31594
31595

Lockheed MC-130E Hercules
7SOS Rhein Main

FY64
40523
40555
40561
40566

European based US Army Aircraft

Serial		Serial		Serial	
Bell AH-1S (FM)		15264	3 B Co	15679	3-4 Avn
Cobra		15266	2 ACR	15682	8 B Co
2-4 Avn, 3-4 Avn, Mainz		15275	503 C Co	15683	501 B Co
3-3 Avn, 2-3 Avn, Giebelstadt		15286	2 ACR	15689	2 ACR
2nd Armoured Cavalry		15289	8 B Co	15701	2 ACR
Regiment: Feucht		15290	2 ACR	15710	503 B Co
11th Armoured Cavalry		15292	3-4 Avn	15716	503 C Co
Regiment: Fulda		15293	501 C Co	15717	3 B Co
3rd Aviation Battalion		15295	2 ACR	15721	3 C Co
(Combat), 'B' Co:		15315	503 B Co	15736	3 C Co
Giebelstadt		15316	3 C Co	15741	503 C Co
3rd Aviation Battalion		15321	3-4 Avn	15745	8 B Co
(Combat), 'C' Co:		15322	501 B Co	15757	503 C Co
Schweinfurt		15324	501 C Co	15764	3 B Co
8th Aviation Battalion		15328	503 B Co	15769	8 C Co
(Combat), 'B' Co:		15335	11 ACR	15771	503 B Co
Mainz-Finthen		15348	3 C Co	15772	8 B Co
8th Aviation Battalion		15350	3-3 Avn	15776	503 C Co
(Combat), 'C' Co:		15356	11 ACR	15784	8 B Co
Mainz-Finthen				15789	501 C Co
308th Attack Helicopter		*FY67*		15790	3-3 Avn
Battalion,		15450	2 ACR	15805	501 B Co
Hanau		15452	8 C Co	15815	501 B Co
501st Aviation		15455	2 ACR	15822	2 ACR
Battalion (Combat),		15457	503 C Co	15829	501 C Co
'B' Co: Ansbach		15459	2 ACR	15833	3-3 Avn
501st Aviation		15460	8 B Co	15842	501 B Co
Battalion (Combat),		15470	11 ACR	15852	308 AHB
'C' Co: Illesheim		15473	11 ACR	15860	3-4 Avn
503rd Aviation		15475	11 ACR	15863	3 C Co
Battalion (Combat),		15477	3 C Co		
'B' Co: Hanau		15479	3 B Co	*FY70*	
503rd Aviation		15480	503 B Co	15947	18 AHB
Battalion (Combat),		15489	3-4 Avn	15950	501 C Co
'C' Co: Hanau		15490	503 B Co	15951	503 C Co
		15491	3-4 Avn	15952	11 ACR
FY68		15497	2 ACR	15958	11 ACR
15007	8 B Co	15506	501 B Co	15959	3-4 Avn
15015	3-3 Avn	15508	501 C Co	15961	8 C Co
15036	503 C Co	15512	3 B Co	15970	3 B Co
15038	501 B Co	15520	501 C Co	15971	3 C Co
15046	501 B Co	15522	3 B Co	15995	2 ACR
15057	10 AHB	15528	3 B Co	16012	3-3 Avn
15069	501 B Co	15530	3 B Co	16016	3 C Co
15084	503 B Co	15535	3-3 Avn	16048	3 C Co
15085	2 ACR	15540	3-4 Avn	16054	501 B Co
15092	2-227 AvCo	15548	3 B Co	16091	501 B Co
15093	8 B Co	15551	501 C Co		
15104	2-4 Avn	15565	3-3 Avn	*FY69*	
15105	2 ACR	15571	8 B Co	16411	3 C Co
15106	3 B Co	15572	11 ACR	16422	501 B Co
15110	503 B Co	15587	501 C Co	16426	2 ACR
15112	501 C Co	15593	11 ACR	16429	2-3 Avn
15113	308 AHB	15610	2 ACR	16432	503 B Co
15116	2 ACR	15613	8 C Co	16433	2-4 Avn
15131	3-4 Avn	15614	2-4 Avn	16434	503 B Co
15134	501 B Co	15617	503 B Co	16436	503 C Co
15142	11 ACR	15621	2 ACR	16439	11 ACR
15152	501 B Co	15633	501 C Co	16445	8 B Co
15173	501 B Co	15642	8 C Co		
15180	503 B Co	15643	2 ACR	*FY68*	
15208	503 C Co	15650	503 B Co	17023	503 C Co
		15652	503 B Co	17028	503 B Co
FY66		15658	11 ACR	17047	11 ACR
15249	503 B Co	15659	2 ACR	17049	8 B Co
15250	2 ACR	15662	11 ACR	17062	503 C Co
15252	11 ACR	15664	3 C Co	17063	503 B Co
15254	2 ACR	15665	3-4 Avn	17070	501 C Co
15261	2 ACR	15666	11 ACR	17074	503 C Co
15263	8 B Co	15675	11 ACR	17076	501 B Co
				17078	2-4 Avn

Serial		

17079	503 B Co	
17082	503 C Co	
17085	503 C Co	
17087	501 C Co	
17088	11 ACR	
17092	503 B Co	
17095	3-4 Avn	
17100	501 B Co	
17101	308 AHB	
17104	501 B Co	
17105	501 C Co	
17108	501 C Co	
17111	3-4 Avn	
17112	503 B Co	

FY71

20998	11 ACR	
21014	503 C Co	
21028	503 C Co	
21033	2 ACR	
21035	2 ACR	

FY78

23089	3 C Co	
23095	11 ACR	
23118	2-3 Avn	
23119	1-2 Cav	

FY79

23189	3 B Co	
23190	3 B Co	
23194	3 B Co	
23199	3 C Co	
23200	3-3 Avn	
23235	3-3 Avn	

FY81

23526	11 ACR	
23527	11 ACR	
23528	8 C Co	
23529	3-4 Avn	
23530	3-4 Avn	
23531	8 B Co	
23533	3-4 Avn	
23534	3-4 Avn	
23535	8 B Co	
23536	3 B Co	
23537	3 B Co	
23538	3 B Co	
23539	3-3 Avn	
23540	2-3 Avn	

Grumman V-1 Mohawk

†1MIB, Wiesbaden
‡2MIB, Stuttgart

14239	(FY64)	RV-1D†
14244	(FY64)	RV-1D‡
14246	(FY64)	RV-1D‡
14248	(FY64)	RV-1D†
14256	(FY64)	RV-1D†
14267	(FY64)	RV-1D†
14268	(FY64)	RV-1D†
14269	(FY64)	RV-1D†
14273	(FY64)	RV-1D†
15930	(FY68)	OV-1D‡
15931	(FY68)	OV-1D
15943	(FY68)	OV-1D†
15956	(FY68)	OV-1D‡
15960	(FY68)	OV-1D†
15962	(FY68)	OV-1D†
16993	(FY68)	OV-1D†
16996	(FY68)	OV-1D‡
17004	(FY69)	OV-1D‡
17008	(FY69)	OV-1D‡

17019	(FY69)	OV-1D†
18910	(FY67)	OV-1D†
18900	(FY67)	OV-1D†
18904	(FY67)	OV-1D
18908	(FY67)	OV-1D†
18921	(FY67)	OV-1D†
25865	(FY62)	OV-1D†
25878	(FY62)	OV-1D†
25891	(FY62)	RV-1D‡
25895	(FY62)	RV-1D†
25897	(FY62)	RV-1D†
25902	(FY62)	OV-1D‡
25903	(FY62)	RV-1D

Beech C-12 Super King Air
($=C-12C, *=C-12D, †=RC-12D, ‡=C-12F)

25AvCo, Stuttgart;
HQ/USEUCOM;
56AvCo, Vicenza
207AvCo Heidelberg
Corps of Engineers, Wiesbaden
62AvCo, Wiesbaden
1MIB, Wiesbaden
2MIB/330 ASACo, Stuttgart

22253$	(FY73)	25AvCo
22254$	(FY73)	7 Corps
22255$	(FY73)	6AvCo
22260$	(FY73)	Corps of Eng's
22261$	(FY73)	VCorps
22262$	(FY73)	Berlin Bgde
22550$	(FY76)	HQ/USEUCOM
22556$	(FY76)	56AvCo
22557$	(FY76)	207AvCo
22564$	(FY76)	56AvCo
22931$	(FY77)	6AvCo
22932$	(FY77)	6AvCo
22944$	(FY77)	56AvCo
22950$	(FY77)	207AvCo
23126$	(FY78)	207AvCo
23127$	(FY78)	207AvCo
23128$	(FY78)	207AvCo
23141†	(FY78)	1MIB
23142†	(FY78)	1MIB
23143†	(FY78)	1MIB
23144†	(FY78)	2MIB/330ASA Co
23371†	(FY80)	2MIB/330ASA Co
23373†	(FY80)	2MIB/330ASA Co
23374†	(FY80)	2MIB/330ASA Co
23375†	(FY80)	1MIB
23376†	(FY80)	2MIB/330ASA Co
23377†	(FY80)	1MIB
23378†	(FY80)	2MIB/330ASA Co
23542†	(FY81)	1MIB
24380†	(FY84)	207AvCo
51264‡	(FY85)	1MIB
51268‡	(FY85)	1MIB

Beech U-21A King Air
*EU-21A

18000*	(FY66)	56AvCo
18010	(FY66)	56 AvCo
18013*	(FY66)	7 Sigs Bgde
18014	(FY66)	56 AvCo
18019	(FY66)	56 AvCo

18021	(FY66)	56AvCo
18025	(FY66)	56 AvCo
18027*	(FY66)	7 Sigs Bgde
18030	(FY66)	7 ATC
18049	(FY67)	56AvCo
18058	(FY67)	5 Corps
18078	(FY67)	7 Corps
18080	(FY67)	56 AvCo
18116	(FY67)	56 AvCo

Boeing-Vertol CH-47C Chinook
* ACo, 5 Batt, 159 Av Reg't Schwabisch Hall;
‡ ACo, 6 Batt, 158 Av Reg't Coleman Barracks

15002	(FY70*)	
15012	(FY70)‡	
15020	(FY70)*	
15829	(FY68)‡	
15831	(FY68)‡	
15838	(FY68)	
15846	(FY68)*	
15847	(FY68)	
15849	(FY68)‡	
15851	(FY68)	
15856	(FY68)*	
15865	(FY68)*	
15867	(FY68)*	
15868	(FY68)*	
15990	(FY68)*	
15995	(FY68)*	
15997	(FY68)*	
16006	(FY68)*	
16008	(FY68)‡	
16009	(FY68)	
17114	(FY69)*	
17116	(FY69)*	
17117	(FY69)*	
17118	(FY69)*	
17126	(FY69)	
18516	(FY67)‡	
18531	(FY67)	
18533	(FY67)‡	
18548	(FY67)*	
20950	(FY71)	
20952	(FY71)	
20953	(FY71)	
20954	(FY71)‡	
22283	(FY74)‡	
22284	(FY74)‡	
22285	(FY74)‡	
22286	(FY74)	
22291	(FY74)‡	
22293	(FY74)	
22677	(FY76)‡	
22678	(FY76)‡	
22679	(FY76)‡	
22681	(FY76)*	
22684	(FY76)*	
23394	(FY79)*	
23395	(FY79)	
23396	(FY79)*	
23398	(FY79)‡	
24734	(FY85)	
24735	(FY85)	
24736	(FY85)	
24737	(FY85)	
24739	(FY85)	
24740	(FY85)	
24742	(FY85)	

US Army (EUR based)

Boeing-Vertol CH-47D Chinook

* A Co, 5 Batt, 159 Av Reg't Schwabisch Hall
† 205 AvCo, Mainz-Finthen

FY86
61671†
61672†
61673†
61674†
61675†
61676†
61677†
61678†

FY87
70071†
70072†
70073†
70075†
70076†
70077†
70078†
70079*
70080*
70081*
70082*
70083*
70084*
70085*
70086*
70087*
70088*
70089*
70090*
70091*
70092*
70093*
70094*
70096 158 BCo
70097 158 BCo
70100 158 BCo
70101 158 BCo
70103 158 BCo

Sikorsky UH-60A Blackhawk

3rd Aviation Battalion (Combat), 'D' Co and 'E' Co: Giebelstadt
8th Aviation Battalion (Combat), 'D' Co: Mainz-Finthen
4th Aviation Co: Wiesbaden
48th Aviation Co: Wiesbaden
203rd Aviation Co: Wertheim
205th AVIM Battalion: Hanau
207th Aviation Co: Heidelberg
57th Aviation Co: Hanau
21st Aviation Co: Giebelstadt
159th Med Det (HA), Lemwerder
15th Med Det (HA), Grafenwohr
63rd Med Det (HA), Landstuhl
236th Med Det (HA), Gablingen
357th Avn Det/SHAPE, Chievres
421st Medical Co: Nellingen
394th AVIM Battalion: Nellingen
421st Medical Co, 1st Platoon: Wiesbaden
421st Medical Co, 2nd Platoon: Schweinfurt

421st Medical Co, 3rd Platoon: Wiesbaden
421st Medical Co, 4th Platoon: Darmstadt
501st Aviation Battalion (Combat), 'D' Co and 'E' Co: Ansbach
503rd Aviation Battalion (Combat), 'D' Co and 'E' Co: Hanau
2nd Armored Cavalry Regiment, 4th Sqn, Feucht
11th Armored Cavalry Regiment, Fulda

FY77
22723   159 Med Det
22727   63 Med Det

FY78
22969   63 Med Det
22986   236 Med Det
22990   159 Med Det
22991   421 Med Co
22995   63 Med Det
22996   236 Med Det
22997   159 Med Det
23000   159 Med Det
23001   63 Med Det
23003   159 Med Det
23271   236 Med Det

FY80
23425   21 AvCo
23427   21 AvCo
23428   21 AvCo
23431   21 AvCo
23432   21 AvCo
23433   21 AvCo
23434   236 Med Det
23436   21 AvCo
23438   21 AvCo
23439   21 AvCo
23440   21 AvCo
23441   21 AvCo
23442   21 AvCo
23443   21 AvCo
23444   21 AvCo
23489   203 AvCo
23490   21 AvCo

FY81
23548   203 AvCo
23551   159 Med Det
23568   205 AvCo
23571   21 AvCo
23572   48 AvCo
23573   57 AvCo
23575   48 AvCo
23578   48 AvCo
23579   48 AvCo
23580   48 AvCo
23581   503 E Co
23582   48 AvCo
23583   503 E Co
23584   57 AvCo
23585   357 Avn Det
23586   503 E Co
23587   48 AvCo
23588   48 AvCo
23589   48 AvCo
23590   48 AvCo
23591   48 AvCo
23592   48 AvCo
23593   48 AvCo
23594   501 E Co

23595   501 E Co
23596   15 Med Det
23597   48 AvCo
23598   48 AvCo
23599   48 AvCo
23602   57 AvCo
23603   503 E Co
23604   503 E Co
23605   57 AvCo
23606   503 D Co
23607   4 AvCo
23608   501 E Co
23609   503 E Co
23610   503 E Co
23613   501 E Co
23614   503 E Co
23615   503 E Co
23616   4 E Co
23617   503 E Co
23618   503 E Co
23622   21 AvCo
23623   8 D Co
23624   8 E Co
23625   8 E Co
23626   8 E Co

FY82
23660   501 E Co
23661   501 E Co
23662   501 E Co
23663   501 E Co
23664   501 E Co
23665   8 E Co
23666   8 E Co
23667   8 E Co
23668   4 AvCo
23669   4 AvCo
23672   203 AvCo
23673   203 AvCo
23674   203 AvCo
23675   421 4 P1
23676   421 2 Pl
23682   4 AvCo
23683   8 E Co
23684   8 E Co
23685   4 AvCo
23686   4 AvCo
23690   501 E Co
23691   501 E Co
23692   21 AvCo
23693   501 E Co
23694   501 E Co
23695   203 AvCo
23696   203 AvCo
23697   203 AvCo
23698   203 AvCo
23699   203 AvCo
23700   207 AvCo
23701   207 AvCo
23702   501 D Co
23703   203 AvCo
23704   203 AvCo
23705   203 AvCo
23706   203 AvCo
23707   203 AvCo
23720   63 Med Det
23721   203 AvCo
23722   203 AvCo
23723   421 4 Pl
23726   63 Med Det
23727   421 4 Pl
23729   15 Med Det
23730   421 Med Co
23731   421 4 Pl

Serial		Serial		Serial	
23733	421 4 Pl	24577		24289	
23735	421 Med Co	24579	48 AvCo	24290*	
23736	421 Med Co	24581	236 Med Det	24291*	
23737	421 4 Pl	24583	357 Av Det	24292*	
23738	421 2 Pl	24584	357 Av Det	24293*	
23739	421 4 Pl			24294*	
23740	421 Med Co	*FY87*		24295*	
23741	63 Med Det	24642	2 ACR	24296*	
23743	421 2 Pl	24643	2 ACR	24297*	
23744	501 E Co	24644	2 ACR	24298*	
23745	421 Med Co	24645	2 ACR	24299*	
23746	421 2 Pl	24646	2 ACR	24302*	
23749	421 Med Co	24647	2 ACR	24303*	
23750	421 Med Co	24656	2 ACR	24304*	
23751	421 Med Co	24657			
23753	421 Med Co	26000	2 ACR	*FY85*	
23754	421 Med Co	26001	2 ACR	25397	
23755	421 Med Co	26002	2 ACR	25398	
23756	421 Med Co	26003	2 ACR	25460	
		26004	2 ACR	25469	
FY85				25471	
24390		*FY88*		25472	
24392		26019	158 B Co	25473	
24417		26021	158 B Co	25474	
24418	21 AvCo	26024	203 AvCo	25475	
		26025	203 AvCo	25476	
FY86		26026	203 AvCo	25478	
24498	357 Avn Det	26027	203 AvCo	25479	
24530		26028	203 AvCo	25480	
24531		26050	8 AvCo	25481	
24532				25482	
24538	207 AvCo	**McD AH-64A Apache**		25483	
24544	207 AvCo	* 2/6 Cav, Ildesheim		25484	
24550	63 Med Det			25485	
24552	48 AvCo	*FY84*		25486	
24553	48 AvCo	24218*		25487	
24554	48 AvCo	24257*		25488	
24551	15 Med Det	24258*			
24555	421 Med Co	24259*		*FY86*	
24565	21 AvCo	24260*		8981	
24566	21 AvCo	24262*		8983	
24570	21 AvCo	24263*			

European based US Navy Aircraft

Grumman C-2A Greyhound
(VR-24 Sigonella)

162144	[JM24]
162145	[JM25]
162153	[JM21]
162155	[JM26]
162159	[JM22]

Lockheed †P-3A/EP-3E/ *UP-3A Orion
(VQ-2: Rota)

148888	[JQ-23]
149668	[JQ-21]
149677	[JQ-20]*
150494	[JQ-25]
150502	[JQ-22]
150503	[JQ-26]
150505	[JQ-24]
151368	[JQ-27]†

Beech UC-12M Super King Air
8C: NAF Sigonella
8D: NAF Rota

3838	[8D]	(163838)
3839	[8D]	(163839)
3841	[8C]	(163841)
3842	[8D]	(163842)
3844	[8D]	(163844)

NA CT-39G Sabreliner
(VR-24 Sigonella)

159361	[31]
159362	[32]
159363	[33]

Lockheed C-130F/KC-130F* Hercules
(VR-22: Rota)

148892	[JL 05]*
149790	[JL00]
149794	[JL01]
149797	[JL02]
149801	[JL03]
150687	[JL04]*

US based USAF Aircraft

The following aircraft are normally based in the USA but are likely to be seen visiting the UK from time to time. The types are in numerical order, commencing with the E-**3** and concluding with the C-**141**. The aircraft are listed in numerical progression by the serial actually carried externally. Fiscal year information is provided, together with details of mark variations and in some cases operating units.

Serial	Wing
Boeing E-3 Sentry	
552 AW&CW	
963 AW&CS (bk)	
964 AW&CS(r)	
965 AW&CS(y)	
966 AW&CS(TS) (bl)	
FY80	
00137	E-3C y
00138	E-3C y
00139	E-3C y
FY81	
10004	E-3C y
10005	E-3A y
FY71	
11407	E-3B bl
11408	E-3A bl
FY82	
20006	E-3C y
20007	E-3C y
FY83	
30008	E-3C r
30009	E-3C bk
FY73	
31674	E-3C Boeing
31675	E-3B r
FY75	
50556	E-3B bk
50557	E-3C m
50558	E-3B b
50559	E-3B r
50560	E-3B bk
FY76	
61604	E-3B r
61605	E-3B r
61606	E-3B
61607	E-3B b
FY77	
70351	E-3B bk
70352	E-3B bk
70353	E-3B bl
70354	E-3B bk
70355	E-3A bk
70356	E-3B y
FY78	
80576	E-3B bk
80577	E-3B r
80578	E-3B bk
FY79	
90001	E-3A bl
90002	E-3B bl
90003	E-3A r
Boeing E-4B	
1ACCS/55SRW	
31676	(FY73)
31677	(FY73)
40787	(FY74)
50125	(FY75)

Serial	Wing
Lockheed C-5A Galaxy	
(*ANG, Air National Guard	
†AFRES, Air Force Reserve)	
60 MAW: Travis AFB, California	
137 MAS/105 MAG*: Stewart AFB, New York	
433 MAW/68 MAS†: Kelly AFB, Texas	
436 MAW: Dover AFB, Delaware	
439 MAW/337 MAS†: Westover AFB	
443 MAW: Altus AFB, Oklahoma	
459 MAW: Andrews AFB, Maryland	
FY70	
00445	433 MAW†
00446	60 MAW
00447	439 MAW†
00448	436 MAW
00449	60 MAW
00450	60 MAW
00451	60 MAW
00452	436 MAW
00453	436 MAW
00454	436 MAW
00455	436 MAW
00456	436 MAW
00457	436 MAW
00458	443 MAW
00459	60 MAW
00460	436 MAW
00461	60 MAW
00462	60 MAW
00463	436 MAW
00464	436 MAW
00465	436 MAW
00466	436 MAW
00467	436 MAW
FY66	
68304	433 MAW*
68305	433 MAW†
68306	433 MAW†
68307	436 MAW
FY67	
70167	60 MAW
70168	433 MAW†
70169	60 MAW
70170	137 MAS
70171	433 MAW†
70173	436 MAW
70174	436 MAW
FY68	
80211	60 MAW
80212	137 MAS
80213	60 MAW
80214	436 MAW
80215	MAW†
80216	60 MAW
80217	436 MAW
80219	433 MAW†
80220	436 MAW
80221	433 MAW†
80222	433 MAW†

Serial	Wing
80223	433 MAW†
80224	137 MAS*
80225	439 MAW†
80226	60 MAW
80228	60 MAW
FY69	
90001	443 MAW
90002	433 MAW†
90003	436 MAW
90004	433 MAW†
90005	60 MAW
90006	439 MAW
90007	60 MAW
90008	137 MAS/105 MAG*
90009	60 MAW
90010	60 MAW
90011	60 MAW
90012	60 MAW
90013	439 MAW
90014	443 MAW
90015	137 MAS/105 MAG*
90016	433 MAW/68 MAS†
90017	439 MAW†
90018	60 MAW
90019	439 MAW†
90020	60 MAW
90021	436 MAW
90022	60 MAW
90023	60 MAW
90024	60 MAW
90025	60 MAW
90026	436 MAW
90027	436 MAW
Lockheed C-5B Galaxy	
FY83	
31285	433 MAW
FY84	
40059	443 MAW
40060	60 MAW
40061	436 MAW
40062	60 MAW
FY85	
50001	436 MAW
50002	60 MAW
50003	436 MAW
50004	60 MAW
50005	436 MAW
50006	60 MAW
50007	436 MAW
50008	60 MAW
50009	436 MAW
50010	60 MAW
FY86	
60011	443 MAW
60012	443 MAW
60013	436 MAW
60014	60 MAW
60015	436 MAW
60016	60 MAW
60017	436 MAW
60018	60 MAW

Serial	Wing	Serial	Wing	Serial	Wing
60019	436 MAW	60035 ‡		76477	93 BW
60020	60 MAW	60036 ‡		76478	42 BW
60021	443 MAW	60037 ‡		76480	93 BW
60022	443 MAW	60038 ‡		76483	93 BW
60023	443 MAW			76484	42 BW
60024		*FY87*		76485	97 BW
60025		70117 †		76486	93 BW
60026	60 MAW	70118 †		76487	93 BW
		70119 †		76488	320 SW
FY87		70120 †		76489	320 BW
70027	436 MAW	70121 ‡		76490	416 BW
70028	436 MAW	70122 ‡		76491	93 BW
70029		70123		76492	93 BW
70030		70124		76495	93 BW
70031	436 MAW			76497	320 BW
70032	60 MAW	*(FY79)*		76498	416 BW
70033	436 MAW	90433 *		76499	93 BW
70034		90434 *		76500	2 BW
70035		91710 *		76501	416 BW
70036		91711 *		76502	93 BW
70037		91712 *		76503	2 BW
70038		91713 *		76504	97 BW
70039		91946 †		76505	93 BW
70040		91947 †		76506	2 BW
70041		91948 †		76508	2 BW
70042		91949 †		76509	2 BW
70043		91950 †		76510	42 BW
70044		91951 †		76511	93 BW
70045				76512	2 BW
		Boeing C-18A/EC-18B*		76513	320 BW
McDonnell-Douglas KC-10A		(Air Force Systems Command)		76514	93 BW
Extender				76515	BW
*2 BW		*FY81*		76516	416 BW
†22 ARW		10891*	4950 TW	76517	97 BW
‡68 ARW		10892	4950 TW	76518	97 BW
		10893		76519	2 BW
FY82		10894	4950 TW	76520	2 BW
20191 †		10895	4950 TW		
20192 ‡		10896*	4950 TW	*FY58*	
20193 †		10897		80158	93 BW
		10898*		80159	320 BW
FY83				80160	416 BW
30075 *		**Grumman C-20B/*C20C**		80162	97 BW
30076 †		**Gulfstream III**		80163	93 BW
30077 ‡		89 MAW Andrews AFB		80164	416 BW
30078 †				80165	BW
30079 *		*FY85*		80166	93 BW
30080 †		50049*		80167	97 BW
30081 *		50050*		80168	93 BW
30082 *				80170	416 BW
		FY86		80171	93 BW
FY84		60200		80172	320 BW
40185 †		60201		80173	2 BW
40186 *		60202		80175	379 BW
40187 †		60203		80176	416 BW
40188 *		60204		80177	2 BW
40189 †		60205		80178	97 BW
40190 *		60206		80179	93 BW
40191 †		60403*		80181	BW
40192 ‡				80182	320 BW
		Boeing VC-25A		80183	97 BW
FY85		89 MAW Andrews AFB		80184	2 BW
50027 †		(Air Force One)		80185	97 BW
50028 *				80186	42 BW
50029 ‡		*FY86*		80189	320 BW
50030 ‡		68000		80190	2 BW
50031 *				80191	2 BW
50032 *		**Boeing B-52G**		80192	93 BW
50033 *		**Stratofortress**		80193	416 BW
50034 *				80194	BW
		FY57		80195	42 BW
FY86		76468	320 BW	80197	320 BW
60027 *		76469	320 BW	80199	97 BW
60028 ‡		76470	93 BW	80200	2 BW
60029 ‡		76471	379 BW	80202	42 BW
60030 ‡		76472	93 BW	80203	320 BW
60031 ‡		76473	320 BW	80204	BW
60032 ‡		76474	379 BW		
60033 ‡		76475	2 BW		
60034 ‡		76476	320 BW		

USAF (US based)

Serial	Wing	Serial	Wing	Serial	Wing
80205	BW	92593	320 BW	*FY60:* **C-130B**	
80206	93 BW	92594	93 BW	00294	731 TAS†
80207	93 BW	92595	2 BW	00295	731 TAS†
80210	2 BW	92596	42 BW	00296	731 TAS†
80211	93 BW	92598	42 BW	00299	731 TAS†
80212	2 BW	92599	93 BW	00300	731 TAS†
80213	320 BW	92601	416 BW	00303	731 TAS†
80214	93 BW	92602	416 BW	00310	731 TAS†
80216	2 BW				
80217	379 BW	**Lockheed SR-71A Blackbird**		*FY80:* **C-130H**	
80218	2 BW	9SRW/99SRS		00320	158 TAS*
80219	93 BW	No 4 Det: RAF Mildenhall		00321	158 TAS*
80220	93 BW			00322	158 TAS*
80221	43 SW	*FY64*		00323	158 TAS*
80222	2 BW	17956		00324	158 TAS*
80223	93 BW	17958		00325	158 TAS*
80224	42 BW	17959		00326	158 TAS*
80225	42 BW	17960		00332	158 TAS*
80226	42 BW	17961			
80227	2 BW	17962		*FY70:* **C-130E**	
80229	93 BW	17963		01259	317 TAW
80230	320 BW	17964	Det. 4	01260	435 TAW
80231	416 BW	17967		01261	317 TAW
80232	42 BW	17968		01262	317 TAW
80233	2 BW	17971		01263	317 TAW
80234	320 BW	17972		01264	435 TAW
80235	320 BW	17973		01265	317 TAW
80236	93 BW	17974		01266	317 TAW
80237	379 BW	17975		01267	317 TAW
80238	93 BW	17976		01268	317 TAW
80239	416 BW	17979		01269	317 TAW
80240	42 BW	17980	Det. 4	01270	317 TAW
80241	42 BW	17981		01271	435 TAW
80242	93 BW			01272	317 TAW
80243	97 BW	**Lockheed C-130 Hercules**		01273	317 TAW
80244	93 BW	**$ — EC-130, £ — HC-130**		01274	435 TAW
80245	416 BW	**• — LC-130, § — MC-130**		01275	317 TAW
80247	379 BW	**‡ — WC-130**		01276	317 TAW
80248	93 BW	* — ANG: Air National Guard			
80249	379 BW	105 TAS Tennesse ANG		*FY81:* **C-130H**	
80250	93 BW	109 TAS Minnesota ANG		10626	700 TAS†
80251	42 BW	115 TAS California ANG		10627	700 TAS†
80252	97 BW	130 TAS West Virginia ANG		10628	700 TAS†
80253	320 BW	135 TAS Maryland ANG		10629	700 TAS†
80254	93 BW	139 TAS New York ANG		10630	700 TAS†
80255	320 BW	142 TAS Delaware ANG		10631	700 TAS†
80257	320 BW	143 TAS Rhode Island ANG			
80258	93 BW	144 TAS Alaska ANG		*FY68:* **C-130E**	
		154 TAS Arkansas ANG		10934	317 TAW
FY59		155 TAS Tennesse ANG		10935	435 TAW
92564	93 BW	156 TAS North Carolina ANG		10937	317 TAW
92565	320 BW	158 TAS Georgia ANG		10938	435 TAW
92566	416 BW	164 TAS Ohio ANG		10939	317 TAW
92567	416 BW	167 TAS West Virginia ANG		10940	317 TAW
92568	416 BW	180 TAS Missouri ANG		10941	317 TAW
92569	2 BW	181 TAS Texas ANG		10942	317 TAW
92570	42 BW	183 TAS Mississippi ANG		10943	435 TAW
92571	BW	185 TAS Oklahoma ANG		10947	435 TAW
92572	93 BW	187 TAS Wyoming ANG		10948	314 TAW
92573	42 BW	† — AFRES: Air Force Reserve		10949	314 TAW
92575	93 BW	63 TAS, Selfridge, Michigan		10950	314 TAW
92577	97 BW	64 TAS, Chicago O'Hare, Illinois		*80950*	
92578	93 BW	95 TAS, Milwaukee, Wisconsin			
92579	BW	96 TAS, St Paul, Minnesota		*FY61:* **C-130B**	
92580	2 BW	301 ARRS, Homestead, Florida		10948	731 TAS†
92581	2 BW	303 TAS, March, California		10949	156 TAS*
92582	2 BW	327 TAS, Willow Grove,		10950	156 TAS*
92583	93 BW	Pennsylvania		10951	757 TAS†
92584	416 BW	328 TAS, Niagra Falls, New York		10952	164 TAS*
92585	320 BW	356 TAS, Rickenbrocker, Ohio		10954	303 TAS†
92586	2 BW	357 TAS, Maxwell, Alabama		10956	303 TAS†
92587	97 BW	700 TAS, Dobbins, Georgia		10957	303 TAS†
92588	2 BW	731 TAS, Peterson, Colorado		10958	303 TAS†
92589	379 BW	757 TAS, Youngston, Ohio		10959	757 TAS†
92590	2 BW	758 TAS, Pittsburgh,		10960	303 TAS†
92591	BW	Pennsylvania		10961	164 TAS*
92592	320 BW	815 WRS, Keesler, Missouri		10963	164 TAS*
				10964	757 TAS†
				10966	187 TAS*

Serial	Wing	Serial	Wing	Serial	Wing
10967	303 TAS†	21793	115 TAS*	31582	21 TAS
10968	303 TAS†	21794	337 TAS†	31583$	43 ECS [SB]
10969	303 TAS†	21795	154 TAS*	31584$	43 ECS [SB]
10971	757 TAS†	21798	154 TAS*	31585$	43 ECS [SB]
		21799	115 TAS*	31586$	41 ECS
FY61: **C-130E**		21801	115 TAS*	31587$	41 ECS [DM]
12358	115 TAS*	21803	63 TAS†	31588$	43 ECS [SB]
12359	115 TAS*	21804	154 TAS*	31590$	43 ECS [SB]
12360‡	53 WRS	21806	96 TAS†	31592$	41 ECS
12361	314 TAW	21807	337 TAS†	31594$	43 ECS [SB]
12362	314 TAW	21808	314 TAW	31595$	43 ECS [SB]
12363	314 TAW	21810	337 TAS†	31597	21 TAS
12364	314 TAW	21811	115 TAS*	31598	21 TAS
12365‡	53 WRS	21812	109 TAS*		
12366‡	53 WRS	21816	63 TAS†	*FY53:* **C-130A**	
12367	115 TAS*	21817	109 TAS*	33132	95 TAS†
12368	314 TAW	21818$	7 ACCS [KS]	33135	TAS†
12369	314 TAW	21819	7405 OS		
12370	115 TAS*	21820	337 TAS†	*FY63:* **C-130E**	
12371	314 TAW	21821	314 TAW	37764	328 TAS†
12372	115 TAS*	21822	7405 OS	37765	314 TAW
12373	115 TAS*	21823	337 TAS†	37767	314 TAW
		21824	154 TAS*	37768	314 TAW
FY61: **C-130B**		21826	115 TAS*	37769	314 TAW
12634	135 TAS*	21827	314 TAW	37770	328 TAS†
12635	187 TAS*	21828	7405 OS	37771	314 TAW
12636	156 TAS*	21829	109 TAS*	37773$	193 SOS*
12638	156 TAS*	21830	63 TAS†	37776	314 TAW
12639	135 TAS*	21832$	7 ACCS [KS]	37777	345 TAS
12640	156 TAS*	21833	115 TAS*	37778	314 TAW
12643	187 TAS*	21834	96 TAS†	37779	317 TAW
12645	135 TAS*	21835	96 TAS†	37781	314 TAW
12647	303 TAS†	21837	109 TAS*	37782	62 MAW
		21838	337 TAS†	37783$	193 SOS*
FY64: **C-130H**		21839	96 TAS†	37784	62 MAW
14854‡	53 WRS	21842	115 TAS*	37786	314 TAW
14859$	41 ECS	21844	96 TAS†	37788	62 MAW
14861‡	815 WRS	21846	109 TAS*	37790	314 TAW
14862$	41 ECS	21847	96 TAS†	37791	314 TAW
14863£	301 ARRS	21848	96 TAS†	37792	62 MAW
14865£		21849	337 TAS†	37793	314 TAW
14866‡	53 WRS†	21850	337 TAS†	37794	314 TAW
		21851	115 TAS*	37795	314 TAW
FY64: **C-130E**		21852	96 TAS†	37796	314 TAW
17680	314 TAW	21855	314 TAW	37799	314 TAW
17681	435 TAW	21856	109 TAS*	37800	345 TAW
18240	435 TAW	21857$	7 ACCS [KS]	37803	345 TAS
		21858	337 TAS†	37804	345 TAS
FY82: **C-130H**		21859	21 TAS	37805	328 TAS†
20054	144 TAS*	21860	337 TAS†	37806	314 TAW
20055	144 TAS*	21862	115 TAS*	37807	317 TAW
20056	144 TAS*	21863$	7 ACCS [KS]	37808	314 TAW
20057	144 TAS*	21864	109 TAS*	37809	317 TAW
20058	144 TAS*	21866	337 TAS†	37811	345 TAS
20059	144 TAS*			37812	345 TAS
20060	144 TAS*	*FY62:* **C-130B**		37813	317 TAW
20061	144 TAS*	23487	757 TAS†	37814	435 TAW
		23493	757 TAS†	37815$	193 SOS*
FY72: **C-130E**		23495	135 TAS*	37816$	193 SOS*
21288	21 TAS	23496	303 TAS†	37817	328 TAS†
21289	345 TAS			37818	345 TAS
21290	21 TAS	*FY83:* **C-130H**		37819	345 TAS
21291	314 TAW	30486	139 TAS*	37820	314 TAW
21292	314 TAW	30487	139 TAS*	37821	317 TAW
21293	314 TAW	30488	139 TAS*	37822	328 TAS†
21294	314 TAW	30489	139 TAS*	37823	317 TAW
21295	314 TAW	30490●	139 TAS*	37824	
21296	314 TAW	30491●	139 TAS*	37825	
21298	314 TAW	30492●	139 TAS*	37826	327 TAS†
21299	345 TAS	30493●	139 TAS*	37828$	193 SOS*
		31212§	AFSC	37829	317 TAW
FY62: **C-130E**				37830	314 TAW
21784	154 TAS*	*FY73:* **C-130H**		37831	314 TAW
21785	109 TAS*	31580$	41 ECS	37832	327 TAS†
21786	109 TAS*	31581$	41 ECS [DM]	37833	327 TAS†
21787	154 TAS*				
21788	154 TAS*				
21789	337 TAS†				
21790	154 TAS*				
21791$	7 ACCS [KS]				
21792	115 TAS*				

USAF (US based)

Serial	Wing
37834	327 TAS†
37835	314 TAW
37836	314 TAW
37837	345 TAS
37838	314 TAW
37839	314 TAW
37840	374 TAW
37841	314 TAW
37842	62 MAW
37845	317 TAW
37846	317 TAW
37847	314 TAW
37848	327 TAS†
37849	317 TAW
37850	314 TAW
37851	62 MAW
37852	328 TAS†
37853	327 TAS†
37854	62 MAW
37856	328 TAS†
37857	314 TAW
37858	62 MAW
37859	
37860	314 TAW
37861	314 TAW
37863	328 TAS†
37864	314 TAW
37865	
37866	314 TAW
37867	327 TAS†
37868	21 TAS
37869$	193 SOS*
37871	317 TAW
37872	374 TAW
37874	62 MAW
37876	314 TAW
37877	
37879	21 TAS
37880	314 TAW
37881	
37882	314 TAW
37883	327 TAS†
37884	317 TAW
37885	435 TAW
37887	314 TAW
37888	314 TAW
37889	21 TAS
37890	317 TAW
37891	62 MAW
37892	327 TAS†
37893	62 MAW
37894	314 TAW
37895	
37896	314 TAW
37897	
37898	314 TAW
37899	317 TAW
39810	317 TAW
39811	314 TAW
39812	314 TAW
39813	314 TAW
39814	314 TAW
39815	314 TAW
39816$	193 SOS*
39817$	193 SOS*

FY84: C-130H

Serial	Wing
40204	700 TAS†
40205	700 TAS†
40206	142 TAS*
40207	142 TAS*
40208	142 TAS*
40209	142 TAS*
40210	142 TAS*
40211	142 TAS*
40212	142 TAS*
40213	142 TAS*
40475§	AFSC
40476§	AFSC

FY64: C-130E

Serial	Wing
40495	317 TAW
40496	317 TAW
40497	21 TAS
40498	317 TAW
40499	317 TAW
40500	310 MAS
40501	317 TAW
40502	435 TAW
40503	21 TAS
40504	317 TAW
40510	62 MAW
40512	62 MAW
40513	314 TAW
40514	21 TAS
40515	21 TAS
40517	317 TAW
40518	314 TAW
40519	62 MAW
40520	345 TAS
40521	62 MAW
40523§	7 SOS
40524	62 MAW
40525	317 TAW
40526	314 TAW
40527	435 TAW
40529	317 TAW
40530	314 TAW
40531	317 TAW
40533	314 TAW
40534	21 TAS
40535	314 TAW
40537	317 TAW
40538	314 TAW
40539	317 TAW
40540	317 TAW
40541	317 TAW
40542	317 TAW
40544	21 TAS
40550	435 TAW
40552‡	WRS
40553‡	53 WRS
40554‡	53 WRS
40555§	7 SOS
40556	21 TAS
40557	314 TAW
40560	314 TAW
40561§	7 SOS
40562§	8 SOS
40566§	7 SOS
40569	314 TAW
40570	317 TAW

FY54: C-130A

Serial	Wing
41631	143 TAS*
41634	180 TAS*
41635	155 TAS*
41637	155 TAS*
41638	95 TAS†
41639	155 TAS*
41640	105 TAS*

FY74: C-130H

Serial	Wing
41658	17 TAS
41659	17 TAS
41660	463 TAW
41661	463 TAW
41662	463 TAW
41663	463 TAW
41664	463 TAW
41665	463 TAW
41666	463 TAW
41667	463 TAW
41668	463 TAW
41669	463 TAW
41670	463 TAW
41671	463 TAW
41673	463 TAW
41674	463 TAW
41675	463 TAW
41676	17 TAS
41677	463 TAW
41679	463 TAW
41680	463 TAW
41681	463 TAW
41682	463 TAW
41684	463 TAW
41685	463 TAW
41686	463 TAW
41687	463 TAW
41688	463 TAW
41689	463 TAW
41690	463 TAW
41691	463 TAW
41692	463 TAW
42061	463 TAW
42062	463 TAW
42063	463 TAW
42065	463 TAW
42066	17 TAS
42067	463 TAW
42069	463 TAW
42070	463 TAW
42071	17 TAS
42072	463 TAW
42130	463 TAW
42131	17 TAS
42132	17 TAS
42133	463 TAW
42134	463 TAW

FY55: C-130A

Serial	Wing
50003	758 TAS†
50004	105 TAS*
50008	758 TAS†
50010	758 TAS†
50015	155 TAS*
50018	180 TAS*
50022	4950 TW
50023	64 TAS†
50025	63 TAS†
50026	105 TAS*
50027	63 TAS†
50031	17 TYS
50033	17 TAS
50035	64 TAS†

FY85: C-130H

Serial	Wing
50011§	AFSC
50012§	AFSC
50035	357 TAS†
50036	357 TAS†
50037	357 TAS†
50038	357 TAS†
50039	357 TAS†
50040	357 TAS†
50041	357 TAS†
50042	357 TAS†

FY65: C-130H

Serial	Wing
50962$	41 ECS
50963‡	53 WRS
50964‡	815 WRS†

Serial	Wing
50966‡	53 WRS
50967‡	815 WRS†
50968‡	53 WRS
50969‡	815 WRS†
50972‡	815 WRS†
50974£	102 ARRS*
50976‡	53 WRS
50977‡	815 WRS†
50978£	102 ARRS*
50980‡	815 WRS†
50984‡	815 WRS
50985‡	53 WRS
50989$	41 ECS

FY85: **C-130H**

Serial	Wing
51361	181 TAS*
51362	181 TAS*
51363	181 TAS*
51364	181 TAS*
51365	181 TAS*
51366	181 TAS*
51367	181 TAS*
51368	181 TAS*

FY66: **C-130P**

Serial	Wing
60217£	(55 ARRS)
60220£	67 SOS
60221£	129 ARRS*
60223£	67 SOS
60224£	129 ARRS*

FY86: **C-130H**

Serial	Wing
60410	758 TAS†
60411	758 TAS†
60412	758 TAS†
60413	758 TAS†
60414	758 TAS†
60415	758 TAS†
60418	758 TAS†
60419	758 TAS†

FY56: **C-130A**

Serial	Wing
60471	105 TAS*
60473	64 TAS†
60475	64 TAS†
60478	143 TAS*
60479	95 TAS†
60483	180 TAS*
60485	105 TAS*
60487	178 FIS*
60493	152 TFTS*
60494	155 TAS*
60495	155 TAS*
60496	95 TAS†
60498	155 TAS*
60500	64 TAS†
60503	105 TAS*
60507	95 TAS†
60508	63 TAS†
60511	186 FIS*
60517	105 TAS*
60518	105 TAS*
60522	64 TAS†
60523	105 TAS*
60524	155 TAS*
60525	356 TAS†
60529	105 TAS*
60531	123 FIS*
60537	64 TAS†
60543	105 TAS*
60544	105 TAS*
60547	105 TAS*
60550	143 TAS*
60551	

FY86: **C-130H**

Serial	Wing
61391	180 TAS*
61392	180 TAS*
61393	180 TAS*
61394	180 TAS*
61395	180 TAS*
61396	180 TAS*
61397	180 TAS*
61398	180 TAS*
61699§	AFFTC

FY87: **C-130H**

Serial	Wing
70023§	AFSC
70024§	AFSC
70125§	
70126§	
70127§	

FY57: **C-130A**

Serial	Wing
70453	155 TAS*
70455	143 TAS*
70457	155 TAS*
70459	155 TAS*
70460	63 TAS†
70463	155 TAS*
70464	105 TAS*
70465	155 TAS*
70466	95 TAS†
70469	95 TAS†
70470	95 TAS†
70471	180 TAS*
70473	143 TAS*
70474	TAS†
70476	64 TAS†
70477	64 TAS†
70479	TAS†
70480	TAS†
70481	96 TAS†
70482	TAS†
70510	328 TAS†
70511	143 TAS*
70512	143 TAS*
70513	143 TAS*
70514	143 TAS*
70515	143 TAS*
70516	TAS†
70519	TAS†
70520	328 TAS†
70521	328 TAS†
70524	143 TAS*

FY57: **C-130B**

Serial	Wing
70525	167 TAS*
70526	6514 TS
70529	167 TAS*

FY87: **C-130H**

Serial	Wing
79281	64 TAS†
79282	64 TAS†
79283	64 TAS†
79284	64 TAS†
79285	64 TAS†
79286	64 TAS†
79287	64 TAS†
79288	64 TAS†

FY88: **MC-130H**

Serial	Wing
80191	
80192	
80193	
80194	
80195	

FY58: **C-130B**

Serial	Wing
80711	135 TAS*
80714	187 TAS*

Serial	Wing
80715	135 TAS*
80716	6514 TS
80720	187 TAS*
80723	731 TAS†
80725	167 TAS*
80726	164 TAS*
80727	167 TAS*
80728	156 TAS*
80729	156 TAS*
80731	164 TAS*
80732	167 TAS*
80733	164 TAS*
80734	187 TAS*
80735	167 TAS*
80736	164 TAS*
80738	731 TAS†
80740	167 TAS*
80741	167 TAS*
80742	156 TAS*
80744	187 TAS*
80746	156 TAS*
80747	167 TAS*
80749	164 TAS*
80750	167 TAS*
80751	156 TAS*
80752	167 TAS*
80753	167 TAS*
80754	187 TAS*
80755	135 TAS*
80757	731 TAS†
80758	135 TAS*

FY78: **C-130H**

Serial	Wing
80806	185 TAS*
80807	185 TAS*
80808	185 TAS*
80809	185 TAS*
80810	185 TAS*
80811	185 TAS*
80812	185 TAS*
80813	185 TAS*

FY88: **C-130H**

Serial	Wing
81301	130 TAS*
81302	130 TAS*
81303	130 TAS*
81304	130 TAS*
81305	130 TAS*
81306	130 TAS*
81307	130 TAS*
81308	130 TAS*

FY88: **C-130H**

Serial	Wing
84401	95 TAS†
84402	95 TAS†
84403	95 TAS†
84404	95 TAS†
84405	95 TAS†
84406	95 TAS†
84407	95 TAS†
84408	95 TAS†

FY79: **C-130H**

Serial	Wing
90473	TAS*
90474	TAS*
90475	TAS*
90476	TAS*
90477	TAS*
90478	TAS*
90479	TAS*
90480	TAS*

FY59: **C-130B**

Serial	Wing
91524	757 TAS†
91525	164 TAS*

151

USAF (US based)

Serial	Type	Wing	Serial	Type	Wing	Serial	Type	Wing
91526	731 TAS†		00341	KC-135R	340 ARW	10303	KC-135A	93 BW
91527	731 TAS†		00342	KC-135Q	9 SRW	10304	KC-135R	384 BW
91528	156 TAS*		00343	KC-135Q	380 BW	10305	KC-135R	305 ARW
91529	167 TAS*		00344	KC-135Q	376 SW	10306	KC-135R	384 BW
91530	731 TAS†		00345	KC-135Q	9 SRW	10307	KC-135R	19 ARW
91531	731 TAS†		00346	KC-135Q	9 SRW	10308	KC-135R	384 BW
91532	757 TAS†		00347	KC-135R	384 BW	10309	KC-135R	19 ARW
91533	156 TAS*		00348	KC-135A	416 BW	10310	KC-135R	384 BW
91535	757 TAS†		00349	KC-135A	509 BW	10311	KC-135R	93 BW
91536	135 TAS*		00350	KC-135A	416 BW	10312	KC-135R	384 BW
91537	731 TAS†		00351	KC-135A	305 ARW	10313	KC-135R	93 BW
			00353	KC-135R	19 ARW	10314	KC-135R	19 ARW
FY69: **C-130N**			00355	KC-135A	416 BW	10315	KC-135R	384 BW
95820£	67 SOS		00356	KC-135A	376 SW	10316	KC-135R	319 BW
95823£	67 SOS		00357	KC-135A	305 ARW	10317	KC-135R	384 BW
95826£	67 SOS		00358	KC-135A	410 BW	10318	KC-135R	384 BW
95827£	67 SOS		00359	KC-135R	19 ARW	10320	KC-135A	42 BW
95831£	67 SOS		00360	KC-135A	93 BW	10321	KC-135A	410 BW
			00362	KC-135A	305 ARW	10323	KC-135A	376 SW
FY59: **C-130B**			00363	KC-135A	376 SW	10324	KC-135R	93 BW
95957	187 TAS*		00364	KC-135A	410 BW	10325	KC-135A	42 BW
			00365	KC-135R	28 BW	10326	EC-135E	4950 TW
FY69: **C-130E**			00366	KC-135A	410 BW	10327	EC-135Y	CinC CC
96566	435 TAW		00367	KC-135R	28 BW	10329	EC-135N	4950 TW
96579	314 TAW		00371	NC-135A	4950 TW	10330	EC-135E	4950 TW
96580	317 TAW		00372	C-135E	4950 TW			
96582	435 TAW		00374	EC-135E	4950 TW	12662	RC-135S	6 SRW
96583	435 TAW		00375	C-135E	4950 TW	12663	RC-135S	6 SRW
			00376	C-135E	8 TDCS/	12665	WC-135B	55 WRS
					SpWg/	12666	WC-135B	55 WRS
Boeing C-135 Stratotanker					CinC CC	12667	WC-135B	55 WRS
* Air National Guard:			00377	C-135A	4950 TW	12668	C-135C	89 MAW
108 ARS Illinois ANG			00378	C-135E	55 SRW	12669	C-135C	4950 TW
116 ARS Washington ANG						12670	WC-135B	55 WRS
117 ARS Kansas ANG			*FY61*			12671	C-135C	89 MAW
126 ARS Wisconsin ANG			10261	EC-135L	305 ARW	12672	WC-135B	55 WRS
132 ARS Maine ANG			10262	EC-135L	4 ACCS	12673	WC-135B	55 WRS
133 ARS New Hampshire ANG			10263	EC-135L	305 ARW	12674	WC-135B	55 WRS
145 ARS Ohio ANG			10264	KC-135A	42 BW			
147 ARS Pennsylvania ANG			10265	KC-135A	97 BW	*FY64*		
150 ARS New Jersey ANG			10266	KC-135A	97 BW	14828	KC-135A	509 BW
151 ARS Tennessee ANG			10267	KC-135A	97 BW	14829	KC-135A	42 BW
168 ARS Alaska ANG			10268	KC-135A	379 BW	14830	KC-135A	5 BW
191 ARS Utah ANG			10269	EC-135L	305 ARW	14831	KC-135A	5 BW
197 ARS Arizona ANG			10270	KC-135A	410 BW	14832	KC-135A	96 BW
† AFRES, Air Force Reserve:			10271	KC-135A	5 BW	14833	KC-135A	97 BW
72 ARS bl Grissom AFB, In			10272	KC-135R	340 ARW	(44833)		
314 ARS r Mather AFB, Ca			10274	EC-135H	6 ACCS	14834	KC-135A	340 ARW
336 ARS y March AFB, Ca			10275	KC-135A	97 BW	14835	KC-135A	42 BW
			10276	KC-135R	384 BW	14836	KC-135A	376 BW
FY60			10277	KC-135R	340 ARW	14837	KC-135A	93 BW
00313	KC-135R	410 BW	10278	EC-135A	28 BW	14838	KC-135A	97 BW
00314	KC-135A	410 BW	10279	EC-135L	305 ARW	14839	KC-135A	19 ARW
00315	KC-135A	2 BW	10280	KC-135R	380 BW	14840	KC-135A	380 BW
00316	KC-135A	93 BW	10281	KC-135A	93 BW	14841	RC-135V	55 SRW
00318	KC-135A	416 BW	10282	EC-135H	10 ACCS	14842	RC-135V	55 SRW
00319	KC-135A	379 BW	10283	EC-135L	305 ARW	14843	RC-135V	55 SRW
00320	KC-135A	379 BW	10284	EC-135H	22 ARW	14844	RC-135V	55 SRW
00321	KC-135R	28 BW	10285	EC-135H	10 ACCS	14845	RC-135V	55 SRW
00322	KC-135R	19 ARW	10286	EC-135H	10 ACCS	14846	RC-135V	55 SRW
00323	KC-135A	380 BW	10287	EC-135A	28 BW	14847	RC-135U	55 SRW
00324	KC-135A	7 BW	10288	KC-135A	93 BW	14848	RC-135V	55 SRW
00325	KC-135A	379 BW	10289	EC-135A	4 ACCS	14849	RC-135U	55 SRW
00326	KC-135A	379 BW	10290	KC-135R	97 BW			
00327	KC-135A	376 SW	10291	EC-135H	10 ACCS	*FY62*		
00328	KC-135A	7 BW	10292	KC-135R	384 BW	23497	KC-135A	416 BW
00329	KC-135A	93 BW	10293	KC-135R	384 BW	23498	KC-135A	93 BW
00331	KC-135A	379 BW		[RT]		23499	KC-135R	19 ARW
00332	KC-135A	320 BW	10294	KC-135R	28 BW	23500	KC-135R	340 ARW
00333	KC-135A	380 BW	10295	KC-135R	340 ARW	23501	KC-135A	42 BW
00334	KC-135A	96 BW	10297	EC-135A	28 BW	23502	KC-135A	509 BW
00335	KC-135Q	380 BW	10298	KC-135R	19 ARW	23503	KC-135A	42 BW
00336	KC-135Q	376 SW	10299	KC-135A	410 BW	23504	KC-135R	19 ARW
00337	KC-135Q	380 BW	10300	KC-135A	22 ARW	23505	KC-135A	509 BW
00339	KC-135Q	9 SRW	10302	KC-135A	42 BW	23506	KC-135R	19 ARW
						23507	KC-135R	340 ARW

Serial	Type	Wing	Serial	Type	Wing	Serial	Type	Wing
23508	KC-135R	340 ARW	23585	EC-135C	55 SRW	38031	KC-135A	305 ARW
23509	KC-135A	509 BW				38032	KC-135R	28 BW
23510	KC-135R	340 ARW	24125	C-135B	58 MAS	38033	KC-135A	305 ARW
23511	KC-135R	384 BW	24126	C-135B	89 MAW	38034	KC-135A	5 BW
23512	KC-135A	416 BW	24127	C-135B	89 MAW	38035	KC-135A	93 BW
23513	KC-135A	416 BW	24128	RC-135X	6 SRW	38036	KC-135R	19 ARW
23514	KC-135A	416 BW	24129	TC-135W	55 SRW	38037	KC-135A	2 BW
23515	KC-135A	410 BW	24130	C-135B	89 MAW	38038	KC-135A	93 BW
23516	KC-135A	93 BW	24131	RC-135W	55 SRW	38039	KC-135A	379 BW
23517	KC-135A	7 BW	24132	RC-135W	55 SRW	38040	KC-135R	384 BW
23518	KC-135A	305 ARW	24133	TC-135S	6 SRW	38041	KC-135A	2 BW
23519	KC-135A	416 BW	24134	RC-135W	55 SRW	38043	KC-135A	42 BW
23520	KC-135A	340 ARW	24135	RC-135W	55 SRW	38044	KC-135A	7 BW
23521	KC-135A	93 BW	24138	RC-135W	55 SRW	38045	KC-135A	92 BW
23523	KC-135R	19 ARW	24139	RC-135W	55 SRW	38046	EC-135C	55 SRW
23524	KC-135A	380 BW				38047	EC-135A	4 ACCS
23525	KC-135A	93 BW	26000	VC-137C	89 MAW	38048	EC-135C	55 SRW
23526	KC-135A	416 BW	*FY72*			38049	EC-135C	55 SRW
23527	KC-135A	410 BW	27000	C-137C	89 MAW	38050	EC-135C	55 SRW
23528	KC-135A	96 BW				38051	EC-135A	4 ACCS
23529	KC-135A	509 BW	*FY63*			38052	EC-135C	55 SRW
23530	KC-135R	19 ARW	37976	KC-135R	319 BW	38053	EC-135C	55 SRW
23531	KC-135R	340 ARW	37977	KC-135R	19 ARW	38054	EC-135C	55 SRW
23532	KC-135R	509 BW	37978	KC-135R	305 ARW	38055	EC-135J	9 ACCS
23533	KC-135R	384 BW	37979	KC-135R	340 ARW	38056	EC-135J	9 ACCS
23534	KC-135R	19 ARW	37980	KC-135A	305 ARW	38057	EC-135J	9 ACCS
23537	KC-135R	376 SW	37981	KC-135A	340 ARW	38058	KC-135D	305 ARW
23538	KC-135R	509 BW	37982	KC-135A	93 BW	38059	KC-135D	305 ARW
23539	KC-135A	93 BW	37984	KC-135R	340 ARW	38060	KC-135D	305 ARW
23540	KC-135R	28 BW	37985	KC-135R	42 BW	38061	KC-135D	305 ARW
23541	KC-135R	340 ARW	37986	KC-135A	416 BW	38871	KC-135A	305 ARW
23542	KC-135A	7 BW	37987	KC-135A	410 BW	38872	KC-135A	509 BW
23543	KC-135R	19 ARW	37988	KC-135A	509 BW	38873	KC-135A	320 BW
23544	KC-135A	2 BW	37990	KC-135A	305 ARW	38874	KC-135A	319 BW
23545	KC-135A	380 BW	37991	KC-135R	28 BW	38875	KC-135A	7 BW
23546	KC-135R	340 ARW	37992	KC-135A	416 BW	38876	KC-135A	93 BW
23547	KC-135R	93 BW	37993	KC-135A	319 BW	38877	KC-135A	93 BW
23548	KC-135R	93 BW	37994	EC-135G	305 ARW	38878	KC-135A	5 BW
23549	KC-135A	93 BW	37995	KC-135R	19 ARW	38879	KC-135A	22 ARW
23550	KC-135R	19 ARW	37996	KC-135A	305 ARW	38880	KC-135A	509 BW
23551	KC-135R	93 BW	37997	KC-135R	319 BW	38881	KC-135A	380 BW
23552	KC-135R	19 ARW	37998	KC-135R	380 BW	38883	KC-135A	305 ARW
23553	KC-135R	319 BW	37999	KC-135R	384 BW	38884	KC-135A	376 SW
23554	KC-135R	19 ARW	38000	KC-135A	22 ARW	38885	KC-135A	410 BW
23555	KC-135R	410 BW	38001	EC-135G	28 BW	38886	KC-135A	96 BW
23556	KC-135R	340 ARW	38002	KC-135R	28 BW	38887	KC-135A	93 BW
23557	KC-135R	19 ARW	38003	KC-135R	93 BW	38888	KC-135A	410 BW
23558	KC-135A	376 SW	38004	KC-135A	379 BW	39792	RC-135V	55 SRW
23559	KC-135A	379 BW	38005	KC-135A	2 BW			
23560	KC-135A	93 BW	38006	KC-135A	305 ARW	*FY55*		
23561	KC-135A	340 ARW	38007	KC-135A	379 BW	53118	EC-135K	8 TDCS
23562	KC-135A	410 BW	38008	KC-135R	19 ARW	53119	NKC-135A	55 SRW
23563	KC-135A	96 BW	38009	KC-135R	305 ARW	53120	NKC-135E	4950 TW
23564	KC-135R		38010	KC-135A	22 ARW	53122	NKC-135E	4950 TW
23565	KC-135A	305 ARW	38011	KC-135A	410 BW	53124	NKC-135E	4950 TW
23566	KC-135A	22 ARW	38012	KC-135A	97 BW	53125	EC-135Y	CinC CC
23567	KC-135A	2 BW	38013	KC-135A	340 ARW	53127	NKC-135E	4950 TW
23568	KC-135R	340 ARW	38014	KC-135A	22 ARW	53128	NKC-135E	4950 TW
23569	KC-135R	19 ARW	38015	KC-135A	416 BW	53129	EC-135P	6 ACCS
23570	EC-135G	4 ACCS	38016	KC-135A	416 BW	53130	KC-135A	7 BW
23571	KC-135R	93 BW	38017	KC-135A	22 ARW	53131	NKC-135E	4950 TW
23572	KC-135A	416 BW	38018	KC-135A	410 BW	53132	NKC-135E	4950 TW
23573	KC-135R	340 ARW	38019	KC-135A	22 ARW	53134	NKC-135A	USN/FEWSG
23574	KC-135A	410 BW	38020	KC-135R	19 ARW	53135	NKC-135E	4950 TW
23575	KC-135A	42 BW	38021	KC-135A	5 BW	53136	KC-135A	2 BW
23576	KC-135A	2 BW	38022	KC-135A	416 BW	53137	KC-135A	2 BW
23577	KC-135A	305 ARW	38023	KC-135A	2 BW	53139	KC-135A	92 BW
23578	KC-135A	42 BW	38024	KC-135R	384 BW	53141	KC-135E	126 ARS*
23579	EC-135G	4 ACCS	38025	KC-135R	340 ARW	53142	KC-135A	93 BW
23580	KC-135A	42 BW	38026	KC-135A	22 ARW	53143	KC-135E	197 ARS*
23581	EC-135C	55 SRW	38027	KC-135A	42 BW	53145	KC-135E	314 ARS†
23582	EC-135C	4 ACCS	38028	KC-135A	305 ARW	53146	KC-135E	145 ARS*
23583	EC-135C	55 SRW	38029	KC-135A	380 BW			
23584	EC-135J	9 ACCS	38030	KC-135R	305 ARW			

USAF (US based)

Serial	Type	Wing	Serial	Type	Wing	Serial	Type	Wing
FY85			71429	KC-135E	117 ARS*	71512	KC-135E	336 ARS†
56973	C-137C	89 MAW	71430	KC-135A	92 BW	71514	KC-135A	376 SW
56974	C-137C	89 MAW	71431	KC-135E	126 ARS*			
			71432	KC-135A	92 BW	72589	KC-135E	55 SRW
FY56			71433	KC-135E	197 ARS*	72590	KC-135A	5 BW
63591	KC-135A	380 BW	71434	KC-135E	116 ARS*	72591	KC-135A	410 BW
63592	KC-135A	305 ARW	71435	KC-135A	92 BW	72592	KC-135A	5 BW
63593	KC-135E	133 ARS*	71436	KC-135E	133 ARS*	72593	KC-135A	96 BW
63594	KC-135A	93 BW	71437	KC-135A	93 BW	72594	KC-135E	108 ARS*
63595	KC-135A	22 ARW	71438	KC-135E	72 ARS†	72595	KC-135E	147 ARS*
63596	NKC-135A	USN/FEWSG	71439	KC-135A	92 BW	72596	KC-135A	5 BW
63600	KC-135A	93 BW	71440	KC-135R	319 BW	72597	KC-135A	92 BW
63601	KC-135A	93 BW	71441	KC-135E	108 ARS*	72598	KC-135E	336 ARS†
63603	KC-135A	2 BW	71443	KC-135E	132 ARS*	72599	KC-135E	509 BW
63604	KC-135E	117 ARS*	71445	KC-135E	145 ARS*	72600	KC-135E	116 ARS*
63606	KC-135E	132 ARS*	71447	KC-135A	93 BW	72601	KC-135A	97 BW
63607	KC-135E	151 ARS*	71448	KC-135E	168 ARS*	72602	KC-135A	7 BW
63608	KC-135E	340 ARW	71450	KC-135E	132 ARS*	72603	KC-135E	336 ARS†
63609	KC-135E	151 ARS*	71451	KC-135A	2 BW	72604	KC-135E	126 ARS*
63610	KC-135A	92 BW	71452	KC-135E	197 ARS*	72605	KC-135A	93 BW
63611	KC-135E	145 ARS*	71453	KC-135A	7 BW	72606	KC-135E	150 ARS*
63612	KC-135E	126 ARS*	71454	KC-135A	92 BW	72607	KC-135E	147 ARS*
63614	KC-135A	93 BW	71455	KC-135E	151 ARS*	72608	KC-135E	147 ARS*
63615	KC-135A	320 BW	71456	KC-135A	509 BW	72609	KC-135A	379 BW
63616	KC-135A	96 BW	71458	KC-135E	108 ARS*			
63617	KC-135A	42 BW	71459	KC-135A	93 BW	*FY58*		
63619	KC-135A	42 BW	71460	KC-135E	117 ARS*	80001	KC-135A	93 BW
63620	KC-135A	5 BW	71461	KC-135A	2 BW	80003	KC-135E	108 ARS*
63621	KC-135A	7 BW	71462	KC-135R	28 BW	80004	KC-135A	379 BW
63622	KC-135E	132 ARS*	71463	KC-135E	117 ARS*	80005	KC-135A	93 BW
63623	KC-135E	336 ARS†	71464	KC-135E	145 ARS*	80006	KC-135E	191 ARS*
63624	KC-135A	42 BW	71465	KC-135E	108 ARS*	80008	KC-135E	145 ARS*
63625	KC-135A	305 ARW	71467	KC-135A	2 BW	80009	KC-135A	5 BW
63626	KC-135E	147 ARS*	71468	KC-135E	336 ARS†	80010	KC-135A	93 BW
63627	KC-135A	2 BW	71469	KC-135A	42 BW	80011	KC-135A	305 ARW
63630	KC-135E	. ARS*	71470	KC-135A	376 SW	80012	KC-135E	191 ARS*
63631	KC-135E	117 ARS*	71471	KC-135A	19 ARW	80013	KC-135E	72 ARS†
63632	KC-135A	92 BW	71472	KC-135A	93 BW	80014	KC-135E	108 ARS*
63633	KC-135A	509 BW	71473	KC-135R	384 BW	80015	KC-135A	380 BW
63634	KC-135A	93 BW	71474	KC-135A	509 BW	80016	KC-135A	92 BW
63635	KC-135A	93 BW	71475	KC-135E	197 ARS*	80017	KC-135E	145 ARS*
63636	KC-135A	376 SW	71476	KC-135A	11 SG	80018	KC-135A	305 ARW
63637	KC-135A	42 BW	71477	KC-135A	340 ARW	80019	EC-135P	6 ACCS
63638	KC-135E	197 ARS*	71478	KC-135E	151 ARS*	80020	KC-135E	116 ARS*
63639	KC-135A	96 BW	71479	KC-135E	336 ARS†	80021	KC-135A	93 BW
63640	KC-135E	132 ARS*	71480	KC-135E	108 ARS*	80022	EC-135P	6 ACCS
63641	KC-135E	117 ARS*	71481	KC-135E	168 ARS*	80023	KC-135A	340 ARW
63642	KC-135A	92 BW	71482	KC-135E	117 ARS*	80024	KC-135E	126 ARS*
63643	KC-135E	151 ARS*	71483	KC-135R	93 BW	80025	KC-135A	305 ARW
63644	KC-135A	92 BW	71484	KC-135E	197 ARS*	80027	KC-135A	97 BW
63645	KC-135A	92 BW	71485	KC-135E	151 ARS*	80028	KC-135A	410 BW
63646	KC-135A	92 BW	71486	KC-135A	93 BW	80029	KC-135A	97 BW
63647	KC-135A	305 ARW	71487	KC-135A	92 BW	80030	KC-135A	42 BW
63648	KC-135E	145 ARS*	71488	KC-135A	2 BW	80032	KC-135E	150 ARS*
63649	KC-135A	2 BW	71490	KC-135A	7 BW	80033	KC-135A	305 ARW
63650	KC-135E	133 ARS*	71491	KC-135E	145 ARS*	80034	KC-135A	410 BW
63651	KC-135A	92 BW	71492	KC-135E	151 ARS*	80035	KC-135A	93 BW
63652	KC-135A	42 BW	71493	KC-135A	7 BW	80036	KC-135A	96 BW
63653	KC-135A	92 BW	71494	KC-135E	168 ARS*	80037	KC-135A	410 BW
63654	KC-135E	132 ARS*	71495	KC-135E	197 ARS*	80038	KC-135A	379 BW
63656	KC-135A	93 BW	71496	KC-135E	197 ARS*	80040	KC-135E	150 ARS*
63658	KC-135E	117 ARS*	71497	KC-135A	92 BW	80041	KC-135E	72 ARS†
			71499	KC-135A	93 BW	80042	KC-135Q	380 BW
FY57			71501	KC-135E	116 ARS*	80043	KC-135E	191 ARS*
71418	KC-135A	93 BW	71502	KC-135R	319 BW	80044	KC-135A	93 BW
71419	KC-135A	92 BW	71503	KC-135E	151 ARS*	80045	KC-135Q	380 BW
71420	KC-135A	7 BW	71504	KC-135E	72 ARS†	80046	KC-135Q	380 BW
71421	KC-135E	116 ARS*	71505	KC-135E	132 ARS*	80047	KC-135Q	380 BW
71422	KC-135E	72 ARS†	71506	KC-135A	42 BW	80049	KC-135Q	380 BW
71423	KC-135A	92 BW	71507	KC-135E	145 ARS*	80050	KC-135Q	380 BW
71425	KC-135E	151 ARS*	71508	KC-135R	28 BW	80051	KC-135A	93 BW
71426	KC-135E	. ARS*	71509	KC-135E	147 ARS*	80052	KC-135E	336 ARS†
71427	KC-135A	93 BW	71510	KC-135E	191 ARS*	80053	KC-135E	314 ARS†
71428	KC-135E	133 ARS*	71511	KC-135E	314 ARS†	80054	KC-135Q	9 SRW
						80055	KC-135Q	9 SRW

Serial	Type	Wing	Serial	Type	Wing	Serial	Type	Wing
80056	KC-135A	93 BW	86970	VC-137B	89 MAW	91516	KC-135E	117 ARS*
80057	KC-135E	108 ARS*	86971	VC-137B	89 MAW	91517	KC-135R	93 BW
80058	KC-135E	314 ARS†	86972	VC-137B	89 MAW	91518	EC-135K	8 TDCS
80059	KC-135A	5 BW	*FY59*			91519	KC-135E	126 ARS*
80060	KC-135Q	380 BW	91444	KC-135A	92 BW	91520	KC-135Q	9 SRW
80061	KC-135E	108 ARS*	91445	KC-135E	116 ARS*	91521	KC-135R	340 ARW
80062	KC-135Q	9 SRW	91446	KC-135R	28 BW	91522	KC-135A	410 BW
80063	KC-135A	93 BW	91447	KC-135E	72 ARS†	91523	KC-135Q	9 SRW
80064	KC-135E	314 ARS†	91448	KC-135E	133 ARS*			
80065	KC-135Q	380 BW	91449	KC-135A	7 BW	**Lockheed C-141B Starlifter**		
80066	KC-135A	2 BW	91450	KC-135E	133 ARS*	(*ANG, Air National Guard		
80067	KC-135E	108 ARS*	91451	KC-135E	72 ARS†	†AFRES, Air Force Reserve)		
80068	KC-135E	108 ARS*	91452	KC-135E	116 ARS*	60 MAW: Travis AFB, California		
80069	KC-135Q	376 SW	91453	KC-135R	93 BW	62 MAW: McChord AFB,		
80070	KC-135A	376 SW	91454	KC-135A	42 BW	Washington		
80071	KC-135Q	9 SRW	91455	KC-135R	28 BW	63 MAW: Norton AFB, California		
80072	KC-135Q	376 SW	91456	KC-135E	126 ARS*	183 MAS, 172 MAG*: Jackson		
80073	KC-135A	96 BW	91457	KC-135E	147 ARS*	Field AFB, Mississippi		
80074	KC-135Q	9 SRW	91458	KC-135R	340 ARW	437 MAW: Charleston AFB, S		
80075	KC-135A	93 BW	91459	KC-135R	28 BW	Carolina		
80076	KC-135A	93 BW	91460	KC-135Q	9 SRW	438 MAW: McGuire AFB, New		
80077	KC-135Q	9 SRW	91461	KC-135A	92 BW	Jersey		
80078	KC-135E	150 ARS*	91462	KC-135Q	380 BW	443 MAW: Altus AFB, Oklahoma		
80079	KC-135A	96 BW	91463	KC-135A	376 SW	756 MAS, 459 MAW†: Andrews		
80080	KC-135E	191 ARS*	91464	KC-135Q	376 SW	AFB, Maryland		
80081	KC-135A	42 BW	91465	KC-135R	319 BW			
80082	KC-135E	116 ARS*	91466	KC-135A	319 BW	*FY61*		
80083	KC-135A	509 BW	91467	KC-135Q	380 BW	12778	438 MAW	
80084	KC-135Q	9 SRW	91468	KC-135Q	9 SRW			
80085	KC-135E	336 ARS†	91469	KC-135A	380 BW	*FY63*		
80086	KC-135Q	9 SRW	91470	KC-135Q	9 SRW	38075	60 MAW	
80087	KC-135E	150 ARS*	91471	KC-135Q	376 SW	38076	438 MAW	
80088	KC-135Q	9 SRW	91472	KC-135A	97 BW	38078	437 MAW	
80089	KC-135Q	9 SRW	91473	KC-135E	191 ARS*	38079	437 MAW	
80090	KC-135E	314 ARS†	91474	KC-135Q	9 SRW	38080	438 MAW	
80091	KC-135A	5 BW	91475	KC-135A	42 BW	38081	62 MAW	
80092	KC-135A	379 BW	91476	KC-135A	2 BW	38082	62 MAW	
80093	KC-135A	42 BW	91477	KC-135E	72 ARS†	38083	438 MAW	
80094	KC-135Q	9 SRW	91478	KC-135R	19 ARW	38084	63 MAW	
80095	KC-135Q	9 SRW	91479	KC-135E	126 ARS*	38085	63 MAW	
80096	KC-135E	314 ARS†	91480	KC-135Q	9 SRW	38086	62 MAW	
80097	KC-135A	93 BW	91482	KC-135R	384 BW	38087	63 MAW	
80098	KC-135R	93 BW	91483	KC-135A	7 BW	38088	60 MAW	
80099	KC-135Q	9 SRW	91484	KC-135E	147 ARS*	38089	443 MAW	
80100	KC-135A	7 BW	91485	KC-135E	150 ARS*	38090	438 MAW	
80102	KC-135A	96 BW	91486	KC-135A	319 BW			
80103	KC-135Q	9 SRW	91487	KC-135E	108 ARS*	*FY64*		
80104	KC-135A	92 BW	91488	KC-135A	509 BW	40609	62 MAW	
80105	KC-135A	92 BW	91489	KC-135E	191 ARS*	40610	437 MAW	
80106	KC-135A	22 ARW	91490	KC-135Q	9 SRW	40611	437 MAW	
80107	KC-135E	191 ARS*	91492	KC-135A	319 BW	40612	437 MAW	
80108	KC-135E	314 ARS†	91493	KC-135E		40613	437 MAW	
80109	KC-135A	96 BW	91494	KC-135E	133 ARS*	40614	172 MAG*	
80110	KC-135A	319 BW	91495	KC-135R	19 ARW	40615	437 MAW	
80111	KC-135E	126 ARS*	91496	KC-135A	7 BW	40616	438 MAW	
80112	KC-135Q	9 SRW	91497	KC-135E	150 ARS*	40617	63 MAW	
80113	KC-135A	96 BW	91498	KC-135A	92 BW	40618	437 MAW	
80114	KC-135A	96 BW	91499	KC-135E	133 ARS*	40619	63 MAW	
80115	KC-135E	150 ARS*	91500	KC-135A	42 BW	40620	459 MAW†	
80116	KC-135A	96 BW	91501	KC-135A	92 BW	40621	438 MAW	
80117	KC-135Q	9 SRW	91502	KC-135A	42 BW	40622	172 MAG*	
80118	KC-135Q	509 BW	91503	KC-135A	42 BW	40623	438 MAW	
80119	KC-135A	5 BW	91504	KC-135Q	9 SRW	40625	438 MAW	
80120	KC-135R	319 BW	91505	KC-135E	133 ARS*	40626	438 MAW	
80121	KC-135A	93 BW	91506	KC-135E	147 ARS*	40627	438 MAW	
80122	KC-135A	92 BW	91507	KC-135A	93 BW	40628	438 MAW	
80123	KC-135A	379 BW	91508	KC-135A	410 BW	40629	437 MAW	
80124	KC-135A	305 ARW	91509	KC-135E	133 ARS*	40630	437 MAW	
80125	KC-135Q	9 SRW	91510	KC-135Q	376 SW	40631	437 MAW	
80126	KC-135A	305 ARW	91511	KC-135R	19 ARW	40632	172 MAG*	
80128	KC-135A	5 BW	91512	KC-135Q	9 SRW	40633	438 MAW	
80129	KC-135Q	9 SRW	91513	KC-135Q	9 SRW	40634	63 MAW	
80130	KC-135A	7 BW	91514	KC-135E (RT)	55 SRW	40635	62 MAW	
			91515	KC-135R	384 BW	40636	443 MAW	
						40637	459 MAW†	

USAF (US based)

Serial	Wing	Serial	Wing	Serial	Wing
40638	438 MAW	50276	437 MAW	60176	443 MAW
40639	438 MAW	50277	63 MAW	60177	63 MAW
40640	172 MAG*	50278	443 MAW	60178	437 MAW
40642	443 MAW	50279	437 MAW	60179	63 MAW
40643	60 MAW	50280	443 MAW	60180	63 MAW
40644	437 MAW	59397	443 MAW	60181	63 MAW
40645	459 MAW†	59398	443 MAW	60182	63 MAW
40646	437 MAW	59399	62 MAW	60183	438 MAW
40648	60 MAW			60184	63 MAW
40649	437 MAW	59400	443 MAW	60185	172 MAG*
40650	438 MAW	59401	437 MAW	60186	443 MAW
40651	437 MAW	59402	443 MAW	60187	437 MAW
40653	63 MAW	59403	60 MAW	60188	60 MAW
		59404	63 MAW	60189	60 MAW
FY65		59405	438 MAW	60190	172 MAG*
50216	459 MAW†	59406	63 MAW	60191	60 MAW
50217	437 MAW	59408	437 MAW	60192	63 MAW
50218	437 MAW	59409	438 MAW	60193	63 MAW
50219	60 MAW	59410	443 MAW	60194	437 MAW
50220	437 MAW	59411	438 MAW	60195	437 MAW
50221	438 MAW	59412	438 MAW	60196	437 MAW
50222	438 MAW	59413	438 MAW	60197	62 MAW
50223	438 MAW	59414	63 MAW	60198	63 MAW
50224	438 MAW			60199	438 MAW
50225	63 MAW	*FY66*		60200	63 MAW
50226	459 MAW†	60126	438 MAW	60201	63 MAW
50227	62 MAW	60128	63 MAW	60202	437 MAW
50228	62 MAW	60129	62 MAW	60203	437 MAW
50229	62 MAW	60130	172 MAG*	60204	438 MAW
50230	60 MAW	60131	437 MAW	60205	63 MAW
50231	60 MAW	60132	438 MAW	60206	62 MAW
50232	62 MAW	60133	438 MAW	60207	443 MAW
50233	60 MAW	60134	63 MAW	60208	63 MAW
50234	60 MAW	60135	437 MAW	60209	437 MAW
50235	62 MAW	60136	63 MAW		
50236	438 MAW	60137	63 MAW	67944	60 MAW
50237	62 MAW	60138	63 MAW	67945	437 MAW
50238	60 MAW	60139	63 MAW	67946	63 MAW
50239	60 MAW	60140	438 MAW	67947	437 MAW (*70947*)
50240	62 MAW	60141	62 MAW	67948	438 MAW
50241	62 MAW	60142	62 MAW	67949	63 MAW
50242	60 MAW	60143	63 MAW	67950	438 MAW
50243	62 MAW	60144	437 MAW	67951	62 MAW
50244	62 MAW	60145	62 MAW	67952	63 MAW
50245	60 MAW	60146	443 MAW	67953	437 MAW
50246	60 MAW	60147	60 MAW	67954	438 MAW
50247	60 MAW	60148	60 MAW	67955	437 MAW
50248	62 MAW	60149	437 MAW	67956	437 MAW
50249	60 MAW	60150	63 MAW	67957	63 MAW
50250	60 MAW	60151	60 MAW	67958	63 MAW
50251	60 MAW	60152	437 MAW	67959	63 MAW
50252	60 MAW	60153	459 MAW†		
50253	62 MAW	60154	443 MAW	*FY67*	
50254	60 MAW	60155	438 MAW	70001	63 MAW
50255	62 MAW	60156	63 MAW	70002	437 MAW
50256	60 MAW	60157	438 MAW	70003	443 MAW
50257	62 MAW	60158	62 MAW	70004	437 MAW
50258	62 MAW	60159	459 MAW†	70005	63 MAW
50259	60 MAW	60160	437 MAW	70007	438 MAW
50260	60 MAW	60161	62 MAW	70009	60 MAW
50261	438 MAW	60162	438 MAW	70010	437 MAW
50262	443 MAW	60163	437 MAW	70011	437 MAW
50263	62 MAW	60164	172 MAG*	70012	437 MAW
50264	62 MAW	60165	62 MAW	70013	438 MAW
50265	60 MAW	60166	438 MAW	70014	437 MAW
50266	437 MAW	60167	437 MAW	70015	63 MAW
50267	437 MAW	60168	437 MAW	70016	437 MAW
50268	60 MAW	60169	438 MAW	70018	62 MAW
50269	437 MAW	60170	443 MAW	70019	438 MAW
50270	437 MAW	60171	63 MAW	70020	438 MAW
50271	459 MAW†	60172	63 MAW	70021	438 MAW
50272	437 MAW	60173	438 MAW	70022	63 MAW
50273	437 MAW	60174	459 MAW†	70023	63 MAW
50275	437 MAW	60175	63 MAW	70024	438 MAW

Serial	Wing	Serial	Wing	Serial	Wing
70025	443 MAW	70028	63 MAW	70164	60 MAW
70026	437 MAW	70029	63 MAW	70165	438 MAW
70027	438 MAW	70031	60 MAW	70166	443 MAW (VIP)

Civil Registered Aircraft in Military Service

Serial	Serial	Serial
Antonov AN12 (Yugoslav Government) YU-AIC/7331	**Grumman Gulfstream III** (Government of Saudi Arabia) HZ103 HZ108 HZ-MS3	**North American Sabre 75A** (Federal Aviation Administration) N52 N53
Boeing 747SP-27 (Omani Government) A40-SO	**Ilyushin IL-76T/IL-76M*** (Government of Iraq) YI-AIK	N56 N58 N60 N62 N65
Boeing B-707-138B (Government of Saudi Arabia) HZ123	YI-AIL YI-AIM YI-AIN YI-AIP	**North American Sabre 40** (Federal Aviation Administration)
Dassault Falcon 20F (Flight Refuelling Ltd/FRADU, Hurn) N900FR	YI-AKO* YI-AKS* YI-ALO* YI-ALT*	N86 N87 N88 N89
N901FR N902FR N903FR N904FR	**Lockheed C-130H Hercules** (Government of Saudi Arabia) MS019 HZ114	**North American F-100F Super Sabre** FR Aviation, Bournemouth for Flight Systems Inc
N905FR N906FR N907FR N908FR N909FR	HZ115 HZ116 HZ117	N416FS (stored) N417FS N418FS (stored)
G-FRAA (N118R) G-FRAB (N27RX) G-FRAC (C-FYPB) G-FRAD (G-BCYF) G-FRAE (N910FR) G-FRAF (N911FR)	**Lockheed P-3 Orion** (NOAA) N42RF (159773) WP-3D N43RF (159875) WP-3D	

Addendum

Serial	Type (code/other identity)	Owner, Operator, Location or Fate	Notes
ZH107	Boeing Sentry AEW1	MoD(PE) for RAF	